A "Yankee" in
the "Texas Army"

Dennis A. Connole

Hamilton Books
A member of
The Rowman & Littlefield Publishing Group
Lanham • Boulder • New York • Toronto • Plymouth, UK

Copyright © 2008 by
Hamilton Books
4501 Forbes Boulevard
Suite 200
Lanham, Maryland 20706
Hamilton Books Acquisitions Department (301) 459-3366

Estover Road
Plymouth PL6 7PY
United Kingdom

Library of Congress Control Number: 2008921411
ISBN-13: 978-0-7618-3982-8 (clothbound : alk. paper)
ISBN-10: 0-7618-3982-8 (clothbound : alk. paper)
ISBN-13: 978-0-7618-3983-5 (paperback : alk. paper)
ISBN-10: 0-7618-3983-6 (paperback : alk. paper)

♾️™ The paper used in this publication meets the minimum
requirements of American National Standard for Information
Sciences—Permanence of Paper for Printed Library Materials,
ANSI Z39.48—1992

In Memory of my father,
Dennis "Joe" Connole
(1919–1990)

Contents

List of Maps

Preface

What you are about to read did not originally start out as a book. It began simply as an inquiry into my father's military background during World War II, a promise I made to myself shortly after his death. Dennis "Joe" Connole of Worcester, Massachusetts, spent four years, three months, and seventeen days in the U.S. Army between March 1941 and June 1945. My original intent was to gather whatever information I could find about the units he served with, the campaigns and battles in which he participated, and the extent of his combat experiences. The purpose of my quest was to compile all of this information into a file, along with supporting materials and documents—pictures, newspaper articles, a copy of his discharge papers, unit patches, medals, and other related material—that I could pass on to my children and grandchildren. Over time, as more and more information surfaced, my investigation gradually evolved into a major research and writing project. This volume is the result.

The search to find my father's past has taken many twists and turns along the way and has resulted in a number of startling revelations. What I ultimately discovered about my father from existing personnel and medical records on file with the U.S. Department of Veterans Affairs (VA), formerly the Veterans Administration, far exceeded the scope of my intended purpose.

I believe that my father's story is one worth telling. It is the story of how young men who experience the brutal horrors of combat are forever changed. For many, the painful memories of traumatic experiences in battle leave deep psychological scars, resulting in years of emotional pain and suffering. Repeated, intrusive recollections of friends killed or wounded, grossly mutilated bodies or horrendous wounds, as well as other disturbing images, sounds, or feelings, come back to haunt them on an almost daily basis. Individuals re-experience these traumatic events through recurring thoughts, vivid flashbacks, and troubling nightmares.

Post-traumatic Stress Disorder (PTSD) is the term used by the psychiatric profession to describe the symptoms that result from a person having faced a traumatic event or ordeal outside the usual human experience. This often debilitating psychological condition is one of a number of anxiety disorders recognized by the American Psychiatric Association (APA). Research data has confirmed that combat-related PTSD can persist for many years, sometimes for a lifetime. The healing process for many wartime soldiers was a gradual one; some, like my father, never completely recovered.

Although there have been numerous reports by members of the medical profession of military veterans suffering from PTSD-like symptoms dating back to the Civil War, psychiatric professionals had made very little progress in understanding the root causes and treatment of post-traumatic stress. It was only after researchers carried out a number of extensive scientific studies during the post-Vietnam War period that the syndrome entered wide public consciousness as a legitimate psychological disorder. Finally, after years of controversy, the APA added PTSD to its list of "Anxiety Disorders" in the third edition of the *Diagnostic and Statistical Manual of Mental Disorders* in 1980. Since that time, continuing research has led to significant progress in the diagnosis, prevention, and treatment of post-traumatic stress.

During the course of my investigation, I have discovered that writing about a parent can be a very emotional and sometimes painful endeavor. At first, it troubled me to think that by revealing certain information about my father's military and personal background, I might be guilty of invading his privacy and that of the family. For a time, I contemplated leaving out certain facts and information. Whether to do so proved a difficult decision. Finally, after much deliberation, I opted to omit nothing—to be completely honest and open—to reveal all the facts as they are. I based my decision partly on conversations and correspondence with many combat veterans who shared their feelings with me about how deeply the war affected them, and also, after reading numerous first-person accounts dealing with the same subject, which are discussed in later chapters.

My subsequent findings over the course of my research have helped me to understand my Dad as a father and as a person, and why he was the man he became after the war. "A labor of love" is an overused cliché, but I can honestly say the journey has been that and more.

Dennis A. Connole
Worcester, Massachusetts

Acknowledgments

Along the way, I have received assistance from many people in the research and writing of this book. Without their time and effort, I could have not completed the project. I would like to express my deepest appreciation to the following individuals, organizations, government agencies, and libraries.

First, I would like to thank my colleagues at South High Community School, who answered my many questions regarding grammar, word usage, mechanics, and style—Mary Reynolds, Tom Nolan, Steven Silverman, Carolyn Martello, and Stu Friedman. I would especially like to thank Michael O'Sullivan, who edited the first draft of the manuscript, and Mary Reynolds, who edited several of the chapters and made numerous suggestions and changes to help improve the manuscript.

Lieutenant Colonel Leonid Kondratiuk (U.S. Army Ret.), Director, Massachusetts National Guard Museum and Archives in Worcester, was an immense help during the course of my research and kindly edited several of the chapters. His professional expertise was invaluable. I would also like to thank Archivist Kent DeGroodt. Both were always friendly and helpful in locating resource materials and providing information about the military in general. My sincere thanks to Robert W. Brickman, a member of my father's heavy weapons company, Company D, 141st Infantry, 36th Division, who also read several of the chapters and provided valuable information.

Next, I wish to thank the staff members at the following institutions and agencies: the Worcester Public Library, especially Nancy Gaudette, Worcester Room Librarian; the Worcester Historical Museum, especially Julia Barrow and Robyn Christensen; the National Archives and Records Administration (NARA), College Park, Maryland; the U.S. Military History Institute, Carlisle Barracks, Carlisle, Pennsylvania, particularly the Friends of the Omar N. Bradley Foundation; and Jackie Belisle, the Resource Sharing Library Assistant for the Central Massachusetts Regional Library System, who provided assistance in tracking down hard-to-find books, articles, and reference materials.

I would like to thank Cecilia Thurlow, who did the final editing and proofreading of the manuscript, for her perceptive criticisms and commentary.

The excellent job of restoration, repair, and enhancement of the collection of photographs used in the book is the work of two individuals: Robert McMahon of McMahon Photography in New York City and Michael Amir of Michael's Photo Center of West Boylston, Massachusetts.

Paolo Carotenuto, a photojournalist with the newspaper *Liberazione* in Rome, provided much help and information about his hometown of Velletri and the people of the region, including his family, during the German occupation. It was during the battle for Velletri, that many of the replacements who joined the 36th Division in the spring of 1944, including my father, saw their first action—where the "rookies" underwent their "baptism of fire." Paolo is the author of a wonderful book about the 36th Infantry Division titled, *23 maggio-2 guigno 1944, La Battagglia di Velletri (March 23–June 2, The Battle of Velletri)*, published in 2004. Thank you Paolo for all your help.

My sincere gratitude to the 36th Division Veterans' Association, especially Gary Butler, Raymond Wells, Robert Faught, Alfred Dietrick, Leonard Wilkerson, and Brian Schenk, who answered my many research questions, helped locate resource materials, and provided hard-to-find articles from past issues of the 36th Division Association's quarterly newsletter, *The Fighting 36th Historical Quarterly* and (after 1993) *The T-Patcher Newsletter*; to Patti Stickle, daughter of William G. "Gregg" Wiley (I-141), the moderator of the association's website, for all her help and for providing articles from her father's collection of the *Quarterly;* and to Gloria Beer (widow of Robert Wear, Company H, 141st Infantry, killed in action on August 25, 1944), who also provided me with past copies of the newsletter.

I am grateful to everyone on the association's Message Board who helped with my research at one time or another: associate members—relatives, like myself, trying to find information about fathers, grandfathers, and uncles—people with a general interest in the 36th Division, history buffs, and also many WWII veterans of the division. Those who were especially helpful include Ron Graves, Greg Colmar, Greg Smith, Terry Rosenbluth (son of David Rosenbluth), Bob Kennedy, Paul Hinkle, and Pieter Oosterman.

Thanks to Tony Mancinone of Windsor, Ontario, Canada, who provided information about his wife's uncle, Edward Slavinski, of Company D, 141st Infantry (see Chapter 14, "The Battle of Nunziatella").

I am deeply indebted to the 36th Division veterans and members of their families whom I have interviewed and corresponded with over the past several years. They have graciously provided me with information as well as many wonderful, sometimes moving and heart warming, stories that have greatly enriched the book. First, the veterans of Company D, 141st Infantry, and family members, who so kindly gave of their time, especially Jack Wilson, Arlis Sizemore, Ernest Smeltzer, Joe Catropia, William A. Hawkins, John Paul Jones, H. Glenn Scott, Robert Brickman, Walter Loster, Ray Osborne, Jr., William Claude Harrelson, Charles Hulse, Peter Androne, Charles Castor (son of Marvin Castor), Edward Langdon (son of Ernest Langdon), and Reneta Benenati (widow of Carl Benenati).

Other members of the division and their families to whom I am grateful include John Hockenbury, David Rosenbluth, Terry Rosenbluth (son of David Rosenbluth), Michael Stubinski, Morris Courington, George Ferguson, Rex Hoon, George Bennett, Johnny Lane, Arthur Rogers, James Flannery, Johnnie Carr, James Robinson, William Hartung, Sr., Rosaire Rajotte, Charles Golub, Robert Bunker, George Ferguson, Charles Price, George Bennett, Greg DeRiggi, Beth DeRiggi, David McKee, and those individuals of the 36th Division Association mentioned above.

There are a number of veterans from the 26th Division who provided information and stories contained in the book. I would like to thank Sulo Ruuska, Guido Fratturelli, Nicholas Renzetti, Jack Judge, and Romeo LeBlanc.

Without the help of these men and women, I would never have been able to write my father's story. A number of the accounts and stories in the book have come from the men of Company D, 141st Infantry, many of whom I consider close friends. With the telling of each real life story by the veterans, history came alive for me. They took me back in time and gave me a real sense of what it must have been like for my father. I would like to express my heartfelt thanks and appreciation to all.

My wife and I have attended a number of 36th Division reunions over the years and we have become close friends with many of the veterans and their wives. A special thanks to our good friends, Jack and Judy Wilson, Arlis and Evelyn Sizemore, Ernest and Sara Smeltzer, John and Sylvia Hockenbury, and to all the members of the Midwest and 141st Infantry chapters of the 36th Division Association and their wives and companions who have attended the reunions over the past several years. You have made us feel so welcome and the gatherings so enjoyable.

I think of the connection between my father and these men with whom he served and fought alongside, and I feel extremely close to them. I remember being at one of the Midwest Chapter reunions, when Arlis Sizemore, a member of my father's mortar platoon, pointed to a photograph of Blue Beach, the landing site of Company D during the invasion of southern France and said, "Your Dad was right there with us." It made me feel so proud. It means so much to me that I could get to know Arlis and the other men in my father's company. Thank you all for the kindness and friendship you have extended to my wife and me. You will always be in our hearts.

I would like to thank the members of my family who provided information: my father's sisters, Helen Palumbo, Margaret Connole, and Betty Mitchell; my sisters, Kathleen Senior and Deborah Coakley; and my brothers, Joe and Rick. Also, my nephew Lieutenant Colonel Kevin Coakley, a career officer in the U.S. Army, who helped me with information about the military.

Finally, to my wife Joyce; my son Dennis, and daughter-in-law, Gail; my daughter Jill, and son-in-law, Ralph Streete; and my grandchildren, Alexis, Anthony, Sydney, and Dominic Connole, Samantha and Nichole Gambaccini, Jordan, Diana, and Melanie Streete; thank you for your love and support.

If I have forgotten to thank anyone, my sincerest apology. I am solely responsible for any errors or omissions.

World War II magazine published a shortened version of Chapter 14: The Battle of Nunziatella titled "A Bloody Encounter North of Rome," vol. 30, no. 5 (September 2005), 34–40.

Introduction

Joe Connole arrived in Italy in early March 1944, landing at Naples where he received an assignment to the 141st Infantry Regiment, 36th "Texas" Division, a mobilized Texas National Guard unit. Thus, my father ended up becoming a "Yankee" in the "Texas Army." "The Fighting 36th" was one of the most distinguished and decorated combat divisions of World War II. During his sixteen months with the division, he participated in the Rome-Arno, southern France, and Rhineland (Germany and Austria) campaigns. Connole earned the Purple Heart for shrapnel wounds received on June 12, 1944, near the town of Nunziatella, Italy, sixty miles north of Rome. He spent twenty-two days convalescing in an Army hospital in Naples before returning to his unit to train for the invasion of southern France ("Operation Anvil-Dragoon") which took place on August 15, 1944.

My father left Germany for the United States on June 17, 1945, and returned home to his family: his wife Michelina (Palumbo), known to friends and family as "Mickey" or Mary (her chosen American name), and children, Dennis, born February 9, 1943, and Richard, whom he had never seen, born April 8, 1944.

Joe Connole was just an ordinary soldier. He was one of thousands of young Americans, many just boys in their teens, who entered the military prior to or shortly after the outset of World War II. Most were recent high school graduates and just getting a start in life when the military buildup and the eventual outbreak of war disrupted their worlds. Many of these men ended up overseas in combat roles where they served courageously and with honor. Every day, they fought the enemy and fought to evade death. They were scared, but they continued to fight on, sometimes for months at a time without relief. Frontline units served under the most inhospitable and grueling conditions imaginable. Today they are called heroes—and they are—but at that time, they did not think of themselves as such. All these young men wanted to do was to go over, get the job done, and return home to begin the task of rebuilding their lives.

My Dad was one of the lucky ones who came back to his wife and family. He led a full life, helped raise five children, had eleven grandchildren, and two great grandchildren. In early 1948, he went to work for the Boston & Maine Railroad as a conductor and later a brakeman. He worked his way up the ladder and in the mid-1960s, the railroad promoted him to the position of Yardmaster for the Worcester Freight Terminal on Prescott Street. Joe Connole held this important position until he retired at age sixty-four in 1983, after 35 years on the job. His loving wife Mary passed away from a malignant brain tumor in 1981. The couple was happily married for thirty-nine years. After finally quitting smoking at the age of sixty-nine, a habit he most likely picked up in the Army, Joe Connole died of lung cancer one year later on August 9, 1990.

Shortly after my Dad passed away, family members were going through his personal effects and found several campaign and other medals, including a Bronze Star, Combat Infantryman Badge, and the Purple Heart, in a bureau drawer. These happened to be replacement medals, which my father obtained from the Army's Military Awards Branch in the early 1980s. The originals were long since gone, most probably lost or discarded during a family move from one place to another over the years. My younger sister Kathleen told me that she remembered the day the replacement medals arrived in the mail. My father placed them on the kitchen table to show her. "He acted so proud," she said, as he explained the significance of each award and told her of the campaigns in which he had participated.

A certificate from the "War Office" accompanied the Bronze Star Medal authorizing the award "by Executive Order 11046 of 24 August 1962," to Pfc. Dennis J. Connole for "meritorious achievement in ground combat against the enemy during World War II in the European-African-Middle Eastern Theater of Operations." The certificate is dated "30 November 1984."

President Franklin D. Roosevelt authorized the medal in 1944, "for heroic or meritorious achievement of service . . . in connection with operations against an opposing armed force." General George C. Marshall suggested to the president in a memorandum that the decoration be awarded to "any person serving in the military" that "distinguishes, or has distinguished, himself in combat . . . particularly the Infantry riflemen who are now suffering the heaviest losses . . . and enduring the greatest hardships." Marshall wanted to use the Bronze Star as a means of "raising the morale of combat troops."

In 1948, President Harry S. Truman authorized "the retroactive award of the Bronze Star Medal to soldiers who had been awarded the Combat Infantryman Badge or the Combat Medical Badge during World War II." President John F. Kennedy further amended the 1944 executive order in 1962, to include those serving with friendly forces during the war.

The sight of the medals brought me back to the time I was about four years old, when I first discovered the originals in a nightstand drawer in my parent's bedroom (see Chapter 1, "The War Souvenirs"). Also found among my father's effects was a copy of his discharge papers along with several pictures of him in uniform. It was at this time that I made the promise to myself to check into his service records.

Over the years, my father was reluctant to discuss the war with anyone, myself included. He belonged to the Vernon Hill American Legion Post No. 435 in Worcester and it is possible he would talk on occasion with other ex-servicemen, but I have no way of knowing for sure. This attitude was typical of many veterans who upon discharge made the conscious decision to forget the war, and move forward. Many, like my father, spent the rest of their lives trying to put the violence and horror of the war behind them. Occasionally he might mention the war in passing, a place he had been or, on rare occasions, tell a brief story about a particular incident, usually a humorous one that something reminded him of, but never did he mention any experiences under fire.

Even though the promise to check on my father's military background crossed my mind at times, I never seemed to take time to begin. There were, in the end, two factors that provided the impetus for me to take that initial step. The World War II era has always fascinated me, and I have read many books on the subject over the years. In 1998, after completing *Goodbye Darkness* by William Manchester, I decided it was time to start my search. Manchester's memoir is, in my opinion, one of the most superbly written and extremely moving books about one man's combat experiences. This also coincided with the first year I had access to a computer and the Internet, which, I would soon discover, is an incredible resource for doing research of this type.

Thus began my quest to discover all that I could about my father's military service. Initially, I started gathering whatever information was immediately available. First, I called my sister Kathleen to borrow a scrapbook in which my mother kept mementoes and remembrances pertaining to the war years. Neatly pasted in the scrapbook were photographs, newspaper articles about my father and other family members in the service from the local *WorcesterTelegram* (morning newspaper) or *Evening Gazette* (which my mother failed to date), poems clipped from magazines, and other items of interest.

One particular article from the Worcester newspaper titled "Connoles in Service"–(c. 1943) contained information on five members of the Connole and Palumbo families, with a picture of each, who were serving in various branches of the military. This included my father; my Uncle Matthew J. "Mitt" Palumbo, my mother's brother, who was married to my father's sister Helen, both serving in the U.S. Army; my Uncle Albert P. Connole, my father's older brother who was in the U.S. Navy; and my Aunt Elizabeth A. "Bette Ann" or "Bette" Connole, an older sister who was in the Coast Guard Women's Reserve. The article listed their current assignments, where stationed at the time, and how long they had been in the service.

The clipping reported that Joe Connole was a Private serving in "a provisional Military Police (MP) unit" with the 181st Infantry Regiment, 26th Division, stationed in Saco (pronounced "Soco"), Maine, on Coast Patrol duty (see Chapter 2, "26th 'Yankee' Division, 1941–1943"). There were two photographs of my father in uniform. The pictures are small; actual size is 2 1/4 x 2 1/4-inches with a 1/4 inch white border, probably taken with an old Kodak box-type "Brownie" camera. In one, my father is wearing the uniform of an MP. On his left arm is a black brassard with the letters MP in white lettering. He is standing, a web belt around his waist with a holster and .45-caliber pistol at his side. Unfortunately, this picture is slightly out of focus. The notation on the back of the second photo reads, "Pvt. Dennis Connole 1941."

One interesting picture, cut out of a fan magazine, shows my Uncle Mitt, a musician in the 181st Infantry Regimental Band, and several other soldiers surrounding Hollywood star Deanna Durbin. The caption reads, "The soldiers of Camp Edwards swamped Deanna with autograph requests as mementoes of a happy occasion." She was part of a USO tour group performing at the camp in 1942.

There were also two wedding notices from the newspaper, one of my parents' marriage on February 12, 1942, with a picture of my mother in her wedding gown, and the other announcing the marriage of my Uncle Mitt and Aunt Helen, with a picture of the couple on their wedding day. There was an article with a picture of my father in uniform reporting that he had been "wounded in action" by "shrapnel" in Italy on June 12, 1944, and hospitalized. The article does not indicate the name of his outfit, a common practice during the war. The scrapbook also contained the birth notices for my brother Rick and me, a brief article announcing my father's return home by air on June 17, 1945, as well as several other clippings and items about the war.

I was aware that my father was a member of the 36th "Texas" Division, but had no knowledge of the regiment or company in which he served. I called my brother Joe, the executor of the estate, and he sent me a copy of his discharge papers. There was an entry listing the unit he was with at the time he separated from the service—Company D, 141st Infantry, 36th Infantry Division. Later, I learned that he was a member of a mortar platoon.

Armed with this meager information, I sat down at the computer one day in October 1998, and went on the World Wide Web. I typed in "141st Infantry Regiment, 36th Division" not knowing what to expect. Much to my surprise, a web page for the 36th Division Veterans' Association appeared on the screen. The site contained a wealth of information about the division and attached units. I also discovered that there was a Midwest as well as a 141st Infantry Regiment Chapter, and I sent applications to join all three as an Associate Member. Shortly thereafter, I received a membership card to the 36th Division Association along with a copy of the organization's quarterly newsletter, the *T-Patcher*. Later I received newsletters for the two chapters.

I began by posting messages on the Association's "Message Board," seeking information and asking if anyone knew my father. I inquired where I might be able to get copies of his military records. I received replies from many helpful individuals with whom I corresponded by mail and e-mail. I eventually made contact with two men from the 36th Division who remembered my dad, one who knew him well.

The website also posted a list of books pertaining to the division. I purchased several, including *The Fighting 36th: A Pictorial History,* and sent for a number of others through Interlibrary Loan (ILL). The *Pictorial History* is a reprint of the original, published in Germany shortly after the war in 1945. The back section of the history contains a division roster by unit, "compiled by unit personnel sections shortly after the conclusion of the war." I looked for company D and found my father's name. One of the veterans had mailed me a copy of the page several weeks earlier. The entry reads, "CONNOLE, Dennis J., Pvt. 34-B Providence Street [his mother's address], Worcester, Mass." His discharge papers list him as a Pfc.

I spent many hours reading the text and studying the photographs, hoping possibly to find a picture of my father. I believe that the photograph taken in St. Croix, France, in November 1944 (pages not numbered) is that of my father with two other GIs riding in a trailer towed by a jeep. Arlis Sizemore, a member of my father's platoon, said that this was exactly how the men of the mortar squads traveled. He believes he recognizes the man next to my father in the trailer as another member of the platoon.

Several members of the 36th Division Association were most helpful, never failing to answer my many questions and provide needed information. These included Mr. Leonard Wilkerson, then Membership Secretary; Mr. Raymond Wells, then Vice President of the 141st Infantry Chapter; Mr. Alfred Dietrick, editor of the *T-Patcher Newsletter*; and Mr. Gary Butler, who maintained the 36th Division website.

Mr. Wilkerson sent me a list of current members of the association who served with Company D. I wrote a letter to everyone on the list, and waited anxiously. I received many wonderful replies from the men telling me about the regiment and Company D, a heavy weapons company, the basic organization of the company, and the role of the unit in a combat battalion. I am still corresponding with a number of the men and we meet every year at reunions. My wife Joyce and I have attended seven reunions of the 36th Division Midwest Chapter and two of the 141st Infantry Chapter in the past eight years, and we have become close friends with many of the veterans, their wives, and other family members.

Mr. Wells informed me that I could write to the National Personnel Records Center (NPRC) in St. Louis, Missouri, for copies of my father's military records, but not to be too hopeful as a fire that occurred in 1973 had destroyed 80 percent of the files from World War II. An estimated 16 to 18 million files for U.S. Army personnel discharged from November 1, 1912 to January 1, 1960, were lost. The fire burned for several days before being contained. An investigation in 1975, never fully determined the exact cause of the blaze. Approximately three months later, I received a letter informing me that the records of Pfc. Dennis J. Connole were lost. The news was most discouraging. I felt I had reached a dead end.

I mentioned my bad fortune to several of my e-mail pals from the association's message board and someone suggested I write to the U.S. Department of Veterans Affairs (VA) in Philadelphia for information. He informed me that if my father had applied for a service-related disability after the war, there was a good possibility the agency might have copies of his military records on file. It took approximately eight long months for the agency to comply with my request. I had just about given up all hope, when one day a large manila envelope, approximately two inches thick, arrived in the mail.

It turned out that shortly after the war in 1945, my father had indeed submitted a claim for a partial disability pension for "a war-related nervous disorder" (see later chapters). The file contained my father's medical history, as well as copies of a number of his military records and other documents from the National Personnel Records Center, thought to be lost in the 1973 fire. At the time he applied for the disability, the VA sent for copies of the NPRC records, and they became part of his permanent VA file.

A few weeks later, I telephoned the Philadelphia office about some missing information. After checking the documents, I realized that several records continued over to the backside of a number of pages, which the clerk failed to include. At that time, I inquired about the long delay in receiving the records, and the VA employee informed me that the agency had difficulty locating the folder. It seems that someone had misplaced the file and following a lengthy search, the agency eventually found it at the Regional Office in Boston.

I spent hours poring over the massive file. The amount and type of information was astounding. The contents of certain medical records, which contained details of my father's days in combat, came as a complete surprise. I soon came to realize how profoundly the war had affected him. The information contained therein helped to fill many of the gaps in my research as well.

Still later, I was able to obtain copies of the monthly "History of Operations" reports (also referred to as "After Action Reports" and "Operations Reports") for the 141st Infantry Regiment from the National Archives and Records Administration (NARA), which chronicled the day-to-day operations of each unit. These detailed reports were a tremendous help, providing me with information about the regiment's movements and engagements. I also obtained the "Morning Reports" (M/Rs) for Company D and several other companies of the 181st Infantry from the NPRC in St. Louis, which provide a casualty list for each day, KIAs, WIAs, LWAs (Light Wounds) and MIAs, as well as the location of the unit and a brief report on the day's location and action.

Chapter One

The War Souvenirs

My father arrived home from the war on June 17, 1945. At the time, my mother, my brother Richard (Rick), and I were living in the third-floor apartment of my grandmother, Lucia "Lucy" Palumbo, at 18 Shamrock Street, off Shrewsbury Street, in the predominantly Italian section of Worcester. My grandmother had been a widow since the death of her husband Antonio on March 15, 1941. After my parents married on February 12, 1942, my mother had continued to reside at home while my father was away in the service. I have no memory of my father's homecoming from the Army.

Shortly after my father returned from overseas, my parents moved to a rented apartment a short distance away on Shelby Street. About one year later, in 1947, the family, which now included my sister Maureen Deborah, or "Debby" as we called her, moved from Shelby Street to 10 Peace Avenue. Debby was born on November 7, 1946. Our new apartment was in a temporary veterans' housing project known as Lincolnwood, located on the outskirts of the city near Lake Quinsigamond. We lived at this location until 1951 (see Chapter 24, "Home Again").

My sister Debbie's crib was located in my parents' bedroom at the far end of the apartment, and Rick and I would occasionally go into the room to see her when she awoke from sleep or a nap. I remember being fascinated by my father's Army uniforms neatly arranged on hangers in the open closet. There was a wool olive-drab (OD) "ETO" (European Theater of Operations) or "Eisenhower" jacket, named for General Dwight D. Eisenhower. Ike had the garment patterned after a British battle jacket, which he admired and had reproduced for his personal use. In 1944, the Quartermaster Corps (QMC) copied the design and issued the short-waisted jacket (it extended to the hips) for wear in the ETO. Originally, the designers intended the jacket for winter wear, under the field jacket as part of a layering system. Eisenhower's command restricted the jacket to "non-combat wear only." Next to the jacket, on separate hangers, were two olive-drab, wool dress shirts over pairs of wool trousers.

I used to stand and stare at the multi-colored ribbons that were pinned over the left pocket of the Eisenhower jacket. Above the ribbons was my father's light blue Combat Infantryman's Badge. Centered over the right pocket, was a brass pin depicting a standing eagle with wings spread inside a wreath, worn by veterans to denote an honorable discharge. My father pointed to it one day, and told me it was a called a "ruptured duck." The military issued the pin to all personnel upon separation from active duty after World War II. As the story goes, upon receiving the pin, some GI made a comment that the bird looked more like a ruptured duck, and the name stuck. I did not know exactly what my father meant at the time, but he thought it amusing. The pin signified that the person wearing the badge was officially out of the service and this authorized him or her to wear the uniform for six months after their discharge date.

There was an olive-drab "overseas" or "garrison cap" tucked under the left shoulder loop. On the flap of the right pocket was a deep blue rectangular ribbon with a gold border, which I now know to be a Presidential Unit Citation awarded to the 1st Battalion, 141st Infantry Regiment for "heroism, gallantry, and esprit de corps" during the Invasion of southern France on D-Day, August 15, 1944. On the left sleeve of the jacket was a blue arrowhead patch with a large "T"—that of the 36th "Texas" Division. I asked my father about the patch and he told me the "T" stood for Texas. In my young mind, I associated Texas as the place where gun-toting cowboys lived on ranches and tended large herds of cattle. At this age, in the days before television, I was listening to the Lone Ranger on the radio and playing cowboys and Indians with neighborhood friends.

Sitting on the floor directly below the uniform was a pair of late World War II-style combat boots—light brown—with the tops, called "cuffs," flopping over to the right. Two buckles secured the cuffs. The wearer bloused the wool dress pants or fatigues into the boots. The new type of boot eliminated the need for the standard issue canvas leggings worn earlier. Developed in 1943, the Quartermaster Corps first introduced the 10-inch boots in both Italy and North Africa one year later.

I also remember my father having a web belt with a canteen and ammunition pouches. I tried to shorten it up so that it would fit around my waist, but it was too large. In a back corner of the closet, standing on end, was a tightly packed canvas duffel, or garrison bag, olive-drab in color. The bag had a wide strap and handle for carrying. The top of the bag had four flaps that folded over the open end to hold the contents in place. Three of the flaps had metal eyelets or grommets. Attached to the remaining flap was a metal loop about two inches in length, which passed through the eyelets. At the end of the carrying strap was a clip that hooked onto the elongated metal loop to secure the flaps.

One day, I must have grown tired of playing with my toys, and as any youngster will do, I began exploring the house. While my mother was busy in the kitchen, I went into her room and started poking around. I pulled open one of the nightstand drawers. Inside, stacked neatly were several large packets of what appeared to be paper money, two cigar boxes with lids, along with several smaller boxes. As I remember, paper bands, about two inches wide, held the bills tightly together. The bands looked the same color as a brown paper bag with some type of printing on them. Each packet was approximately two to two and one half inches thick and contained crisp new bills.

I knew it was not U.S. paper currency by its large size, approximately 4 x 5 or 4 x 6 inches as I remember, but I was not sure what kind it was at first. I asked my mother about the money, and she said my father brought it back from overseas and that it was not worth anything because Germany had lost the war. I seem to remember her saying it was German money. She told me that I should not be "snooping" around in her bedroom drawers, but she did not forbid me from going in the room again.

I mentioned the packets of money to Jack Wilson (D-141), one of the 36th Division veterans at the October 2006, reunion of the 141st Infantry Chapter of the 36th Division Veterans' Association in San Antonio, and he related a story about the capture of a German payroll truck somewhere near Montelimar, France, in August 1944. In an article titled "Honorary Texans," Paul D. Hinkle (L-141) wrote that after the battle of Montelimar, his outfit went down to the valley floor after the area was cleared of Germans and walked among the wrecked vehicles and equipment. He said they "found a paymaster's bus loaded with French francs from the Bank of France; we were told that only francs from the Bank of Morocco were good, so we threw them to the wind, only to find out later they were good." Another veteran of the 36th, James A. Nasso (K-142), wrote that he remembers a time in southern France when his squad entered "a beautiful house" the Germans had been using as a headquarters. "We found stacks of money and did not know if it was good or just invasion money." They also "found several beautiful uniforms of very high [ranking] officers." It appeared as if the Germans "left in a hurry as it was all left very neat." Nasso suspected that the occupants might have booby-trapped some of the items left behind. He said, "We just made a mess of the place."

One of the cigar boxes contained all kinds of German Army pins, medals, insignias, emblems, ribbons, badges, and other decorations of all sizes and shapes—souvenirs from the war. There was also a beige or khaki colored armband with a black swastika. I distinctly remember a small, thin black wallet, or billfold, approximately 3 x 5 inches that held a picture of a young-looking German in uniform on one side and an identification card on the other covered in clear plastic. A search revealed it contained nothing else.

One of the items I was most fascinated with was a very large, actually huge, gold ring. It was flat on the top surface and had no outside markings of any kind. There was some lettering imprinted on the inside of the band. The hole was larger than an ordinary man's finger—and I remember thinking that the person who owned it must have been a giant of a man. Without exaggerating, if I curled up my fingers I could almost fit my entire hand through the hole. The ring was excessively heavy. No one told me so, but I knew in my mind that my father had taken these items off the bodies of dead German soldiers. Did my father kill them? I wondered.

The other cigar box contained loose paper money and coins of all different shapes and sizes, presumably from the countries to which my father had traveled while in the Army. There were different denominations, some very colorful with pictures of kings, queens, presidents, and other government officials. The coins were silver, copper, and steel. Most were round; a few were hexagonal or octagonal while others had holes in the middle. The second box contained my father's identification, or "dog" tags, on a chain, some Army patches, one the YD patch of the 26th Division and another of the 1st Coast Artillery (see Chapter 2, "26th "Yankee" Division, 1941–1943"), a tarnished brass U.S. Army belt buckle, and numerous other items.

For a kid my age, it was like discovering a treasure chest. Before I learned to read, and in the days before television, playing with the war souvenirs was something that kept me occupied, often for hours at a time. I examined them closely and lined them all up in rows on the bed. Sometimes I would pin several of the medals to the front of my shirt.

In the drawer were a number of smaller silk-lined boxes that contained my father's campaign and other medals. The only one I remember in any detail was the Purple Heart, because of the pretty purple ribbon and heart with gold border and profile of General George Washington. My mother told me that my father was awarded the medal because of wounds he received in Italy. "Did he get shot?" I asked. "No," she said, "it was from shrapnel." "What is shrapnel?" She replied, "They are pieces of metal from an exploding shell." "What is a shell?" was my next question, and on and on. The questions were endless, but she patiently answered each one as best she could. When I finished playing with the souvenirs, I was always careful to put everything back in its proper place.

One time, my brother and I were with my father on the bed play wrestling. He was tickling us and throwing us up in the air, to our great delight. We were jumping all over him and laughing wildly. He had no shirt on. I do not re-member if I saw the pink scars on his shoulder blade, or whether I asked him where he had been wounded. I think I came right out and asked him. He pointed at two curved scars on his left scapula, one approximately two and one-half inches long, and a second smaller one, just inside the first. Then, he leaned over and opened the drawer to the nightstand, reached inside one of the cigar boxes and pulled out a small metal container with a lid that held the two pieces of metal, the shrapnel that caused the wounds. They were shiny, with jagged edges, and though not too large, felt very heavy in my small hand. He said that the Army doctor gave them to him as a souvenir of the war.

One day my father was out of the house and I was playing in his room. He came home unexpectedly and I did not hear him come in. He entered the room and caught me with the drawer open and the souvenirs all over the bed and floor. I was sitting there with my back to the door and he startled me. I was very embarrassed that he caught me in the room. He became very angry and told me that he did not want me going in the drawers or touching his things ever again. Then he ordered me out of the room. My head hung down as I walked into the kitchen. My mother could see that I was hurt. I heard her tell my father that I was just curious and that I was not doing them any harm. After that incident, I had to be very careful whenever I went into the bed-room.

One day my curiosity about what was in the duffel bag got the best of me. The bag bulged from its contents so tightly that I had trouble getting the metal clasp undone. I opened the top and pulled out some khaki shirts and pants, un-der which were some olive-drab underwear and socks. That was as far as I dared to go. The clothing was packed so tightly, I knew that if I pulled every-thing out I would never be able get it all back inside.

I remember being very nervous, expecting my father to come in the room at any moment. I re-closed the top of the bag, having a very difficult time stuffing everything back inside and getting the top flaps secured over the loop that held the clip. To my dismay, I could not snap the clip back into place and started to panic. I almost gave up. I put all my weight on top of the bag and pushed as hard as I could. Finally, I managed to secure the clip and breathed a deep sigh of relief. I did not want my father to know that I had been touch-ing his things against his wishes.

When I was a little older, I brought my two best friends from the neigh-borhood, Jimmy Louney and Pat Thibaud, over to the house and I took them into my parents' bedroom to show off the souvenirs. "Wow," Jimmy ex-claimed, all excited. "Did your father have to kill some Germans to get the medals?" "Yes," I bragged, not really knowing for sure. They grilled me, "How many did he kill?" "How did he kill them?" "Did he shoot them?"

Both Jimmy and Pat's fathers were veterans of the U.S. Navy and had served aboard ship in the Pacific Theater. One day when I was at Jimmy's house, he showed me some of the things his father had brought back from the war. Mr. Louney had several large shells of different sizes. I believe that some were antiaircraft shells, although I did not know that at the time. Jimmy told me that they were not dangerous because his father had removed the powder. He twisted the round and pulled it out of the shell to show me that it was empty.

The shells sat on a small, three-tiered mahogany stand. On the shelves and neatly arranged on the wall behind the stand were several framed photographs of his father and some of his shipmates in their uniforms, some white and some blue. All were wearing white sailor caps and smiling broadly for the camera. There were different poses, some against the ship's railings, others next to the big deck guns.

In 1951, we moved from Lincolnwood to an apartment at 43 Great Brook Valley Avenue in a newly constructed all brick veterans' housing project called the Curtis Apartments, so named for Ephraim Curtis, the first settler of Worcester (originally named Quinsigamond Plantation) who built a house and trading post on Lincoln Street. The housing complex is located off Route 70, a short distance from our Lincolnwood apartment.

After we moved to "Great Brook Valley" or "Great Brook," as the veterans' project became known (today people refer to it as "the Valley"), the boxes containing the war souvenirs and other items were gone from the original drawer, and I never saw them again. Years later, I asked my father what ever became of the war souvenirs. "I got rid of them," was his reply. No other explanation. My guess is that he needed money and sold them.

In 1954, my father took out a VA loan for $6,500 and purchased a three-family house, sometimes called a "three-decker" or a "triple-decker," at 50 Paine Street, in the lower Lincoln Street neighborhood. My siblings and I lived in the house until we married.

Worcester has many nicknames, including "The City of Seven Hills," "The Heart of the Commonwealth," and the "The City of Three Deckers." The three-decker house originated in the New England states, with the peak construction period occurring between 1880 and 1910. The exact origin of these unique three-story apartment buildings is unknown. Historians believe the wood-framed structures to be a "mutation of the Mansard-style row house." Three-deckers provided inexpensive housing for a like number of families in a relatively small vertical space. My father rented out the second and third floors for extra income. Both parents lived in the house until their deaths, my mother in 1981, and my father in 1990.

Behind the house on Paine Street was a large three-car garage, originally an old barn with a hayloft above. Many of Worcester's three-deckers have barns, which were used to shelter horses and carriages in the days before the automobile. The barn had a door near the peak of the roof with a large beam above, at the end of which was a metal ring for attaching the tackle used to haul bales of hay up to the loft.

On the second floor of the barn, which the family used as an attic, my mother kept a very large old-fashioned wooden chest that had an arched top with slats in which she stored her keepsakes. On the front, in the center, was a large, round, hinged brass lock that would not close because of the rectangular bolt that jutted out of the hasp in the locked position. The key to the chest was long lost. The chest had two large brass clasps on either side of the lock that held the cover shut. A floral print silk cloth lined the inside.

Under the lid was a large removable tray, about eight inches deep, divided into several compartments. Beneath the tray, my mother kept several plastic garment bags containing her wedding dress and veil, along with a number of other items of clothing and personal effects. The chest also contained several scrapbooks she had compiled over the years, her high school diploma, and the like. One of the scrapbooks, I remember, contained pressed flowers and small bouquets glued to the pages. Neatly printed below were a date and a short note explaining the significance of each—her high school prom, graduation, wedding, and various other occasions. There were a number of greeting cards, invitations, thank you notes, as well as other mementoes.

Another of the scrapbooks, mentioned earlier, contained photographs, articles, prayers, and poems that she had cut out of newspapers and magazines, with numerous other items relating to the war. This scrapbook, found among my father's effects after he passed away in 1990, is still in my possession.

Sitting in the tray were several thick packets of letters, arranged by date, which my father had written to his wife during the war. My mother had lovingly tied each of the packets together with pretty colored ribbons, secured by neat little bows.

When I was about eleven or twelve years old, my mother and I went looking for something in the barn, and she went over to the chest and opened the lid. She picked up a packet of the letters, removed the bow, and opened one of the envelopes. As she stood there quietly reading the letter to herself, her eyes welled up and tears rolled down her cheeks. I touched her hand and asked what was wrong. She wiped the tears away and said, "This is one of the letters your father wrote to me during the war." She told me that he wrote almost every day to tell her how much he loved and missed her. As she continued to read the letter, she smiled and a warm glow came over her face, her eyes still wet from the tears.

"Your father was a very sweet and loving person before he went overseas," were her exact words. And then she said, "He is not the same person that went off to fight in the war." She pursed her lips and said with a sigh, "He came back a changed man."

"How," I asked her. She paused for a few seconds trying to think of a way to explain it to me and replied, "The war hardened him."

I knew exactly what she meant. She said that when she met him at the airport upon his return from overseas, after being away for about eighteen months, that he looked like he had aged ten years. The details of this incident are indelibly imprinted on my mind.

Later, as a curious teenager, I remember reading some of the war letters. To me they were very sentimental and to read them was quite embarrassing. In professing his love for her, my father's letters contained tender, loving expressions of affection and endearments, which seemed completely out of character. I had never seen this side of him. He always acted the tough guy and was very stern with my brother Rick and me. It was a bit of a shock, to say the least. I found it hard to believe that my father had written the letters. It was obvious from his words that he was very much in love with my mother and missed her greatly.

When my father had the dilapidated barn torn down in the late seventies or early eighties, the chest and its contents went into our enclosed front porch, where it remained until after my mother died. No one in the family knows what happened to the chest. I would dearly love to have those letters in my possession today. It was not until I read *V-Mail: Letters of a World War II Combat Medic*, by Pfc. Keith Winston (Chapel Hill, North Carolina, 1985), that I realized their potential value and interest to my siblings and me. *V-Mail* is a poignant book, which portrays the life and times of an American GI and is taken from a collection of correspondence to his wife Sarah and children. Sarah Winston selected and edited her husband's letters for publication after his death.

My father's letters home would have provided information about the war and as much of his role as a soldier that the censors would allow. They might have been very insightful regarding his thoughts and his frame of mind at various times during the war. Although it is quite possible that he may not have wanted to reveal too much to his wife, not wanting to cause any undue worry or concern.

The memory of the incident with my mother that day in the barn has stayed with me all through the years. Her husband's participation in the war had resulted in a profound change in his pre-war behavior and personality. In a sense, the man she married never returned. Someone else came back in his place. It is reasonably safe to conclude that the sheer horror, the brutality, and senselessness of war had a detrimental and lasting effect on every man who has spent any length of time in a combat role. The wounds these men suffered were not of the body but of the mind.

I am now convinced that what happened to my father during the war had a tremendous psychological impact on him. Initially, my sole purpose was to find out what I could about his military background. As the work progressed and more information concerning his medical background came to light, I found myself making more of a conscious attempt to discover how much of an influence his combat experiences might have had on his post-war personality and behavior. Maybe then, I would have a better understanding of what happened to him and why he had changed.

Chapter Two

26th "Yankee" Division, 1941–1943

Dennis Joseph Connole graduated from Worcester's St. John's Catholic High, an all boys' school, in June 1939. At the time, the family was living in an apartment at 34-B Providence Street in the Vernon Hill section of the city. St. Johns Parochial School, a three-story red-brick structure, was located on Temple Street, across from St. John's Church, in the block between Green, Harding, and Winter streets. The Diocese of Worcester constructed the main building, "commonly referred to as the 'Old Building,'" in 1891, and the adjacent "New High School," which housed the gymnasium, in 1924, to alleviate overcrowding.

Classes for grades nine to twelve were held in the new building and on the first floor of the main building. The grammar school, which was co-ed, occupied the second floor and the auditorium was on the third floor. Nuns from the Sisters of Notre Dame de Namur taught classes at the grade school, and the Brothers of St. Francis Xavier, commonly known as the Xaverian Brothers, at the high school level.

St. John's High School moved to the nearby community of Shrewsbury, Massachusetts, in the early 1960s. In the mid-1970s, the diocese demolished the main building. All that remains on the old site is the boarded-up former High School/Gymnasium building. An automobile dealership purchased the property sometime after the school closed and for many years used the structure as a storage warehouse.

I remember my father telling me what strict disciplinarians the Xaverian Brothers were, and how they, in his words, "would not tolerate any guff from any of the students." For the slightest infraction of the rules, "the brothers would invite a student to step out into the hallway for a little talk." Of course, the brothers would be sure to leave the door slightly ajar, he said. In the hall, hidden from the view of the others in the classroom, they were not afraid to give the deserving student "a good backhand," or "bang his head against the wall just to get his attention," before issuing the offender a stern warning. My father would smile and say, "There were no smart alecks at St. John's."

John F. "Jack" Judge of Worcester, who served with the 26th "Yankee" Division in Company C, 181st Infantry, was a classmate of my father's at St. John's from the fourth to the tenth grade. Jack related a story about a classmate named George _____, "who was acting out in Brother Robertus's class one day." Brother Robertus taught Religion and Latin. "George," he says, "was a big tough kid." The brother "came up behind him and gave him a smack in the back of the head with a textbook." He said to the brother, "You think you're tough! If you didn't have that collar on, I'd knock your block off." Robertus "was just a little guy," Judge said. "He weighed no more than 120 pounds." What George did not know was that he "was a former amateur featherweight boxing champion." Brother Robertus said, "Why don't you meet me down in the basement [referred to by the students as "The Dungeon"] after school and I'll take the collar off?"

That afternoon, when the final bell rang, teacher and student walked silently down the stairs to the basement. Judge says that the basement had no lights except that from the narrow windows around the foundation. All the kids in the class crammed around the windows looking through the panes in eager anticipation of the match, with lots of pushing and shoving to get into position for a good view. "They fought bare-knuckled, and Brother Robertus gave George a pretty good beating," Judge said. "When it was over, the two shook hands and, after that, they were the best of friends."

Judge also mentioned another teacher at the school named Brother Peter, whom he remembered as being "a very tough individual." He "was about five feet eight inches tall and weighed maybe 160 pounds. No one misbehaved in Brother Peter's classroom." He "was an excellent basketball player," Judge recalled.

When Jack was in his junior year, his family moved out of the neighborhood and he had to transfer to Commerce High, one of the city's four public secondary schools. "If you lived in the parish, the tuition was free," Judge said. His family could not afford the sixty dollars a year, a goodly sum in those days, which it would cost to allow him to continue at the school.

John "Long John" Foley, a World War II veteran, was another student at St. John's during the prewar depression days, graduating in June of 1942. In an 1994 article in the *Worcester Telegram & Gazette* titled, "Remembering Days Gone By/Forgotten St. John's Gym Sparks Memories" by sports reporter John Gearan, Foley reminisced about his school days at St. John's. "Back then, things were simpler, 'Nobody had any money to make things complicated,' Foley observed. 'I wore the same pair of trousers to school for four years . . . honest.'"

In those days, Gearan noted, "St. John's students were mostly raggedy Catholic city kids." The neighborhood, located next to the New York, New Haven & Hartford (commonly referred to as the New Haven) Railroad tracks, "was a gritty mix of factories, businesses and tenements," most of which have long since "been torn down for parking."

Foley was a star player for the "Pioneers" basketball team from 1938 to1942. Gearan described him as "a 6-foot-5 center with a deadly hook shot." Coach Buster Sheary, a local legend and former college all-star at Catholic University in Washington D.C., appointed Foley captain of the team in his senior year. The Pioneers "would often scrimmage the Holy Cross team and beat the collegians." During Foley's tenure with St. Johns, the team "was invited to several eastern seaboard tournaments." After the war, Foley went on to play basketball for Notre Dame University where he "excelled."

Foley remembers that the gymnasium had no heat in the winter during practice and the team did not have warm-up suits. He wore a sweater his mother had knitted for him to practice and tossed it on the sidelines after working up a sweat. The St. John's game uniform was "all wool, itchy and washed only once a year at the end of the season," yet Foley says he "took great pride in putting it on." The locker room downstairs had only one showerhead. "At home, few had showers and the Saturday night bath was a routine," Foley said.

Upon graduating from high school in 1938, Dennis, or "Joe" as his friends knew him, set out to find a steady job. Very few, if any, young men or women in my father's working-class neighborhood on Providence Street went on to college in the 1930s, unless it was on a sports scholarship. College was never a consideration. Shortly thereafter, Joe Connole found employment with the New Haven Railroad as a laborer with the title of "shipping checker." His duties included "loading and unloading freight cars; sorting incoming packages for delivery; following up on lost freight; checking merchandise, and assisting the shipping clerk." Although the job was an entry-level position, the railroad was an excellent place to work during the prewar Depression years. The work was steady, the companies paid a decent wage, and even more important, there was always a good chance for advancement.

There were seven children in the Connole family: Catherine, the oldest; Albert; Margaret "Peg"; Helen; Bette Ann or Bette; my father Dennis; and the youngest, Rita. Albert was a Petty Officer in the U.S. Navy during the war and served on a cruiser assigned to convoy duty in the North Atlantic. Seaman 2-c Betty Ann was a member of the Coast Guard Women's Reserve, stationed in Palm Beach, Florida, and later in New York City as part of an intelligence unit.

My grandfather, Dennis Francis Connole, known as "Dinny" Connole, was born in 1883. He came to America from Ireland in 1908 in search of a better life. Dinny later met and married my grandmother, Margaret Considine. Margaret was sixteen years old when she came over with family friends in 1907. By coincidence, Dinny and Margaret had grown up in two towns only four miles apart in County Clare, my grandmother in Ennis and my grandfather in Raheen.

The two immigrated to the United States and eventually ended up in the city of Worcester, where they met through mutual friends and fell in love. Dinny, age twenty-nine, and Margaret, age twenty-one, were married on June 10, 1912, and their first child, Catherine, was born the following year. The marriage certificate lists Dennis's occupation as "drop forger" and Margaret's as a "corset operative." Dinny worked at the Wyman-Gordon Company in Worcester.

Dinny Connole died at age forty-two of Pancreatic Cancer in 1927. My father was only seven years old at the time. The family went through some difficult times after Dinny's untimely early death. His wife Margaret was six months pregnant with Rita at the time. For a while, my grandmother, with seven children to raise, was forced to go on the welfare rolls in order to survive. My Aunt Helen says her mother "received five dollars per week."

In 1929, the family had to leave their second-floor apartment in a three-family house at 112 Harding Street, a short distance from St. John's High School, because they could no longer afford the rent. My grandmother contacted John C. Mahoney, a local politician and a friend to the Irish community, and he found them a nice apartment in another three-decker at 34-B Providence Street. Mahoney served as Mayor of Worcester from 1932 to 1935.

Margaret found work at the New England Corset Company at 140 Green Street. Each morning she would walk to the factory building pulling a small wagon, pick up a load of unfinished corsets, and cart them home where she and her older daughters would sew the buttons on the garters. The next morning she would haul the finished garments back to the company to collect her pay and pick up a new batch. When the corset factory closed in 1930, she went to work at the Donohue Modern Laundry located at 154 Green Street.

"Four or five days a week," my aunt Helen said, her mother, "pushing a baby carriage with her two youngest children, would walk to Worcester's west side," about five miles away, where many of the city's more affluent citizens lived. She worked for several families "mending and ironing clothes." Helen paused, "So the family could eat."

As soon as the Connole children were old enough, they had to go out and find work to help support the family. Helen said that as a young boy, her brother Albert sold newspapers on the corner of Chatham and Main streets outside Liggett's Drug Store, a very busy intersection in downtown Worcester.

Albert had to leave school in February 1933, during his junior year to help with the family's finances. He went to work full-time as a "clerk" for the Front Street Market, "a branch of the Worcester Market" (631 Main Street). The store was located at the end of Front Street near Washington Square, which fronted Worcester's Union Station. The Brockelman Brothers, a local family, owned and operated the market, one of three in the city. Helen described it as "a very large market." She said the family would walk to the store every Friday to shop for groceries for the week and Al would pay the bill. He may have received a discount as part of his employment. Helen said, "Al was a wonderful son and helped the family out as much as he could." He was a city of Worcester police officer for many years, retiring with the rank of Sergeant in 1969.

To earn a little extra money, the older girls of the family would babysit for some of the Jewish families in the area. The Providence Street neighborhood was at the time predominantly Jewish. Water Street, about a block away, served as the business district for the Jewish community. My grandmother's house was located two doors away from Shaarai Torah East, 32 Providence Street, one of the neighborhood's many synagogues. My Aunt Helen said that she and her sister Peg babysat for the Rabbi's children.

Helen and her siblings "turned over every cent" of their earnings to my grandmother. Keeping the money or any part of it for themselves was never even a consideration. "My mother might give us each a quarter allowance for the week," she remembered.

Helen said, "We never knew we were poor. My mother worked very hard to support us. Fortunately, there was never any sickness in the family. We were all healthy. The good Lord must have been looking down on us." As a young child, I would occasionally stay over at my grandmother's apartment and remember her as being a meticulous housekeeper.

In the winter, my Uncle Al and my father would walk down Vernon Hill to the New Haven Railroad freight yard on Franklin Street "with a burlap sack to pick up scattered pieces of coal that had fallen from the railroad cars." They lugged their heavy load back home to feed the furnace so there would be heat in the house. "Some days," my father said, "we came home empty-handed." He told me this story many times. If a train of cars loaded with coal just happened to be sitting in the yard, they might have helped themselves to some of the contents, but my father would never admit to this.

My Aunt Helen says that her mother held Irish dances in their home every Saturday night, charging the guests a small admission fee. Two large sliding doors separated the two main rooms of the apartment, converting the living room and the dining area into one large open space. The family moved the parlor furniture and dining room table off to the side and placed kitchen chairs around the perimeter walls to provide additional seating.

During the week, the entire family helped out, baking and making home-made beer to sell to the men. Remember, this was during the Prohibition Era. "Sometimes the bottles were only hours old when the guests arrived," Helen said. There was cake and tea available for the women.

My grandmother was an excellent concertina player and provided the music. Helen said that her mother hired a violinist named Tom Louney to accompany her on Saturday nights and paid him fifty cents. Most of the people in attendance were Irish. Many, she said, worked at Worcester State Hospital on Belmont Street. At the time, Helen said, there was no place to go in the city to hear the music and songs of their homeland. An Italian family lived on the first floor and a Jewish family on the third; they had a standing invitation to attend at no charge.

How well I remember my father or his sisters coaxing my grandmother to play Irish jigs and reels at family gatherings. Despite having tremors caused by Parkinson's disease, she played extremely well. While Margaret played, she was all smiles and never seemed to tire. All the grandchildren would get up and dance. We called her Nana. Margaret passed away in 1960 at the age of sixty-eight.

World War II officially began on September 1, 1939, when Germany invaded Poland. Sixteen days later, on September 17, Soviet troops crossed the Polish border and attacked the beleaguered country from the east. By late September, the military high command along with officials of the Polish government had escaped into exile. Hitler and Stalin partitioned the country, with the Soviets occupying the eastern third. Following the defeat of the Polish Army, Hitler's powerful war machine in turn easily crushed the defenses of Denmark, Luxembourg, the Netherlands, Belgium, Norway, and France. On June 10, 1940, Italy entered the war on the side of Germany and declared war on Great Britain and France.

One month later, on July 11, 1940, Herman Goering's Luftwaffe began an all-out attack on British ports, airfields, and industrial centers, thus commencing the Battle of Britain. Beginning in August 1940, Luftwaffe bombers carried out a series of "attacks on the population and air defenses of major British cities, including London by day and by night." The "Blitz," from "blitzkrieg," the British name for the sustained attacks, lasted until mid-May 1941. The fighting soon spread to Greece and North Africa.

At this time, a majority of the people in the United States believed the country should remain neutral. President Franklin Delano Roosevelt and other interventionists urged support of the nations fighting the Axis powers, "short of war." Isolationists, opposed to any kind of U.S. aid to the nations fighting against Germany, accused the president "of steering the nation into a war it was not prepared to fight."

On March 11, 1941, Congress approved the "Lend-Lease Act," proposed by Roosevelt, empowering the Chief Executive to supply raw materials, equipment, weapons, and food "on a cash-and-carry basis" to "any nation deemed vital to U.S. security," principally to the United Kingdom, Soviet Union, and China. As German victories continued to mount, isolationist sentiment, originally strong, began to slowly evaporate. Following the Japanese surprise attack against Pearl Harbor the movement ceased to exist altogether.

During the late 1930s, the U.S. military was woefully undermanned and unprepared. America needed men and materials to bring the Army up to strength in the event circumstances forced the country to enter the war. On July 1, 1940, Congress enacted the Selective Training and Service Act, the first peacetime draft in U.S. history. President Roosevelt signed the bill into law on September 16, 1940. The legislation required all male citizens between the ages of twenty-one and thirty-five to register with one of 6,443 local draft boards manned by unpaid civilians from individual communities.

The first "Selective Service draftees," later referred to as "selectees," short for "Selective Service trainees," or "inductees" (the terms were used as synonyms for "draftees"), entered the Army on November 18, 1940. The act imposed a penalty for "draft dodgers" of up to five years imprisonment and a $10,000 fine. The period of service was initially set for one year, which the government extended in August 1941, to eighteen months.

Twenty-one-year-old Joe Connole received his draft notice on January 6, 1941. He reported to the local U.S. Army Induction Center on Lamartine Street in Worcester to begin his one year of active-duty training on March 12, 1941, approximately nine months before the Japanese attack on Pearl Harbor. After the swearing in ceremony, the draftees and "enlistees" (volunteers) boarded a train at Union Station for Camp Edwards on Cape Cod to begin thirteen weeks of basic training with the 181st Infantry, a regiment of the recently mobilized 26th Massachusetts National Guard, known as the "Yankee" Division (YD). At the time, the YD, a square division, consisted of four regiments—101st, 104th, 181st, and 182nd Infantry (the configuration would change to three regiments when the Army triangularized the division in February 1942). The companies comprising the battalions of the 181st Infantry, were located in Worcester and the surrounding towns of Worcester County in central Massachusetts.

Following the basic training period, which ended in mid-August, the trainees began four weeks of advanced infantry training. The training program consisted of "Brigade field exercises," involving the use of the Regimental Combat Teams (RCTs) as a whole, with supporting units—a Field Artillery Battalion, an Engineer Battalion, and a Medical Battalion—participating. The 26th Division history defines a Combat Team as "the basic foundation for providing a highly mobile, self-sufficient, shock-producing, and well-balanced striking force." This "highly flexible organization . . . could be adjusted by adding or detaching supporting troops to the Infantry Regiments as the situation required." The second phase of the advanced training program involved the introduction of new "Blitz[krieg] tactics" being employed by German forces in Eastern Europe.

From August 19 to September 12, 1941, the division participated in the U.S. Army VI Corps maneuvers—a "tactical affair"—at Fort Devens, Ayer, Massachusetts, in northern Worcester County. The field exercises, which extended over the terrain north of Fort Devens into New Hampshire to a point just south of the city of Nashua, marked the beginning of a "very rugged" three weeks of training for the troops of the division. The primary purpose of the Devens exercises was to coordinate mechanized attacks—those carried out by armored vehicles, including light and medium tanks, half tracks, and scout cars—with infantry tactics "in a two-sided maneuver."

Sixth Corps Headquarters designed the Devens maneuvers as a precursor to the U.S. Army war games (General Headquarters or GHQ maneuvers) scheduled for the Carolinas from October 2 to December 3, 1941. For the first time, division forces would take part in large-scale simulated combat exercises involving troops and units from other divisions. According to historian Christopher R. Gabel, the "fundamental goal" of GHQ planners "was to make the maneuvers as much like real war as possible in order to test and train under near battle conditions."

The training exercises conducted by the War Department in Louisiana and the Carolinas during the summer and fall of 1941, were the largest mass maneuvers and gathering of troops since World War I, with "nearly half" of the Army's total manpower, approximately 500,000 troops (fighting men plus support personnel), participating "in these enormous field exercises."

After more than two months of strenuous training, the troops of the 26th Infantry Division departed North Carolina and returned to Camp Edwards, arriving on Sunday, December 6, 1941. The men awoke on the morning of December 7, 1941, and prepared to go on leave. Many, who had completed their one year of active duty, were eligible for immediate discharge. A considerable number had already left the camp for home the previous evening. By noontime, the camp was all but deserted with the exception of a few officers and enlisted men from each unit left behind to secure the area. At 2:25 that afternoon, the almost unbelievable news that the Japanese had attacked Pearl Harbor came over the airwaves. Throughout the camp, men "filled with tenseness," remained glued to every available radio listening to the latest news bulletins.

Following the declaration of war against the Axis powers by Congress on December 8, 1941, the War Department charged the 26th Division with the responsibility of guarding the New England coast and parts of Long Island, New York, later expanded to include the entire east coast of the United States as part of the country's "home defense." Given the fear and paranoia of the time, there was great concern among government and military officials about the threat of a German invasion, as well as the possibility of incursions by Nazi spies and saboteurs on American shores. The troops of the division bivouacked on the beaches and pulled sentry duty along the eastern seaboard from the Canadian border to the Florida Keys.

The 181st Infantry was responsible for securing the coast from the Canadian border south to the Massachusetts-New Hampshire line; the 101st covered the Boston Sector to the Connecticut-Rhode Island line; the U.S. Navy patrolled the Connecticut coast, from Quonset Point, Rhode Island, west to the Naval Base at New London; and Coast Guard personnel patrolled the Washington, D.C. area, as well as all areas around all Naval bases. The 104th Infantry patrolled the remainder of the east coast from North Carolina southward to Key West, Florida, a distance of more than 1,000 miles.

The 181st Infantry spent approximately twenty months on Coast Patrol duty from January 1942, until November 1943 (interrupted by three months of combat training at Camp Edwards beginning in March 1942). Joe Connole was a member of Company H, 2nd Battalion, stationed in Saco (pronounced Soco), Maine. The regiment patrolled the coast from Machias, Maine, near the Canadian border, to the Massachusetts-New Hampshire line. During this period, my father volunteered to serve with a provisional Military Police (MP) Unit.

Beginning in 1943, the Navy and Coast Guard, having increased their numbers to full war strength, began to assume more and more of the Coast Patrol duties. One by one, the War Department relieved the remaining 26th Division units from patrol duty assigning them to various military bases in the east to undergo combat training and exercises. In January 1943, the Eastern Defense Command decided to separate the 181st Infantry, from the 26th Division and leave it on Coast Patrol in the New England Sector. This left the triangular division with only two regiments.

In May 1943, the entire division (minus the 181st Infantry) reassembled at Camp Gordon, Georgia, where it remained until July 1943. The War Department added a third regiment, the 328th, to replace the 181st, bringing the division back up to full strength. Over the next 11 months, the 26th moved several times, participating in additional training exercises and combat maneuvers in preparation for an overseas assignment. The division shipped out to the European Theater on August 24, 1944.

Foot and motor patrols remained in effect along the eastern seaboard until the fall of 1943, when both the Army and the Coast Guard gradually phased them out. By this time, United States military forces had successfully carried the war to the enemy to the point where the maintenance of a domestic defensive force was no longer necessary. The military replaced regular beach patrols with cavalry reconnaissance groups, which served as a mobile reconnoitering and striking force.

On November 30, 1943, the War Department relieved the 181st Infantry from duty within the New England Sector and assigned the unit to "AGF & XIII Corps," Fort Dix, New Jersey. The regiment proceeded from original stations by motor transport and assembled at Fort Devens, Massachusetts on December 4, 1943. The troops of the unit left Fort Devens the same day and proceeded by rail to Fort Dix, arriving at their destination on December 5, 1943. Division issued many of the men a thirty-day "delay en route" order that allowed them to go home and spend the Christmas holidays with their families before reporting to their units at Fort Dix. Twenty-four-year old Pvt. Dennis "Joe" Connole was one of the lucky ones and this was the last time he would see his family until after the war.

In February 1944, the U.S. Army ordered all enlisted men (EMs) from the 181st Infantry to report to Replacement Depot #1 (known to American servicemen as a "repple-depple"), at Fort Meade, Maryland. The majority went to Italy as replacements. Among this group was my father. The Non-Commissioned Officers (NCOs) were sent to Indiantown Gap, Pennsylvania, where they were "cataloged and 'held on the shelf'" until a combat outfit had a particular need for their Military Occupation Specialty (MOS). When a slot opened up due to battlefield losses, units selected NCOs from the pool.

At Fort Dix, the Army officially inactivated the 181st Infantry Regiment, effective February 8, 1944.

The original invasion of the European mainland began on September 9, 1943, when Allied forces landed at Salerno, Italy ("Operation Avalanche"). During the winter of 1943–44, the advance up the Italian peninsula toward Rome by Lieutenant General Mark W. Clark's U.S. Fifth Army had stalled. Fighting against entrenched and heavily fortified enemy positions in the rugged, mountainous terrain, the American divisions suffered heavy casualties and were badly in need of replacements. The majority of the 181st Infantry Regiment's enlisted men shipped out to the European Theater of Operations (ETO) in early February for reassignment to one of the decimated combat divisions.

Chapter Three

Overseas

On February 27, 1944, Pfc. Joe Connole boarded the USS *General Alexander E. Anderson* (AP-111), a U.S. Navy troop ship, for transport to the European Theater of Operations (ETO). From November 25, 1943, to March 21, 1944, the *Anderson* made four round-trip transport voyages out of Norfolk, Virginia, to ports in North Africa and back, a distance of approximately 8,240 nautical miles. Designed to carry 5,289 passengers and 118,175 cubic feet of cargo, the *Anderson* had a crew complement of 43 officers and 464 enlisted men.

The United States Maritime Commission (MC) named the vessel in memory of Major General Alexander Edward Anderson, "a distinguished soldier" who rose up through the ranks to become a commanding officer of the "Fighting Irish" 69th Regiment, 42nd Division. Anderson fought on the Western Front during World War I and won the D.S.C., D.S.M., Croix De Guerre with star and palm and the Legion of Honor. The War Department appointed Anderson commander of the 86th "Blackhawk" Infantry Division upon its activation on December 15, 1942. He died suddenly just ten days later on December 24, 1942.

Constructed by the Federal Shipbuilding and Dry Dock Company of Kearney, New Jersey, the USS *A.E. Anderson,* which had a displacement of 20,175 tons fully loaded, was the second of eleven General class of ships built by the MC between 1943 and 1945—the first was the USS *General John Pope* (AP 110)—all named for generals. The MC designed this class of vessel to transport a minimum of 5,000 infantry troops, both regular Army units and replacements, with all necessary equipment. The U.S. Navy placed the ship in "full commission" on October 5, 1943. The same day, "a virgin crew" took the *Anderson* out on a nineteen-day shakedown cruise with Captain William E. Miller in command.

Ships included in the General class had a unique hull design, identified as the P2, with "a distinctive clipper bow." The superstructure had two pole masts and a pair of racked stacks. Driven by two steam-turbine engines, with 18,700 shaft horsepower, and twin screws, the P2s were extremely fast and highly maneuverable. With a top speed of 20.6 knots, these ships sailed the high seas without escort and could outrun any submarine. The P2s "had two independent engine rooms so that . . . if hit while plying enemy submarine in-fested waters," the vessels still "had a chance to navigate."

In the event of a catastrophic sinking resulting from a torpedo strike or bombing by enemy aircraft, it was "an unspoken secret" that the APs did not have the capacity to assure survival of the 5,289 passengers and a crew of 507. Aboard the APs, designed to land dockside in a deep harbor, there were a limited number of lifeboats.

Armament aboard the *Anderson* consisted of four single 5-inch/.38 caliber dual purpose (DP) gun mounts designed for both surface and antiaircraft use; sixteen 1.1-inch/.70 caliber quadruple heavy machine gun mounts for air de-fense; and twenty, single 20mm antiaircraft guns. Naval historians consider the 5-inch/.38 caliber deck gun one of the most effective shipboard weapons employed during World War II.

Troops boarded the USS *Anderson* for the February 27 voyage at the "south side Pier #6, Chesapeake and Ohio Railroad Piers, Hampton Roads Port of Embarkation [P.O.E.], Newport News, Va." When the trains pulled into the station at the P.O.E., Transportation Corps personnel with red-and-gold armbands marched the troops directly to the ship. Red Cross volunteers, young women, were on hand to serve coffee and doughnuts and a U.S. Army band ("port band") was on hand to give the troops a rousing farewell. Mili-tary Historian Lee B. Kennett says that the band "played First World War tunes such as 'Over There' and songs representing the states that the National Guard divisions were from." Few of the men had ever been abroad and ship travel was a novel experience.

Kennett says the men had their unit designation chalked on the front of their helmets and that "boarding was done 'by the numbers.'" GIs, carrying or dragging heavy barracks bags or a duffel bag, weapon, and loaded down with backpack, gas mask, web-belt with canteen, bayonet, and other gear, struggled up the steep-angled gangplank. "As each man came forward his last name was called, he answered with his first name and initial, and he was checked off." Once onboard, ship's personnel directed the men to their assigned berth, "which," Kennett says, "was usually far deeper into the bowels of the ship than [they] imagined it would be." In some quarters, bunks were positioned right up against the ship's hull with only three-quar-ters of an inch of steel between the men and the open ocean. Many feared that if a torpedo struck they would not be able to make it topside before the ship sank.

U.S.S. General Alexander E. Anderson (AP-111).

Dennis J. Connole (c.1942).

The training of "Army lookouts and gun crews," made up of volunteers, took place on the same day. The ship got underway at 10 A.M., on the twenty-eighth, and "steamed independently" (not part of a convoy—see Rajotte below) toward its destination "in accordance with COMFIVE's secret letter Serial # UG-19, 25 February 1944." Once at sea, the ship's commander opened the sealed order disclosing the *Anderson*'s destination—Oran, Algeria, North Africa.

Three days out of port (March 1), the transport encountered a "moderate to strong SW'ly gale, with vessel yawing to rough westerly seas," that lasted through March 4. Many of the young GIs had never set foot on a ship before and seasickness became a major problem.

On March 3, 4, and 6, assigned gun crews took part in "target and spotting practice," expending 752 rounds ("49 r[oun]ds AA 5?-38; 253 r[oun]ds, 1.1"; and "450 r[oun]ds 20mm") of ammunition. The weather cleared on March 5, "with light winds, calm sea, with long rolling W'ly swells." The *Anderson* arrived at its destination in Oran, on March 9, 1944, after eleven days at sea. Slower Liberty Ships averaged twenty-six to twenty-eight days for the same voyage. William E. "Gene" Hamelman, a crewmember onboard the "Andy" during the fourth voyage, remembers the cruise as being "pretty routine."

While onboard the *Anderson,* a U.S. Navy surgeon treated my father for a blocked eustachian tube (VA File). The doctor diagnosed the problem as a case of "otitis media," a common middle-ear infection, generally caused by bacteria or viruses, resulting in the buildup of fluid, and prescribed medication. Symptoms include pain, fever, hearing loss, and in some cases, loss of appetite, vomiting, tinnitus, or a dizzy feeling. The attending physician's report states "blocked Eustachian tube, bulging of ear drum."

Rosaire "Ross" Rajotte, a native of Northbridge, Massachusetts, was another member of the 181st Infantry, 26th "Yankee" Division who, like my father, later served with the 36th "Texas" Division (A-141). Rajotte also sailed overseas aboard the USS *A.E. Anderson*, about one month earlier than my father did, on January 22, 1944. The P.O.E. was Newport News, Virginia. He wrote,

"After the Army inactivated the 181st Infantry at Fort Dix in early 1944, the men of the regiment received orders to ship out to various locations overseas, primarily to Italy, as replacements for Army Ground Troop Units."

Rajotte remembers that the USS *A.E. Anderson* was not part of a convoy. Two British destroyers led the way and U.S. Navy patrol aircraft flew overhead part of the way for protection. He claims there were 8,000 soldiers onboard; if correct, this number far exceeded the ship's official capacity. "We were all cooped up," Rajotte said. Samuel F. "Sam" Kibbey of Ypsilanti, Michigan, a sergeant with Company K, 143rd Infantry, said the ship he sailed over on "was so jam-packed, I didn't know whether I was a sardine or a soldier," a comparison used by a number of others who made similar voyages. The ship carried troops across and wounded GIs and German POWs back.

Officers and NCOs issued a stern warning about throwing anything at all overboard—food or trash, including something as small as a cigarette butt—which, supposedly, might leave a trail and give the ship's position or direction away. The 141st regimental history reported that one man on the S.S. *Brazil,* "was fined $15.00 for throwing an apple core over the side." For this reason, shipboard regulations did not allow smoking anywhere above deck. Below deck, the smoking lamp was lit from sunup to sunset. The ship's strict regulations prohibited lights of any kind during the hours of darkness, for obvious reasons, and did not permit any noise or loud talking.

Men passed the time reading, writing, or otherwise relaxing in quarters or on deck. Books were passed around and read over and over again. Small groups lounged around, as much as the cramped conditions would allow, chatting, telling stories, and cracking an occasional joke or pulling pranks. Some men relieved the monotony by joining one of the marathon card or dice games in quarters or on deck. Several days out of port, officers passed out booklets and other literature containing useful information about the language and customs of the country of destination.

Under such crowded conditions, the ship's ventilation system was insufficient, "and the compartments," Kennett says, "became hot and dank." Most men preferred to spend their time up on deck during the daylight hours to escape the smoke-filled, stuffy, foul-smelling quarters. The men perspired profusely in the cramped sleeping quarters. After several days at sea, the stench from perspiration-soaked clothes and unwashed bodies, combined with that of vomit, became almost unbearable. Men found it difficult to sleep amidst the ship's noises and a constant chorus of snoring. In the cramped holds, tempers sometimes flared and fights broke out.

"At nightfall, the ship's public address system announced 'All troops lay below,' and the decks were cleared," Kennett wrote. Guards patrolled the decks continuously to ensure that troops obeyed the order. Officers, however, were allowed to roam the decks freely, a source of deep resentment among the enlisted men.

Troops lined the ship's railings, mesmerized by the constant wave action and the endless horizon. Some hung on the rails, vomiting endlessly. Near sunset, men stared at the ocean, transfixed by the eerie bluish-green fluorescent glow in the water, created by the ship's bow wave or wake.

One can only imagine what it must have been like for the men heading overseas and to war. As the ship carried them farther and farther from their homeland, many sat in quiet solitude thinking about that "special person" they were out with the last night of leave, or the saddened faces of parents and siblings when they last said their good-byes. Some were preoccupied with what the future had in store. A few prayed silently that a miracle would occur and the war would suddenly end. If the chilling thought that many might never come back did enter their minds, it was quickly suppressed.

Berthing accommodations for the enlisted men were the same on every ship, wrote Kennett. Tiers of fold-down "canvas and metal-frame bunks, six feet long and two feet wide, suspended by chains or standees and stacked one above the other—as many as six high," lined every bulkhead and compartment. In some parts of the ship, the aisles between rows of bunks were so narrow a person had to walk sideways. There was a "two foot space between bunks," making it difficult to shift position or roll over. To make matters worse, each man had to share the limited bunk space with all of his equipment. Men used their life preservers as a pillow and arranged barracks bag and equipment into some semblance of order so as to be as comfortable as possible. The men slept fully clothed and kept their life jackets within easy reach in case of an emergency. Kennett says that "some men slept in their life-saving vests."

On some of the more crowded transports, there was double and even triple bunking—men had to sleep in shifts, which meant giving up their bunk to another GI during specified sleep periods, wrote Kennett. Periodic announcements echoed throughout the ship, warning all U.S. Army personnel to carry their life jackets with them at all times when moving about the ship.

Rajotte said the men had no duties and were free to go anywhere unrestricted on the ship. The only requirement was that the replacement companies take a turn on deck doing calisthenics for at least one hour each day. The Officer of the Day (OD) lined the men up three rows deep on each side of the deck and then turned the exercise duties over to a non-com.

The crossing hazards—German "wolf pack" submarines and mines—were a constant threat to the convoys. The troop ships zigzagged their way across the Atlantic, changing course every fifteen minutes, to present a difficult target for

U-boats prowling the high seas. This turned what normally would have been a four- to five-day trip for one of the speedy Navy transports into one of eleven to fourteen days or for many of the convoys as long as twenty-eight to twenty-nine days. Most men decided they had little control over the situation, so it was not worth worrying about. Rajotte said that after a while he "stopped thinking about it."

The weather, according to Rajotte, was unseasonably mild all the way over and, fortunately, seas were calm. It was January, but Rajotte remembers the conditions on deck as being sunny and warm for most of the voyage. In spite of the fair weather, a considerable number of the men suffered from bouts of seasickness. "I did not get seasick, but a lot of the guys were very ill," Rajotte remarked.

The troops were also required to participate in mandatory "abandon ship drills," conducted daily. Navy crewmembers directed each group to a designated spot on deck for assembly in the event of an emergency. During the drill, officers checked the men to see that their Mae West life jackets were on correctly and adjusted properly, and instructed them on the proper procedures to follow if the ship was sinking. Officers warned the men that during bad weather the deck of a ship could be a hazardous place and to use caution when moving about. If, during the voyage, anyone fell overboard he would be left behind. The risk to the thousands of troops aboard and the millions of dollars' worth of goods and supplies was just too great a chance to take.

The troops ate twice a day—breakfast and supper. There were so many men onboard mess cooks served the meals in shifts. It was one continuous chow line from early morning until late in the evening. Cooking went on all the time and a constant odor of food permeated the ship, much to the dismay of the seasick soldiers. Even on deck, one could not escape the smell of food cooking.

After crossing the Atlantic, the convoys passed through the Gibraltar Strait, twenty-two miles long and eight miles wide, between the coast of Tangier, French Morocco, on the south, and the southern coast of Spain on the north, and entered the high seas of the blue Mediterranean. On clear days, passengers and crew caught a beautiful view of the famous Rock of Gibraltar, 426 meters high (1,397 feet). Gibraltar is a territory of the United Kingdom. The USS *Anderson* proceeded through the "mine-swept channel" of the straits between 8:57 and 10:31 P.M., on March 8, 1944, giving passengers a view of the rock just before sunset, which must have been a spectacular sight.

The troop transports continued on, hugging the North African coast, to dock at the great French Port at Oran, Algeria, or another of the Allied Mediterranean ports. Upon exiting the strait, the *Anderson* rendezvoused with the British destroyers HMS *Witherington* (D 76) and HMS *Wishart* (D 67), for escort to their final destination. At 11:43 A.M., on March 9, the *Anderson* entered the mine-swept channel on the approach to the city of Oran, Algeria, docking at "Berth #10" at 1:05 P.M. The main body of troops commenced debarking at 4:45 P.M.

The passengers marched to an enclosure about five miles outside of Oran where they bivouacked for several days awaiting passage to Italy. Following the layover, officers and noncoms herded the men onboard waiting transport vessels, primarily freighters of foreign registry, that ferried them to the harbor at Naples, a three- to four-day trip.

Ross Rajotte made the voyage aboard an Australian ship, the name of which he says he has long since forgotten. There were no bunks. The only sleeping accommodations were hammocks suspended from the steel framework inside the ship's compartments. This was a "unique experience" for most, Rajotte said, and for the first several days everyone had to help each other climb in and out of the swinging cots without flipping over and out again, landing hard on the steel floor. He says the Aussie sailors got a big kick out of watching the Americans trying to master the tricky procedure. It must have been a comical sight, something out of a Three Stooges movie. During the day the men placed their barracks bags in the hammocks so members of the ship's crew could swab the floors.

"It was a rough voyage in quarters 'below the waterline,' made worse by the horrid food that caused [the men's] stomachs to retch in protest," Rajotte recalled. "Guys would no sooner finish eating when they would throw it all up—they just could not keep the food down," he commented. "The voyage took several days but it seemed like an eternity."

The men's opinion of the food on the voyage between North Africa and Italy was unanimous: it was bad. Jack Clover (Hq. 2nd Bn., 143) of Columbus, Ohio, wrote, "We had sailed from Africa on a limey boat which basically served lousy mutton and mint sauce and tea. This food made C Rations taste like eating at the Waldorf." Allen E. Stern (B-142) from Brooklyn, New York, wrote, "We were put on a British boat headed for Italy. She was so old, I was always expecting them to run up the sails. We slept in hammocks suspended over the mess tables. The food was terrible." Stern says he managed to trade "some American cigarettes (African price $3 a pack)," for some decent food from the officers' mess.

During Rajotte's voyage to Naples, the ship's claxon horns wailed and the PA announcer shouted orders for the crew to man their battle stations. Word quickly got around that a German U-boat had fired a torpedo at the ship. Rajotte later spoke with one of the ship's crewmen, who informed him that the torpedo missed the stern by a mere six feet. He said the incident seemed to be no big deal to the sailor, almost as if it were a common occurrence.

Sulo Ruuska, who like my father was originally a member of Company H, 181st Infantry, 26th Division, traveled from Oran to Naples on the Polish Freighter SS *Sobieski*, a "passenger-cargo" vessel converted to a troop carrier. An all-British crew manned the ship. "What a tub she was!" declared George A. Benton (A-143), another GI who sailed aboard the *Sobieski*. Ruuska spoke with several members of the crew, who told him they had not been home to England in more than five years. Early one morning, a British officer called over the ship's speakers for the crew to fall in on deck for a first-class inspection. Ruuska could not help but notice that their dress uniforms were tattered and frayed and their assorted footwear well-worn from age.

Ruuska said that the American troops had had only one decent meal during the voyage; the rest of the time, "we were served a gruel-like slop that tasted just awful." Ruuska remembers the small loaves of bread served with each meal being full of cockroaches. "The cooks baked them right into the bread." When Ruuska broke open one of the loaves, he thought the dark spots were raisins at first, but upon closer inspection discovered what they really were. He threw the bread in the garbage along with most of the meal.

One day Ruuska went below deck to visit his friend, Nicholas J. "Nick" Renzetti (H-181) of Boston, who was pulling K.P. (Kitchen Police) duty in the galley. Nick was washing the seemingly endless stacks of dirty dishes (probably used in the officer's mess as enlisted men ate out of their mess kits) and utensils in a large double-welled stainless-steel sink. Renzetti explained how he scraped the food off the plates, dipped them in soapy water, and rinsed them under hot running salt water. He then handed the clean dishes to an Indian kitchen worker, who dried them with a bed sheet. The sheet was dragging on the slop-covered floor. The stoves and ovens were working twenty-four hours a day, causing the temperature of the galley to hover close to 100 degrees. The Indian, who wore only a loincloth and turban, was sweating profusely. "Every so often, he took the sheet, wiped his face and armpits and went right on drying the plates," Renzetti said with a laugh.

As Ruuska and Renzetti talked, a line of cockroaches came out of a crack in the wall and crawled across a small, narrow shelf about four inches wide just above the back of the sink. Nick, pointing, said, "Watch this." The insects started coming out of the wall in greater and greater numbers, forming a wide column. Thousands emerged and for several minutes marched, as if in military formation, toward a second opening in the opposite wall, into which the rear of the long column eventually disappeared. "They'll be back," said Nick, as he continued washing the plates. "And sure enough," Sulo said, "after a while they reversed direction and went back into the hole from which they came." "Where did they go?" Sulo asked. "Who the hell knows?" was Nick's reply.

During the voyage, a huge storm began brewing. As the tempest increased in intensity and fury, the ship pitched and rolled violently in the mountainous swells. A Dutch destroyer, escorting the *Sobieski* for protection, led the way. "The waves got so high, the destroyer went down into a trough and all we could see was the top of the mast," Sulo said. Men became violently seasick—including Ruuska. "Many could not make it to the head and threw up all over themselves and the floor." The ship was pitching so badly, men were slipping and sliding all over the place on the slick, vomit-covered floors. The quarters reeked from the vile odor.

Outside, the gale-force winds howled and a continuous chorus of loud creaks, groans, and other mysterious noises echoed throughout the troop's quarters, sounding as if the vessel would suddenly break apart at any moment. Each time the stern came out of the water, the ship shuddered and the propellers made a loud whirring noise as they sped up. When the ship finally arrived at Naples on the fourth day, Ruuska, who weighed not more than 110 pounds, was so weak he could not lift his barracks bag. One of the men in his group carried the bag off the ship and helped throw it up on the truck for him.

Calvin R. Wilson of Kansas City, Missouri, sailed from Newport News in April 1944, aboard the SS *Benjamin Franklin,* a Liberty-type troop transport. The *Franklin* was part of a large convoy of ships crossing the Mediterranean. Eighteen-year-old Wilson volunteered as an assistant gunner for one of the 20mm antiaircraft guns on the bridge. Near Algiers, in the Mediterranean Sea, the transport came under attack by several German torpedo bombers. "Our ship was equipped with torpedo nets, thank God," Wilson said.

During the attack, the Naval Air Guard, flying top cover for the convoy, received credit for downing two of the enemy aircraft. Two days later, the ship made a scheduled stop at a Sicilian port. As the Franklin was preparing to enter the harbor, the ship's crew raised the protective steel anti-torpedo nets that hung from the sides of the vessel. Entangled by its fins in the starboard side net was a live torpedo. The Navy commander pulled the vessel out of the convoy and diverted her to Malta, about 100 miles away, where a British demolition team disarmed the device and removed it from the net. "We rejoined the convoy at Sicily, and proceeded on to Naples Harbor," Wilson said. In May 1944, Pvt. Wilson drew an assignment to Company F, 142nd Infantry, just in time for the breakout at Anzio.

Chapter Four

Replacements Join the
36th "Texas" Division

The 36th Division was originally a Texas National Guard outfit made up almost entirely of citizen-soldiers from the "Lone Star state." The division, commanded by Major General Fred L. Walker, was the first Allied force to land on the continent of Europe when it hit the beaches at Salerno, Italy, on September 8, 1943. Between the date of the landings and February 27, 1944, when the Fifth Army relieved the 36th from the fighting at Monte Cassino, the division had experienced a considerable reduction in numbers. During this period, division troops had spent a total of 104 days (out of 171) on the front lines.

Continued fighting between November 15, 1943, and December 27, 1943, resulted in heavy losses. Despite strong opposition and severe winter weather—during one period it rained for seventeen consecutive days—division forces captured Mt. Maggiore, Mt. Lungo, and the village of San Pietro Infine. The German Bernhardt or "Winter Line" ("Winterstellungen"), an indepth series of fortified defenses, passed directly through the hillside town of San Pietro, blocking the Allied entrance to the Liri Valley, considered the best avenue of advance toward Rome. Historian Robert L. Wagner described the capture of San Pietro as "the key to breaching" the outer defenses of the Winterstellungen. Total battle casualties for the division during the month of December numbered 1,169 killed, wounded, and missing, while non-battle casualties (sickness, disease, and injury) totaled 2,186. Following the Battle of San Pietro (December 8–17), the 143rd Infantry Regiment was at twenty-seven percent of full strength and required 1,100 replacements; the 141st Infantry was at fifty-seven percent of full strength; and the 142nd at sixty-three percent of full strength.

Fifth Army pulled the 36th Division out of the line in early January for two weeks of "training and refitting." During this period, II Corps units (3rd, 34th, and 45th Divisions) made good progress pushing forward to the Rapido River, part of the Gustav or Cassino Line, the last major defensive barrier of the Winter Line. At this juncture in the campaign, Lieutenant General Mark W. Clark, Fifth Army Commander, proposed sending one infantry division to spearhead the assault, crossing the Rapido near San Angelo and then driving up the Liri Valley in the direction of Rome. Defending the main line of resistance (MLR) behind the Rapido was the numerically superior 15th Panzer Grenadier Division, considered one of the best German units in Italy. For the mission, set to begin on January 21, Clark chose the 36th Division.

The "ill-conceived" and "poorly planned" operation, "designed by Corps and Army Commanders," which called for a direct frontal assault across an unfordable river against a well-entrenched and determined enemy, ended in complete disaster. The physical odds—difficulties of terrain and severe winter weather—proved insurmountable. At the main crossing point, the swift-flowing Rapido averaged twenty-five to fifty feet across and ten to fifteen feet deep with vertical banks varying in height from three to six feet. Approaches to the river consisted of flat, soggy marshland, which hampered all movement. The Germans had cleared "all vegetation of any importance" on both sides of the river and heavily mined the areas. In addition, units of the division lacked sufficient boats, bridging equipment, and training in river crossings. Failure of the mission resulted in 2,128 casualties, including 155 killed, 1,052 wounded, and 921 missing or captured, one of the worst defeats suffered by the Americans during the war.

My father joined the 36th Infantry Division at Maddaloni, Italy, on March 18, 1944. Maddaloni, a supply depot and bivouac area for the 141st Infantry, was located about four miles from the Royal Palace at Caserta, approximately eighteen miles north of Naples. The decimated units of the 36th arrived at Maddaloni on March 6, 1944, to undergo an "intensive rebuilding and refitting program" out of the line. In March, the division received 1,350 enlisted men as replacements and an additional 750 the following month, with smaller numbers arriving from time to time. In time, as more and more men from other states joined the division as replacements, the 36th gradually evolved into an "All American" division.

The "good old boys" from Texas had strong patriotic feelings for their home state. Ross Rajotte (A-141) was one of the first of the replacements assigned to the decimated 36th Division in early February 1944. His first impressions were that "the Texans were still fighting the Civil War. They were the Rebels and we were the Yankees," he said. Many of the original Texas-bred T-Patchers still harbored a basic distrust of all northerners. It did not take long, however, for the north and south to come together and become fast friends. The boys from Texas soon learned that their counterparts from other areas of the country were not much different from themselves, except maybe for the way they spoke and eventually accepted them into the fold. The GIs found that they all had the same basic goal in mind—to defeat the enemy as quickly as possible and, God willing, return home safely.

When relieved at Cassino, the 36th Division moved by truck to a rest area near Pratella for several days and from there to the town of Caserta, the "Versailles of Naples," for a five-day period of Rest and Recuperation (R&R). The troops bivouacked in pyramidal tents near the Royal Palace. The palace, dating to 1752, "served as the hub of the 5th Army rest center." The "arc-like wing" extending to the left of the palace provided quarters for the battle-weary GIs. At the rest camp, they exchanged their tattered and mud-stained combat uniforms for a new set of clothes, took long hot showers, ate three delicious hot meals a day, and slept as long as they wished. Throughout their relaxing stay, the division provided plenty of group activities and great entertainment. "But what the men welcomed the most," stated *The Fighting 36th Pictorial History,* "was relief from the nervous tension synonymous with battle, the high strung feeling that wears down morale."

Movie star and singer Marlene Dietrich came to Italy in March 1944, on a USO tour, "to brighten the spirits of [the] battle-worn GIs." Nightclub comedian and singer Danny Thomas emceed the show. The program featured slow, sultry songs by Dietrich, plus music, comedy, and dancing by Milton Frome and Lynne Mayberry. Later that month, the USO troupe stopped at Maddaloni and put on a show for the 36th Division troops. After the performance, the group stopped by the K Company, 141st Infantry mess for chow. An account of the visit published in *The Fighting 36th Historical Quarterly* in 1996 noted that Dietrich "seemed to enjoy the GIs' company (maybe not the chow) as much as they enjoyed such a vivacious and beautiful lady."

During the spring thaw, the bivouac area at Maddaloni turned into a vast sea of mud, knee-deep in many places. A late winter storm in early April covered the area with two inches of snow. As the days grew longer, the cold, rainy weather soon ended and temperatures began to increase steadily. The bright Mediterranean sunshine dried and cracked the mud, eventually turning it into a fine-powdery gray dust, volcanic in origin. The wind, combined with heavy vehicular and foot traffic, churned up thick, billowing clouds of the minute particles, which swept across the grounds of the encampment, coating everyone and everything. The ever-present dust irritated eyes, nose, and throats and made breathing difficult.

Each company drew a specific number of sorely needed replacements to fill the diminished ranks. Officers assigned these to each of the depleted platoons as needed. The Division G-3 Section (Operations and Planning) scheduled training exercises from dawn to dusk five days a week, conducted under the direction of the officers and NCOs. The "greenhorns" or "rookies" had a lot to learn—but they had good teachers, combat-wise infantrymen with plenty of experience who tried to teach them what they needed to know to survive in combat.

The under-strength units welcomed the addition of the replacements. During the training period, the new men had a chance to mix with the veterans of the division, with whom they would very soon be fighting alongside. After a short adjustment period, the new boys fit right in. Many of the battle-hardened troops took the rookies under their wing and looked out for their welfare. Replacements trained side-by-side with the "old men" of the outfit and, in the process, picked up many valuable tips about staying alive. Strong bonds of friendship soon developed between the new and the experienced men.

Joe Connole was a Yankee, one of many that joined the Texas Army in early 1944, and became an "adopted Texan." Originally assigned to a rifle company (VA File), regimental headquarters later reassigned him to Company D, a heavy weapons company, 141st Infantry, and placed him in the mortar (3rd) platoon. It is likely his superiors made the change because of his prior experience with mortars in the 26th Division. "This is not the way the Army usually operated," said Romeo LeBlanc with a bit of cynicism. LeBlanc was with my father as a member of Company H, 181st Infantry, 26th Division. "Usually if someone is trained in a particular MOS [Military Occupation Specialty], the Army would place them in a totally unrelated field. If someone is trained as a cook, they were certain to end up as a truck driver, or vice versa." The simple fact of the matter, he said, was that, "men were sent where needed, despite previous training." Edward A. Chrobak, another "Yankee" who ended up in the 36th Division, was a member of E Company, 142nd Infantry. Chrobak was a native of Sutton, Massachusetts. After basic training, the Army sent him to Georgia for training with a field artillery unit. "I ended up as a rifleman," said Chrobak.

When my father joined Company D, 141st Infantry, the Commanding Officer (CO) was 1st Lt. Robert "Bob" Arn, and 2nd Lt. William A. Hawkins of Mebane, North Carolina, was the Executive Officer (XO). After Arn received a wound on May 31, 1944, Hawkins took over as CO. Lieutenant Ralph J. Eastberg, of Menominee, Michigan, commanded the 1st (machine gun) platoon. Lt. Robert Brickman of Holstein, Iowa, was the leader of the 2nd (machine gun) platoon. The mortar (3rd) platoon leader was Lt. William V. Church of Lenoir, North Carolina. John Paul Jones of Dallas, Texas, was the Supply Sergeant for Company D.

On April 9, 1944, the 141st moved to Celzi-Forino, near Avellino and Naples, where the training program resumed. The remainder of the month was devoted to mountain training, river-crossing problems, and amphibious landings. While the infantry troops of the battalion were out on the small-arms live-fire ranges, the heavy weapons companies conducted mortar and machine gun field-firing exercises at a secluded spot along the seashore south of Naples. The purpose of the exercises was to improve skills and accuracy of personnel as well as to instruct and familiarize replacements, having little or no experience, with the operation and capabilities of the weapons. Firing problems for the machine gun squads included stationary known distance targets (100 to 800 yards) as well as moving targets. Mortar platoons set up their weapons on the beach and practiced firing at targets bobbing up and down on rafts out in the bay.

Charles Golub (K-143), a native of Worcester, Massachusetts, joined the Army in 1943. After completing 13 weeks of basic infantry training at Camp Wheeler near Macon, Georgia, in March 1944, he received orders to report to the overseas processing center at Camp Patrick Henry, Newport News, Virginia. Golub sailed to Italy on the USAT *Alexander Hamilton,* a U.S. Army Transport. The embarkation point was Hampton Roads. Onboard the ship, he said, was a company of Nisei soldiers, Japanese Americans from Hawaii on their way to join the 442nd Infantry Regiment, later attached to the 36th Division.

Golub's ship went directly to Italy, landing at Brindisi, on the heel of the boot, a major Allied supply port. "On the docks," he said, "there were tons of supplies, stacked four and five stories high, plus all types of new vehicles, armament, and equipment." That evening the troops marched to the train station and loaded up on boxcars for the trip to Naples, arriving early the next morning. At Naples the troops transferred to two and one-half ton (deuce-and-a-half) GMC transport vehicles and trucked to a replacement depot (referred to by GIs as a "repple depple") in Santa Maria, a little town about fifteen miles to the north, where they stayed for approximately ten to twelve days. Eighteen to twenty thousand infantry troops crowded the camp awaiting assignment to a line outfit. "There was a lot of confusion at the camp," Golub remembered. "Long parallel rows of pup tents covered the grounds as far as the eye could see."

While at Santa Maria, training personnel conducted a live demonstration of captured German weapons for the newly arrived soldiers. The officers would show a comparison between a particular weapon and the American equivalent. "I remember the German machine pistol" (MP 38/40), said Golub, "it could fire 600 to 650 rounds per minute. A clip held maybe 30 or 40 rounds [it actually held 60 rounds]—bur-r-r-r-p, bur-r-r-r-p—the clip emptied in seconds." Thus, the weapon got its name—the "Burp gun." "This was followed by the U.S. Browning .30-caliber [M1919] light machine gun, tap, tap, tap—400 to 500 rounds per minute," Golub said. "Then came the German version [MG 42], bur-r-r-r-r-r-p, bur-r-r-r-r-r-p, bur-r-r-r-r-r-p—up to 1,550 rounds per minute. No comparison." Next, the U.S. Browning .50-caliber (H1921) heavy machine gun was contrasted with the German heavy machine gun, and "again there was no comparison," he said. In terms of sheer firepower, the German weapons were by far much superior. "It was a very dramatic presentation." Golub says that the effects of the demonstration were very devastating for the morale of the young replacements. "I remember my buddies saying, what chance do we have against weapons like this? We'll be slaughtered."

After several days, noncoms lined up the troops and handed them a slip of paper with the name of their assigned division, regiment, and company. Golub ended up in Company K, 143rd Infantry, 36th Division. "We left Santa Maria by truck and traveled for four or five hours into the mountains to a place called Celzi-Forino." Golub described Celzi-Forino as "two small towns that had merged into one large community." "I remember the road to Celzi being paved with white crushed rock and as the trucks moved along they kicked up huge rolling clouds of white dust. When we arrived at our destination, the soldiers were all covered with white powder and looked like ghosts." Major R.K. Doughty of Walpole, Massachusetts, a staff officer with the 141st Infantry S-2 (Intelligence) Section wrote, "On April 4th we moved to Celzi a small town just inland from Naples but reached by road that, in those days, twisted and turned, corkscrew fashion, over the mountains. The terrain compared closely with that part of Italy, lying along the coast between Gaeta and Anzio, where we expected to re-enter combat."

For the next several weeks, the unit underwent mountain training exercises. Forino, a medieval village surrounded by high, craggy cliffs "provided excellent ground" for the rigorous training. "From there," Golub said, "the outfit [143rd] went to the nearby town of Avellino, about sixteen or seventeen miles north of Salerno." After leaving Avellino, units traveled by truck to the Bay of Naples south of the city where amphibious training took place. Troops practiced going ashore in all types of landing craft. "Finally," he said, "we were sent to Anzio."

When Ross Rajotte's ship docked in Naples Harbor, the men assembled on deck and were addressed by the captain with a bullhorn. While Ross was a member of the 181st Infantry, he met and became friends with a young man named Manley Black from Pierce, Florida. Ross says that Manley "was a loner, who kept pretty much to himself." Black was a very religious young man who always carried his pocket edition of the New Testament wherever he went. "One of the reasons he liked me was because I was religious too," Ross said. "He trusted and confided in me." After a brief speech, the captain wished the American soldiers "good luck and good hunting." Manley was very offended by the captain's remark. He told Rajotte, "What is the matter with that man? These are not animals were going after, these are humans." "No," Rajotte said softly, "but someone has to stop Hitler."

Noncoms marched the soldiers to a replacement depot near Naples. Upon arrival, the officers lined the troops up in formation and informed them that there was an immediate need for replacements at the front. An NCO handed each man a slip of paper with the name of their assigned outfit. Rajotte and Black both drew assignments to the 36th Division: Company A, 141st and Company E, 142nd Infantry Regiments respectively. Rajotte went to one of the officers and requested that the two men be allowed to remain together, but was informed that this would not be permitted.

Several months later while in France, Rajotte happened to run into some of the men from Black's regiment and began making inquiries into his friend's whereabouts. He spoke with one of the soldiers in Easy Company, who informed him that his buddy had been killed in action by shrapnel a few weeks earlier. The loss of his close friend came as a shock and left young Rajotte devastated. One day on the trip overseas aboard the USS *A.E. Anderson,* Black confided to Rajotte, "I had a premonition last night. I won't be coming back." Speaking with Ross Rajotte by telephone almost sixty years later, the fondness he had for his companion Manley Black was clearly evident as his voice trailed off and began to crack.

In 1942, while stationed at Westerly, Rhode Island, on Coast Patrol Duty with the 26th Division, Black had fallen in love with and married a local girl named Aurelia Dinwoodie, from the nearby town of Bradford. After the war, Rajotte wrote the young widow a long letter offering his condolences and explaining what he knew about Manley's final moments in action. Other than the official notification from the War Department that Manley died in the service of his country, she knew nothing concerning the circumstances of his death. She was very appreciative of Rajotte's kind gesture. For many years after the war, Rajotte corresponded with Aurelia, who had remarried, and in 1997, she came to his home in Northbridge to visit her first husband's Army buddy.

Ross related an amusing story that happened while he was at the replacement depot. The memory of the incident stayed with him all these years. There were signs posted all around the place that read, "URINATING ON THESE GROUNDS IS PROHIBITED." One of the soldiers, a country boy, asked him what the sign meant. He chuckled and said, "Don't pee on the ground."

The need for replacements by the 36th Division was so critical that trucks waited at the staging area, engines running, to pick up the troops as soon as they arrived. NCOs loaded Rajotte and the other new men on two and one-half ton GMC transport trucks that carried them over muddy, rutted dirt roads to a base camp at the foot of "Hill 593" (Monte Calvaro), part of the "Snake's Head" ridge, northeast of Monte Cassino. The trucks averaged only fifteen miles per hour under blackout conditions, taking more than three hours to cover the forty-five-mile trip.

After dismounting, a two-man detail from each company, one leading and one at the rear, directed the new men up the mountain trail to the unit's position. The group spent all night making the long, arduous climb to the summit. When the replacements reached the top near dawn, a sergeant greeted the group and told the exhausted men to "dig in," but to stay low and curtail all movement to prevent detection by enemy snipers and artillery observers. Rajotte's company was dug in all along the forward slope of the mountain, with the Germans similarly positioned some forty to fifty yards distant.

Harassing fire from artillery and mortars was a constant threat to American positions. Enemy gunners "practically dropped the mortars in your back pocket," Rajotte wrote. GIs on the line had to keep their heads low or fall victim to deadly accurate fire from enemy snipers ever watchful for some careless soldier. Another hazard was the threat of automatic weapons fire. If a man raised his head but a few inches, Rajotte said, it resulted in "a rain of machine gun bullets." Observers watched for any telltale movement that would give a position away. Wounded men lay for hours before medics could attend to them. "You could hear the cry of wounded men in pain," Rajotte said. Emptying bowels or bladder during the daylight hours posed a major problem. Most of the GIs used their all-purpose helmets and tossed the contents over the side of their hole and down the edge of a cliff. This was Rajotte's introduction to combat.

Every Saturday morning, after a week of hard training and conditioning, the troops were required to undergo a rigorous and detailed field inspection. After inspection, the troops received weekend passes. GIs headed for the nearest bars and cafes. For many, the main interest was women. Some of the guys visited the area's picturesque towns and other nearby attractions and places of interest. Military officials had declared the city of Naples "off limits" for most of the winter months because of epidemics.

On Sunday, April 21, 1944, Joe Connole and several of his buddies visited the ruins of Pompeii. In A.D. 79, Mount Vesuvius buried the ancient city, which at the time had a population of 25,000 inhabitants, under twenty to twenty-four feet of ash and dust, smothering to death thousands who were unable to make it to safety. Archeologists had begun "organized excavations" at the site, beginning in 1860.

The group had an early breakfast in the mess hall at 6 A.M., left Caserta by passenger train at 7 A.M., and arrived at the gates of the walled city three hours later. From ten to twelve o'clock, representatives of the American Red Cross escorted individual groups on a guided tour, explaining every aspect of the city's historical development and cataclysmic demise. Among my father's estate papers was a tattered and yellowed ticket stub, kept as a remembrance of that day.

One of the highlights of the trip was a visit to the huge oval amphitheater, where officials of the city placed condemned prisoners at the mercy of a host of wild beasts to provide sport for the inhabitants. This is the oldest known arena, constructed in 89 to 75 B.C., which held 20,000 spectators, almost the entire population of the city.

The ruins were a very popular attraction for the servicemen stationed in Italy. Was it because there were so many history-minded young men in the military, or might it have been the infamous "works of art" that drew large numbers of American GIs to the site? Pompeiian's it seems were very fond of erotic images depicting either the loves of the gods or priapic prowess. Throughout the city, inhabitants richly adorned the walls and floors of private houses and other buildings with mural paintings, mosaics, and other forms of artwork.

There were colorful illustrations depicting the techniques of experienced prostitutes; figures displaying a huge phallus; or scenes of bestial coupling arranged side by side with idyllic images of romantic love. Venus, the Roman "goddess of love and nature," was the "protectress" of Pompeii. In all her many guises, Venus ruled supreme, and her exquisite naked form could be found almost everywhere in the city—paintings, statues, and even a magnificent temple. The people expected her to protect the city and bring them good luck and prosperity. Ernie Pyle, who made it a point not to miss the tour while in Italy, referred to the erotic images as "dirty pictures." He and his companions spent three hours touring the ruins and, he wrote, "decided we enjoyed it." Some of the stops along the tour route may have been very embarrassing to the mostly young female Red Cross volunteers, or did they decide to by-pass certain buildings, homes, and other sensitive locations?

Following the two-hour tour, the soldiers ate lunch, which included "sandwiches and coffee." A note on the ticket reminded soldiers to be sure to bring their canteen cup. The train departed Pompeii at 12:45 P.M., and arrived back at Caserta at 4:15 P.M.

On March 18 to 19, 1944, Vesuvius flared up with its most violent eruption in seventy-two years, depositing nearly a foot of ash in some places. Huge billows of lava dust, ash, and smoke from the volcano's crater surged skyward some thirty to forty thousand feet and many miles across. During the night, Vesuvius put on a dazzling display, as brightly colored flames spewed forth, turning the sky blood red; rivers of red lava snaked their way down the sides of the cone. American GIs were in awe of the majestic sight.

After nearly three months out of the firing line, Fifth Army Headquarters scheduled the 36th Division back at the front. On May 22, the division moved aboard troop- and tank-landing craft from Naples to the Anzio beachhead. The boats landed under cover of smoke screens and the troops closed into their assigned bivouac areas. Approximately 70,000 troops and 18,000 vehicles shared the beachhead. The 141st Regimental assembly area was located about three miles northeast of the town proper. The history of the 141st Infantry notes that the arrival of the division at the Anzio beachhead "could hardly be called a secret." Axis Sally, known to GIs as the "Berlin Bitch" or "Sultry Sally," broadcasting from Rome, announced the division's arrival.

One 36th Division GI commented, "Sally had the most beautiful, sexy voice you ever heard." First Lieutenant William A. "Buck" Rodgers of Silesia, Montana, with the S-3 Section, 2nd Battalion, 142nd Infantry, said Axis Sally played popular American dance tunes, "with lots of Bing Crosby," that made the men long for home. Between songs, she would tease them with chatter about their wives and sweethearts running around with the 4-Fers back in the states, while they were away fighting and dying for Uncle Sam. Rodgers wrote to his mother that the Germans did not understand American psychology. The daily broadcasts only made the men "more content to be here, since it serves as a reminder of all the things that we are fighting for." Sally "constantly reminded" the GIs, Rodgers told his mom, that the Jews were behind the war "for their own selfish purposes, and all the time she is talking, I am standing with my arm looped over the shoulder of Mr. [Warrant Officer Irving] Young, a Jew and one of the grandest men I have ever met."

At Anzio, the troops stayed in foxholes on the beach. The men dug square or rectangular holes about shoulder deep and covered them with two tent halves. The average foxhole was big enough for two men, others could accommodate as many as six and more. It was an easy task digging in soil, which was almost pure sand, but it had several disadvantages including frequent cave-ins that occasionally buried one or more of the occupants. Sometimes the concussion from the big guns would start the walls sliding in. "In a good dugout," wrote Pyle, "a man could keep both warm and dry."

Warren Taney, an engineer with Company B, 111th Engineer Combat Battalion, attached to the 36th Division, provided a vivid description of what it was like for the troops on the Anzio Beachhead:

> We haven't done anything since we landed here except sweat out an air raid every night and the Anzio Express[,] a big railroad gun, 280mm [which] shoots a projectile of 550 lbs. Sure sends chills up one[']s spine, but these air raids are of the worst nature. They fly over your area at night dropping a few flares and those flares hang in the sky for many minutes. They light the whole area and you could just about read a newspaper. You just lay in a foxhole or wherever you are and hope they don't drop anything on you. What a horrible sound those bombs make when they come down and also those anti-personnel bombs, which cover quite a large area.

"Anzio Annie" was the name given by the GIs to the large 283mm (11-inch) caliber "Krupp K5 series" RR gun that shelled the Allied units penned up inside the Anzio Beachhead. The piece weighed 218 tons and had a 70 foot 6-inch long barrel with a range of thirty-eight miles. The Americans discovered later that Annie was actually a pair of guns. The Germans named them "Robert" and "Leopold" (See Chapter 13).

As if that was not bad enough, the troops at Anzio had to contend with falling flak that, Taney says, killed and wounded some of the "fellows near us." Thousands of American antiaircraft batteries opened up during an air raid. He explained that a number of the shells failed to explode until they hit the ground, most likely due to malfunctions and defects. The shells were set to detonate at a specific elevation as the aircraft fly overhead, and it is possible that a certain percentage failed to reach the desired height, then fell to earth and exploded on contact.

John Paul Jones, the Supply Sergeant of Company D, 141st Infantry, said that many of the young replacements would come over to the company command post where the supply area was located, seeking advice. "I would tell them, 'get your ass down and start digging.'"

One day a "new kid" came over to Jones while he and his men were excavating a huge pit for one of the supply tents. "About two-thirds of the tent was set below the surface of the beach." The "rookie" was standing there with his hands in his pockets when all of a sudden a German shell (probably an 88mm) went whistling overhead and exploded a short distance away. Very calmly, Jones said to the young man, "Son, did you hear that?" The kid nodded. Jones barked, "Now get the Hell over in your own area and start digging." Jones explained to me, "If a German forward observer saw a man walking around they would fire a few rounds, thinking there might be others nearby."

German railway gun similar to Anzio Annie. "Seventh Army, La Coucourde, France, a 27 CM Schneider and Co., German Railway Gun, vintage of 1918 that has reached the end of the line. The Air Force took care of this Big Bertha. 163rd Signal Corps Photo Company" (111-SC-193882).

At the 2006 reunion of the 141st Infantry Chapter of the 36th Division Veteran's Association in San Antonio, Texas, Arlis Sizemore (D-141) related a story about the day the company arrived at Anzio. Arlis says he was "shooting craps with a bunch of guys" in his platoon. "We just got paid a couple of days before." "All of a sudden," he said, "we heard a strange whooshing sound." The sound continued to increase in intensity. "Someone yelled, 'Its Anzio Annie,' and everyone scattered." Jack Wilson, sitting next to Arlis at the reunion said, "It sounded like a box car flipping end over end through the air with its doors open." Arlis, running full tilt, spotted a foxhole nearby. He dove in headfirst and landed on top of his buddy Glenn Scott, who "let out a few choice words." "Scottie," he said, "was the only one in the group whom had the foresight to dig a deep hole for protection." It turned out "the shell was a dud, but it still shook the ground violently," Arlis remembered.

The Anzio breakout (Operation "Buffalo") commenced at 7:30 A.M., on May 23, 1944, with the 1 and 5 British Divisions, the American 34th and 45th Divisions, and the 36th Engineer Combat Regiment leading the initial attack. The 3rd and 36th Divisions, and the 1st Armored Division, plus the 1st Special Service Force, were in reserve.

Chapter Five

The "Stovepipe Platoon"

When Joe Connole joined Company D, 141st Infantry, 36th Division, as a replacement at Maddaloni, Italy, in March 1944, his first assignment was to a rifle company (VA File). Shortly thereafter, the company reassigned him to the mortar or "stovepipe" platoon, very likely a result of his prior training with the weapon. GIs referred to the mortars as stovepipes. There are a couple of possible explanations for the origin of the nickname. During the prewar training period (Carolina and Louisiana Maneuvers) and in the early days of the war, many U.S. Army divisions were equipment-poor. Units trained with broomsticks for rifles, wooden machine guns, and substituted a length of stovepipe attached to a board to simulate a mortar tube and base plate. Another possibility for the use of the term is the fact that the barrel looks like a length of stovepipe.

It was my father's good fortune to draw an assignment to a mortar squad, and this was, most probably, a major contributing factor in his having survived the war. Everyone who is in an area of the front lines during battle is in mortal danger. The mortar platoon, however, sets up the weapons some distance behind the line companies and generally operates from a safe firing position, usually behind a building, in a gully or ditch, or dug in. As a result, the men in the mortar platoon had a somewhat better chance of survival than a frontline rifleman or member of a machine gun squad. A number of veterans who served in a mortar platoon have echoed this very sentiment.

Wayne C. Kirby, an 18-year old from Ellenwood, Georgia, was a member of Company D, 142nd Infantry. While undergoing basic training at Camp Shelby, Mississippi, Kirby trained as a machine gunner. Kirby fancied himself as being "very good with the gun" and he boasted, "was equally proud of myself." Even before Kirby completed basic, he proved that he was proficient enough to receive a promotion to the position of "first gunner with a P.F.C. [Private first class] rating." When Kirby joined Company D, 142nd Infantry as a replacement in Italy on the day before Christmas 1943, much to his surprise and dismay, the First Sergeant assigned him to the mortar platoon. Despite vehement protests that he "never had any training on a mortar," Kirby was told, "Don't worry about that, you're in the 3rd platoon, just don't worry."

Fifty years later, he was still wondering how he ended up in a mortar platoon after being a machine gun specialist out of basic training. "I sometimes believe my life might have been saved that cold Christmas Eve when the sergeant said, 'Don't worry you're in the 3rd platoon, now.'" "I say this," Kirby wrote, "because I think a machine gunner's chances of survival are not as good as a mortar man's." During a discussion on this very subject at a reunion of the 36th Division Midwest Chapter at Dayton, Ohio, in 2002, Ernest R. Smeltzer, a member of a machine gun platoon in my father's company (D-141), commented that "a machine gunner's life span in combat was about two minutes—I sure fooled 'em," he said with a wry smile.

Kirby reflected on this unusual turn of events. Was it a "stroke of fate" that decided his destiny? "Was it good luck? Was it God's will? Or was it a dumb sergeant? It's still puzzling, but I like to believe that I know the answer." In the end, Kirby says he "learned to be a good mortar man." His expertise with the weapon led to his eventual promotion to the rank of Section Sergeant.

John E. McFall (E-141) was another replacement who joined the 36th at Maddaloni. McFall said that when he reported to the company Command Post (CP) for squad assignments the sergeant called for a volunteer for the 60mm mortars. In an article titled "An Infantryman's Concerns About Survival," published in *The 36th Division Historical Quarterly*, he wrote, "I had always liked the mortar and volunteered. I figured this duty would increase my odds for survival over being in a rifle squad."

Arlis D. Sizemore from Wooten, Kentucky, a corporal with Company D, 141st Infantry, said that the platoon leader, Lieutenant William V. Church approached him one day and asked if he wanted to become a forward observer, which meant being up at the front with the riflemen. "The job came with sergeant stripes," Sizemore pointed out. "I told him I wanted to stay back with the mortars." Church replied, "I don't blame you." Arlis was another veteran who credited being in a mortar platoon with having saved his life.

In spite of statements by the above individuals that a chance assignment to a mortar platoon may have been a major factor in their having escaped death or serious injury during the war, there was an element of danger that many could not deny. George L. Ferguson of Hollis, Long Island, New York, a sergeant with Company M, 141st Infantry, was a member of a machine gun platoon. He wrote, "We in our company had a friendly rivalry with the mortar men as we called them 'rear echelon.'" He explained, "Most of he boys on the front lines, who did the bulk of the fighting, despised rear echelon soldiers, who slept in nice warm tents or commandeered houses, hotels, etc., ate hot meals every day, and almost never got their uniforms dirty. Of course, this was in jest," he added, "as we knew when the platoon opened up with their mortars there was sure to be return fire from enemy mortars or artillery."

Cartoonist Bill Mauldin, in his book *Up Front*, had this to say about mortars:

> Mortars [60 and 81mm] are the artillery of an infantry company. Outside of the bazooka, they carry more viciousness and wallop per pound that any weapon the infantry has. The guys who operate them are at a big disadvantage. Because of the mortar's limited range, they have to work so close to the front [unlike artillery] that they are a favorite target for snipers, patrols, shells, and counter-mortar fire. Knocked-out mortar positions earn Iron Crosses for ambitious young Herrenvolk.

Mauldin bemoaned the fact "that the Germans make them too," and that is "the worst thing about mortars," he complained.

Historian Michael D. Doubler, in his book *Closing With the Enemy*, also spoke of the dangers faced by the men in the mortars stating, "The purpose of an infantry regiment's mortars and assault guns was to support the rifle platoons. Consequently, these weapons . . . became favorite targets for German artillery, tanks, and other heavy weapons," and "gun crews often suffered heavy casualties."

The mission of the battalion heavy weapons company during World War II was to provide close and continuous fire support to the infantry companies. Standard procedure was for the company commander to attach one or more machine gun or mortar squads to each of the rifle companies. The job of the machine gun squads was to lay down fields of fire in the attack or in defense of a position. Mortars serve as the Battalion Commander's own personal artillery.

Unlike the machine guns, which provided direct sweeping fire, the mortar is used for high angle, or indirect, fire only. Mortar crews utilize the weapon to "throw shells over hills, into gullies, and other places," referred to as targets in defilade, that the infantry could not reach using direct fire from small arms and machine guns. The weapon fires a shell high into the air, which then drops almost straight down on top of the enemy. Mortar fire was invaluable against dug in enemy troops and entrenched positions, such as a bunker or dugout with overhead protection.

Each of the three battalions of an infantry regiment has three rifle companies and one heavy weapons company, i.e. 1st Battalion consists of rifle Companies A, B, and C, and heavy weapons Company D; 2nd Battalion consists of Companies E, F, and G, and heavy weapons Company H; and 3rd Battalion of Companies I, K, L, and heavy weapons Company M. Each of the heavy weapons companies has three platoons, two heavy machine gun (water cooled), and one mortar platoon. The U.S. Army Table of Organization and Equipment (TO&E) for an infantry heavy weapons company called for a full complement of 8 officers and 158 enlisted men.

The 3rd platoon, armed with 81mm "heavy" mortars, had three sections, each with two squads. The platoon was equipped with six guns, one per squad. At full strength, there were fifty-six men in the mortar platoon.

A mortar squad consisted of a squad leader (sergeant) and seven or more enlisted men: one gunner (Corporal), one assistant gunner, a "base plate man," and five or six ammunition bearers (a Pfc. or Pvt.). The TO&E identified each man in the squad by number, 1, 2, 3, and so on. The gunner was No. 1; the assistant gunner No. 2; the base plate man No. 3, and the ammunition bearers, No. 4, 5, 6, etc. Normally, it was the gunner's job to carry the barrel and his assistant the bipod (see below).

The 81mm mortar is a smoothbore, muzzle-loading, high-angle fire weapon weighing 136 pounds. The mortar consists of three main components, the barrel at 44.5 pounds, the base plate at 45 pounds, and the bipod at 46.5 pounds. Broken down, the gun's component parts form separate loads, the weight of which is manageable enough for one man to carry, but by no means an easy task.

The barrel is 49.5 inches long, with a base cap that has a removable firing pin threaded into the center.

The bipod consists of the legs, elevating apparatus, and traversing mechanism assembly. To raise and lower the barrel, which decreases or increases the distance a shell travels (range), the gunner adjusts the "elevation apparatus" by turning the gear handle until the barrel is at the desired angle. Set at an elevation of between 45 degrees and 85 degrees, the weapon has a range of between 250 and 4,500 yards (approximately 2 1/2 miles).

The gunner uses a second hand crank to move the barrel right or left to provide traversing fire (limited to 5 degrees right or left). For greater movement of traverse, the gunner lifts the legs of the bipod up and swings the gun so that it aims in the proper direction.

The base plate is made of a pressed-steel body with welded ribs and braces. The plate functions to spread the recoil shock to the ground. After two or three rounds, the base firmly seats itself. The plate is equipped with a socket to accommodate the spherical projection at the base of the barrel. The socket allows a full 360-degree traverse without the need to move the base plate. The base plate has an attached handle and two loops for carrying purposes (see below).

Prewar photograph of 81mm mortar squad conducting a simulated fire mission (c. 1939 or 1940). Prior to WWII, only trainees wore khaki uniforms.

"24 JAN 1944, RAPIDO RIVER AREA, ITALY. AN 81mm. MORTAR FIRES AS MORE AMMUNITION IS HELD READY AT AN ADVANCE 141ST INFANTRY REGIMENT POSITION." Mortar crew of Company D, 141st Infantry. From left to right, unknown, (no first name) Lucio, Cpl. Arlis D. Sizemore of Wooten, Kentucky, Staff/Sgt. Buben D. Clarke of Roslin, Tennessee, unknown, unknown. 163rd Signal Photo Company (111-SC-187098).

An 81mm mortar crew of the 315 Infantry, 79th Division, passes through La Haye du Puits, France, July 4, 1944. First man is carrying the barrel. Second man from right is carrying the base plate. Notice protective shoulder pads worn by members of the crew. Men at rear are wearing bib-like ammunition bags used to carry up to six mortar rounds (111-SC-191372).

An 81mm mortar squad of Company D, 141st Infantry. Sandbagged emplacement near Haguenau, France, March 9, 1945. At the sight is Corporal John E. Richards of Pompton Lakes, New Jersey. With round in hand, Pfc. Ernest Dolloff of Hamilton, Texas, waits for command to fire. March 9, 1945 (111-SC-364270).

The 81mm mortar crew (same as fig. 5.4) of Company D, 141st Infantry, prepares to fire a mission in the Haguenau area of France. March 9, 1945 (111-SC-259590).

The 81mm projectile is a "tear-drop shaped bomb with fins at the rear to give stability in flight." Mortar ammunition is classified into three basic types: High Explosive (HE), Chemical (Smoke), and Training. There were two types of high explosive rounds: HE light, for use against personnel, and HE heavy, for use in the demolition of enemy shelters and defenses. HE shells weigh between 6.87 and 15.05 pounds, depending upon the size of the charge. The "lethal radii" of a mortar shell, "based upon standard 1939–45 HE bombs," was "49 feet (a diameter of 98 feet) at an angle of 70 degrees." Just before firing, the assistant gunner removes the safety wire (cotter pin) from the fuse, which is located in the nose.

There were two types of detonating impact fuses—"superquick" and "delay." Superquick fuses detonate on impact, while delay fuses are designed to allow penetration of a bunker or dugout, or building before detonating, therefore producing a demolition effect.

Smoke shells (11.4 pounds) contain white phosphorus (WP), referred to by GIs as "Willy Peter," a solid substance that ignites upon exposure to air. The mortar platoon leader employed smoke "for the purpose of blinding enemy observation, and to prohibit him from the delivery of aimed fire on advancing troops." It may also be used to protect an exposed flank, to screen a withdrawal, or in support of a counterattack.

The exploding WP shell disperses small particles of phosphorus, which can cause serious burns if the substance comes in contact with the human body. For this reason, WP was "also classified as casualty producing."

For drill purposes, the gun crew used training rounds (6.92 pounds) which contain no bursting charge and are recoverable. These are used to determine accuracy only. For safety purposes, all projectiles were color coded: yellow for HE; gray with a narrow yellow band for smoke; and blue for training.

The propelling charge consists of two parts: the "primary charge" and the "secondary charge." The primary charge is a shotgun cartridge ("primary cartridge") located in the center of the tailpiece, while the "secondary charge" consists of "propellant increments," smokeless powder contained in cloth bags that are attached to the base end of the mortar projectile (up to six) by the ammo bearers to increase the distance the shell travels.

When the assistant gunner drops the shell down the barrel, the primary cartridge strikes the fixed firing pin. The primary charge explodes igniting the secondary charge, propelling the shell from the tube.

An 81mm mortar can fire 30 to 35 rounds per minute for short periods and 18 rounds per minute for a sustained period. Arlis Sizemore (D-141) reported, "Sometimes the barrel got so hot the paint blistered. At night, it glowed a fiery red." A single mortar squad could lay down a devastating barrage in support of a line company.

(1st Lt.) Robert F. Spencer, from Charlestown, Indiana, the mortar platoon leader of Company H, 143rd Infantry, called the 81mm mortar "The Biggest Little Artillery Piece of the Infantry [in] WW II." To quote James W. "Bill" Robinson, Jr. (A-141) of Boston, "God Bless the mortar platoon. Those boys in mortars saved our ass on more than one occasion," he said with a chuckle.

One of the gunner's duties is to set up the mortar and align it to hit the target. The assistant gunner assists in mounting the weapon and, once the weapon is ready to fire, loads the rounds upon orders from the gunner. Ammunition bearers see to it that the gun crews have an ample supply of shells.

Under ordinary circumstances, mortar crews used jeeps towing one-quarter-ton trailers to transport weapons, ammunition, and equipment any distance. The TO&E indicates that the mortar platoon had seven jeeps and six trailers assigned to it. Robert "Bob" Bunker of New Brunswick, New Jersey, a staff sergeant with Company M, 143rd Infantry wrote:

> Each squad had a jeep with a trailer used to haul the weapons, extra ammunition, and other equipment. The majority of the time, however, the men carried this assigned equipment on their backs. This was especially true in Italy, in the mountains and when fighting was heavy. Seldom, if ever, were vehicles kept close to the front lines. They were too valuable.

In Italy, the Germans almost always held the high ground. This all changed after the invasion of southern France. During the latter period, Bunker says, "We used the jeep and trailer a great deal to transport our weapons and equipment, because of the periods of rapid advance when the Germans were in retreat and resistance was relatively light or non-existent."

(T/Sgt.) George N. Morse of Denton, Montana, at one time a forward observer with Company M, 141st Infantry, wrote:

> We liked to have the mortar positions about a thousand yards behind the front line where jeeps could be gotten close to them as they could use up a lot of ammunition at times and if they were too far back it cut down on the accuracy. The guns had a range of about two miles. Of course, like everything else there never was a perfect position.

In rough terrain, where jeeps could not navigate, gun crews had to lug the parts of the mortar for some distance to get the weapon into position for firing.

Each ammo bearer usually carried six rounds of ammunition, called a "clove." The load consisted of either High Explosive (HE) light rounds, or four HE heavy rounds, or smoke (see below). When reserves became low, the ammo bearers would go back to the designated supply point in a rear area to pick up a fresh supply. Because the mortars used a tremendous amount of ammunition, the platoon leader tried to locate a site that would be accessible by jeep.

Each squad member in a heavy weapons platoon had an assigned job to do, which included carrying specific parts of the gun and/or ammunition. Several veterans mentioned that the men shared in the duties of lugging the equipment from place to place. Walter T. Loster of Chicago, Illinois, a Pfc. with Company D, 141st Infantry says, "We all took turns carrying ammunition, heavy guns, and heavy mortars." Loster was a member of a machine gun platoon.

George Ferguson (M-141) wrote:

> I'm glad that when I was a private I didn't have to carry a base plate. Besides the base plate, the poor private was carrying his web belt with canteen and ammo for his rifle, his rifle and probably his light pack. Although we mostly carried a blanket roll. Think Civil War rebel infantry.

"At any rate," Ferguson concluded, "what a load for an average guy."

When Earl A. Mansee of Houston, Texas, first joined the 36th Division, his first assignment was with Company H, 141st Infantry. The platoon sergeant chose Pvt. Mansee to carry the base plate. "I soon found out how heavy an 81mm base plate can weigh after shouldering it for hours at a time. Those forced marches were a new experience that was not soon forgotten." During training at Camp Blanding, Florida, Mansee wrote, "We lost the M.P. Company" and division picked a number of men to form a "new platoon." "I don't know how I was selected, but I was only too glad to shed that 81mm mortar base plate."

Robert Bunker was at one time a "base plate man" with Company M, 143rd Infantry. "I carried it over my pack." "The trouble was," he wrote, "if you had anything in the pack that was crushable, it was." One day on the battlefield, Bunker says he picked up a "small side pack" (a lightweight canvas gas mask bag with strap that went around the waist—the men discarded the mask), in which he carried anything the weight of the plate might damage. "This worked quite well," he said.

(Lt.) Harold L. Bond of Newtonville, Massachusetts, the leader of the mortar platoon, Company M, 141st Infantry, had an "Italian boy from New York City" (Brooklyn) in his platoon named Ralph J. DeLuca, who was a base plate man. One day in Italy, De Luca called out, "Look what I've got, Lieutenant." He had found a mule wandering about which had broken loose from his handler during a shelling and was trying to train the animal to follow him around. His plan was to teach the mule to carry the base plate for him. "He was pretty sure that he would never have to carry his part of the mortar again," wrote Bond.

A few days later, a mule train, "which had come up the mountain in the morning," began the return trip after dark with its "dreadful load of dead." As the train passed by the mortar position, one of the drivers spotted his lost mule. The muleskinner went over to DeLuca and tried to get the animal back. At first, DeLuca "resisted him, but after a while even he could see that it was more important for food and ammo to come up than that he have a mule to carry his part of the mortar," Bond said.

To ease the burden of carrying gun parts and ammunition, supply issued a number of accessory equipment items (see photo on p. 49). Squad members carrying the barrel and bipod wore special protective shoulder pads, fastened together with straps, and designed to slip over the neck. The Number 3 man in the squad carried the base plate on his back by means of a special V-shaped strap that fastened to the link and loops of the unit. The strap slipped over the shoulders. Attached to the strap was a pad, approximately 1 1/2-inches thick, that the carrier positioned to soften the load on his back and make it more comfortable.

One day, wrote Bond, DeLuca "had lost the straps that are used by the mortar crewmen to fasten the heavy base plate of the weapon to the back when it had to be carried any distance." DeLuca said, "To hell with the straps, I ain't no mule. Let somebody else worry about carrying the stinking base plate." Then he remarked sarcastically, "We'll shoot the bitch without it!"

The barrel, because of its unwieldy length and bulk, is probably the most burdensome part of the weapon to carry. Arlis Sizemore (D-141) tells the story of how his best friend and fellow mortar crewmember Herman G. "Glenn" Scott of Statesville, North Carolina, dropped the barrel of his weapon into the ocean off the coast of Naples, Italy. The incident occurred during one of the landing exercises while training for the southern France invasion in the summer of 1944. Sizemore and Scott had been together since basic training at Camp Shelby, Mississippi and became close friends. Scott was coming down the bow ramp of an LCI (Landing Craft Infantry) when the incident occurred. "The ramps," Sizemore said, "were not too steady and had a rope railing that you hung onto." When Scott went to shift the heavy, cumbersome barrel from one shoulder to the other, it slipped out of his hands and "went over the side into the water."

"Boy did Captain [a 1st Lieutenant at the time] Church give him hell," said Sizemore with a chuckle as he related the incident. Church, who was usually even-tempered, and not easily excitable, was all over Scott. "He was asked what if we were in action in southern France and the mortar had to be replaced?" Sizemore said, "Scotty never dropped his mortar again!"

In a telephone conversation with Glenn Scott in September 2004, I mentioned the incident as told by his friend Arlis, and he had a good laugh. He added that, "Lieutenant Church stripped to his pants, jumped in the water, and dove for the barrel." Scott says, "He came up with it on his second dive." Church, he said, "was one of the best-liked officers in the company." Sizemore echoed Scott's respect for the man as well.

"Ammunition bags," constructed from a strip of reinforced canvas, had six pockets, three in front, and three in back, to carry the rounds and evenly distribute the weight. The carriers had a central opening for the head. John F. McFall of Kansas City, Missouri, a Pfc. with Company E, 141st Infantry, who was the No. 2 ammunition bearer for a 60mm mortar squad, described the bags as "bib-like containers . . . not unlike the yoke signs 'EAT AT JOE's' we used to see in the comics." This was a smaller version of the ones used by the 81mm ammunition bearers. McFall wrote, "When we would pause in our advance we would usually remove these carriers and place them on the ground beside us. Unless this was done we couldn't lie prone or even crouch low."

Robert Bunker (M-143) claims that the "ammo carriers, with a clove of six shells weighing 52 pounds, were worse off than the men who carried the parts of the gun." In addition, he said, each crewmember had to carry his regular load of equipment—pack, weapon (carbine), and other gear. David H. McKee of Detroit, Michigan, an ammo bearer with Company M, 143rd Infantry wrote, "Our shoulders would really get sore after carrying this ammunition for miles at a time up and down the mountains as they would not let us travel on the roads as they were probably mined or zeroed in by artillery."

Members of the mortar squad followed a regular training schedule of instruction and drill. This was necessary due to the high number of replacements. A number of the new men had received some prior training, others none at all. The purpose of mortar drill was to teach each member of the team his regular assigned duty in executing movements with equipment and serving the weapon during firing. Training began with preparatory instruction, geared to teach the individual soldier to perform in a proscribed manner. Training personnel conducted a series of demonstrations eventually followed by hands-on exercises.

Initially, each soldier performed the required exercises without regard to time. Development of accuracy was the most important consideration during the training exercises. Once crewmembers attained the habit of exactness, they practiced for speed until they were able to perform each test with the required accuracy in the allotted time.

The platoon sergeant familiarized the trainees with the duties of the other crewmembers by rotating assignments. This way, if the squad lost one or more of its members in battle, the others could step right in and take over. Once the crewmembers became proficient in drilling exercises, they began live fire training.

As the rifle companies advanced rapidly in a fast action, it was sometimes necessary for the crew to move the weapon to a new position as quickly as possible to provide continuous fire support. Platoon sergeants trained the crews to carry this out with the utmost speed and efficiency. The drill consisted of setting up the weapon, sighting it, and then dismantling it and moving to a new position (Bond). Each crew repeated this exercise over and over, grumbling all the time as they did so.

As leader of the mortar platoon, the lieutenant (or the platoon sergeant), would determine a suitable location for the placement of the guns, usually in defilade, which afforded adequate protection from direct fire and where it would be more difficult for the enemy to locate visually. Robert Bunker (M-143) wrote, "We always tried to get a good defiladed spot, if possible, in setting up the guns. This could be behind a building you could fire over, a deep hole position, etc. The mortar being a high angle of fire weapon could get into places the artillery could not." If time and conditions permitted, the crew dug in and sandbagged a large pit for protection.

After the crew sets the weapon up, the gunner establishes an "initial direction of fire" by driving a stake in the ground at the forward part of the base (a "base stake") and an "aiming stake" about 25 yards forward of that. Using the sight, the gunner aligns the two stakes to a specific compass heading (azimuth). In order to lay out protective fields of fire in front of the rifle companies, the platoon leader pre-registers the gun to a number of potential or key targets, a building, a crossroads, or a likely avenue of approach such as a trail, a draw, etc. As soon as the platoon leader establishes communications (radio or telephone) with the gun crew, he provides estimates of range and direction and calls for initial fire. After observing where the shell hits, he would send back corrections. The stakes enable the crew to shift the weapon to a specific heading in the quickest possible time and bring fire on the enemy (see Bond below).

The use of mortar fire on the battlefield requires the coordinated efforts of both the "indirect fire team" and the mortar squad. The Indirect fire team consists of a Forward Observer (FO) and a Fire Direction Center (FDC), referred to as the "nerve center" of the team. Since the gun crew generally fires the weapon from the defilade and cannot observe the target, the indirect fire team gathers and applies the data required by the mortar squad to carry out its assigned mission.

The forward observer takes up a position on the front line from which he is able to detect and locate potential targets. He determines the target and initiates a call for fire to the FDC. A radio-telephone operator (Pfc.), equipped with an SCR 300 (Signal Corps Radio) radio backpack, or a field telephone, relays the map grid coordinates of the target from the FO to the Fire Direction Center (FDC). Located a short distance from the gun, the FDC is manned by a Tech/5, the "fire direction chief," and a second radio-telephone operator who receives the call for fire. The FDC evaluates the information from the FO and uses a "plotting board" to compute the firing data, then directs and adjusts the fire of the weapon.

The Tech/5 issues a set of instructions, called a "fire command," to the weapons crew. The first command is the "initial fire order," and those issued thereafter are "subsequent fire orders." Each command contains the necessary data to fire the weapon—type of shell and charge, deflection (direction), range, and number of rounds. The FDC conveys each element of a fire order to the gun crew in a specific sequence:

1. Type of shell and fuse—HE light, quick
2. Deflection—ZERO
3. Aiming point—STAKE
4. Range—1100 (Yds.)
5. Number of rounds—ONE ROUND

The gunner repeats the order and makes the necessary adjustments as his assistant is preparing the shell for firing. The assistant gunner places the end of the shell inside the barrel and holds it with both hands. Upon receiving the command "FIRE" from the squad leader, the assistant gunner releases the round.

When the initial round hits the target area, the FO sends corrections to the FDC to adjust the fire. The Tech/5 made the necessary computations and issues a "subsequent fire order." He precedes the second order with the command "fire for adjustment." This contained only the data the gunner needed to change in correcting errors in deflection (right or left) or range (25 yards or multiples thereof):

1. Deflection—LEFT 25 (Yds.)
2. Range -1200 (Yds.)
3. ONE ROUND

When the second round hits, the observer makes the final corrections, and again sends the information to the FDC. The Tech/5 once again processes this information and issues the necessary data to the crew:

1. Range-1225 (Yds.)
2. FIVE ROUNDS

The command "fire for effect" follows the instructions. In this particular case, a volley of five rounds would be the number needed to destroy the target.

There are two types of "fire for effect": fixed (a point target) and distributed. During fixed fire, "the gunner fires a specific number of rounds without changing the lay of the mortar between rounds." For distributed fire, the gunner "manipulates the mortar for elevation [range] or deflection [right or left] between each round," to cover a target area having a specific width and depth, for example 50 x 50 yards. As shown in Table 5.1, it would take nine rounds to cover the designated target area.

George Morse wrote, "From September 1943 until April or May 1944, all communication we had was by telephone or hand held radios." The radios, he says, "were practically useless as the range was short and they were line of sight." The "sound powered telephones we had worked pretty well. They were good for about five miles, but of course, the lines were subject to enemy mortar and artillery fire." On their way to establish an Observation Point (OP), Morse and his radioman had to string wire from the FDC to the forward position. "The Germans intermittently shelled the trails and the lines often got knocked out."

Just before Morse went to Anzio in May 1944, the company received the new (Signal Corps Radio) SCR 300 radios. After getting the improved radio equipment, the FOs used the telephones only "occasionally." The observation team had "to keep the SCR 300 radios in a protected place if possible and couldn't use them on the forward slopes as [the signal was] too easy for the enemy to pick up." Once the Germans obtained a fix on the transmitter using a direction finder, they would shell the OP.

It was necessary for the mortar platoon leader to locate the Observation Post on or very close to the front lines to be able to have a clear, unobstructed view of the entire battlefield. "As an observer," Robert Bunker wrote, "you selected the highest spot to set up your OP, which gave you observation on the line and [you] worked from there." Enemy artillery and mortar observers knew this as well. They would pre-register the coordinates of elevation points that an American observer might choose as an OP, and periodically called for

Table 5.1.

1150 Yds.	9	8	7
1125 Yds.	6	5	4
1100 Yds.	3	2	1

fire on these positions. "So, on the OP you had to be very careful and make sure you had a place (foxhole, etc.) [in which to take cover] when 'incoming mail' was a possibility." The Germans were on constant watch to detect the slightest movement and pinpoint a forward observer's position, wrote Bunker. "It could get pretty rough if they spotted you."

Sgt. Carl G. Benenati of Dunkirk, New York, a member of Company D, 141 Infantry, was wounded in the Vosges Mountains by a German 88mm flak gun while directing fire from the 81mm mortars on enemy positions. Benenati was with his radioman, Pvt. Angelo J. Barca of Yonkers, New York. Years later, at a 36th Division Association reunion, Benenati explained to former mortar squad member Arlis Sizemore what happened the day he was hit. "We stayed on the radio too long. The Germans got a fix on the signal and zeroed in on our position." A shell landed close by the OP, severely wounding both men. Arlis says, "Neither man ever returned to the company." After a lengthy recuperation period at a hospital in Naples, Benenati was reclassified "limited service."

At times, in order to have what Bond referred to as "a useful OP," it was necessary to site the position well out in front of the infantry lines. Bond described one such OP overlooking Hill 593 near Monte Cassino in his book, *Return to Cassino*. Due to the nature of the terrain, the lieutenant and one of his sergeants, James Haney, had to carefully crawl seventy-five yards beyond the frontline through thick scrub growth to be able to see down a steep incline into a ravine in front of the riflemen. The brush protected the two men from observation by the enemy.

After finding a suitable position for the OP, Bond and Haney took turns digging in. Bond wrote, "the ground was covered with small scrubby brush, and the soil was extremely rocky," which made digging "almost impossible." The Germans had been mortaring the American positions steadily through the day and Bond could see the shells exploding near some New Zealand troops who were dug in along the crest of a nearby ridge off to his left adjacent to the 36th Division sector. Infantry troops "had little protection against high-trajectory fire," wrote Bond. "We had to work carefully and slowly, for too much movement would surely draw enemy fire." One kept watch through the binoculars for signs of enemy activity, while the other "slowly and painfully dug." The two men continued to dig for more than three hours, piling the rocks and soil up behind the bushes in front of the position for added protection.

Before dark, Bond sighted the mortars on several likely targets and had the gun crews put stakes in front of the guns to mark the compass headings. To Bond's left, in front of the New Zealanders, there was a draw covered by thick scrub brush and oak trees, "which looked like a place the Germans might choose to use for a counterattack." Bond radioed estimates of range and direction, and the crew "put a shell into the middle of it with only two tries."

Early the next afternoon, the lieutenant "heard a sudden burst of fire" coming from the New Zealander's side of the line. The Germans, using the thick tangle of vegetation for cover, were coming through the draw Bond had registered the day before. This made it difficult to see them or to estimate the size of the force, but "from the amount of shooting," he said, "it was obvious this was a counterattack of some size."

Bond immediately grabbed the phone and called for fire. The men spun the gun around and sighted it on the stakes set up the previous day, and within one minute, the first round was on its way. The shell was right on target. Bond ordered the crews "to fire six more, and in a matter of seconds there followed the frightful, crunching explosions of seven shells right in the draw where the Germans were attacking." When the firing stopped, everything suddenly went quiet. Heavy black smoke rose in the air from the explosions and drifted slowly away on a slight breeze. It was then, that Bond could hear "the agonized cries and shrieks of wounded men." The mortars had stemmed the attack.

Jack W. Wilson of Newburg, Indiana, a staff sergeant with the 2nd machine gun platoon of Company D, 141st Infantry, wrote "We [machine gun and mortar squads] would be attached to either A, B, or C Company. These were the rifle companies. Sometimes we would not see any of our first or third platoon members for a week or two, sometimes longer." Wilson said, "We were the forgotten stepchild of the battalion." The NCOs of the rifle companies had little regard, or consideration for the attached heavy weapons squads and assigned every lousy detail that came up to the men of Company D. With regard to this unfair practice, most non-coms felt they had an obligation to protect the interest of their own troops and, at every opportunity, tried to spare them from unwelcome work details or duties. "The only time we were together was in a rest area," Wilson said. During this time, he explained, the men usually stayed with a small circle of friends in their squad and had at best only a passing acquaintance with some of the others in the company. Raymond A. Osborne, Jr. of Basset, Virginia, another member of Company D, wrote, "We did not get to see each other very much, although we were very close when we were together."

Chapter Six

The Stalled Italian Campaign Resumes, May 1944

On May 11, 1944, the American Fifth and British Eighth Armies launched a massive spring offensive (code-named "Diadem") against the "Gustav or Cassino Line," in what was the initial phase of the Allied plan for the destruction of the German armies south of Rome. Allied Command massed fourteen divisions against the German defenses, with the 6th South Africa Armored Division in reserve. The Gustav Line, which extended across Italy's "waist," the narrowest portion of the peninsula south of Rome, was part of the German's "Winterstellungen" or "Winter Line," a fortified series of mountains and rivers, so named because the Germans hoped to hold the line at least throughout the winter. General (Field Marshal) Albert Kesselring, Commander of the German forces in Italy, believed the Winter Line would halt any further allied advance up the boot indefinitely. It had been 1,500 years since an invading army had seized Rome from the south.

The "key" to the Gustav Line was Monte Cassino, a rocky spur of the Apennine Mountains known as the Cassino massif. Located seventy-five miles southeast of Rome, Monte Cassino soared 1,700 feet above the surrounding Liri valley. Military strategists considered this "superb natural fortress" to be "one of the most formidable defensive positions in the world." Atop the mountain sat the ruins of Monte Cassino Abbey, the 1,400-year-old Benedictine monastery, reduced to a pile of rubble by Allied bombers on February 15, 1944. The Abbey was the birthplace of the Roman Catholic Benedictine order, founded by St. Benedict of Nursia in A.D. 529. Observation from the heights of Cassino dominated all approaches from the south during daylight hours. A single vehicle or small cluster of soldiers would draw deadly accurate artillery fire.

"In peacetime," 36th Division historian Robert L. Wagner wrote, the Italian Military College, "reputedly, had used this six- or seven-mile area to demonstrate to its officers the 'perfect defensive position.'" Historian David G. Chandler, in his *Guide to the Battlefields of Europe*, wrote that the battle of Cassino, which he described as "the bitterest in the history of warfare," lasted for four long months. Within just sixteen days after the fall of Cassino, he noted, the Allies captured Rome.

British General Sir Harold R. Alexander, Commander of all Allied Armies in Italy (AAI), concentrated the main assault along the western half of the Gustav Line that stretched for twenty-five miles from the Cassino vicinity to the Tyrrhenian Sea near Minturno. The defense line followed the Garigliano River and then up the Rapido River to the heights above the town of Cassino (pop. 25,000) and ended in the Apennine Mountains. The Rapido River, running generally southwesterly from the hills south of the Cassino area to its junction with the Garigliano River, was the "main defensive barrier" of the Gustav Line blocking the entrance to the Liri Valley. If the Allied armies could crack this sector of the line, it would open the way to the capital city of Rome. An attempt by the 36th Division forces to cross the Rapido on January 20 to 21, 1944, resulted in more than 2,100 casualties.

The second phase of the Italian spring offensive (code-named Buffalo), scheduled to begin on May 23, called for Lt. Gen. Lucian K. Truscott's VI Corps, penned up at Anzio, to punch out of the beachhead ring defended by General Eberhard von Mackensen's Fourteenth Army and link up with Allied forces moving up from the south. Truscott's VI Corps consisted of the American 3rd "Rock of the Marne," 34th "Red Bull," 36th, and 45th "Thunderbird" Infantry Divisions, the 36th Engineer Combat Regiment, 1st Armored "Old Ironsides" Division, plus the First Special Service Force.

General Alexander's Plan called for the British Eighth Army (four British and two Canadian Divisions) to attack the German Tenth Army in the main assault on the Gustav Line southeast of the Rapido River. Simultaneously, the Polish II Corps would capture Monte Cassino, giving the Allies control of the heights from which to direct artillery fire against German defenses. The fall of Cassino would allow the British to move forward along Highway 6, the famed Via Roma, one of two main roads leading to Rome. Lieutenant General Mark W. Clark's U.S. Fifth Army would surge up Highway 7 (the old Appian Way), the second major route to Rome until making contact with Truscott's U.S. VI Corps breaking out of the Anzio beachhead. Clark had twelve divisions under his command, including seven American, three French, and two British. The beachhead troops would then join with Fifth Army forces and race northward in the direction of Valmontone to cut off Route 6, blocking the escape route of the retreating Germans, being chased northward up the highway by the advancing British Eighth Army.

By the May 16, after nearly a week of "bloodthirsty slogging," the German front finally began to crumble. Allied troops were making steady gains in every sector. On the morning of May 18, the Poles captured Monte Cassino at a cost of nearly 4,000 casualties. Losses across the entire front were heavy on both sides, but those of the German armies "were irreplaceable."

In an attempt to stem the advance and bolster the "creaking front," Field Marshal Kesselring brought up one of his crack divisions from the Anzio beachhead perimeter, the 26th Panzer, but the move came too late. The British Eighth Army, "in the old 36th Division sector," crossed the Rapido River and then turned north toward Route 6 to outflank the ruins of the town of Cassino. Wagner wrote, "This time there were six divisions to do the job where the Texas Army had failed in January." Wagner described the initial going as "extremely sticky." By May 16, British and Canadian forces held a bridgehead "only two miles deep at a cost of 4,056 casualties."

On May 17, General Kesselring ordered his divisions to withdraw to the "Adolf Hitler Line," one of two fall-back positions. The heavily fortified Hitler Line was located five to ten miles west of the Cassino defenses. Before the advancing Allied armies could reach the defense line, the Germans hurriedly changed the name to the "Senger Position," after Lt. Gen. Frido Von Senger Und Etterlin, the Corps Commander directing the battle west of the Apennines. Historian Wynford Vaughn-Thomas wrote, "the Fuhrer's prestige could not be jeopardized."

The second fallback position behind the Gustav and Hitler (Senger) Lines was the C-Point, which the Allies named the "Caesar Line." This fortified barrier, the last before the city of Rome, was located on the southern slopes of the Colli Albani or Alban Hills, a distance of between fifteen and twenty miles south of the Eternal City. Anchored on the Via Roma (Highway 6), the Germans based this line on a series of strong points that included the towns of Ardea, near the Tyrrhenian Sea, Campoleone Station, Lanuvio, Velletri, Giulianello, Artena, and Valmontone. The Germans assigned three full-strength units (the 4th Paratroop, and the 65th and 3rd Panzergrenadier Divisions) to hold this line. On May 25, Hitler "grudgingly consented" to Kesselring's request to abandon the Senger Line and pull his troops back to the C-Position.

The American 85th "Custer" and 88th "Blue Devils" Infantry Divisions, fighting their way up the coast along Highway 7, were making slow but steady progress. The two "green" divisions sustained more than 3,000 casualties in the first six days of fighting, but Fifth Army Headquarters quickly brought replacements up to the front to keep the divisions at nearly full strength. American forces continued their advance and by May 19, had moved to within forty miles of the Anzio perimeter. It was time for the breakout from the Anzio beachhead to begin.

Sofia
BULGARIA
Varna
Constanţa
Sevastopol'
Maykop
RUSSIA
Black Sea
Sochi
Pyatigorsk
Vladikavkaz
Grozny
Edirne
Thessaloníki
İstanbul
Karabük
Sokhumi
K'ut'aisi
Samsun
GEORGIA
Tbilisi
Lárisa
Aegean Sea
Bursa
Adapazarı
Trabzon
ARMENIA
Gäncä
Eskişehir
Ankara
Sivas
Erzincan
Yerevan
İzmir
Athens
TURKEY
Erzurum
AZERBAIJA
Kayseri
Aydın
Denizli
Konya
Elâzığ
Van
GREECE
Antalya
Malatya
L. Van
L. Urmia
Khaniá
Adana
Gaziantep
Diyarbakır
Tabriz
Rhodes
Mersin
Urfa
Urmia
Iráklion
Crete
Latakia
Aleppo
Mosul
Arbil
Nicosia
Hamah
Dayr az Zawr
CYPRUS
Tripoli
SYRIA
Kirkuk
Mediterranean Sea
Beirut
Homs
Hamadan
LEBANON
IRAQ
1 - Gaza Strip
2 - West Bank
Haifa
Damascus
Ar Ramadi
Baghdad
Tel Aviv
2
'Amman
Karbala'
Al Kut
Alexandria
Port Said
1
Jerusalem
An Najaf
Al 'Amar
ISRAEL
'Ar'ar
Cairo
JORDAN
An Nasiriyah
Suez
Sakakah
Basra
Al Fayyum
Aqaba
Rafha
Kuwait City
Al Minya
Al Hawiyah
Hafar al Batin
EGYPT
Tabuk
Asyut
Ha'il
Hurghada
Suhaj
Al Jubayl
Luxor
Buraydah
Al Kharijah
Ad Dammam
Idfu
Ar Rass
Al Hufuf
Medina
Riyadh
Aswan
Yanbu' al Bahr
Ad Dawadimi
L. Nasser
Jiddah
Mecca
SAUDI ARABIA
At Ta'if
Port Sudan
Qal'at Bishah
Ad Dabbah
Red Sea
SUDAN
Atbara
Khamis Mushayt
Shandi
Najran
Jizan
Sharurah
Khartoum
ERITREA
Kassala
Asmara
Sanaa
YEMEN
Wad Madani
Dhamar
Al Hudaydah
Al Ubayyid
Sannar
Al Qadarif
Ta'izz
Mek'ele
Ad Damazin
Gonder
Aseb
Aden
Gulf of Aden
Kaduqli
ETHIOPIA
DJIBOUTI
Djibouti
Bahir Dar
Dese
30°E

Anzio to Rome, May 11–June 4, 1944.

To ensure a successful outcome of this phase of the operation, Allied planners reinforced VI Corps by some 90,000 men to bring the total to over 160,000, seven full divisions to the Germans five. Once the initial objective was achieved and the beachhead troops joined up with Clark's Fifth Army, the combined force would push through the Velletri gap, a break between the Alban Hills and Colli Lepini Mountains east of the city, and head north in the direction of Cori and Valmontone. The ultimate objective was to cut off Highway 6, thus trapping the Germans between the British forces moving up from the south and the waiting American forces in a classic pincer movement.

The Allies launched Operation Buffalo at 7:30 A.M., on May 23, with troops breaking out of the forward positions along the entire perimeter. From left to right, the 1 and 5 British Divisions, the American 34th and 45th Infantry Divisions, and the 36th Engineer Combat Regiment, attacked German defensive positions ringing the beachhead. Truscott held the 3rd and 36th Infantry Divisions, 1st Armored Division, plus the First Special Service Force, in reserve. Prior to the breakout, sixty light bombers clobbered German positions in the town of Cisterna, considered the key to the German defenses.

Once again, the operation caught the Germans by surprise. Eight days earlier, on May 16, before the breakout, Kesselring had weakened his defensive ring around the beachhead by committing reserve forces to stem advances in the south. Attacking beachhead units made immediate gains. Still, German resistance was tenacious. Cisterna fell on May 25, at a cost of 476 Americans killed, 2,321 wounded, and 75 missing. Earlier that day, II Corps units pushing up from the south joined with VI Corps troops from the beachhead, "effecting the long-planned and longer-awaited link-up between Fifth Army forces" (Laurie).

After taking Cisterna and Cori, the way was clear for the American forces to cut through the Velletri gap and advance to Valmontone where General Alexander hoped to smash Kesselring's armies. General Clark, however, "had little faith in the feasibility of the plan"—he had a plan of his own. The general wanted to get to Rome as quickly as possible, more specifically, before the cross-Channel invasion of France, which he knew would take place on June 5 or 6. The Fifth Army commander wanted the "singular honor" of liberating the capital city to go to the Americans, who had fought so hard to earn the prize (Laurie).

Clark believed the media had unjustly attributed Allied gains obtained in Italy to British forces. He was concerned that the British would take all the glory while American units were busy engaging the Germans at Valmontone. He ordered Truscott to change directions from north to the northwest toward the Alban Hills and the Caesar Line, the most direct route to Rome. The change upset Truscott, but he obeyed the directive without question, and expected his commanders to do the same.

Clark had doubts about whether the maneuver to take Valmontone would in fact trap the retreating Germans, given that there were a number of alternative routes of escape further inland. Clark could not totally ignore the orders of a superior, so he directed a part, less than one-third (the 3rd Division with attached units), of Truscott's force to continue the offensive toward Valmontone. This unexpected change of plans was a move that generated much controversy, both during the war and for some time after. The British generals were outraged.

The placement of Truscott's divisions in the VI Corps zone of responsibility was as follows: On the far left flank, abreast of the Campoleone Station sector of the Caesar Line was the 45th Division. To the right of the 45th was the 34th Division in a defensive position in front of Lanuvio. The 1st Armored Division was situated south and east of the town of Velletri, on the right flank of the 34th. To the right of the 1st Armored Division was the 85th, then the 88th Division. The 3rd Infantry Division was on the right flank of the 88th, moving in the direction of Valmontone, its advance stopped by the Herman Goering Division.

Truscott sent three American divisions, the 34th, 45th, and 1st Armored, northwest in the direction of Rome to attack along a narrow three-mile front from Velletri to Lanuvio and Campoleone Station south of the Alban Hills. This was the most heavily defended portion of the German line.

After two days of bitter fighting, VI Corps failed to penetrate the enemy defenses. Truscott's forces sustained heavy losses and, by May 28, Clark deemed the operation a failure. On May 29, he brought up Major General Ernest N. Harmon's 1st Armored Division, but it too failed to make a dent in the German defenses. By May 30, the offensive was at a stalemate and the Americans went on the defensive. The drive to Rome had ground to a halt.

Truscott decided to continue the attack by calling up the 36th Division, Major General Fred L. Walker commanding. When Clark had the Texas Division shipped from Naples to Anzio and placed in VI Corps reserve, Truscott voiced his objection. The VI Corps commander had neither faith in Walker's division, nor confidence in his abilities as a commander, but Clark overruled him. The 36th had acquired the reputation among American troops of being a "hard luck" outfit, because of the heavy losses incurred during the winter campaign in the Mt. Lungo-San Pietro area and during the ill-fated Rapido River operation.

Between May 22 and 25, the 36th Infantry Division remained in reserve at a bivouac about three miles northeast of Anzio. Early in the afternoon of the twenty-fifth, Walker received orders from VI Corps Headquarters to move forward to the sector south and east of the city of Velletri and relieve the 1st Armored Division in the line.

Gen. Walker set up his advance CP in a group of ruined farm buildings about two and one-half miles northeast of Cisterna and approximately five miles southeast of the city of Velletri. His *Journal* entry for May 25 reads: "We were not to become involved in serious combat, are to be ready to withdraw on short notice, and to move promptly to exploit a breakthrough anywhere in the VI Corps front."

General Walker positioned the 141st Infantry on the division's far-right flank and the 143rd Infantry on the left flank, with the 142nd in division reserve. At 11 A.M., on May 27, 1944, Walker issued orders for the lead regimental combat teams to cross the Line of Departure (LD) beginning at 3:30 P.M., and advance toward the north in the general direction of Velletri. The division's initial objective was to move to a point parallel to the railroad line and Velletri-Cori Road leading east from the city. For the new replacements like my father, who joined the 36th Division after February 26, 1944, this would be their first chance at possible contact with the enemy. The time was coming closer.

Chapter Seven

Entry into Battle

On the morning of May 27, 1944, Maj. Gen. Fred L. Walker held a meeting with his staff and all field grade officers to outline the directive from VI Corps Headquarters ordering the unit to move up to the battlefront and relieve the 1st Armored Division. Regimental headquarters notified company commanders of the appointed hour and briefed them on the unit's primary role in the overall plan of attack. Company grade officers passed this information down the chain of command to small unit leaders and senior NCOs, who in turn informed subordinates.

Almost immediately upon being alerted to the change of orders from reserve status to frontline duty, the soldiers' anxiety level began to intensify, especially among the new men about to undergo the initiation of battle, Pvt. Joe Connole among them. This was it—the day they had all been waiting for and dreading had finally arrived. After undergoing several weeks of instruction and training with their assigned outfits, the rookie replacements were about to experience the "real thing."

While waiting for zero-hour, the troops checked and rechecked weapons and equipment or otherwise busied themselves doing some routine task in an attempt to avoid thinking about the impending move to the front. But most men found it almost impossible to concentrate on anything else. Replacements, their eyes grown wide, carefully arranged the contents of backpacks—clothing, raincoat, personal items, mess kit, K-rations—filled canteens, "not always with water," and crammed extra clips into ammo pouches. With shaking hands, men fumbled as they fastened grenades by the hand levers to their suspenders and webbing belts. Heavy weapons personnel responsible for parts of mortars or machine guns and ammunition made sure everything was in order. All movement was mechanical, for their conscious minds were detached from all that was going on around them.

As the time of departure grew shorter, the tension mounted and the men became more agitated. Most men found themselves too keyed up to rest or even eat. Some appeared to be dozing, but their nervous systems would not allow sleep to come. Many chain-smoked or chewed gum, anything at all to calm jittery nerves and ease their growing apprehension. While waiting for the clock to tick down, small groups formed and the men sat around chatting quietly. Many "did not talk at all," wrote historian John Ellis, while "others kept up a steady stream of inconsequential banter and feeble jokes in an effort to take their minds off what lay ahead and to convince others, and thus themselves, that they were not afraid."

Some individuals moved off by themselves and sat alone in quiet reflection. These men were lost in private thoughts. Images of friends, family, and home crossed their minds in rapid succession. Some men hurriedly dashed off letters to loved ones—in many instances the last they would ever write. Letters from home, tattered and soiled, were read and reread. The words brought peace and comfort and diverted their attention from the move up to the frontline. Mail was an important part of a soldier's day-to-day existence, essential to morale. Letters kept them going until new ones arrived.

They stared lovingly at photographs of family—parents, siblings, wives, children—and sweethearts, and reminisced of the world they had left behind and to which they longed to return. Lee B. Kennett wrote, "Nostalgia was a common ingredient in soldiers' letters." Letters "created intense feelings" and "the most vivid images" of home and family. Both provided a close link with that other world. During World War II, letters were the only means of communicating with family members.

Most of the time, the news was good—sometimes it was not. Families often shielded sons or relatives from any disturbing news from home, knowing that it was best to keep it from them, unless it constituted some kind of dire emergency. However, this was not always the case. Many a GI received a "Dear John" letter, a term that originated during the war to denote a letter from a woman to a husband or boyfriend informing them that their relationship was over, usually the result of involvement with another man not in the military. An Army psychiatrist quoted by Kennett wrote, "We had a saying, that as many casualties were caused on Guadalcanal by the mail from home as through enemy bullets."

Thoughts of family and home were an immense source of comfort and solace. For many young men away from home for the first time, they sometimes had an opposite effect, bringing on waves of acute homesickness, yet another source of distress. The separation, combined with the thought of possibly never seeing loved ones or their hometown or old neighborhoods ever again, induced an overwhelming state of melancholy. Longings for home and family brought many to the verge of emotional collapse or breakdown, but men were careful not to show their true feelings around anyone other than close buddies.

Many prayed fervently and made solemn promises to their maker, asking that He protect them from all harm. A number of men found that reading passages from pocket editions of the New Testament, issued to all American soldiers, had a calming effect and gave them inner strength. An extremely high percentage of men carried good luck charms, amulets, and talismans, thought to avert harm and bring good fortune.

There were those who wished with all their might that they could be somewhere else, anywhere. The current situation seemed surreal, almost as if it were happening to someone else. They stared straight ahead, their eyes glazed, and repeatedly asked themselves the same questions—How had it come to this point? What am I doing here? How could this be happening to me?

Despite the fact that the threat of war with Japan had occupied newspaper headlines for more than two years, few had ever imagined the disruption and upheaval it would bring to their lives or the lives of almost every American citizen. The nation found itself thrust into the conflict overnight and within a few short months of the declaration of war, hundreds of thousands of young men, the majority of whom had never ventured very far from home, found themselves thousands of miles away in the middle of a war zone.

The majority of the GIs were still teenagers, or barely out of their teens—many just boys. Some had yet to shave. A few short months earlier, they were attending high school or continuing their education at a college or technical school. Recent graduates were embarking on careers or just settling into a new job or career. A few were newly married and thinking about starting a family. Some, including my father, had left pregnant wives behind. There were older married men with children. All had been contemplating the future and were busy making plans and preparations. Following December 7, 1941, most young American males faced the days ahead with a profound sense of uncertainty and foreboding.

While waiting to go into their first action, many of the young single men wondered if they "would ever know a woman before they died."

What concerned most men at the front, especially those going into battle for the first time, was the uncertainty of the situation. The fear of the unknown was ever present. Jack Belden, a war correspondent for *Time* and *Life* magazines, who wrote *Still Time to Die* in 1944, tried to convey to his readers what this state of uncertainty was like for the combat soldier about to enter the line:

> It is everywhere, and its effects are felt even before a battle. Uncertainty exists in the line of march through an unfamiliar country, on the water before an invasion

actually begins, and it exists subjectively in the minds of the men who never know what they are going to meet. But when once met, it is no better. For the uncertainty, instead of melting away in the action, only expands and multiplies a hundredfold.

Unless experienced, the effect of uncertainty, Belden emphasized, can "hardly be imagined." It is a "corrosion that eats away at the armor of the soul."

Belden went on to remind his readers that most ordinary men, "in no matter what branch of life," long for a sense of security. "On the battlefield, there is none, either physical or emotional." A combat soldier lives in a "perpetual state of emotional unbalance." In Belden's opinion, to "operate on a shifting ground of uncertainty tears at every fiber [of] your being"; consequently, one cannot exist very long "in an earthquake of feeling without losing emotional stability."

In every battle, Belden says, "there sits like a king on his throne, uncertainty deified, the uncertainty of the enemy's whereabouts, the uncertainty of falsehood, the uncertainty of surprise, the uncertainty of your own troops' actions, the uncertainty of a strange land, the uncertainty of rescue and the uncertainty of confusion itself." Uncertainty is the "very air in which a battle breathes" and "it is coiled at the heart of every combat." Belden's closing comment on the subject, "So I say that the unknown is the first-born son of combat and uncertainty is its other self."

The array of possible fates resulting from combat filled the men with fear and trepidation. Before them loomed the threat of being killed or wounded or worse. They contemplated the possibility of losing their sight, of being crippled or maimed, or of suffering some other form of hideous mutilation or disfigurement too horrible to imagine. If wounded, would they suffer intense, unbearable pain? These troubling thoughts weighed heavily on their minds and caused intense psychological stress. In a 1944 survey of 300 American volunteer combat veterans of the Spanish Civil War (1936–1940), Yale University staff members John Dollard and Donald Horton found that the "wounds most feared" were those of the "abdomen, eyes, brain and genitals."

The combat soldiers' imaginations tended to run wild, conjuring up all sorts of horrific fates that might befall them during an upcoming operation — an enemy shell seeking them out and in an instant they would be no more; being critically injured by the blast of a land mine; being dismembered by an artillery shell; a sniper's bullet finding its mark; machine gun fire ripping through flesh and bone; or being trapped alive in a burning tank. There was no end to the many possible ways that death could overtake a man in combat. All elicited intense fear and inner turmoil.

Vivid, disturbing scenes of their demise on the battlefield tormented the GIs night and day, depriving them of a single moment of peace. Men tried to block these terrifying images out of their mind, but all too often, they persisted. Suppression of such thoughts and images was all but impossible. In the days and weeks before entry into battle, men experienced bad dreams that often jolted them awake at night, causing fitful, restless sleep.

In combat, premature death is ever present as a distinct possibility. The fear of death was uppermost in the mind of the frontline soldier. Under ordinary circumstances, death seemed remote, far removed from their thus far uncomplicated, happy-go-lucky lives. Death was something that would happen in the distant future. Young people believe that they are invincible. In their relatively short lives, few had ever witnessed death firsthand. All too often, especially in American culture, parents shield their children from the specter of death. Rarely did they witness anyone die. The only dead people they ever saw were relatives—grandparents, elderly aunts and uncles, or other close family members—lying in silk-lined caskets, embalmed, and laid to rest in fine clothes and jewelry. Conversely, the more a person is exposed to death, the more he begins to question his own mortality.

What was for some their greatest fear, "often more powerful that the fear of death itself," Ellis wrote, was the "fear of showing fear." Most of the time a man's mind wrestled with whether he would stand bravely and fight or flee in panic? Or would he "be immobilized by uncontrollable terror?"

Raw replacements entered battle for the first time under differing circumstances. Some of the replacements, like Pvt. Joe Connole, joined the 36th while the division was withdrawn from the line for an extended time, either in a rest phase, training, or while in reserve. In my father's case, this happened in March 1944, shortly after VI Corps Headquarters relieved the division at Cassino. During this period, the unit was undergoing an extensive rebuilding program just prior to the Anzio breakout. Army Researcher Samuel Stouffer noted that this represented "the ideal way for the individual replacement system to operate," in "contrast to the alternative case, in which the replacement first saw his new outfit in the lines, perhaps in the midst of a major offensive."

The men who were fortunate enough to join their units out of the line clearly benefited from the opportunity to assimilate into a preexisting group of combat veterans. This enabled a replacement "to acquire for himself the practical knowledge and skills of battle so that he could function as a member of the team," wrote Stouffer. Under the guidance and tutelage of combat-wise veterans, these men were better able to deal with the conditions of battle and had a much greater chance of survival. In addition, a reasonable period of acclimation tended to rid the replacements of many insecurities, while increasing feelings of self-confidence.

These men were also able to go through a process of social integration—to establish personal relationships in their squad or section. As Stouffer points out, "intragroup ties played a central role in combat motivation." One replacement, Allen E. Stern (B-142), who joined the 36th at Caserta before the Anzio breakout, explained it this way: "During this period, I got to know the boys. I trained with them and went to town with them." The men of Company B "had just come from the worst front of the war—Monte Cassino." These men had been up on the line for seventy-two days and "had earned a 2 1/2-month rest and I was lucky to join them at the beginning." Stern listened attentively as the veterans related stories of combat and he tried to learn as much as he could before the big day arrived.

In addition to these benefits, for the replacements that joined the 36th before the Anzio breakout, there was a gradual introduction to actual combat. During the initial phase of Operation Buffalo, the 36th Division was in reserve and saw only limited action, enabling the new men to ease their way into combat. The 36th followed behind the lead divisions and was primarily involved in mopping up operations. The 36th Division history reported that troops met with only "light resistance" on the first day as it advanced north from Cisterna (May 24). This also held true for the action between May 25 and May 28.

Many of the replacements who went directly to the front lines were not as fortunate. Because of their lack of experience, a high percentage became casualties within a very short time; some did not survive their first day. Men who went into action shortly after joining their outfit had very little opportunity "to become integrated with their units before meeting the test of combat." They lacked "established ties to buddies as well as experience in teamwork with them" which, it would appear, placed them "at a distinct disadvantage in [their] first combat experience," opined Stouffer.

Raymond C. Wells of El Paso, Texas, a Master Sergeant (M/Sgt.) with Company H, 141st Infantry, related that this was a frequent occurrence among the new replacements. Shorthanded units sent men directly to the front lines, usually at night—thrown right into the heat of battle "in the midst of a major offensive." Upon reporting to their units, in almost all cases severely shorthanded, noncoms ordered them right into a particularly dangerous situation or out on a tough assignment, a night patrol, or on outpost duty, "without any satisfactory pre-battle orientation." These novices did not fare well.

Wells spoke about the absolutely "frightful experience," the "sheer terror," that a green replacement was subject to when ordered "to report to his company during the dark hours of the night during an attack." Such was the case with many of the replacements during the advance by units of the 36th across the Rapido River in January 1944. Many of these "young men and boys, or most of them, rather, teenagers," wrote Wells, "never found their companies or knew a soul in their units because in the heat of battle, in the dark, lonely and afraid, the enemy's bullet found them and they were no more." All were "perfect strangers" to the regular men of the company; no one even knew their names. "We sorrowed for these unknown comrades," Wells said, "but only their families, friends, wives or sweethearts at home knew them."

Wells also spoke of the reaction by the young replacements who, upon reporting to their assigned companies, observed firsthand the physiological and psychological impact of prolonged combat stress on the men who had experienced the Hell they were about to undergo. Anthony Harlinski of Mt. Carmel, Pennsylvania, a Pfc. with Company E, 141st Infantry, said that when he joined his new outfit, the first thing that struck him was that "everyone looked older and weary." Another unusual thing about the veteran combat soldiers that he noticed right away, was that "there was no uniformity, everyone dressed to his own convenience."

John E. McFall, a member of Company E, 141st Infantry, who joined the company as a replacement at Maddaloni, wrote, "During bivouac, I noticed many of the men had scars and marks on their body resulting from wounds, some severe. But they had been at Salerno, Altavilla, San Pietro, in the mountains and at the Rapido, and had survived. They seemed to be a good outfit; experienced and quietly confident as accomplished fighting men." McFall's closing remark, "I was determined to learn all I could from them so as not to let my outfit down, and just hope for the best."

Ernie Pyle, the "best-loved" syndicated war correspondent, wrote in his book *Brave Men*, that he "felt sorry" for the men who had to join an outfit when it was in the line. The "best method for replacements to come," he informed his wartime readers, was "when a whole regiment was out of the line for a long rest." This enabled the "new men to get acquainted with the older ones, they could form their natural friendships, and go into their first battle with a feeling of comradeship." A few others arrived during short rest periods, and at least had a few days "to fit themselves into the unit."

The "worst of all," he said, was for a man to be brought directly to the front and then dumped in a foxhole. Pyle wrote a fitting tribute to men who found themselves in just such a situation and somehow managed to endure:

All of us who have had any association at all with the imminence of death know that the main thing a man wants is not to be alone. He wants company, and preferably somebody he knows. To go up to the brink of possible death in the nighttime in a faraway land, puzzled and afraid, knowing no one, and facing the worst moment of your life totally alone—that takes strength.

As I read Pyle's words, I immediately thought of Ross Rajotte, whose story of moving up to the front line on the very night he arrived in Italy has been related in an earlier chapter.

1st Lt. Robert W. Brickman of Holstein, Iowa, wrote, "At Fort Benning we were told the absolute worst time to join a unit was under fire. Sure enough, I was ordered to take over the 2nd platoon [machine gun] of "D" Company [141st] while under fire at Mt. Lungo." Brickman was among "the first wave of replacements for the 36th Division after the landings at Salerno, Italy, on September 9, 1943." He joined Company D in "late September" and assigned "as an extra officer until needed."

Brickman was on duty at the company CP in November when word came down that 2nd Lt. Gordon E. Nelson of Dedham, Massachusetts, 2nd Platoon leader, had been wounded by shrapnel. 1st. Lt. Price, the company XO, said, "Lt. Brickman, go up and take over the 2nd Platoon." Brickman related what happened in a 2002 letter, "I had only a vague notion of the platoon's location and knew nothing of its situation." Price, pointing the way, said, "Follow that ditch. It will lead you to their position." Brickman wrote:

> I ran up the ditch expecting to see Germans behind every rock. I suppose I really had no time to worry about being afraid. About 1,000 yards up the ditch, I came across several members of the platoon whom I recognized. I checked with the section leaders as to the location of the machine gun emplacements and was briefed on what had been happening.

Brickman remained with the 2nd Platoon for more than a year until he left the unit at Bruyeres in northern France after contracting a case of acute hepatitis. Upon release from the hospital, division reassigned him to a non-combat position.

What was the attitude of the battle-hardened veterans toward the replacements? Robert J. Faught of Houston, Texas, a S/Sgt. with Company G, 141st Infantry wrote, "We welcomed them with open arms, as they were sorely needed." Anthony O. Meo (M-141) said, "We were happy to have them, we needed their help and we also could relate to their feelings." Raymond C. Wells (H-141) wrote, "They fit in very well . . . we immediately placed them in a squad with the squad leader to look out for them."

According to Samuel A. Stouffer, studies suggest that this reflected the general attitude of most of the experienced veterans. In November 1945, an Army research team asked 243 returning veteran American infantrymen: "When a replacement comes into an outfit during combat, [do] the veterans usually try to help him out all they can?" Eighty-eight percent agreed.

Stouffer also included the results a survey conducted in August 1944, where researchers asked "a small random group of hospitalized wounded men . . . in the European theater":

> Do you think the men who had been in your outfit for some time tried to pass on what they had learned and tried to be of help to the replacements? (Stouffer, pp. 278–279.)

> 82% They did as much as they could.
> 12% They could have done a little more than they did.
> 6% They could have done a great deal more than they did.

The evidence is clear that most experienced veterans took the new arrivals under their wing as often as possible. At every opportunity, officers and noncoms attempted to pair up the new men with seasoned veterans.

Some of the veterans did admit that there were other, more selfish reasons, why they were happy to see the replacements. Harlinski related, that "since the units were undermanned, they saw us as a [means of] spreading out the risks and duties." The noncoms "wanted the biggest and strongest men in their platoon to carry the heavy equipment." Harlinski wrote of his experience:

> The rookies in the squad would get the most unpleasant jobs, like first scout or automatic rifleman (BAR). The BAR man was glad to change his automatic rifle for a rifle [M-1]. I was elected automatic rifleman and sure was reluctant to give up my new rifle for a beat up, rusty looking BAR. It had no bipod, the front sight was out of line, and the whole gun needed a thorough going over.

This was all part of the initiation process, which every replacement had to endure before the veterans accepted them into the fold.

There were occasions, John Ellis says, when veteran infantrymen and officers treated the newly arrived replacements callously, "especially those who had arrived in a unit only a few days or hours before they were thrown into combat." The fact that they knew no one in the unit to which they were assigned, "as well as the rookies' often infuriating ignorance," Ellis says, "sometimes tempted the veterans and their officers to use them almost as cannon fodder."

Necessity sometimes forced officers and noncoms to send replacements into a particularly dangerous situation. Ellis explained:

> The fast turnover in replacements simply meant that no other troops had been available. In the later stages of the European and Pacific campaigns, casualties were so high that raw soldiers had to be sent out immediately on tough assignments because there was simply no one else to do the job. But their inexperience exacted a terrible toll.

Most of the "rookies only remained such for a very short time." One of two things usually occurred: either they were wounded or killed, "or they soon acquired the instinctive caution of the other veterans."

As zero hour approached, a strange silence set in. After what seemed like only a few seconds, platoon leaders gave the order to move out. Shouts of—"Okay boys, saddle up," "Time's up, let's go," "On your feet"—could be heard up and down the line. The moment that everyone had been waiting for and dreading was almost upon them.

Chapter Eight

Baptism of Fire

At the appointed hour (3:30 P.M.) on May 27, the 141st Infantry began to advance gradually toward the northeast in the general direction of the city of Velletri, two battalions abreast, 2nd on the left, 1st on the right. The 3rd Battalion, in regimental reserve, advanced behind the lead battalions prepared to defend the flanks against counterattack. Two companies of the 805th Tank Destroyer Battalion advanced "by echeloning forward by bounds behind advancing foot troops, one company [12 TDs] with each battalion." Elements of the regimental Cannon and Antitank Companies moved forward with each of the lead battalions. The twelve medium tanks of Company A, 751st Tank Battalion, moved forward on the left flank, maintaining contact with the 143rd Infantry.

The troops of the 141st Infantry encountered no resistance in any sector of the advance and forward progress continued through the afternoon and evening without interruption. The primary means of forward movement was to send aggressive small unit patrols to the front to cover a sector and then to bring the main elements forward where the ground was determined to be clear. Jack L. Clover of Columbus, Ohio, a Pfc. with Headquarters Company, 2nd Battalion, 143rd Infantry, referred to the process as "the usual probing and jabbing patrol activity." Once regimental forces established a new forward assault line and all units were in position, the process would begin again.

Near dusk on May 27, division halted the advance about one mile from the initial objective on a line roughly parallel to the railroad tracks running east from the city of Velletri. Platoon leaders posted sentries and ordered the men to dig in for the night. During the night, scouting patrols brought in eighteen prisoners.

On the morning of the twenty-eighth, the 141st Infantry continued the advance with the 1st and 2nd Battalions again in the lead. It was at this time that the replacements experienced first contact with the enemy—their "baptism of fire." As advancing units closed on the enemy defensive positions, the Germans opened up with harassing artillery and mortar fire that continued throughout the day, becoming heavy at times. Snipers continually harassed the rifle companies with deadly accurate fire. Harold L. Bond, Brigadier General Robert I. Stack's (Assistant Division Commander) aide-de-camp, wrote that the snipers, "dressed in camouflage suits," were "hidden in the trees." Elements of the 2nd Battalion encountered small pockets of resistance, mostly from small arms fire, which they quickly eliminated without serious difficulty. By midday, the regimental line ran southwest to northeast, approximately two and one half miles in front of Velletri at the southeast corner of the city.

Allen E. Stern of Brooklyn, New York, a Pfc. with Company B, 142nd Infantry, who, like my father, saw his first action at Velletri, wrote that his squad surprised and captured four German artillery observers. "Unfortunately," he says, "the radios were still on and Jerry heard us and threw in a bunch of artillery—my first barrage." Stern's squad dug in behind a high ledge for protection. "I found that I could outdig any mole or machine," he quipped.

In an article titled "First Day of Combat," Pvt. John F. McFall of Kansas City, Missouri, Company E, 141st Infantry, another rookie replacement, gives the following account of the action on May 28:

> We left the line of departure in early morning and advanced across farm country. Soon the sound of small arms fire came from the front and the advance slowed. The rate of fire increased and the advance came to a halt. Things heated up. I could distinguish our rifle and automatic weapons fire, and could identify our artillery and heavy mortar fire going overhead as this was an experience from basic training. The rapid fire from German machine pistols and machine guns was new, and the enemy artillery and mortar fire bursting around us was new. The large volume of bullets cracking overhead and past the ear was disquieting to say the least and shrapnel from enemy mortars and artillery exploding in the vicinity made me realize this was the real thing.

Off to the front, McFall said he could hear the clanking of tracks from approaching enemy tanks.

As the shelling intensified, McFall's 60mm mortar platoon dispersed in a small orchard behind a stone farmhouse where they sought some measure of protection from incoming shells. There was no time to dig in. The men hit the ground and assumed as low a profile as they could, taking advantage of any natural depression or hollow in the ground wherever possible.

Several riflemen passed through McFall's position in an apparent hurry to get to the rear. Shortly thereafter, a number of others followed. When he inquired of the men where they were heading, one shouted that there were German tanks to the front and they were withdrawing. The presence of enemy tanks spread fear and panic through the ranks. Paul H. Duffey of Lancaster, Pennsylvania, Company C, 141st Infantry, remarked that small arms fire did not present much of a problem to the advancing troops, "but when we heard tanks rumbling on the road, now that makes you sweat."

McFall and the others in his platoon were tempted to follow, however, they decided to remain in place. They looked to their platoon leader for direction, but could not locate him (he was later found in the rear). The retreating riflemen, most rookie replacements like himself, "seemed to be agitated," he wrote, "telling us the rifle platoons were withdrawing and if we didn't go to the rear, there would be none of our troops in front of us facing the enemy."

It was at that point that the remainder of McFall's platoon decided to go back with them. The men fell back until they came to the sunken farm road (cart path) running parallel to the forward line. Situated at intervals along the road were a number of officers and noncoms to halt the retreat and reorganize the units so they could be returned to the front. McFall commented later that the soldiers that had withdrawn to the rear were in the minority—"Our line had held."

Shortly after noon on May 28, the Germans launched a surprise counterattack toward the southeast, striking directly within the 2nd Battalion, 141st Infantry sector. Heavy concentrations of enemy artillery and mortar fire preceded the attack. The attacking force, consisting of two companies of infantry, four panzers, and several armored personnel carriers, followed closely under the barrage. Due to the nature of the "well-wooded heavily rolling terrain," the advancing units of the regiment did not detect the presence of the enemy force until they were almost upon them. The German tanks managed "to make a quick dart through a covered [sunken] road" in the sector occupied by Company F and come in behind several isolated units. Companies E and G, along the left flank of the battalion, where the fighting was heaviest, had to withdraw several hundred yards to a stronger defensive position. The attack caused a considerable amount of confusion, and resulted in a complete disorganization of the battalion.

At 2:20 P.M., Colonel John Harmony, CO of the 141st Infantry, notified his battalion commanders that he was postponing the advance until the 2nd Battalion had a chance to reorganize. The battalion did not complete the reorganization until just before dark. Harmony ordered the regiment to set up defensive positions for the night.

Aerial photograph of Italian countryside south of Rome. Signal Corps number MM-5-8291. The NARA Special Media Archives Services Division was unable to locate the image. Photograph courtesy of World War II Magazine.

36th Division troops moving up to the line from Anzio Beachhead. A paratrooper (left) watches as a 60mm mortar crew passes. Fourth man from rear is carrying mortar ammunition (111-SC-271282). Photograph courtesy of World War II Magazine.

"Cisterna, Italy, 36th Division, held in reserve at beachhead, move up to Cisterna as mop-up force." Notice 81mm ammo bearers. Several members of the mortar squad are wearing gas mask (discarded) pack in front to carry anything "crushable" (111-SC-347457).

"Anzio area, Italy. 1st Special Service Forces, 1st Regiment Troops moving up railroad tracks on way to foot of the mountains. 25 May 1944" (111-SC-377809).

Enemy forces defending the ground in front of the city of Velletri launched a second counterattack during the night of May 28 to 29. The main effort was against the 143rd Infantry situated on the left flank of the division, but again the 2nd Battalion, 141st Infantry sector, received some attacks. The attacking enemy force on this occasion was judged to be about the size of a platoon (approximately fifty-two men). Security and reconnaissance patrols, active throughout the night, reported that the main force of the enemy was dug in 300 to 600 yards to the front of the 2nd Battalion forward positions.

The 141st Infantry resumed its advance toward Velletri about daylight on the morning of May 29. The advance continued throughout the morning hours. The 2nd Battalion on the left and the 3rd Battalion farther northeast, encountered pockets of resistance from isolated strongpoints, but were able to force the enemy to abandon their defensive positions with little difficulty. To the west of the 36th Division, the 34th and 45th Infantry Divisions were encountering strong opposition from heavily defended enemy positions between Lanuvio and Campoleone Station.

*May 29, 1944. Velletri area, Italy, Pfc. Edward J. Foley, of Methuen, Mass.,
a member of the 1st squad, 1st platoon, Company G, 143rd Infantry.
"Pfc. Foley is an American sniper. He is checking his [Springfield] rifle that
is equipped with a telescopic sight before going up to the front" (111-SC-190378).*

Several features of the terrain hampered the advance by units of the 141st Infantry and made the situation much more treacherous. German forces held the high ground, affording them the advantage of observation and fields of fire. The Americans found themselves continually having to move uphill against well-entrenched defensive positions and weapons emplacements. A commonly voiced complaint among veteran T-Patchers was that throughout the Italian campaign the Germans "always seemed to be on higher ground than we were." German commanders positioned armor, machine gun emplacements, and troop concentrations in such a manner as to be able to cover all major avenues of approach. In addition, the thick vegetation, which included waist-high scrub oak, scattered clumps of trees, and numerous vineyards and olive groves that dotted the surrounding hillsides, severely restricted observation. Engineers, using bulldozers, had to cut trails into makeshift roads, which would enable infiltrating troops and armor to maneuver around enemy strong points. Harold L. Bond referred to the advance as "a slogging, uphill fight."

Advertisement for Weaver Scope from American Rifleman Magazine, *vol. 92, no. 11 (November 1944): 53.* American Rifleman *is the official publication of the National Rifle Association (NRA).*

"27 May 1944, Fifth Army, Velletri area, Italy, Sgt. Everitt W. Bastion, 143rd Infantry, Company E, of the 36th Div., patrols for snipers" (111-SC-271285).

"Nazi snipers captured by U.S. soldiers of the Fifth Army are marched back on Route 7, after being taken in a house on the outskirts of Velletri, Italy. May 27, 1944" (111-SC-183360-S).

Jack L. Clover (Hq., 2nd Bn., 143) described the foliage as "thick and jungle-like." Along the roads and cart paths there were "vineyards by the dozens masking off any real vision." Some of the "grape arbors" were "seven to eight feet tall" and "loaded with grapes." Clover says, "due to the heavy terrain . . . Burp Pistols were ideal." German soldiers "dashed in and spread rapid fire all over hell and back . . . Snipers abounded."

Bond wrote that division troops were "fighting in a mixed terrain of vineyards and woods, now at the beginning of the Italian summer thick with bright green foliage." On May 28, Bond traveled with General Stack to one of the battalion CPs in a clearing in the woods. He could "hear bullets crackling in the air overhead." From his position a short distance behind the lines, Bond said he "could see nothing through the heavy vegetation."

Rifle companies worked the area to the front of their sectors, forming long skirmish lines to the right and left of lead tanks and tank destroyers (TDs). Generally, a rifle company's zone of attack was 200 to 500 yards wide. Concealed by the thick, dense vegetation, enemy machine gunners and riflemen would lie in ambush for the infantrymen to approach their positions and then open up with murderous fire. German gunners and crews would then pick up and run back 50 to 100 yards to wait again. In a like manner, harassing snipers, described in one account as "Nazi varmints," would fire several rounds on the troops from their hiding places, run back and quickly relocate to another vantage point, making it difficult to pinpoint their location. The occasional Italian farmhouse, solidly built of stone, offered ideal protection for enemy troops.

A single concealed sniper in a good location could pin down an entire company and inflict heavy casualties. When snipers halted or impeded the advance, commanders brought up "sniper hunters" in an attempt to locate the shooter's place of concealment. When asked about the use of sniper hunters, Alfred Dietrick of San Antonio, Texas, a Tech/Sgt. with Company B, 141st Infantry, says that one time his platoon was "being sniped at from Mt. Lungo," about two and a half miles northeast of the town of Mignano. The unit was in a defensive position and harassed by the sniper. "The lieutenant radioed company headquarters and they sent over a marksman who had a rifle with a telescopic sight." He scanned the mountainside with his scope, but was unable to detect the location of the shooter.

Raymond Wells, Company F, 141 Infantry, called them "sniper killers." These were men in the company "who were particularly good shots and were issued a rifle with a scope." They "acted just like the rest of us," and their job "was to shoot when the opportunity arose and we could see the enemy." Snipers carried a five shot, bolt action Springfield Rifle (M1903) with a 4X Weaver M330 telescopic sight. The company sent these individuals to the "5th Army sniper school at Caserta," of five weeks' duration, where they took courses in sniper tactics, identification of enemy officers, and the art of camouflage and concealment. The training included hours of practice firing at stationary and pop-up targets, some positioned at distances of up to 600 yards, to sharpen their skills.

Most times, the enemy sniper would get off a couple of quick shots and then move back several hundred feet, making it more difficult to locate and eradicate them. Once advancing forces approximated a sniper's location, commanders sometimes directed machine gun, mortar, and "even artillery barrages" against a persistent marksman. Ellis says that a sniper's "natural habitat was any built-up area." Where "a village or town had been pounded with bombs and shells the heaps of rubble . . . offered excellent cover."

Michael Stubinski was a sharpshooter with Company K, 141st Infantry. His squad was leading a tank company "on the last hill before Velletri" when, through his binoculars, he spotted a couple of Germans about ninety yards away, sprinting toward a nearby house. Stubinski took aim, getting off a couple of quick shots at the soldiers just as they were about to enter the open doorway. To his surprise, the bullets hit high up on the roof. He thinks he may have accidentally snagged the scope on some brush during the advance, knocking it out of alignment. Stubinski had to resight the weapon later.

A Sherman tank commander coming up the road behind Stubinski's position, who had witnessed the action, rotated the nose of his turret and laid a 75mm shell right through the doorway into the building. The resulting explosion enveloped the house in a huge cloud of flames, dust, and smoke. Stubinski was standing only a few feet from the muzzle and the concussion knocked him clean off his feet. "All I saw was dust," he wrote. "My ears didn't stop ringing for several days."

One common problem Stubinski says he encountered with the Weaver sight in Italy, much to his annoyance, was impaired vision caused by moisture getting inside the scope and fogging up the lenses.

Tech/Sgt. Delbert W. Kendall of Oak Park, Illinois, a member of the Anti-tank (A/T) Company, 143rd Infantry, wrote that in Italy "The Krauts had snipers working a lot. With [a] rear-guard action, what better to use?" During a barrage, he said, "you could hear an occasional "piiiiiing." To prevent detection, the "Kraut sniper was . . . cagey enough not to fire when all was quiet." Kendall tells about being on the "receiving end of a sniper," a person described by the editor of the newsletter, (Tech/4) William E. Jary, Jr. (Div. Hq.), as a "sniperee." The incident took place as Kendall's unit approached the city of Velletri:

Our outfit was on the flank waiting for the artillery to zero in on Velletri. I was watching the first smoke shell hit the town, when I felt a crap coming on. I crossed the road into a grape vineyard, dropped my drawers when—piiiiiing, a couple of grape leaves fell shredded to the ground in front of me. Just one shot. I yanked up my pants and hit the dirt, and with my eyes on ground zero down a row of vines, I got a fleeting glance at a pair of legs, and they crawled out of sight, and that was the end of that.

Another time, before pulling out one morning, he propped his mirror on the side of a deuce-and-a-half and was shaving. Kendall said he was "just about finished with one side of [his] jaw, when piiiiiiing! That one thunked through the tarp overhead." He surmised that the "sonofabitch" was "attracted by the glint from my shiny steel shaving mirror."

Kendall commented that some snipers "didn't wait for the sound of artillery fire to cover [their] shots." He remembered another incident that took place on the outskirts of Rome while waiting for orders to move into the city proper:

> A sniper started to take pot shots at [the] men and their vehicles. Like shooting fish in a barrel. Well a coupla shots whizzed overhead and the whole crowd would duck looking much like a present day crowd of spectators in a stadium doing that "wave" bit, sitting then standing etc. in turn. It was a funny sight, that many men ducking in waves.

Kendall says that "the bastards were finally found in a small utility shed along a garden path, two drunken (now deceased) Krauts."

Remarking on the subject of marksmen in his outfit, Kendall wrote, "I know we had a lot of pretty good shooters (besides bull)." His guess was that "the squirrel shooters from Tennessee were the best—cause once a squirrel is shot at and missed, he's one spooky critter to bag."

General Walker wrote in his *Journal* that the German hit-and-run tactics did not fool the "seasoned troops" of the 141st Infantry, who "knew their business." As rifle platoons advanced, the troops routinely raked the heavy brush and stands of trees with continuous small arms and machine gun fire for possible enemy hiding places, after which they rushed in to secure the area. Wick Fowler, a war correspondent with the *Dallas Morning New*, assigned to the 36th Division, wrote that this was "a new tactic the division developed and used in this attack for the first time." Fowler told his readers that the practice reminded him of a "Texas jackrabbit drive, only this time the rabbits fought back." During previous engagements, concealed German gunners would often wait until the infantrymen were well past their positions and then open up from the rear with devastating effect.

General Walker ordered tank and tank destroyer battalions to employ similar tactics of firing into suspected enemy positions. Thomas M. Sherman, a member of Company A, 636th Tank Destroyer Battalion, described the practice in his book *Seek, Strike, Destroy*. Sherman wrote that on the drive toward Velletri, the CO of the 636th ordered his company to move out ahead of the 1st Battalion, 141st Infantry. "The attack jumped off at 3:30 P.M., with the 'A' Company destroyers shooting into houses, trees, and other places that might conceal enemy vehicles or troops."

Sherman reported that on the following day, when the attack resumed, the lead TDs "fired into known and suspected enemy positions, causing many casualties and much damage to enemy material." The destroyers pushed into Velletri "driving the enemy from his well organized, stoutly defended positions on the outskirts of town."

According to Jack L. Clover, another tactic used by the battalions of the 141st Infantry, was to bring "every vehicle up on the line with a [.]50 caliber mount." Clover says the heavy .50-caliber Browning air-cooled machine guns, which could fire 550 rounds per minute, "were used with great success during the Anzio breakout." Instead of "sitting in the rear wasting away," as they had in the past, commanders interspersed the vehicles with the forward echelons "laying down a solid base of fire" to clear the way for advancing frontline troops. The .50-caliber machine guns, combined with small arms and .30-caliber machine gun fire produced a "solid wall" of lead. Commanders also used armored half-tracks, with their turret-mounted quad fifties, at the head of the advancing infantry units. Originally designed for antiaircraft applications, the vehicles were capable of delivering a high rate of concentrated fire (2,200 rounds per minute). These weapons had a devastating effect on enemy forward positions.

At 2 P.M., on May 29, Col. Harmony informed his officers that the regiment would be launching a coordinated push toward the direction of Velletri to begin at 4:30 P.M. An artillery barrage would precede the attack. The big guns began firing at 3 o'clock, causing the German batteries to quickly follow suit. A few minutes later, the 81mm mortar sections added their crump, crump, crump, to the staccato of battlefield noises. Incoming artillery continued to increase in volume. German snipers, who had been silent for most of the afternoon, began firing at any movement that caught their eye.

During the late afternoon, the 1st Battalion (141st), located north and east of the city, "encountered large mine fields in their forward sector," which prevented them from advancing throughout much of the afternoon. Several small units had passed through and out of the area before it was discovered that the

Germans had mined the approach to the outskirts of the city. There is no record of any casualties. Once the battalion flanked the minefields, it made steady forward progress.

Paul Duffey (C-141), a member of the 1st Battalion, wrote that word spread rapidly among the men of his company that they had just passed through the minefield. "That was the correct time to tell us," he affirmed, "after we were out of it." The 2nd Battalion was held up for a time by a concentrated artillery barrage on their position, but continued to press on after the shelling ceased.

By 6 P.M., the 3rd Battalion had cut the railroad line running east from Velletri and established a roadblock on the main highway (Velletri-Cori Road) two miles east of the city. One hour later, the Germans mounted a major thrust by four tanks and an undetermined number of infantry against 1st Battalion positions. Artillery and mortar fire were successful in breaking up the counterattack.

One half-hour before midnight, Division ordered regimental commanders to post guards out in front of the forward lines to provide early warning in the event of another surprise attack and hold their positions throughout the night. Heavy machine gunners carried on a "running duel" with their German counterparts into the early morning hours.

Night patrols sent out by the 141st Infantry captured several prisoners, bringing the total to more than thirty since the advance began. Interrogators gathered much valuable intelligence concerning the enemy's strength and fortified positions within the city from the prisoners, "who talked freely and willingly." Among the group were several Russians, captured by the Germans at the eastern front and sent to Italy. Their captors had forced them to serve as soldiers and put them to work constructing fortifications. Before division forces entered the city, the total number of POWs would reach more than one hundred.

Enemy soldiers who immediately "threw up their hands were taken prisoner," Walker wrote, "those who tried to run away were shown little mercy. It was a matter of survival." Historian John C. McManus, in his book *The Deadly Brotherhood*, noted that some German soldiers "would kill as many Americans as possible and then, after their ammunition was expended and their situation hopeless, would try to surrender." In such instances, it "was understood among American combat soldiers" that "the German soldier would not be taken alive."

McManus included testimony from a number of combat veterans that they had killed Germans when confronted by this type of situation, or who related incidents of retribution by other members of their squad or platoon. All confessed that they had absolutely no qualms about doing so. Some even admitted feeling good about it. Among the veterans he quoted to illustrate this point was Radford Carroll, an infantryman with the 99th Division, who explained, "There was a recognized rule: surrender without fighting and all is well, but you don't fight and kill some of our people and then surrender." McManus closed, "If the enemy abrogated this unwritten agreement, he was to be destroyed."

The advance moved forward once again on the morning of May 30, with the lead battalions moving northeasterly in the general direction of the macadam road at the base of Mount Artemisio (Velletri-Artena-Valmontone Road). Paul H. Duffey (C-141) says he "was up before daylight, as was the rest of the company." The company assembled in the deepest part of the cart path, protected from fire, and made ready for the word to move out. Duffey described the next sequence of events:

> At the predetermined time, the officers were yelling, "Up and Over!" After several minutes of this, and nobody moving, I said loud enough for two Lts. to hear, "If the officers would lead us instead of driving us like cattle, maybe this show would get started." The one Lt. turned to me and said, "If I go over, will you follow?" I said, "Yes, Sir!" He went over the top, and I had to be the third man behind him. They [the men] were ready, but they wanted a leader. The show was on!

The action, Duffey says, was "hot and heavy" as the Germans opened up with "every piece of small arms they had, M.G., rat pistols (burp guns), rifles, everything, and it was furious."

It was a hot, windless day and a big yellow sun burned brightly in the sky. The men were sweating profusely in their woolen ODs. Huge swirling clouds of dust rose from the dry ground behind the moving tanks, trucks, and other vehicles, coating the men's exposed skin and damp clothes. The thick dust made breathing difficult and choked weapons, causing them to malfunction. It did not take long before German artillery and mortar fire began to zero in on the billowing dust clouds. Rounds began exploding all around, stopping the advance as the men quickly dug in for protection.

Officers passed word down the line for C Company to shift left and make contact with A Company. The riflemen were up and running while staying low. An enemy machine gun opened up from behind, and the "slugs" were walking up the far side of the road, coming ever closer all the time. As Duffey hit the ground, he looked back to see "the second (trailing) man's shirt 'pop' and he went down fast—dead." Next, the lead man was hit in the back of the head, the bullet passing right through his helmet. As "he fell to his knees, he put his hand up to his forehead, yelled, 'medic,' and fell flat, dead." The enemy machine gunner "had done a lot of damage," Duffey said. The

Germans killed seven men in the company that day, including the 1st Sergeant, Clyde Henley of Gonzales, Texas, whom Duffey fondly recalled as "a 'top rate' man . . . I knew no one that disliked him."

Duffey says he was walking along a dirt path on the right side of the main highway (Velletri-Cori Road?) when he saw a dead German lying up ahead with his legs on the path and his upper body in the gutter. Just as he was stepping over the dead man's legs, a tank came from behind, swerved slightly toward him, and purposely ran over the German's head with the tank tread. Duffey says, "I don't know if he was angry or if he was trying to upset me, but whatever it was, it didn't bother me." Men quickly became inured to the sights and smells of death.

Toward evening on May 30, the mortar platoon of Company D, 141st Infantry, stopped at a clearing near a small house in the hilly countryside before Velletri. Arlis Sizemore of Wooten, Kentucky, a mortar gunner, says that the "old man" who lived in the home left, and the mortar platoon moved into the dwelling. Platoon leader 1st Lt. William V. Church of Lenoir, North Carolina, instructed the mortar squads to set up the guns for night firing adjacent to the house. Crews placed stakes out to the front of the mortars for firing at a range of between 400 and 1,400 yards.

That evening, Lt. Church selected Arlis to pull a four-hour shift on guard duty beginning at midnight. "All was quiet, and the stars were out," when, just as his stint of duty was about to end, he says, "all hell broke loose." Artillery and mortar shells began exploding all around. When the barrage ended, Germans tanks and infantry troops launched a counterattack against the rifle companies on the front lines.

Forward Observers for the mortar platoon radioed for fire in an attempt to stem the advance. Sizemore says, "We were firing non-stop." Discarded ammunition containers began piling up high on the ground near the gun's position. The initial call was for fire about 1,000 yards out. Enemy infantrymen were advancing so rapidly on the American positions that the mortar shells were exploding behind them. "The FO kept calling for us to 'bring it in,'" Sizemore said. Finally, after several tense moments, combined arms fire from machine guns, mortars, and the rifle platoons was able to slow the advance and the Germans began falling back.

When the mortar crews finally ceased firing, Sizemore says, shells were exploding about 400 yards out. The impact diameter of a 15-pound High Explosive (HE) mortar shell at a range of 1,300 yards is approximately thirty-three yards (98 feet). The minimum safe distance from the near edge of the impact area to the forward defense line is 200 yards. A "short" round, or an "erratic round" (too far right or left), caused by human error on the part of the crew, faulty ammunition, as well as a number of other factors such as, for example, gusting winds, is always a concern and could result in friendly casualties. When friendly troops are within 400 yards of the impact area, the Forward Observer informs the Fire Direction Center (FDC) of the relative danger by including the words "DANGER CLOSE."

The original VI Corps plan called for the 36th Division to be ready to exploit any breakthrough along the Campolioni-Lanuvio-Velletri sector of the Caesar Line southwest of Velletri. By May 27, this did not appear likely. It was in this sector that the Germans had positioned their greatest buildup of troops and armament. Two days earlier, on May 25, Truscott hurled the bulk of the VI Corps forces—the 34th, 45th, and the 1st Armored Divisions—against the heavily fortified line. Repeated frontal assaults by elements of the 34th against a well-entrenched enemy over the previous four days had netted only minimal gains. German forces had pretty well battered the 34th and the division "was showing signs of battle fatigue." By the evening of the 29th, the drive had stalled. The stubborn German defenses held fast and Truscott contemplated bringing up the Texas Army in relief of the 34th Division for another attempt at cracking the line. "It began to look as if there would be no breakthrough for [Walker's] division to exploit," wrote historian Robert L. Wagner. When Walker learned of Truscott's proposed plan on May 28, he was not pleased.

Chapter Nine

Monte Artemisio

The terrain extending north from Anzio is generally flat, rising gently and becoming gradually more hilly as it continues inland toward the Lepini Mountains on the east and the Alban Hills (Colli Albani) on the west, boxing the beachhead against the sea. The "Velletri gap," through which the road from Velletri to Valmontone runs, separates the Alban Hills and the Lepini Mountains.

The Velletri area, part of Italy's "Western Uplands and Plains" region (the country has eight), is rich in agriculture. The northern half of the region, of which Velletri is a part, is known for its grain crops and livestock. Intermittent stands of trees and scrub growth, interspersed with crop fields, mainly wheat, and pastureland, spread out across much of the rural landscape. Located on the steeper slopes, many of which are terraced, are numerous vineyards and olive groves. The countryside is bisected by wooded ravines, some deep, and gullies created by runoff. The lush vegetation afforded waiting enemy troops a distinct advantage. Numerous farmhouses, barns, and outbuildings dot the landscape.

The city of Velletri sits on a high hill (1,300 feet) at the base of Monte Artemisio just above the flat Anzio coastal plain (see photograph next chapter). Velletri marks the terminus, or southern extent of the Alban Hills, a group of volcanic hills that surround Lakes Albano and Nemi, southeast of Rome. These are part of a larger group of hills known as the Colli Laziali. The Alban Hills formed an integral part of the Caesar Line, the last German defensive barrier before Rome.

Mount Artemisio rises abruptly behind the city to an elevation of 3,050 feet (939 meters) at its highest point. Artemisio is a ridge, three and a half to four miles long, running on a southwest to northeast axis. German troops occupied three major prominences atop the bumpy ridge: Maschio d'Ariano (Hill 891) at the northeast end; Hill 931 (having no name), the highest elevation, located several hundred yards (approximately 1,300 meters) down the ridge to the southwest; and Maschio del'Artemisio (Hill 812), "a knob" at the southern end. Enemy artillery FOs atop the mountain had a clear view of the city as well as the surrounding terrain and road network for miles in every direction.

General Mark Clark's decision to once again use the 36th Division in a frontal assault against a heavily fortified sector in the German defenses was deeply disturbing news to Maj. Gen. Fred L. Walker. There was little doubt in the general's mind that such a move would be a mistake on the order of the Rapido River fiasco, which occurred in January 1944, and resulted in 2,128 division-casualties. Clark had insisted on going forward with the Rapido River offensive operation despite Walker's vehement protestations. Contemporary military historians have depicted Clark as "a good general, but a poor tactician."

Clark's only interest was to succeed in attaining the objective—for the American Fifth Army to be the first Allied force to enter the Italian capital, and he cared not, as he had repeatedly shown in past operations, what it would cost in terms of lives lost. Rome was the prize he coveted. Time was running out for Clark and unless he was able to accomplish this goal before the invasion of northern France, his efforts would all be for naught. Once the long-awaited cross-Channel operation began, he knew that the news media back in the States would quickly forget the Italian campaign. Walker felt that Clark's hunger for glory was insatiable and that it had already cost the lives of a considerable number of the men in his division.

U.S. Army Historian Ernest F. Fisher says that when Walker received the troubling news, he began "to search for a possible alternative to simply taking over from the 34th Division an apparently hopeless task." For several days, the general had been trying to find a weakness in the German defenses in his forward sector that he could exploit. Regular reports had been coming in to the Division Command Post (CP) over the previous twenty-four hours from the 141st Infantry, indicating that reconnaissance patrols, sent out to probe the heavily forested slopes of Mt. Artemisio to the right of Velletri, had encountered no enemy resistance.

General Walker himself reportedly made a personal investigation of the area in front of the 141st Infantry positions, by jeep and on foot, and was greatly encouraged. Due primarily to the nature of the steep, rugged terrain on Artemisio's southeastern face, as well as the shortage of troops, General Kesselring decided to leave this section of the Caesar Line, "which he believed secure," only lightly defended. Walker wrote in his *Journal* under the date Sunday, May 28, "It looks to me like this is the place to break through."

"If the 36th Division could climb Monte Artemisio and slip in behind the German defenses . . . Kesselring's grip on the Alban Hills would be broken," wrote Fisher. Such a maneuver would also give division forces control of the heights from which artillery forward observers could call in fire missions on the city and surrounding road network, as well as depriving the Germans of that advantage.

Walker began making tentative plans in the event he was successful in getting Truscott to approve his request for a substitute infiltration maneuver. The general's *Journal* entry for Saturday, May 27, 1944, reads, "I prefer George Washington's theory—avoid fighting the enemy where he is strong; fight him where he is weak."

In his book *Return to Cassino*, Harold L. Bond, a lieutenant with Division Headquarters, provides a different version of the discovery of the existence of this weakly defended sector on Artemisio. Bond credits Brigadier General Robert I. Stack, Walker's second in command, with being the first to detect the gap. He then reported his findings to Walker. Stack, he says, "was constantly looking for some way to break the German's defenses." Bond, Stack's aide-de-camp, rode in a jeep with the general and his driver along the Velletri-Valmontone Road "to the extreme right flank of the division." The party ran into some soldiers of the 1st Battalion, 141st Infantry, dug in on the south side of the road. When Stack questioned the men, they reported that there was no sign of any German troops forward of their position.

The general's map indicated there was "an old wood road" close by leading to the top of Mt. Artemisio, which the Italians had "used for lumbering operations many years ago." The two men parked their vehicle off the road under cover and continued on foot. They walked cautiously along the south side of the paved highway to its junction with the logging road, "keeping well into the cover of the woods." Unused for many years, the road had become "heavily overgrown." Stack followed the road for several hundred yards and, based on his observations, was certain that "a tank-bulldozer could open it up in a short time." Bond wrote:

> The Germans undoubtedly covered this section of their front by patrols, but if we acted quickly we could infiltrate an entire regiment through their lines and get behind them. It would be a risky business; the regiment might be cut off and then systematically destroyed, but to Stack it seemed like a chance worth taking.

General Stack pondered the possibilities for several moments and then jumped in his jeep and the two headed back to division headquarters "as fast as possible" to report this intelligence to Walker.

On the eve of May 29, General Truscott ordered the 36th Division commander to move his troops on the following day to an assembly area to the rear of the 34th Division in front of Lanuvio. The relief of the 34th would take place during the night of May 31 to June 1. When Stack arrived at division headquarters, Truscott happened to be present at the CP discussing the upcoming move with Walker. He broke in at the first opportunity and told the VI Corps commander what he had discovered and that here a breach of the line might be possible. Truscott flat out rejected the plan. He expressed skepticism about committing troops, "which could be used to exploit any breakthrough brought about by more orthodox means."

After Truscott departed, Walker and Stack went to one of the caravans "to talk the whole thing through." Over the next several hours, they met with officers from the division's intelligence (S-2) and engineering sections for their appraisal of the situation. The two men then studied the latest maps and aerial photographs of the area before discussing all possible scenarios on the best way to accomplish such a mission, as well as calculating all possible liabilities and risks. The outcome of the session was that Walker and Stack made the joint decision ("they decided together") to schedule another meeting with the VI Corps commander at the first possible opportunity in an attempt to convince him of the plan's validity.

It is Bond's contention that General Stack never received the recognition he deserved for his part in the discovery of the weakly defended sector, nor was he given credit for "planning the scheme which cracked the Velletri line." The "dispatches from the front which described our division's brilliant maneuver mentioned only the division commander; yet it was Stack who developed the plan for the breakthrough, fought for his ideas, and supervised their execution," Bond wrote.

In Walker's version of the story, he called in Lieut. Col. Oran C. Stovall, the division engineer, and his immediate staff for consultation. Walker explained the current situation and outlined his proposal. The success of the entire operation, in Walker's mind, depended on the construction of a temporary road to the top of Artemisio over which artillery, tanks, and tank destroyers, as well as the necessary supply trains, could ascend behind the infantry regiments. He asked his veteran engineering officer to determine whether a trail or cart path existed that his men could improve into a suitable supply route. After a detailed reconnaissance by himself and his staff, Stovall returned the following day and informed Walker that, in his opinion, the construction of such a road was entirely feasible.

The general made yet another reconnaissance of the sector in front of the 141st Infantry in a Piper Cub artillery spotter to search for evidence of German defensive fortifications or gun emplacements on the heights of Artemisio. Walker detected "almost no field works," nor did he "see any entrenchments or gun positions."

Next, he requested that the division's air photoreconnaissance section make a detailed study of the terrain on the south face of the mountain for recent evidence of German defensive positions. After carefully scrutinizing the latest photographs, the intelligence officer reported only minimal activity. The news confirmed Walker's suspicions. What the general had discovered was a gap, or undefended section, in the main German defenses approximately two miles wide between the left flank of the 1st Parachute Division and the 76th Panzer Corps.

Heavy losses in the defense of Cisterna during the initial breakout from the beachhead had left the Germans without sufficient troop strength to cover the entire defense line. As a result, the Germans had stationed only a token force in the two mile sector, where they believed the Americans would be least likely to attack. General Walker considered this the ideal place to penetrate the German defense line. It was at this point that he decided the time was right to present the idea to Truscott once again.

Walker's plan was simple: he proposed sending two regiments, the 142nd and 143rd (approximately 6,000 men), "with the former in the lead," on a night march through the enemy lines to outflank the city of Velletri. The troops would make the climb to the top of Artemisio to seize Hill 931 and the Maschio d'Ariano (Hill 891). After securing the crest, the 142nd would proceed down the southwestern slope of the ridge to its base, at a point approximately two miles north and west of Velletri, and establish roadblocks across the two remaining routes of withdrawal left to the enemy garrison, the Via dei Laghi and the Velletri-Nemi Road. Once units completed this phase of the operation, the 141st Infantry, in coordination with the 142nd Infantry and 36th Engineer Combat Regiment, would mount a full-scale attack against the city from several directions.

Fisher wrote, "With the enemy garrison virtually surrounded, the 36th Division could then quickly destroy the remaining defenders along this part of the Caesar Line, and the 'shortest' road to Rome would be open." At the same time, the 143rd would continue toward the northwest in the direction of Rome and secure the Alban Hills.

"It was the same sort of flanking maneuver that General Walker advised the higher command to let him make [January 20–21, 1944] at Cassino before the ill-fated Rapido River crossing," wrote correspondent Wick Fowler. In a second attempt to break through the Rapido defenses later that month, the 34th Division, using the end around maneuver proposed by Walker, succeeded in crossing the river at a point farther north and managed to establish a bridgehead (January 30).

When Truscott visited the 36th Division CP on the morning of May 30, Walker broached the subject of the apparent gap in the Mount Artemisio forward sector and apprised the general of the latest intelligence. He outlined his stratagem for exploiting the weakness. Walker detailed the advantages of the plan and emphasized that, if successful, the maneuver would result in far fewer casualties than a direct, head-on assault into the teeth of the German defenses. The corps commander listened attentively, thought about it for a moment, and acknowledged that the idea had some merit. Truscott informed Walker that he could not give his approval without first consulting with Clark. He said he would discuss the matter with his boss and get back to the general within the hour. Wagner wrote, "By advocating a major change in plans General Walker had laid his professional reputation on the line and his future, he felt at the time, was bound up with the success or failure of the pending operation against Velletri."

The call finally came in about 11 A.M., giving Walker the okay to go ahead with the alternate plan. Truscott's "last words were, AND YOU HAD BETTER GET THROUGH!" Walker commented, "I was surprised that Truscott would take that attitude." The two men had known each other for a long time and had had a cordial relationship. He called Truscott's parting words a "veiled threat," meaning that the responsibility was his alone, and if he failed, he would be "on [his] way back to the States." The general was not to be intimidated; he was confident that despite the risks, the plan would "succeed in a big way."

Walker "put the staff to work at once to arrange for the change," scheduled to begin at 4 P.M. His Operations and Planning Section (S-3) had to issue counterorders and new orders, prepared in advance, and deliver them to subordinate commanders posthaste. At 3 P.M., the commander held a conference of unit commanders and their principal staff officers at the division CP located under the railroad tunnel, approximately one mile east of Velletri, and gave them the good news. All in attendance were "greatly pleased and enthusiastic" and considered the change "a challenge." With everyone gathered before a large map on the wall of the command post, Walker presented the details of his plan, using his finger to show the location and trace the movement of the various regiments.

The 142nd, followed by the 143rd, would make the night infiltration up the side of Artemisio, northeast of Velletri, beginning at 10:55 P.M., on May 30, and be at the top by daylight on the morning of May 31. At the appointed time, the 142nd passed through the lines of the 141st. The lead battalion reached the Velletri-Valmontone Road at the base of Mt. Artemisio at 1:30 A.M., and began the steep, arduous 3,000-foot climb to the top of the ridge. The 143rd occupied positions vacated by the 142nd and protected the rear from counterattack. The lead regiment cautiously followed the old logging trail up the lower slopes of the mountain. Spread out on both sides of the old path, troops passed through parallel rows of lush vineyards, which afforded good cover and concealment.

Lieutenant Colonel George E. Lynch of Orlando, Florida, CO of the lead 142nd Infantry, described by Associated Press correspondent Kenneth L. Dixon as "a raw-boned bemoustached West Pointer," issued orders that there would be no rifle fire. The men could keep a full clip in their weapons, but no cartridge in the chamber. "To make certain," officers checked to see that "all rifle barrels were cleared," wrote Dixon. James M. Estepp (E-142) of Chattaroy, West Virginia, said facetiously, "That was enough to scare the hell out of a brave soldier much less an eighteen-year-old coward."

Commanders instructed troops to kill, using only "homemade wire garrottes and bayonets or knives." Lynch authorized the use of hand grenades, but only "as a last resort." The enemy could easily mistake the explosion for an incoming mortar round. The Germans knew the sound of American small arms and a single shot might jeopardize the entire operation. William F. Hartung, Sr. (E-143) wrote in 2004, "We got rid of anything that rattled or shined, painted our faces black, no clips in the rifle, and extra hand grenades." Early detection could possibly result in the slaughter of hundreds, perhaps thousands of men should they be cut off and surrounded by German forces. Officers sent word down the line instructing troops to maintain absolute silence and forbidding all smoking (Kurzman).

Wagner says a "new moon shed a faint glow, giving enough light to pick out the path and any object near it." During the ascent, troops passed an occasional darkened farmhouse. Every so often, the sound of a barking dog broke the silence, setting off "a chain reaction of howls." Now and then, the men could hear a braying jackass off in the distance. Troops passed a dead dog lying in the brush off the side of the trail with its throat slashed, silenced by one of the lead scouts. Farther on, in plain sight, a dead German, who had met the same fate, was propped up against the side of a tree. Off to "the left the men heard the distant chatter of machine gun fire" from "the 141st Infantry Regiment probing the German defenses on the outskirts of Velletri."

The troops of the 142nd and 143rd Infantry "climbed all night long, like Indians," wrote CBS correspondent Eric Sevareid. Infantrymen, spaced at intervals of five yards, "climbed straight up the mountain" carrying "only the minimum of arms and equipment." Men of the heavy weapons companies carried "heavy mortar shells in their bare hands, clutching them to their stomach," while others lugged "weighty metal boxes of ammunition they strapped on their backs." Describing the climb sixty years later, William Hartung wrote, "We scaled a cliff almost vertical."

At about 3 A.M., German planes dropped hundreds of magnesium flares suspended by miniature parachutes "that blossomed directly overhead," illuminating the countryside for miles around. Everyone hit the ground, until one by one the flares flickered and died out. Dixon wrote, "We lay flat and trembling on our bellies for what seemed like hours." During the march, troops encountered several enemy outposts and gun positions, which infantry squads sneaked up on and quietly neutralized, allowing the climb to continue. "Finally," wrote Estepp, "dog-tired, sleepy and hungry, we reached the peak of Artemisio behind Velletri as it broke dawn." The men of the 142nd had not fired a single shot.

Dixon wrote, "We had walked, climbed, skulked, crawled and fought our way some eight circuitous miles to gain the ridge, some three miles behind German lines." Along the way, he said he "passed one or two exhaustion cases. Weariness became a nightmare. So did nervous strain. One man went berserk and had to be gagged until he calmed."

Once at the top, the 142nd Infantry quickly captured Hill 931, the primary objective, surprising and capturing three artillery observers, one an officer, in the middle of his morning bath. From that point, the regiment moved southwest along the crest of Artemisio toward the secondary objective, the 2,500-foot Marchio dell'Artemisio (Hill 812). The trailing 143rd Infantry turned toward the northeast to cover the right flank. Advancing abreast, the 1st and 2nd Battalions of the 142nd encountered light to moderate opposition, mainly from enemy snipers and small patrols. Troops made slow but steady progress along the densely wooded ridgeline, carefully probing as they went to prevent detection or possible ambush.

As soon as the German commanders realized the extent of the infiltration, resistance gradually stiffened throughout the afternoon and enemy troops mounted several strong counterattacks. The Germans quickly assembled a battery of self-propelled guns near Highway 7, west of Velletri, and directed artillery fire called in by the defenders on the mountain against the T-Patchers.

The 143rd Infantry took up positions vacated by the 142nd on Hill 931 and established its command post. The primary objective of the 143rd was Maschio d'Ariano (Hill 891), located several hundred yards (1,300 meters) away at the northeast end of the ridge. As units of the 143rd Infantry advanced, troops "encountered considerable sniper fire." By 2:40 P.M., on May 31, the regiment had eliminated all opposition, including a platoon of engineers entrenched in the ruins of the Castel d'Ariano on the summit of Maschio d'Ariano (Hill 891). The regimental CO had to call upon artillery support to drive the stubborn defenders from the castle ruins.

Following the engagement, the 143rd Infantry continued its march over the mountain toward the north in the direction of Rome to capture Monte Cavo (949 meters), the highest point in the Alban Hills, and Rocca di Papa (Papal Rock), both important German observation points.

When German outposts initially reported the infiltration, they were uncertain as to the strength of the force. A German engineer platoon leader from the Hermann Goering Panzer Division "reported to his battalion commander only that he had been engaged by some American infantry—nothing more," wrote Fisher. Initially, Wagner says, "the Germans had thought the attack was merely an American probing operation of perhaps a company or two." During the afternoon, the German commander dispatched a battalion to wipe out the American force. Kurzman says that the force "was no match for two American regiments" and "was crushed." "By the time the enemy grasped the gravity of their situation, it was too late." Following the engagement, the 142nd made steady progress toward the southwest, along the ridgeline.

Field Marshal Kesselring "was furious with [Generaloberst Eberhard von] Mackensen, [the Fourteenth Army Commander] for allowing the ridgeline to fall and ordered it retaken at all costs." By this time, however, the 142nd was firmly entrenched on the summit and all German counterattacks failed. Kesselring relieved Mackensen of command and replaced him with Lt. General Joachim Lemelsen, commander of the armored forces in Italy (Laurie).

By 7:30 P.M., the 142nd occupied the Maschio dell'Artemisio (Hill 812) at the southwestern end of the ridge, and began moving down the slope to Monte Spina (Hill 731), a lesser elevation below Hill 812, located two miles north and west of Velletri. During the night of May 31 to June 1, elements of the 142nd moved down off Mt. Spina to establish roadblocks on the two major roadways leading out of the city toward the northwest, the Via dei Laghi and the Velletri-Nemi Road, effectively sealing off the two northern escape routes. By sundown on June 1, the entire ridge was in American hands, save for a few small pockets of enemy troops and snipers.

As the last of the troops began the climb, the 111th Engineer Battalion came in behind to begin work on the "twenty-mile-long road up and over M. Artemisio," described by Wagner, as "one of the most extraordinary combat engineering feats of World War II." Three bulldozers, "manned by skilled and determined operators," Kurzman wrote, crawled their way up the side of the mountain "like monstrous beetles, hungrily consuming and then spitting out chunks of earth to pave the way for tanks, big guns, and supplies."

By the evening of May 31, the Americans had completely cut off the garrison inside the city. When the Germans realized the strength of the Artemisio force behind their positions, they began to retreat in large numbers. As dawn broke on the morning of June 1, artillery FOs that accompanied the infantry to the top established themselves on the heights and began calling in fire missions. Spread out below them were the supply arteries supporting the Lanuvio-Velletri sector of the Caesar Line. Scores of trucks, armor, and other vehicles were clearly visible traveling over the road network heading to Rome. Observers had a field day shooting at the lucrative targets below. The battle for the city of Velletri was about to begin.

When Col. John W. "Jazz" Harmony of Sidney, Ohio, CO of the 141st Infantry, reported to the Division CP at 9 A.M., on the morning of May 30, General Walker informed him that the 36th Engineer Combat Regiment would relieve his regiment, scheduled for completion no later than 6 P.M. Harmony's Regimental Combat Team (RCT) would then move to an assembly area north and east of the Velletri-Valmontone Road, in preparation for a direct attack against the city. By 6 A.M., on May 31, all battalions were in position awaiting the order to launch the main assault. The 1st Battalion was situated due east of the city; the 3rd Battalion was on the right flank blocking the Velletri-Valmontone Road; and the 2nd Battalion was in regimental reserve. The attached 36th Engineer Regiment would assist, attacking the city from the south. Walker issued orders for the 141st Infantry "to take the town" beginning at four o'clock in the afternoon of May 31.

Chapter Ten

The Battle for
Velletri–Walker's Masterpiece

On the afternoon of May 31, General Walker charged the 141st Infantry Regiment, under the command of Col. John W. Harmony, with the mission of capturing the city of Velletri. The operation was scheduled to begin the following morning. "Operational instructions," detailing plans for encircling and taking the town, came down from division at 2:45 P.M., and lead units began moving into position at around 4 P.M. The 2nd Battalion would advance north of the town in a westerly direction along the lower slopes of Mount Artemisio to a point one-and-a-half miles northwest of the city. Upon reaching the objective, the battalion would veer south behind the town and sever the Velletri-Nemi Road, running northwest from the city, blocking the enemy's main route of supply and escape. The 1st Battalion would make a direct, frontal attack against the city from the east. The third phase of the plan called for the 3rd Battalion to close out of regimental reserve at 8:30 P.M., and advance on Velletri from the northeast along the Velletri-Valmontone Road.

The 2nd Battalion cut the Velletri-Nemi Road as directed, reaching the objective at about 9:30 P.M. Moving along the high ground north of Velletri, the battalion encountered only light opposition from snipers and isolated pockets of resistance. Regiment notified the 2nd battalion commander to set up and maintain a roadblock with a force of sufficient strength and then move farther south and west to establish a second interdiction on Highway 7 (the Appian Way).

The objective of the 3rd Battalion was to set up a defensive position astride Highway 7, where it turns northwest toward the base of Artemisio, approximately one thousand yards north of the city. Third Battalion arrived at its objective at 1:15 A.M. (June 1). Regiment ordered the battalion to hold its position until first light. All major highways entering or exiting the city were now blocked.

The 1st Battalion, pushing west toward Velletri along the Velletri-Valmontone highway on the afternoon of May 31, ran into heavy opposition in the form of sniper, mortar, and machine gun fire from widely scattered points. The Germans laid minefields throughout the battalion's forward sector, temporarily halting the advance. Strong points of resistance prevented the 1st from clearing or flanking the minefields. Beyond initial gains of 400 to 600 yards, the battalion could make no further progress until engineers cleared lanes through the minefields.

First Battalion repulsed a German counterattack shortly after noon by an infantry unit, estimated at platoon strength, backed by tanks. The strength of the resistance put up by the German defenders prompted the battalion CO to radio regimental headquarters for additional support. Later that day, regiment attached Company K (3rd Battalion) to the 1st Battalion, for reinforcement.

As the troops of the 141st Infantry entered the outskirts of the city, tank, artillery, machine gun and rifle fire greeted them. Tall trees and villas lined both sides of the main road, providing good hiding places for deadly snipers. The Germans positioned machine gun emplacements at strategic points to give gunners greater fields of fire. Houses and buildings became more densely packed as the troops moved into the suburbs ringing the city, increasing the element of danger.

Four Mark VI Tiger tanks zeroed in on vehicles and troops as they approached the junction of the Nemi and Valmontone Roads just east of Velletri. Hidden panzers wheeled out from cover and let loose with their 75mm guns, sending men scrambling into nearby road ditches, ignoring possible antipersonnel mines. As one tank withdrew out behind a building or wall, another pulled out from cover and fired. German tanks held up the advance until TDs and bazooka teams could come forward to neutralize them. Most often, before this could happen, the enemy tanks hightailed it to previously determined safe positions farther in the rear. *Dallas Morning News* correspondent Wick Fowler wrote that during one encounter, a tank destroyer carried on a fifteen-minute duel, "continuous and heavy," with a German Tiger tank and had to demolish a house to get at its quarry.

Jack W. Wilson's (D-141) machine gun squad was advancing with one of the infantry companies on the highway leading to Velletri when he witnessed what he says was "a very unusual incident." "There was a .30 caliber machine gun entrenched on the side of the blacktop highway when a German tank approached from around a bend in the road." The machine gunner, "foolishly," opened up on the tank. "Normally," Jack said, "the bullets would have bounced right off the tank's armor." He "could see the bullets striking the road in front of the tank, when suddenly it burst into flames. The crew bailed out and ran for cover." He surmised that the "tracers must have ricocheted off the road and pierced the fuel tank." It is "also possible," he said, that "the fuel tank was leaking and that either the tracers or sparks ignited the fuel." Wilson could think of no other explanation for what happened.

During the afternoon of May 31, Capt. Robert Arn of Moundsville, West Virginia, the Commanding Officer of Company D, 141st Infantry, received a painful wound to his coccyx bone and had to relinquish command. A bullet or piece of shrapnel had clipped his spine. Arn sent for 1st Lt. William A. "Alan" Hawkins (later promoted to Captain), his Executive Officer (XO). Medics were attending to Arn's wound in the cellar of a nearby building when Hawkins arrived. Arn turned over command of the company before stretcher bearers carried him to an aid station.

History of Operations (May 1944), reported that on the night of May 31, the battalions of the 141st Infantry were in defensive positions prepared to continue the advance at first light. The 1st Battalion, situated astride the Velletri-Valmontone Highway, encountered stiff resistance throughout the night, but managed to hold the ground gained earlier in the day.

The city of Velletri was bombed for the first time by Allied aircraft on September 8, 1943, having been mistaken for Frascati, ten kilometers to the north. The bombing destroyed approximately thirty percent of the city's buildings. The original target was the location of Field Marshal General Albert Kesselring's headquarters in the Villa Aldobrandini in Frascati. Shortly after the bombing, German troops entered the city, at first only a few and later many more. All Italian soldiers and police (Carabinieri) had fled the town a few days before, leaving their weapons behind. After that date, the Allies bombed Velletri and the nearby countryside on an almost continuous basis.

In January, the Herman Goering and the 87th Panzergrenadier Divisions moved in to occupy Velletri. Many of the people left the city to live in homes and other buildings in the surrounding countryside. As many as forty to fifty people, sometimes more, crowded into a single house, while others went up into the hills to live in man-made caves, which were used to store wine barrels, that dotted the countryside among the vineyards.

German soldiers rounded up all remaining able-bodied men and put them to work building up the defenses along the Caesar Line. The Germans transported all others, mostly women, children, and the elderly, by train to the city of Rome and other towns along the rail line. When the people arrived at the railroad station in Velletri, many were frantic. A false rumor had been circulating that the soldiers were about to ship them to a concentration camp in Germany for extermination.

Paolo Carotenuto, born on April 18, 1966, grew up in the city of Velletri and lives in the area today. He works in Rome for the daily newspaper *Liber-*

azione as a graphic designer and journalist. He is the author of a book about the 36th Division and the Battle of Velletri titled, *23 maggio-2 guigno 1944, La Battagglia di Velletri* (*March 23–June 2, 1944, The Battle of Velletri*), published in 2004.

In a letter to the author, Carotenuto related how his grandmother and mother, an infant at the time, were among those at the station. Paolo's grandfather was in the Italian Army. His grandmother was sobbing so hard that the German guards released her and the baby. Mother and child followed the railroad tracks out of the city and went to live in one of the caves in the nearby hills, where many others had taken refuge.

The man-made caves extended into the hillsides at a forty-five-degree angle for some four to five meters, then leveled off and continued for several meters more. The stratum around Velletri is composed of dry, compact volcanic ash covered by approximately one meter of fertile soil. Centuries of pressure have compressed the underlying ash, so if any excavation into the sides of the cliffs is attempted, there is no danger of a landslide or cave-in.

The entrances to the caves are "usually reinforced with cement, stones, and or bricks," Carotenuto wrote. "The entrance appears like a house door." In the center of the beginning of the tunnel are stone steps, with a "cement slipway" on each side. The slipways are just wide enough to enable workers from nearby vineyards to roll the wine barrels into the cave for storage. The Italians have used the excavated chambers for many centuries. In the past, this had been the only way to keep the wine at a constant temperature of eleven degrees Celsius (approximately fifty-two degrees Fahrenheit). Side shafts interconnected some of the tunnels on the left and right.

People who lived in the caves had to endure many hardships. The underground chambers were quite cold and damp, especially during the rainy season. An infestation of fleas, lice, and other vermin plagued the temporary occupants.

Another large group of people lived in what Carotenuto describes as "water ditches," or "natural canals," averaging between four and twelve meters deep. These channels, created by erosion over many centuries, begin high in the mountains and extend for many miles across the countryside. Thick trees and vines form a high vegetative canopy over the ditches, blocking their view from above. The water runs in a streambed at the bottom of the ditch. The people hollowed out chambers into the sides of the channel for sleeping. In one large ditch, the "Fosso S. Nicola," more than 200 citizens hid from the Germans. Both the Italians and German soldiers occupied some of the ditches. The Germans concealed 88mm artillery pieces, self-propelled guns, and other vehicles and weapons in the ditches from Allied strafing and bombardment.

The German high command prohibited fraternization with the Italian populace to prevent any possibility of friction between soldiers and civilians. One of the biggest problems for the Italian people during the occupation period was hunger. They had little or no food and survived by eating grass and roots or whatever else they managed to scavenge. During the early days of the occupation, German troops purchased food from area farmers, paying very little, but most of the time they just confiscated what they needed. Soon there was no food left for anyone.

On February 19, 1944, a German soldier was killed and another severely wounded by two Italians, Amedeo Moretti and Dante Costanzi, after Amedeo caught them attacking his wife inside their house in the area south of Velletri (Contrada Pratolungo). Amedeo wounded one German with a bayonet, but the soldier managed to escape. Dante beat the other German to death with the butt of his rifle.

In reprisal, the Germans took twenty one "innocent citizens" of Velletri prisoner. Two were just teenagers, one thirteen and another nineteen years old. They lined the group up on the edge of a ravine in front of the townspeople for execution by a firing squad. Unbelievable as it may sound, the Germans only wounded some of the men. Eleven among the group survived. They remained under the pile of bodies playing dead until the Germans left the area.

Paolo wrote, "It might seem strange that so many survived the reprisal." After interviewing a number of elderly people in the town who witnessed the incident, he is able to provide a very credible explanation as to why this occurred. It was the belief of a majority of the witnesses that many of the soldiers had serious misgivings about participating in the killing of innocent people purely as a retaliatory measure. There is a high probability, based on the testimony of those present, that they fired with the intention of only wounding the prisoners. Some members of the firing squad, Paolo said, recognized that the fault lay with the soldiers who initiated the assault against the woman, and in doing so, brought about their own misfortune. "When ordered to determine if there were any survivors," witnesses related, "the Germans failed to do a thorough check."

Every year on the anniversary of the atrocity, the citizenry of Velletri hold a commemorative ceremony, "Martiri di Pratolungo" (Martyrs of Pratolungo), in honor of the unfortunate victims. Following the incident, the Italians killed other Germans, but from that time on they were careful to dispose of the bodies so that the officers would think they had deserted. The Italians rescued many Allied pilots shot down behind enemy lines and kept them hidden from German patrols until the partisans could lead them back to friendly lines. Carotenuto claims there were no partisans in the area of Velletri.

At dawn on the morning of June 1, the 141st Regimental Combat Team was poised for the capture of Velletri. The battalions of the regiment had the German garrison occupying the city surrounded on four sides and the carefully prepared trap was about to spring shut. First Battalion was east of the town; 2nd was situated to the west; and the 3rd to the northeast. The 36th Engineer (Combat) Regiment was prepared to advance on the city from the south. The south and east, the direction from which the Germans were expecting the main attack to come, were the most heavily defended parts of the urban area. With escape routes to the west and north sealed, the town was, in effect, encircled and isolated.

Division artillery batteries carried on "a harassing program" of shelling throughout the night and into the early morning hours of June 1. During the day, Forward Observers (FOs) accompanying the 143rd Infantry on Monte Artemisio assisted the 141st Infantry in its advance by calling in missions on targets of opportunity inside the city and the surrounding environs. From their vantage point on the summit of Maschio d'Ariano (on the northeast end of Mount Artemisio), observers had a 200 degree field of observation from the east to the southeast. FOs were having a field day. Below them lay the city and the major arteries supplying the German Fourteenth Army. Forward observers took any detected movement or other activity by enemy vehicles or troops immediately under fire.

Every available forward observer was busy calling in fire missions. At one point, targets were so numerous that additional observers had to be called up from division and VI Corps. Once commanders alleviated the shortage of FOs, artillery batteries began firing on an almost continual basis. In fact, it reached a point where observers were calling in more observed missions than could be executed. FOs concentrated their fire on lines of communication, command posts, and reserve forces.

Jumping off at 4:15 A.M., the 141st Infantry once again began pushing forward toward Velletri proper for the final assault. First Battalion, supported by tanks and M-10 tank destroyers, came under heavy sniper, mortar, and machine gun fire from widely scattered points. Enemy forces mounted a number of strong counterattacks, generally by units of about platoon strength. Small enemy raiding parties were active on the 1st Battalion's right flank.

General Walker personally led the 1st Battalion attack, following closely behind the lead vehicles on the main road with members of his immediate staff. The foot troops of the battalion moved abreast of the road through the cane fields (described as bamboo-like growth) and vineyards. Walker skillfully directed the 1st Battalion units "as though he were playing chess back at division headquarters." The brigadier general moved enthusiastically among the men, shouting words of encouragement and urging them to push on, his two stars clearly visible to any hidden snipers lurking in the vicinity.

At one point, artillery shells began striking all around, forcing the general and his staff to take cover in a small culvert.

When the advance continued, a German self-propelled 88mm gun came around a sharp curve in the road and let loose with two shots. At the same time, several mortar rounds hit close by. Lt. Col. Harold Reese of Philadelphia, Pennsylvania, the division Inspector General, who had been walking out beyond the bend in front of the lead vehicles, was killed instantly by a piece of shrapnel. At first, witnesses mistakenly reported that a sniper's bullet had killed the colonel. Glenn Raithel (Hq., 142nd) wrote, "We learned the Colonel was killed by a mortar shell and not by a sniper, which was some consolation, knowing he didn't suffer." Walker had cautioned his friend several times not to get out in front of the lead infantry units and armored vehicles, thereby exposing himself to enemy shelling and arms fire.

Attached Company K, spearheading the 1st Battalion advance, moved toward the initial objective, "the high ground southwest of Velletri," which B Company had lost the previous day. Throughout the morning, the company experienced "high velocity fire" but suffered no casualties. En route, units of the company captured many prisoners. After a two-hour battle, the company wrested the objective from enemy forces and established defensive positions in preparation for an expected counterattack. One of the radio operators inadvertently broadcast Company K's position and for the next six hours, the enemy responded with a heavy barrage of artillery and mortar fire, resulting in eight casualties.

During the confusion, enemy patrols worked their way around and behind K Company's position in an attempt to infiltrate from the rear. The mortar section of Company D discovered the infiltrating troops sneaking up from behind and drove them off with accurate fire from the mortars. First Battalion went on the offensive again at 3 P.M. Two and one-quarter hours later (5:15 P.M.), units were entering the outskirts of Velletri.

A full-scale assault launched by the 2nd Battalion from the west (behind the town), met with "fierce resistance." Battalion assigned Company F the task of "assault echelon" (lead company) for the battalion, followed by E and G. When the Germans realized the Americans had encircled the town, they launched a last desperate counterattack at 2:40 P.M., in an attempt to break out to the west. Enemy panzers and infantry pounded the forward elements of the 2nd Battalion mercilessly in a vain effort to escape. Aggressive German patrols infiltrated the battalion's forward positions and at one point had Company G completely cut off. Hand-to-hand combat ensued when several units exhausted their ammunition supply.

After fending off the counterattack, the 2nd Battalion continued its advance. Leading elements, supported by tank destroyers, penetrated the town at 4:30 P.M., drawing heavy machine gun and sniper fire.

The 3rd Battalion, advancing on Velletri from the northeast during the morning, ran into stubborn resistance. Two Mark V Panther tanks pinned down Company I, inflicting several casualties. While the CO of the 3rd Battalion waited for tank destroyer support to move into position to clear the way, a strong enemy force tried unsuccessfully to break through the lines of Headquarters Company. During the firefight that ensued, the enemy force suffered heavy losses. Units of the battalion captured seven prisoners and killed or wounded twice that number. Infiltrating enemy detachments and artillery fire from the city slowed the advance considerably during the afternoon and evening hours. Around dusk, 1st Battalion released Company K and the unit rejoined the 3rd Battalion in a defensive position just outside the city limits.

At 10 P.M., June 1, the 3rd Battalion, advancing against heavy resistance, found itself about 500 yards from the city when the order came down to post guards and hold its positions during the night.

Inside Velletri, house-to-house fighting by the 2nd Battalion was continuous through the late afternoon and evening hours of June 1. Defense of the city by the German garrison was tenacious. The Germans positioned machine gun emplacements in bunkers and other fortified enclosures to cover the approach down every street and avenue. The upper floors of practically every building sheltered deadly snipers. At approximately 6 P.M., lead elements of the 141st managed to penetrate to the center of the city.

Company K, attached to the 1st Battalion, was one of the first units to gain a foothold inside the city. Michael Stubinski, a native of Gilbertsville, Pennsylvania, says that a couple of tankers called for him to check out a bunker to their right just before the main square. After maneuvering into position, he shouted for the occupants, if there were any, to give themselves up. When no answer came, he shoved his rifle into the entrance and "let go a few rounds." The tankers "were surprised that I did not stick my head in," he said. The fortification, it turned out, was empty.

Many of the Germans, "hearing us close by, and I'm sure they heard the noise of the tanks also," began to cautiously emerge from the "caves" (formed by the debris from bombed and shelled buildings) and cellars with their hands high in the air. Stubinski approached one group, about a dozen in number, and "asked if anyone spoke Polish." One man stepped forward. "The first thing my captain wanted to know was whether there were any mines in the streets." He answered, "No, there were none." The prisoner informed Stubinski that many of his wounded comrades were below in the cellar and needed immediate medical attention. Stubinski told him that the medics were on their way from the rear area to help.

"20 may 1944, Velletri, Italy. View of Velletri from observation post" (111-SC-360631). Photograph taken several days prior to attack against the city by the 141st Infantry. Monte Artemisio is in background. 163rd Signal Corps Photo Company.

"The entrance arch to the town of Velletri" (Porta Napoletana).
Photograph courtesy of the Imperial War Museum, London (N.A. 15731).

Just then, a formation of surrendering Germans, who were "dressed real sharp," came goose-stepping in cadence down the street toward the main piazza with their heads held high. Their uniforms were spotless and their boots spit-shined to a high gloss. The unit had discarded all weapons. They were "real cocky and sure of themselves," Stubinski said. He believes these were "the officers and technicians who were chased down off the mountain [Artemisio]" by units of the 142nd and 143rd, and sought safety in the city. Stubinski stepped out in front of the group with his hand raised and tried to stop them, but several high-ranking American officers, who had a ringside seat to his rear, were yelling for him to let them continue.

Stubinski says he read an account later in an issue of *The 36th Division Historical Quarterly*, which indicated that General Walker was among the group. Stubinski's reaction was "Hell, I would have kicked them in the shins." Some of the other men in his company may not have been so lenient

"An old lady 74 years of age, who hid in a cellar during the bombardment of the town. She is seen seated on a heap of debris outside her home." June 3, 1944. Photograph courtesy of the Imperial War Museum, London (N.A. 15735).

either and, if it had not been for the presence of all the brass hats, they just might well have been inclined to take somewhat harsher measures to teach the Germans a lesson in humility.

One of the officers among the group spoke perfect English. "Then out of the blue," Stubinski says, "I asked him 'What happened to Max Schmeling?'" The German, who seemed puzzled at first by the question, answered, "Oh, Max Schmeling, the boxer that knocked out Joe Louis?" Stubinski said, "Yes," and the soldier replied, "He's in the paratroops."

The former Pfc. says that later in the afternoon he was involved in the "last attack" on Velletri. His squad was investigating "a hole just behind the town square," where it was suspected German troops might be hiding. When his shouts for those inside to come out and surrender went unanswered, he pulled the pin on a hand grenade and sent it bouncing down the steps. The explosion echoed throughout the square and a huge cloud of gray dust and smoke billowed from the entrance. Inside, he found the bodies of several dead Germans, the victims of earlier artillery and mortar fire.

Groups of German soldiers, realizing they had little chance of retreat, and convinced of the futility of further resistance, would walk up and surrender to the nearest American GI they could find. Eric Sevareid, a correspondent for CBS, tells how twelve fully armed Germans surrendered meekly to a single MP sitting in a jeep, while another seven gave themselves up to an unarmed medic. Regimental (141st) forces inside the city routed hundreds German soldiers from their fortifications and took them into custody. Units came up against pockets of diehards, who refused to quit the fight, and systematically

"The main square of Velletri [Piazza Cairoli] with the church in the background."
June 2, 1944. The fountain (located in foreground) is buried under a pile of rubble.
Photograph courtesy of the Imperial War Museum, London (N.A. 15732).

*A priest (Padre Italo Laracca) returns to Velletri with one of the inhabitants. Photograph
courtesy of the Imperial War Museum, London (N.A. 15736).*

wiped them out. GIs escorted the prisoners to collecting points where guards
held them in cages or compounds. From that point, escort guard companies
brought them to prisoner of war (POW) stockades behind the front lines.

The 141st Infantry regimental POW compound, located only "a few yards"
behind the frontline troops, quickly filled. According to the history of the
141st, the tally was up to 700 prisoners, with many more arriving by the
minute, when headquarters personnel lost count. Company D, 141st Infantry
alone accounted for 103. Regiment sent the overflow to the division POW
stockade on Highway 7, approximately eight miles south of Velletri at Cisterna. Combat units could not spare troops to escort all the prisoners, so they
trudged to the rear unguarded. The number of German POWs sent to the rear
was so great it was impossible to process them all through existing regimental and divisional interrogation facilities. Division shunted large groups farther down the road to Fifth Army POW enclosures at Anzio. Most prisoners

were content, knowing that for them the fighting was over and they would be safely sitting out the rest of the war in a POW camp back in the United States.

An inspection of the enemy's defensive positions, made after Velletri fell, indicated the city was a bastion in the central portion of the Caesar Line. The town was a maze of extensive fortifications, bunkers, tunnels, reinforced dugouts, shelters, and gun emplacements. Russian prisoners who had escaped to the American lines earlier told interrogators that the Germans used them as forced laborers for many months, along with all able-bodied male citizens of the city, on the construction and improvement of defensive positions. The Russians were able to provide the Americans with the location of every major defensive fortification and position.

The combined effectiveness of artillery and armor (tanks and TDs) proved to be a major factor in the overall success of the Velletri operation. This is borne out by the speed and smoothness with which the American forces were able to smash through the intricate and heavily fortified defensive network inside the urban area. After the 143rd and 142nd Infantry Regiments secured the heights behind Velletri, FOs perched on top of Mount Artemisio brought accurate fire to bear directly on enemy troop concentrations, emplacements, and supply lines, before they could do any real damage to advancing American troops and armored vehicles.

Prior to the main attack, commanders used artillery batteries to hammer and soften enemy positions inside the city. Artillery FOs called for delayed fuses so that shells penetrated several floors before exploding, instead of detonating on rooftops, causing greater destruction. Explosions caused buildings to implode and collapse, killing the defending troops. Once the American troops succeeded in entering the city proper, commanders lifted all artillery fire for fear of causing friendly casualties. During the advance through the outskirts and into the downtown area, the lack of artillery forced commanders to make maximum use of organic mortars, which served as their own personal artillery. Forward observers from the 81mm mortar platoon, up front with the line troops, used deadly accurate fire to take out stubborn defensive positions halting or impeding the advance.

The mortar platoons of the 141st Infantry Regiment's heavy weapons companies put on a tremendous display of firepower and played a prominent role in the capture of Velletri. Section leaders directed salvo after salvo of 81mm mortar fire at enemy positions, expending large amounts of ammunition during the afternoon of June 1. Regimental records for the 141st Infantry show that during the three-day period between May 30 and June 1, gunners expended 13,800 rounds of High Explosive (HE) and 495 rounds of smoke. Mortars squads could barely keep up with the demand for fire missions called in by FOs. Drivers had to use very available vehicle to bring resupply up from the dumps.

With units of the 141st Infantry attacking the city from all sides, the Germans found themselves cut off from ammunition and other supplies, unable to receive reinforcements, and with all escape routes sealed. This left the defenders with two choices: either fight to the death or surrender. Although the German high command insisted that field commanders issue strict orders to their troops to "defend to the last," the majority chose to surrender. American commanders found that German troops tended to surrender early if their getaway path was blocked.

The almost constant artillery and mortar fire directed against Velletri during the attack, combined with damage done by previous bombing raids, had left the city a shambles. Scarcely a building remained intact. Piles of rubble and other debris choked city streets. Rotting horse carcasses, wrecked carts, burned-out enemy tanks and overturned vehicles of all types littered the town. Paolo Carotenuto estimates that the war resulted in the destruction of approximately seventy percent of the city's buildings.

After the battle, members of the 141st Infantry observed broken and bloodied bodies, both German and American, lying where they had fallen in every twisted position and form imaginable. Wick Fowler described a scene on the outskirts of Velletri where he estimated more than 200 enemy bodies lay strewn across the field of battle. The smell of death hung in the still summer air. Troops discovered numerous German wounded and dead inside buildings and cellars, a testament to the effectiveness of earlier artillery barrages and mortar fire.

The 1st Battalion (141st), after reaching the outskirts of Velletri on the northwest, received orders to continue through and out of the town. Units of the battalion arrived at the objective at 3 A.M., on June 2, and took up a defensive position on the high ground northwest of the Velletri-Nemi Road, where they bivouacked for the night. Regiment assigned mopping up operations to the 2nd Battalion. By 8 P.M. (June 1), the fighting inside Velletri was pretty much over.

Considering the massive scale of the Velletri-Artemisio operation, total casualties for the 36th Infantry Division were relatively light. The historian for the 141st Infantry Regiment placed the number of dead, wounded, and missing for the division at 339. Despite stubborn resistance by the enemy, the 141st Infantry Regiment incurred few casualties; one man killed and thirty-eight wounded.

Over the previous three days, the men of the 36th Division had had little rest. The T-Patchers had caught only "snatches of sleep" and were "silent with exhaustion" from being constantly on the move. Fowler described them as "weary and dog-tired—infantry style." Harassing enemy artillery barrages and mortar fire throughout the night resulted in fitful sleep at best. Night infiltrations by small units of the enemy caused men to sleep with one eye open. The rest they so richly deserved after the hard-fought victory would not be forthcoming, at least not for the present. With the Alban defenses broken, the beaten and thoroughly disorganized enemy began a hasty withdrawal toward the city of Rome. The 36th took up the pursuit. Orders came down to use every means available to maintain contact with the enemy, to keep them on the run and off balance.

After undergoing their initiation into battle just a few days earlier, the "raw replacements" were thereafter considered "combat veterans" by their comrades, the first step to becoming full-fledged combat soldiers. Army war correspondent Sgt. James E. Farmer, in an article titled "When Doughboys Become Men," printed in the *Indianapolis Star* in April 1944, said the "baptism of fire" these "green and untried" individuals went through (writing about Salerno) "transformed them into gritty combatmen." GIs, Farmer wrote, "have the habit of referring to a soldier who's experienced several combat operations as an old man. He may have just passed 20 years but they consider him old because of what he knows about battle tactics." The "Doughboys of the 36th Division," he writes, "have learned through hard battle experience that a change from garrison soldier to combat soldier is in fact a transition from boy to man."

Men who survived their baptism of fire spent each additional day of combat honing their survival skills until they attuned their senses to the most subtle of danger's warning signals. They eventually learned to avoid situations that spelled danger. This ability was partially learned and partially instinctive, and became more acute over time. Their state or presence of mind in battle was such that they usually could sense if something, or a given situation, was not right. The slightest hint of risk or peril sent a cautionary impulse to the brain. Those who were careless and ignored these warning signals were destined to become casualties. Mistakes could be unforgiving.

General Walker's stratagem during the Velletri operation was an unparalleled success. Walker wrote in his *Journal* under the date of 2 June, "We have succeeded in a big way." Later he added, "We are having success everywhere. This is wonderful. I am proud of the 36th." Lt. Gen. Lucien B. Truscott drove up to the edge of the city in his jeep where Walker was conferring with his staff. Walker approached his superior and said in a calm voice, "You can go in now, General. The town is yours." Walker could have taken a smug attitude, and rightfully so after the condescending way in which Truscott had treated him when last they spoke. Being the gentleman that he was, there was not a hint of bitterness or resentment in the man's voice.

General Mark Clark, accompanied by Truscott, later came to Walker's Command Post (June 4) to congratulate him for the Division's impressive breakthrough. "I'm going to see to it," Clark told Walker, "that you and the 36th Division get credit for this in the newspapers back home. You have done a marvelous job."

Later in the day, Clark changed his mind and ordered the censors at VI Army Headquarters to put a stop order on all stories about Velletri bound for the United States. "So we get no credit again," Walker remarked disappointedly. After D-Day on June 6, the media relegated all press releases about the campaign in Italy to the back pages of most newspapers and major periodicals. It was not until several months later that the media back home published accounts of Walker's stunning victory and the "mild-mannered" Ohioan finally received the recognition in the press that he so justly deserved.

Walker drew a number of well-deserved accolades from many of the correspondents and journalists who witnessed the Artemisio infiltration and subsequent capture of Velletri firsthand. Wick Fowler called it "one of the most brilliantly executed maneuvers of the entire Italian campaign." Kenneth L. Dixon, noted Associated Press correspondent, wrote that the Velletri infiltration "is still considered by military experts to have been the most brilliantly successful combat-line maneuver of the entire war." He called Walker "a master strategist." Sevareid's piece, "On the Standards of the 36th Proudly Inscribe 'Velletri,'" published a few months after the battle, closed with the following commentary:

> Many outfits deserve the credit for the whole operation, but those of us who were present will always remember the men of the 36th, climbing silently in the night behind the enemy, armed with little but their American competence and a personal faith in their quiet, retiring general who has never let them down. If Generals Alexander and Clark received the key to the city of Rome, it was General Walker who turned the key and handed it to them.

Today, the account of Walker's tactics and the capture of Velletri are "used as instructional material at the Army's Command and General Staff College," wrote 36th Division historian Vincent M. Lockhart.

Regarding the successful breakthrough by the 36th, the historian for the 141st Infantry wrote, "It was the greatest victory we had experienced in Italy. After the disaster of the Rapido and the bitterness of the winter campaign, we had at last an opportunity to see our proud enemy humbled and surrendering in large groups." Historian Peter R. Mansoor wrote of the accomplishment that despite past failures of the Italian campaign, the Texas Division had learned a great deal from its experiences. "For the men of the division, Artemisio was not just a battle — it was justice."

Chapter Eleven

The Race for Rome–
Clearing the Alban Hills

After the fall of Velletri, the bulk of the battered German Tenth and Fourteenth Armies began a rapid retreat toward the Eternal City with the 36th Division in hot pursuit. Walker's tactical masterpiece had "produced a great gaping hole in the wall of the German defenses below Rome," and the division "moved quickly to exploit the breakthrough," wrote historian Robert L. Wagner. General Mark W. Clark, commanding the Fifth Army, ordered his corps (II and VI) commanders to execute an aggressive pursuit of the retreating enemy with the intent of inflicting maximum losses in the process.

Opposition by the fleeing Germans was generally of the rearguard type, with occasional instances of resistance at greater strength. German commanders employed mobile infantry units, ranging in size from scattered groups of snipers to a battalion, to fight delaying actions designed to slow the impetus of the attack, which would allow the main army to widen the gap between itself and pursuing Allied troops. Delaying tactics included well-organized strongpoints and roadblocks, reinforced by armored units (tanks, towed 88mm guns, and self-propelled artillery), at key defensive locations, combined with ambushes, and counterattacks.

Enemy rearguard detachments would engage vanguard elements, causing units to deploy. Before advancing Allied forces could concentrate sufficient combat strength to envelop and reduce the blocking line, enemy defenders would quickly disengage and withdraw, usually under cover of darkness, to the next predetermined defensive position. At a number of key locations, German commanders left behind units, comprised mainly of foreign conscripts, deemed dispensable, with orders to "fight to the death." In almost every case, they surrendered at the first opportunity.

Rearguard strategies, plus the extensive use of demolitions by German engineers to destroy bridges and culverts, proved highly effective in obstructing and delaying the pursuit by Allied forces. Kesselring succeeded, through the effective use of delaying tactics, in buying the precious time needed to accomplish his goal and save his two armies from possible annihilation. Thus, Wagner says, the Nazi war machine was able to maintain a presence in the boot for the duration of the war.

On the morning of June 2, the 36th Division continued the advance north of Velletri, between Highway 7 (Appian Way) and Highway 6 (Via Roma), the two major thoroughfares leading to the city of Rome. Orders called for the regiments of the division, moving abreast in a coordinated attack, to make a broad sweep of the remaining Alban Hills, or Colli Albani, between Mt. Artemisio and the Roman Plains (Campagna Romana), which began just north of the town of Marino (approximately thirteen miles south of Rome). Walker ordered the 141st Infantry under its CO, Colonel John W. Harmony, to proceed over the Velletri-Marino Road, known as the "Lakes Road," which parallels Highway 7, approximately two miles to the east, on the division's left flank. The Lakes Road leads to Lake Albano and Lake Nemi (the "Alban Lakes"), two popular summer resort areas southeast of Rome.

The 143rd Infantry would secure the right flank and make a sweep of the countryside to Rocca di Papa ("Papal Rock"), a lesser elevation (700 meters), which Wagner describes as "being part of the last high bluff before the Italian capital." Finally, the 142nd Infantry, in the center, would proceed to Mt. Cavo (949 meters), clearing out any pockets of the enemy in that vicinity.

The primary mission of the 141st Infantry was to secure "the Mt. Alto hill mass" (three prominences—Hills 660, 675, and 680), located due east of Lake Nemi. The Germans were using Mt. Alto as an observation platform to direct artillery fire on the surrounding region. The regiment advanced north astride the Velletri-Mariano Road and moved into position to attack the objective. Just before the attack was set to begin, Allied aircraft strafed and bombed the area, killing eight Americans and wounding twenty-five others. Preparations again got under way for an attack, but just prior to the jump-off time heavy concentrations of friendly artillery fire fell on the lead companies, causing "heavy casualties," and the attack had to be called off (see below).

During the early morning hours of June 2 and 3, the 1st Battalion advanced up the east side of Hill 675 by compass in darkness over rough terrain and took possession of the objective at 2:05 A.M., against negligible opposition. The 2nd Battalion, ordered to clear Hill 660, had a more difficult time with its assignment, as units encountered stubborn resistance in the form of artillery, mortar, machine gun, and small arms fire on the southwest slopes. After overcoming all opposition, the battalion occupied the summit by 9:45 A.M. With Hill 660 secured, the 2nd Battalion passed through the 1st Battalion and went into the attack. The battalion engaged a sizable German unit on the Velletri-Marino Road southeast of Lake Albano. Enemy forces held up the battalion's advance for more than two hours before retreating to the north.

After clearing the Germans from the heights of Mt. Alto, the 1st Battalion reorganized and then continued on to its secondary objective, the town of Nemi. Enemy forces used intermittent artillery concentrations and small arms fire to harass forward elements as they advanced up the highway, but the battalion encountered no definite defensive positions. At 9 A.M., 1st Battalion moved into Nemi "practically unopposed," and remained there for the rest of the day.

Maj. Gen. Fred L. Walker described the June 2 bombing and strafing of 36th Division troops by Allied air support aircraft that resulted in thirty-three casualties, as an "unfortunate accident." Contained in the "History of Operations Company B, 141st Infantry" (also referred to as "Report of Operations" and "After Action Reports") for June 2 is the following brief entry: "During the afternoon the whole area [1st and 3rd Battalion] was strafed and bombed by some unidentified planes believed to be our own." The company clerk listed four men in Company B as killed and five wounded, all enlisted. One bomb fell near the 3rd Battalion command group and another on I Company's position ("causing about 30 casualties"). The After Action Report for Company I states that the unit "suffered heavy casualties from friendly planes bombing" the company area (no totals provided). Eyewitnesses from Company A indicated that a total of four aircraft were involved in the attack, killing one man and wounding another in the unit.

Michael Stubinski (K-141) wrote, "We feared our own air force more than the enemy," a sentiment voiced by many GIs throughout the Italian Campaign. The division was moving so fast, the flyboys mistook American units for German troops in retreat. "We [Company K] had many casualties," Stubinski wrote. "Bombs fell on the 3rd Battalion medical aid station set up in the hills north of Velletri and one of the doctors lost a leg." On June 2, 3rd Battalion Headquarters reported that the "area was . . . bombed and strafed by low-flying unidentified planes. Capt. [Joseph A.] Burke [spelled Burk on the 1945 roster] of the Battalion Medical Detachment was seriously wounded as a result of this strafing." Possibly this was the doctor mentioned by Stubinski.

Walker called the incident of June 2 a "tragedy" and blamed the situation on "inexperienced pilots," who were "careless in identifying troops on the ground." The general had absolutely no confidence in close support of infantry by the air corps, remarking, "Our own artillery does a better job."

Walker concluded in his *Journal* that air support "can help best by bombing enemy reserve formations and artillery positions." The overall success of the Velletri operation, he wrote sadly, "was lessened" by the unfortunate incident. Such "accidents," he said, were a detriment to the morale of the infantry troops.

After reading the After Action Reports for the various companies, one has to question Walker's contention that artillery did "a better job" in support of ground troops. On the same day as the bombing and strafing (June 2), the CO of Company I Headquarters reported that friendly artillery fire fell in the area, causing an additional casualties (no totals provided). The clerk of Company I wrote, "Despite these setbacks morale of the troops remained high." This assertion seems hard to believe under the circumstances. Thirty plus men out of a company of approximately 185 at full strength (the number was probably far fewer with recent battle losses) figures out to be a very high percentage of casualties. Two days later, on June 4, American artillery shells fell on trucks transporting Company E just outside of Rome, killing five and wounding twenty (see below).

During the afternoon of June 3, the 142nd Infantry launched an assault against Monte Cavo, three-and-a-half miles from the town of Rocca di Papa, located inside the extinct volcano's caldera. The 2nd Battalion approached from the south, while 1st Battalion picked its way up the western slopes under steady sniper fire. Atop the mountain sat a large stone villa with several smaller houses and outbuildings, surrounded by a six-foot-high ivy-covered wall that enclosed a central compound. A "reduced company" of the enemy, well supplied with weapons, including machine guns and mortars, garrisoned the villa.

The attacking force wiped out all resistance shortly before dark after a fierce battle in which the mortars and machine guns of the heavy weapons companies were brought to bear against enemy positions. Enemy losses were considerable; with twenty defenders killed and another thirty captured. Amazingly, during the final assault, the Americans did not suffer a single casualty. While the defenders of Monte Cavo were holding up the 142nd Infantry, the main body of the enemy withdrew rapidly toward the north and northwest.

On the morning of June 4, the 142nd Infantry received orders from division headquarters to capture the village of Rocca di Papa. The regiment moved into the town without opposition. Division issued further orders for the 143rd to reduce the town of Grottaferratta, located about three miles west of Rocca di Papa and approximately twelve miles from Rome on the Velletri-Marino Road. By noon, regimental forces cleared the defenders from the town, capturing seventy prisoners in the process.

Division assigned the mission of taking the town of Marino, "the last major obstacle before Rome," to the 141st Infantry. Regiment designated the 3rd Battalion as attack echelon. Operations (S-3) used every available means of transportation to shuttle the companies of the battalion forward. The column of transport vehicles, supported by elements of the 636th Tank Destroyer Battalion, "with their three-inch guns," and the 751st (medium) Tank Battalion, moved rapidly toward the northwest in the direction of the objective. Meanwhile, the 2nd Battalion was advancing up the highway on foot, with the 1st Battalion following close behind in reserve.

The 3rd Battalion, in the lead, moved into position to attack the town from the southeast, while the 2nd Battalion prepared to strike from the south and southwest. With support from division artillery, the two battalions attacked simultaneously against stronger resistance than had been anticipated. The combined force neutralized all opposition and secured the town at approximately 1:30 P.M. Pursuit of the main body of the German forces was so close, forward artillery observers reported that the enemy fled north just as the battalions began moving through the town to mop up the usual snipers and small groups left behind to cover the withdrawal.

Michael Stubinski (K-141) wrote, "The battle for Marino was the German's last stand before Rome." Just before the main assault got under way, a German patrol captured one of the sergeants in Company K along with his walkie-talkie (SCR 300 Radio). Stubinski explained that there were four of the backpack radios to a company identified, in this case, by Top 1, Top 2, and so forth. When interrogated by his captors, the sergeant told them his call name was Top 5, which he knew would immediately alert the company that the Germans were trying to trick them. A German, speaking perfect English, radioed the company CP, identified himself as Top 5, and reported that the way was clear and that it was safe for the rest of the company to advance on the town. Company K, the lead element, deployed and began cautiously moving into the outskirts.

The Germans had positioned machine guns at key locations to cover all arteries approaching the center of the town and snipers occupied the upper floors of buildings ready to ambush unsuspecting American troops. While Company K medic Pfc. Robert J. "Red" Briscoe of Trenton, New Jersey, was giving aid to a sniper casualty, a German machine gunner, having total disregard for the bright red cross on a white circle clearly visible on Briscoe's helmet and armband, opened fire from a nearby house, cutting him down. Stubinski, who witnessed the incident, has no doubt that the callous act was "intentional." Staff Sgt. Peter F. Nicoulin of Union City, New Jersey, incensed at what happened, made an individual attack against the machine gun nest in an attempt to take it out. He also died.

The platoon leader, Stubinski says, ordered a machine gun squad to work its way around to the left rear of the house and set up the weapon. He then called up a bazooka team and ordered the gunner to start throwing rockets through the doors and windows. The enemy machine gun crew, in an attempt to get away, bolted out the back door of the house and was mowed down. During the battle, which lasted more than four hours, Company K inflicted heavy casualties on the enemy and captured twenty prisoners.

Stubinski wrote, "After the shooting stopped, the Germans called for a cease-fire and sent some medics in an ambulance truck to pick up their dead and wounded." Under normal circumstances, the Americans would have allowed the Germans to go about their business unmolested. As their ambulance was retreating, the BAR man in Stubinski's squad "leveled his weapon and opened fire on the truck without warning." The others in the group immediately followed suit. "Everyone was so bitter over the loss of Red Briscoe and the others," Stubinski wrote, "we blew up the truck and the battle was over." After the Germans left, a joyous population began emerging from their shelters; they "were all over, throwing flowers and giving us what little they had, hugging and kissing us," he said.

Once beyond Marino, all enemy resistance vanished. At 1 P.M., on June 4, Walker issued a general order for all units of the division "to proceed to Rome." Most of the men had been without adequate rest for more than four days and were exhausted. Walker motorized the 2nd Battalion, 141st Infantry, using every available vehicle at his disposal. Company C, 1st Battalion, rode atop the lead tanks and TDs. The limited number of transport vehicles forced the rest of the division, "including 1st [less Company C] and 3rd Battalions, 141st RCT; 142nd RCT; and 143rd RCT," to make the long trek from Marino to Rome on foot, a distance of approximately fifteen miles. The division proceeded along the Lakes Road leading out of the Alban Hills to the level Roman Plains (Campagna Romana) stretching out before the city.

First Lieutenant William A. Hawkins, the CO of Company D, wrote in his History of Operations report for June 1944, "We detrucked [south of Marino], deployed, assumed the offensive and attacked the town. Marino fell this afternoon and the company in march formation moved through and beyond the town en route to Rome. Bivouac[k]ed south of Rome for the night."

As the various units of the Fifth Army converged on the Roman capital, heavily congested traffic along Highways 6 and 7, the two major north-to-south thoroughfares, as well as on all secondary roads, caused numerous slowdowns and stoppages. All Allied units were competing for the coveted place in history that awaited the first unit to enter the Eternal City. Walker firmly believed that this unique honor should go to the 36th, because of the division's success in cracking the Alban Hills defenses. He made up his mind to do everything in his power to attain the distinction for the men of his division, even if it meant disobeying orders. Dan Kurzman says Walker was convinced that Clark was determined to deprive his division of the glory it deserved. In Kurzman's words, "He would show Mark Clark."

As partially motorized units of the 36th Division raced across the Roman Plains on Highway 7, they passed the Claudia Aqueduct, which in ancient times carried water from the Alban Hills to the city. Tall, dark-green cypress trees, evenly spaced, lined both sides of the roadway. Just beyond the trees lay the many ruins of Roman tombs from the classical period. Overhead, the troops could hear the whoosh-whoosh sound of artillery shells going in both directions.

First Lieutenant Julian H. "Duney" Philips (G-143), in "Rome-Plus Twenty Days," provides a brief description of what it was like for those units without the benefit of transportation. He wrote, "The sun was out and it was a very hot day. This wasn't a leisurely march, it was more like a forced march, but no one was complaining. If ever a division was on a roll, the 36th was." Throngs of friendly Italians came out of their homes and lined the highway cheering and applauding. As the T-Patchers passed by, groups of happy people thanked the men and offered wine, water, and food.

Emerging from the Alban Hills, the long column followed the Velletri-Marino Road (Lakes Road) as it turned west toward its junction with Highway 7, the point beyond which the level Roman Plains extend to the outskirts of the city. By turning north on Highway 7, Walker knew that he would be going out of his assigned sector, which he was not authorized to do. The only chance the general had of beating the other divisions to Rome was to take the fastest, most direct route.

Columns of escaping Germans heading north on the primary and secondary roads were without advantage of cover and concealment and provided a plethora of easy targets for strafing and bombing by American aircraft. Low flying fighters and fighter-bombers, chopped the fleeing columns to pieces. Wrecked and smoldering vehicles and other equipment littered both sides of the road. Dead Germans, in various attitudes of death, lay sprawled along the sides of the highway where they had fallen, stopped in their futile attempt to make it to safe cover. They had little chance of escaping the torrent of bombs and bullets. A thick coat of gray dust kicked up by the ceaseless line of traffic, shrouded the lifeless, almost ghostlike corpses. Some bodies were still sitting in the cabs of their vehicles, others hanging from the sides of trucks in grotesque positions, many charred black.

The hot Mediterranean sun accelerated the process of decomposition. Swarms of huge bluebottle and other species of flies, buzzing loudly, feasted on the exposed parts of decaying bodies. Passing soldiers gagged on the stench of putrefying flesh, and water streamed from their irritated and swollen eyes. The rank odor was so thick it inflamed nostrils and created a foul, acrid taste in their mouths. Men covered their faces with dirty handkerchiefs to keep from gagging. It was of little help. Their insides began to heave and vomit welled up, the acid burning their throats. Some men became sick and remained so for many hours, and in some cases for days afterward.

Most of the German bodies, says Michael Stubinski (K-141), were without shoes or boots, the needy Italians having removed them. Correspondent Eric Sevareid, with the 85th Division on Highway 6, witnessed a refugee child kicking viciously at the body of a German officer, until a young peasant woman shoved him aside and pulled off the dead man's boots. Small groups of displaced Italians passed by on the shoulders of the road as they headed back to their deserted homes in the south. They were pushing or pulling an assortment of carts and wagons transporting their meager belongings. Many of the women balanced huge bundles high on their heads, while dragging little children by the hand.

Hordes of German prisoners of war moved to the rear on foot and by truck, clogging the narrow roadways. Warren E. Taney, Company B, 111th Combat Engineer Battalion, wrote in his diary: "We have captured around 30,000 prisoners so far; we see truckload after truckload go by." Service companies needed every available vehicle for the forward movement of troops and supplies, without which the advance would stall. The POW situation exacerbated a serious transportation shortage.

Michael Stubinski wrote in his memoirs that, as the German prisoners were marching past them to the rear, some of the men "were tripping and humiliating them." Escort guards prodded prisoners who did not move fast enough with the butt of a rifle or a boot to the backside. Given the circumstances, one can understand the GIs committing vengeful acts against the POWs, having seen many good men in their outfits, close buddies, wounded and killed. During moments of great grief and sorrow, many men had uttered solemn vows to avenge the death of a foxhole buddy. Friendships in wartime were like marriages, almost sacrosanct. When a close pal received a life-threatening wound or died in battle, it created a deep sense of personal loss and severe emotional distress.

Despite all Stubinski had seen and experienced, he was not a vindictive person and had no desire to participate in the abusive behavior. Stubinski admitted that he actually "felt sorry" for the prisoners, many of whom "were young Italians in German uniforms, 17–18 years old. There were many Poles, Russians, Austrians, all nationalities." All had been conscripted—forced to fight for the Wehrmacht, and were, in a sense, "prisoners of the Germans" before their capture by the Americans, he said.

Details of the next series of events are provided by historian Dan Kurzman in his book *The Race for Rome*. The lead column of the 36th Division arrived at the intersection of the Lakes Road and Highway 7, and was just about to swing north toward the objective when it ran into units of the 1st Armored Division. General Walker and Major Carthel N. "Red" Morgan, CO of 1st Battalion, 141st Infantry, met with Col. Louis V. Hightower, commander of the 3rd Battalion, 1st Armored Regiment, 1st Armored Division, who was at the head of the formation. The colonel insisted that his division had the right of way. He ordered Walker to remain in place until after the unit had passed and then fall in at the rear of the column.

Walker knew full well that Hightower's orders were valid, but he was not about to sit calmly by the side of the highway and watch as his chance to be the first division to enter the gates of the city slipped slowly away. His immediate thought was, "Since when did a colonel give orders to a general?" Kurzman writes, "Walker imperiously placed his hands on his hips" and informed the colonel that the directive was unacceptable. No, he would not follow, the 36th would take the right half of the road, and his tanks could take the left. Hightower was incensed. Outranked, he had no choice but to obey.

Both forces raced down Highway 7 side by side, nearly pushing each other off the road on a number of occasions. On the outskirts of the city, a force of the 85th Division, traveling cross-country from Highway 6 on the east, threatened to cut in front of the two columns and block their line of advance. The resulting traffic jam brought a halt to all movement. Col. Donald E. Carlton, Truscott's Chief of Staff, called his counterpart with the 85th to warn him that if his troops "tried to cross Truscott's highway they might be greeted by gunfire" (from his troops). Confusion and chaos reigned.

General Truscott personally drove to the scene in an attempt to restore order and get the troops moving once again. The VI Corps commander confronted Walker and inquired in a gruff voice, "Fred, what are you doing outside your sector boundary?" Walker did not respond, knowing full well that he had disobeyed orders so that his troops could reach Rome more swiftly. Truscott ordered Walker's column off the highway, forcing it to detour onto a narrow secondary road (the Via Tuscolana from Frascati) running between Highways 6 and 7, approximately one to two miles to the north, which would take them to the outskirts of the city.

As leading elements of the 36th entered a densely populated suburb on the southeast side of Rome, they encountered heavy mortar and sniper fire. An enemy rearguard unit had been waiting in ambush. House-to-house fighting ensued, slowing progress to a crawl. The bodies of four T-Patchers soon lay sprawled on the sidewalk, the work of deadly snipers. While the column was being held up, friendly artillery fire, determined by Walker to have come from a 1st Armored Division battery to the south, fell on the trucks transporting Easy Company, 141st Infantry (mentioned earlier), killing five and wounding twenty men. Walker's obvious contempt for those responsible for the senseless death of his men is reflected in his closing remark, "I have no patience with trigger-happy people."

Enemy fire hit one of the lead tanks attached to the 36th and it sat burning in the middle of the street with its crew trapped inside. "Not a pleasant sight," wrote a saddened Walker. The lieutenant who commanded the tanks could not control himself and became hysterical at the tragic demise of his men. He began shouting and weeping uncontrollably. The young officer was wringing his hands and cursing the war, his superiors, and the general, standing a short distance away within earshot. "No longer able to command," Walker wrote, "I sent him with an escort to the hospital." His final *Journal* comment was, "Poor fellow. 'Shell shock' is the term sometimes applied to this hysteria."

First Lieutenant Duney Philips, who made the exhausting trek from Marino on foot with the 2nd Battalion, 143rd Infantry, detailed some of the events that occurred along the way in his diary. As the foot soldiers marched in a file down each side of Highway 7, jeeps and three-quarter and two-and-one-half-ton trucks began pulling through the column and around each other in a mad scramble to gain the lead. "From time to time," he wrote, "the large trucks would move close to our men and they would jump in the ditch to keep from being hit." The regiment, Philips says, had not run into an enemy rearguard all morning. He found it hard to believe that the Germans had pulled out without a fight.

At about 2 P.M., the faint outline of the city, shrouded in a thick haze, came into view far off in the distance. "Each step took us closer to Rome," Philips wrote, "but where were the Germans?" Coming to a point about 800 yards from the built-up area on the outskirts, a column of Sherman tanks, following close behind the infantry, pulled out of formation and moved out in front to go tearing down the home stretch in a mad dash for the city limits. "We began eating the dust and cussing every tank that ran past the walking infantry."

Philips was watching the tanks speeding down the highway, when a perfectly placed German artillery shell hit the last one in line. Armor plates flew high into the air as the machine exploded in a huge ball of smoke and flames. German batteries had the road zeroed in. The crippled tank blocked the road preventing any retreat. Then a second tank exploded followed by a third.

Spread out on both sides of the highway for some distance were standing fields of wheat ready for harvest. Philips signaled for the platoon to move off to the left side of the road and ordered his men to "get underground fast." "Those guns could turn on us any minute," he shouted. When the lieutenant looked up again, the jeeps, trucks, and tanks that had pulled ahead of the infantry earlier had reversed direction and were barreling down the road in a panic, like "scared rabbits."

Technical Sergeant Thomas M. Sherman was a Recon Sergeant with Company A, 636th Tank Destroyer Battalion, attached to the 36th Division. During the race for Rome, the job of the TDs was to clear out any pockets of resistance encountered along the route of march. First Lieutenant Robert E. Graham, the CO of Company A, received a radio message from battalion "to send a platoon of tank destroyers [4] to clean out [some] snipers and a self-propelled gun that was blocking Highway 7 into Rome." Graham ordered Sherman to take a jeep and escort Sgt. Donald V. Bynum's platoon to the enemy position. The platoon came to a backup in the road and swung out of line to move to the head of the column. Sherman "noticed that all of the vehicles held officers from 'rear echelon' units." These, Sherman noted, "were advance quartering parties from their units out to grab choice housing for themselves."

Sherman was heading past the stopped vehicles, when a major flagged him down and told him to wait in line. He tried to explain his orders to the major, but the officer stood in front of the jeep and refused to let him pass. Finally, an indignant Sherman asked the major, "Do you want us to clear the road or are you going to do it with this bunch of yours?" Sherman described what happened next:

> The major glared at me and asked, "Who sent you?" Well he was a Major so I said, "Col. Graham." The men in the destroyers started yelling at me saying, "We don't want the gun or the snipers[;] let him have them." Others called, "Let[']s stay here, it might be dangerous up there." There were other similar remarks and the Major continued to block our path so I said, "We might as well go back and tell Col. Graham that this Major wouldn't let us go by. What did you say your name was?" The Major stepped out of our way and said, "Go ahead." That Major didn't like it too well but we went ahead and Sgt. Bynum and his men soon neutralized the road block wiping out the machine guns, and forced the self-propelled gun to withdraw.

Sherman mused, "I never did tell Bob Graham about the promotion I gave him."

Right around dusk, all enemy resistance in front of Walker's position ceased. Kurzman says that at that time several women came out of their houses into the streets and reverently covered the bodies of the dead GIs with flowers from their gardens. They stood weeping over the slain men, making the sign of the cross and praying quietly. American and British troops drew into the outskirts of the city and awaited orders to go in. All vehicular traffic came to a standstill. Harold Bond says that the "vehicles, crowded too closely together for safety, stretched back in the road as far as the eye could see, across the plains and into the [Alban] hills." Meanwhile units of the German Fourteenth Army were streaming through and out of the capital as they made their escape to the north.

Bond says exhausted infantrymen threw down their packs and immediately dropped off to sleep on the sidewalks and steps of nearby buildings, drivers in their jeeps, and tankers in the streets alongside their tanks. Soon darkness set in. Supply brought up food rations and small fires flickered throughout the area where men heated K-rations and coffee. Division headquarters staff arrived with General Walker's caravans and set up a command post near the lead vehicles. Officers dispersed units and established security for the night. Division notified unit commanders to make all necessary preparations for the advance to continue at approximately 4:50 A.M., on June 5.

Division troops without benefit of transportation continued the march over the Appian Way. The 2nd and 3rd Battalions, 141st Infantry, exhausted and thirsty, having made the long, grueling trek from Marino, closed into their assigned assembly area at approximately 10:00 P.M. It was not until well after midnight that the last of the units arrived. Footsore, tired and thirsty, the haggard troops had walked more than ten miles carrying full packs, weapons and other gear. Water and rations had been in short supply during the day's march. A thick layer of road dust covered their uniforms and combined with perspiration to form a layer of chalky paste on exposed parts of the body.

Chapter Twelve

The Eternal City

At about 10 P.M., on the night of June 4, General Walker received a call from Colonel Donald E. Carlton (VI Corps) inquiring as to the location of the 36th Division forces. Walker responded that he was on the southeast edge of Rome. Everyone is on the "near edge" (southwest), Carlton shouted into the phone. "The general (Truscott) wants somebody on the far side of Rome. He wants to report that the VI [Corps] has taken Rome. Do you understand?" "Yes, Sir," replied Walker. In his *Journal* he wrote, "Not a direct order, but an implied one." Walker scheduled a conference with his staff and artillery and infantry commanders for 11:00 P.M. He explained the situation and issued orders for the division to continue through and out of the city, commencing at 2:00 A.M. The G-3 (Operations and Planning) section initiated plans to provide transportation for the entire division, but this proved impossible to implement because of the severe shortage of vehicles.

After the briefing, the general lay on his bunk to catch a couple of hours of much needed sleep. Ever sensitive to the needs of the men under his command, the commander found this order a difficult one to issue. The troops were in bivouac, many units having just arrived, thinking they were about to get a well-deserved night's rest after more than a week of continuous fighting.

Truscott, on orders from Clark, had burdened Walker with an extremely dangerous assignment. "His 36th Division," explained Kurzman, "was to risk the dangers of a night march through Rome without even a compensatory taste of its pleasures and chase the Germans northward—another typical 'hard luck' assignment." In the absence of accurate intelligence, Walker admitted he had absolutely no idea what to expect. Would the Germans fight for possession of the city? Had German units blocked the main arteries with heavily defended barricades?

In his *Journal* Walker outlined some of the logistical problems faced by the division. There was no local police force (Polizia Municipale) to direct traffic. Rome's streets were a maze, with no discernable pattern, and therefore no definitive route of march could be established beforehand. Division G-2 (Intelligence Section) had supplied commanders with maps, but they would be useless in the dark. There would be no directional signs, streetlamps, or lights in any of the buildings. Darkness and danger lurked down every city street and around every corner.

During the previous afternoon (June 4), the divisions constituting Clark's Fifth Army were in position on the outskirts of the city awaiting orders to go in. Clark sent the following dispatch to his commanders (Kurzman):

> We are now approaching Rome. Do not know if the Krauts are going to defend. It is urgently desired that private and public property in Rome not [be] damaged. Firing into Rome depends on Krauts. If opposed, Battalion Commanders and higher Commanders have power to eliminate same by fire and movement.

Would American troops be facing only blocking tactics by rearguard units to protect the retreat of the Germans through Rome to the north? Or would the German High Command order an all-out defense of the city to allow for their battered armies to regroup and fortify the next defensible position, the Gothic Line?

In the case of the latter, the Americans would have to fight for every street and every building, which would likely result in a high rate of both civilian and military casualties and could delay the advance for an indefinite period. The capital city, one of the world's great historic places, with its magnificent architecture and ancient monuments, which stand as reminders of Rome's past glory, could not possibly escape the devastation that would most certainly occur if the Americans fought for possession of the city by a series of street-by-street offensive actions.

There was one thing of which Clark was certain: if he wanted to take Rome before the start of the Normandy invasion, set to begin in two days' time, he had to make his move and make it fast. The clock was ticking for the Fifth Army commander, who was well aware that if the Germans decided to defend, his chance for glory would in all probability be lost. Clark had to take possession of the city, and he had less than two days accomplish the task. Once the cross-channel invasion got under way, the media would bury all reports about the southern front in the back pages of the world press.

Clark's answer to the dilemma was to employ one of his divisions as a probing and reconnoitering force to gather vital intelligence regarding the strength of the German defenses within the urban area. This would enable the general to make an accurate assessment of the present situation and consider his options. If Clark waited until morning, it just might be too late. His choice to carry out this dangerous mission, for whatever reason, was the 36th Division. The commander might just be placing Walker in a near impossible situation. Whether the Germans ordered the city defended or employed rearguard actions to ensure the safe evacuation of the retreating troops, the 36th could essentially be facing a potential disaster on the magnitude of the Rapido River fiasco.

Michael C. Doubler, in his book *Closing With the Enemy*, describes "urban combat as a rigorous and costly form of warfare that should be avoided," and that "offensive operations were fraught with difficulties." Military planners and tacticians have long been aware that urban warfare is usually more dangerous and costly to the attacking force than to the defenders. Enemy units would be waiting in ambush down every street, around every corner, from high above in the upper floors, and on the rooftops of buildings.

To attempt a mission of this type and magnitude, especially at night, was sheer folly. If the Germans decided to defend, it would be utter suicide. Yet, that is what Clark was proposing. Militarily, the hastily conceived operation would have had little chance of succeeding against even lightly defended emplacements. Accurate fire from a single, well-positioned tank or artillery piece, machine gun positions, or even a lone sniper, could delay or disrupt, and possibly even halt the advance by attacking forces for a considerable length of time.

There are several possible motivations behind Clark's decision to send in the 36th Division. In Walker, he would have a scapegoat should the mission fail, and it would provide the commander with a reason to replace him. If Walker succeeded, and the way was clear, Clark would take all the credit in the press, something he had done at Velletri.

Clark was well aware of the hazards associated with a night operation in an urban setting. The general obviously had absolutely no qualms about sacrificing the troops of the 36th to obtain the critical intelligence needed to determine his next possible move. Would Clark have used the military might at his disposal to drive the defenders out and take possession of the city? One can only speculate what he might have done to achieve his goal. As the general had demonstrated many times in the past, he was more interested in personal glory than in the welfare of the troops under his command. If successful, the history books would record only the glorious victory; the number of men it would cost to take the objective—in this case T-Patcher lives—would be just a footnote to the battle.

Unknown to General Walker or anyone at Fifth Army and VI Corps Headquarters, Hitler had already made the decision not to defend the city. General

Kesselring had personally briefed Hitler by telephone about 4 P.M., on June 3, regarding the status of the current situation. The commander made it clear to the German leader that all hope was lost. With the Allies knocking on the door of the city, time was becoming critical. Hitler must allow the troops occupying Rome to leave before it was too late. Upon being apprised by Kesselring of the current predicament, the Fuhrer grudgingly agreed to declare Rome an open city to spare the ancient capital from almost certain ruin. The Allies had no knowledge of Hitler's decision until the very end. The field marshal was one of the few military leaders whose judgement Hitler trusted, because, in the past, Kesselring had always been forthright and truthful in his assessment of any given military situation. Unlike others among his commanders who, Kurzman says, "found it a healthy policy to tell the Fuhrer what he wanted to hear."

On the morning of June 4, Kesselring issued a memorandum, "for his officers only," announcing: "The Fuhrer has ordered the city of Rome should not become a scene of battle because of its importance as a place of culture." Kesselring had nothing to gain from putting up a defense inside the urban area. The Americans would simply surround the outskirts and trap the defending troops, which would result in untold and unnecessary losses to men and materials. The German commander's primary concern was to salvage what he could of his armies and move them to the next fortified defensive position—the Gothic Line. It was in the mountains beyond the Arno River that he believed he could hold off the Allies indefinitely, a feat he was able to accomplish. Hitler, Kurzman says, made it clear to his commander that if Allied troops or partisans tried to hinder the evacuation in any way, the Fourteenth Army would defend Rome until the last German departed.

The decision to abandon the city was completely out of character for the German leader, considering the massive devastation wrought by the German war machine upon other European cities. Hitler's decision came as a great surprise to many. Duney Philips (G-143) wrote, "Everyone thought he would get pleasure out of seeing [the city] turned into a pile of rubble." To do so most certainly would have been extremely unpopular with the German people, a great many of whom were Christians. At a time when the tide of war was turning in favor of the Allies, public opinion was a major concern and must have weighed heavily on Hitler's final decision.

Walker's plan was simple. He designated assembly areas for each of the three combat teams about five miles northwest of the city. Orders called for regimental commanders to get to their assigned areas "with the least possible delay." The general instructed each commander to impress as many Italian civilians as necessary to act as guides and advisers to assist in navigating the units through the urban maze. The 36th Division task force would proceed as a column of combat teams in the following order, 142nd, 141st, and last, the 143rd, the lead regiment to pass the initial point (IP) by 2 A.M. Once inside the city, if commanders met with resistance they were free to take appropriate action to counter such opposition.

A platoon of four tanks at the head of the main column would establish the route of advance. The partisans provided two of their members, Roman citizens who knew the city well, to ride on the turret of the lead tank and direct the driver through the streets. The 36th Reconnaissance Troop led the main procession, followed by the remaining tanks and TDs. Next in line was the 1st battalion, 142nd Infantry, in two and one half-ton trucks, prepared to dismount and fight at a moment's notice. The Operations Section (G-3) used every available vehicle — three-quarter and two and one half-ton trucks, half-tracks, jeeps with trailers, mess vehicles, as well as any others that the staff could press into service — to transport as many troops as possible. Walker said he saw sixteen men riding on a jeep and one half-ton trailer.

Infantrymen not on trucks or jeeps filled every available space on tanks, tank destroyers, artillery pieces, anything with wheels. Three men, Walker says, were perched on the tube of a Howitzer with several others on the trails (the two rear legs that support and stabilize the weapon during firing). The trails folded together to form the hitch that attached to the truck or tracked vehicle towing the howitzer.

Behind the motorized column, soldiers on foot marched in two files. Division troops had already marched the better part of the 100 miles and more of ground covered since leaving the Anzio beachhead on May 28.

Division placed personnel from Headquarters Company, 142nd Infantry, at strategic locations along the route of advance to ensure that the main column proceeded in an orderly fashion and that units did not become separated. Walker, in his jeep, was up front of the column with the lead vehicles, his usual place when his division was executing an advance or during a battle. Antitank guns, cannon, and artillery were located at the rear of the column.

The long column proceeded cautiously, without lights, along deserted streets in the pitch-black darkness. Walker could hear "soft applause" coming from open windows and balconies above the streets. A bright moon rose in the clear night sky, but the buildings and trees that lined the route effectively blocked out all light. Lt. Harold L. Bond, riding in General Stack's jeep near the head of the column, says that he "kept a close eye on the lead tank and the deserted streets in front of it, wondering what would come next." Everyone was uneasy. The column passed down empty streets along row after row of shops and houses with the windows shuttered. Bond says, "There was no noise in the city, except for the rumble of our tanks and the sound of trucks behind us." At about 4:30 A.M., a sliver of gray light appeared on the horizon off to the east.

After the column had gone only a few miles, much to Walker's relief, it became evident that the German troops had evacuated the city. Thousands of eyes peered out apprehensively from behind closed blinds, unsure of the conquering army's attitude. There was hesitancy at first on the part of many to leave the safety of their homes. Families came out into their courtyards and gathered before every gate, waiting, while trying to summon the courage to venture out into the street. Shortly after sunrise, men, women, and children, many still in their nightclothes and slippers, began to appear. Cautiously at first, a few at a time, the people began drifting out of the courtyards into the streets to welcome the American troops. They stood on the sidewalks and watched as the long line of vehicles and footsore soldiers passed before them. Tired infantrymen, marching like robots, shuffled along. They could only smile and wave back at the people as they continued on in silence.

A beautiful bright sunny day broke over the Eternal City on the morning of June 5. The crowds continued to grow as people from the outlying districts streamed into the center of the city to take part in the long-awaited celebration. By 9 A.M., it seemed that the entire Roman populace lined the streets along the division's route of march. After years of Fascist rule and nine months of German occupation, food shortages, and deprivation, the Italians were overjoyed that liberation had finally arrived. It was a most festive and happy occasion. Huge crowds of elated Italians, dressed in their best clothes, stood waving and cheering wildly. Above the noise and applause of the cheering crowd could be heard shouts of "BRAVO AMERICANI!" "VIVA ITALIA!" "VIVA AMERICA!"

Everywhere there was rejoicing. People young and old were kissing and hugging each other. The men, sporting broad smiles, exchanged long handshakes and slapped each other affectionately on the back. Groups of people sang and danced in the streets. Young mothers held babies up for passing soldiers to kiss. Correspondent Eric Sevareid expressed the mood of the people uniquely, "There was a gladness in all eyes." Individuals whispered in prayer, "Thanks be to God, the war is finally over," while others stood silently, with tears of joy flowing freely and unashamedly.

Major R.K. Doughty of Walpole, Massachusetts, a staff officer with the 141st Infantry S-2 (Intelligence) Section, wrote that the reception received by the liberating forces "exceeded anything that Cecil B. DeMille ever put together for a Hollywood spectacular." Doughty likened the "mood," to that of "Mardi Gras." People thrust bottles of wine and bread into the hands of the "dog-tired troops" as they shuffled past. Fresh fruit, ripe cherries, and tomatoes, which the hungry Romans could hardly spare, were generously offered the conquering heroes. These gifts were a delicacy to the men who had had only C- and K-rations to eat for more than a week. The soldiers, in turn, passed out chewing gum, chocolate, sugar, and American cigarettes that had not been available in Rome for many months.

*"Smiling Italians approve the Allied entry into Rome, Italy.
Fifth Army, June 5, 1944" (111-SC-190313).*

Women and children pelted the marching troops with roses; some threw bouquets of flowers or placed garlands around the soldiers' necks. Many people waved tiny American and Italian flags. Everywhere people flashed the V for Victory sign. The occupants in the upper floors of apartment buildings along the major thoroughfares showered the endless procession with a continuous rain of confetti.

Warren Taney's (B-111) diary entry for June 5 reads in part:

> We were all amazed at the beautiful buildings and girls. Seemed more like our cities than any we have been in since the U.S. Not being bombed or shelled, the streets were clean and the people looked none the worse for the price of war, [un]like most of the cities and hamlets that we had gone through. They were short of food but were getting along fairly good.

Kurzman noted, that aside from the railroad yards, about ninety-five percent of Rome remained undamaged. Many people greeted the troops in English,

"American infantry pass through Rome, Italy. Fifth Army, June 5, 1944."
Building dubbed the "wedding cake" by G.I.s is in center of photograph
(111-SC-190908). According to Arlis Sizemore, Company D, 141st Infantry
entered Rome at approximately 8:00 a.m. and "marched about fifteen miles"
to a bivouac area north of the city.

Taney said, having learned the language in Italian schools. More than a few
shouted that they had relatives living in the United States or had been to
America themselves.

Troops and vehicles moved single file down narrow lanes as the crush of
cheering civilian crowds reduced wide boulevards to a single lane. R.K.
Doughty, riding in General Walker's jeep near the head of the column, said
that the "press of people, many of whom rode on the hoods of our vehicles,
was so great that it was practically impossible to maintain even a semblance
of march discipline." Crowds of people would surge into the streets in front
of the vehicles, causing drivers to slam on their brakes to keep from injuring
someone.

The division had entered the center of Rome on the Via Prenistina. After
turning right on the Via Appia Nuova, the column proceeded down a slight
grade and made its way past the ancient ruins of the Coliseum, its empty arches

"G.I.s GET A HELPING HAND . . . Italian children in Rome, Italy, lend a helping hand to tired Fifth Army Infantrymen, by carrying some of their equipment. June 5, 1944" (111-SC-190447-S).

and columns aglow in the morning light. American GIs were in awe of its monumental size and grandeur. The vast elliptical structure, designed to hold 50,000 spectators, was the equivalent of a twelve- to fifteen-story structure. A short distance farther on was the Imperial Forum on the left and, diagonally across the street, the triumphant Column of Trajan, forty meters high. On the edge of the Forum stood the ruins of the Basilica of Constantine.

Soon the column entered the Piazza di Venezia, Rome's busiest intersection. At one end of the square stood Victor Emmanuel II's gigantic monument to the Italian victory in World War I. The white marble structure was a memorial to the unknown Italian soldier. "The soldiers would soon dub this 'the wedding cake,' instinctively recognizing its tasteless extravagance," wrote Bond.

Groups of armed partisans with red, white, and green armbands of the CLN-National Liberation Committee, waved Italian flags. Communists wearing the red hammer-and-sickle armbands and carrying red banners marched through the city to tumultuous applause. Old vehicles, jam-packed with the freedom fighters, careened wildly through the streets, their compatriots hanging precariously off the running boards, waving clenched fists in the air.

It was just about daybreak when leading elements of the 36th Division crossed the Tiber over the Sant'Angelo Bridge, the most well known of all the Roman bridges, lined with its many statues of angels. General Walker was relieved to find that the Germans had destroyed none of the seventeen bridges over the Tiber. It had been uncertain whether the Germans would blow all the bridges and make a stand on the north bank of the river.

The column turned left on the Via della Conciliazione and followed the west bank of the Tiber until it came to St. Peter's Square, the majestic colonnaded court built by the sculptor and architect Giovanni Lorenzo Bernini. At the head of the piazza stands St. Peter's Basilica, "the premiere church of Roman Catholic Christendom," capped by the magnificent dome designed by Michelangelo. In the center of the piazza are two fountains and a tall Egyptian obelisk, brought to the city in the first century. The lead tanks clanked noisily across the cobblestones of the deserted square and came to an abrupt halt. As the sun peered above the horizon, its rays glistened off the golden dome of the Basilica and the buildings glowed orange-yellow in the morning sunshine, an incredibly beautiful sight.

Not wanting "to create an international incident" by violating the neutrality of the Vatican, wrote Kurzman, assistant division commander Brig. Gen. Robert I. Stack, at the head of the column, checked his map and ordered the lead tank to turn down a side street heading out of the square to the right. The Italian guides, who spoke very little English, protested vehemently, but the impatient Stack curtly brushed them aside and gave the command to exit.

Gesticulating wildly, they tried unsuccessfully to explain in their limited English that the street ended in a cul-de-sac. When Stack finally realized his mistake, he tried to get the convoy turned around, but a mass of frenzied Italians swarmed around every vehicle blocking passage. The entire division, strung out for blocks throughout the city, slowly ground to a halt "like a great steel accordion," Kurzman wrote.

Wild crowds of cheering, laughing people swirled around the jeeps and other vehicles and mingled with troops on foot. Among the crowd were many "attractive" Italian women "dressed in fashionable clothes and wearing make-up." To the "sex-starved GIs," wrote Eric Morris, the beautiful women "looked like Hollywood film stars." Corporal Wade Jones, a reporter for *Stars and Stripes*, wrote that the young ladies of Rome "look like the best of American women" and "are extremely glad to see us" (Adleman). The beautiful young signorinas could hardly restrain themselves. They smothered the GIs with hugs and kisses and the soldiers responded in kind. Soldiers drank freely of the wine offered them by happy Romans, knowing, of course, that it would be impolite to refuse.

Walker's jeep, a short distance behind General Stack, inched its way forward through the sea of humanity. Bond, an eyewitness to the incident, says that the general was "furious at Stack" for having taken a wrong turn. His men were liberally partaking of the many gifts of wine and food and "carousing" with the women while the Germans were escaping to the north, Kurzman wrote. It took leading elements several hours to reverse direction and get back on the right street, past Vatican City, toward their destination on the northern limits of the capital.

When the long column ground to a halt, the men of Company K, 141st Infantry, marching through the city, found themselves in the Palazzo di Venezia under the window of the brown stone building where Mussolini gave his speeches. Mike Stubinski says that he and some of his squad mates were near the great fountains in the square (Fontana di Trevi), "the ones that people threw coins into." Many of the men removed their boots and waded in the pools to soothe tired, aching feet. Not having had a shower in several weeks, several members of the company stripped to the waist and began to sponge bathe. Hot and sweaty, the cool water provided a welcome relief.

Many in the company had not shaved since the unit had been committed to battle near Velletri and were sporting a heavy growth of whiskers. An elderly Italian man approached Stubinski with straightedged razor in hand and offered to give him a shave. Using a bar of soap for lather, the gentleman skillfully shaved him clean. For his services, Stubinski gave the old man a K-ration package, which was very gratefully accepted.

While passing through the city, Stubinski said he saw "beating after beating of collaborators, and some Germans left behind to sabotage, etc." Women who had dated or lived with German soldiers had their heads shaved and were paraded through the streets before a hostile crowd. The angry people expressed their contempt by shouting vile epithets and viciously attacked or spat upon the despised women.

Eric Sevareid wrote of the violence he witnessed following the liberation of the city. "Vigilantes were in operation at every corner," he said. Numbers "of tough-looking young men, wearing the banner of their underground political group," went about the business of ruthlessly exacting the long awaited vengeance against the "tyrants." He watched in horror as the groups dashed about the city killing, beating known Fascists and German sympathizers, and destroying their property. "There was a frightening look in their eyes, an expression of sheer bloodlust and hatred. The hunt was on."

Rifle and pistol shots and bursts of automatic weapons fire split the air. "A terrified man ran out of one [of the shops], his hands in the air. He was slugged and kicked and went stumbling through the street with blood running down his face." Sevareid says he "tried to tell himself that these present victims had done frightful things to countless others, that savage oppression must result in savage release. But it remained a sickening thing to see."

In "A Personal View of World War II," Allen E. Stern of Company B, 142nd Infantry, provides the reader with an idea of what the American GIs looked like to the Italian people:

> Rome was a beautiful city and the people welcomed us joyously as we rode through. We were a seedy bunch, and as we were sitting on our Jeep trailer, a little girl came up to Raymond McGuire [the 1945 roster for B-142 lists a Raymond B. Magwire of Windsor Locks, Connecticut?], a gentleman and a college professor from Vermont, to give him some flowers. In his torn greasy clothes, a two week stubble of hair on his shaved head and a wad of tobacco distorting his face, he must have been a frightening sight. She burst into tears!

Most Italians paid no mind to the unkempt and scraggly appearance of their American liberators.

Charles A. Golub of Worcester, Massachusetts, was a member of Company K, 143rd Infantry. The platoon leader chose Golub and another member of his squad for a detail to direct units of the 143rd as they passed through and out of the city. The sergeant in charge stationed the men at one of the many piazzas in the heart of the urban area. The drop-off, as he recalled, took place between 8:30 and 9 A.M. Shortly thereafter, a crowd of about fifty or sixty smiling Italians surrounded the two young soldiers and milled about, shouting praises and patting them on the back.

"A young lady of about seventeen or eighteen, the most beautiful girl I had ever seen," Golub said as we chatted in his Worcester neighborhood market, "came out of the crowd to greet us." After more than fifty years, the memory of this attractive young woman brought a soft smile and a noticeable twinkle to his eyes when he related the story. She stepped forward and spoke to them in impeccable English, "Welcome to Rome. We thank you for liberating us from the Germans." She explained that her mother was an American citizen and her father was Italian. They had come to Rome for a visit when the war broke out, stranding them in Italy.

The girl presented the two men with a large pitcher of "yellow wine," which they took turns sipping. They were at the checkpoint for several hours and not a single vehicle came by, which caused them some concern, but after having consumed some of the wine, it no longer mattered, Golub said.

Several young children came up and stood gaping at the two GIs in wide-eyed wonderment, curious about their weapons and equipment and strange American uniforms. They pointed and chatted excitedly among themselves as they checked out the two soldiers from every possible angle. Golub and his buddy pulled some sugar cubes out of their breast pockets, those that come in K-ration packages, and began passing them out to the children. Several men, seeing the sugar, pushed forward and grabbed the cubes out of their hands, jostling them in the process, and then ran off. Golub was concerned for the children's safety and decided against passing out any more of the sweets.

After a while, the hot midday sun, combined with the effects of the wine, made the two men a bit tipsy. "We got very dizzy," Golub said. The long foot marches over the past several days, plus the lack of adequate sleep, began to take its toll. A little old woman came by and sensing their condition, asked them, "Siete stanchi?", her two hands pressed to the side of her face in the universal gesture for sleep. She went inside her home, which was close by, and came back carrying a large comforter and handed it to them. Golub spread the blanket on the sidewalk next to the building, and the two weary soldiers, who by now had finished most of the wine, lay down and were soon fast asleep.

The next thing they knew, they heard shouting and opened their eyes. By now, it was late afternoon. The truck that dropped them off earlier in the day had returned to pick them up. The sergeant yelled down at them, "Come on, you guys, get the hell up, it's time to go."

The jam of traffic and the hordes of civilians prevented all units of the 36th Division from clearing the city limits until late afternoon. Near the western outskirts, a well-organized enemy delaying force held up the advance for several hours to give the last of the fleeing German vehicles time to clear the city limits. Walker learned later that his Texas Army had been the first division to pass all the way through with all of its men and equipment. The general noted in his diary, obviously with great satisfaction, "My men are happy and proud of their achievement and I am proud of them."

After moving into their assigned areas northwest of the city, the regiments went into bivouac for a much-needed rest. When Walker reported to Truscott, the VI Corps commander assured him that the division would remain in place at least for the night. Sixth Corps established a bridgehead north of the Tiber River six miles deep and twenty miles wide, the British 1 and 5 Divisions on the left, U.S. VI and II Corps in the middle, and the French Expeditionary Corps (FEC) on the right. After being continuously on the move for more than forty-eight hours, the tired and weary men of the division settled in, most dropping off to sleep immediately. They were too exhausted to eat. It would be a brief respite.

No sooner had Fifth Army Headquarters personnel and other rear echelon units settled themselves into comfortable billets in Rome, when the order came down from Army Command declaring the city off limits to combat troops (June 5). American MPs established roadblocks on every road at the city limits, allowing only vehicles and troops on "official business" to enter. It was not until Allied Command relieved the 36th Division from the fighting in Italy on June 25, that the infantry troops were finally allowed to visit the city.

In his *Journal*, Walker expressed annoyance with the directive. "This is not the way to treat the men who made it possible for the high command to sleep in clean, comfortable beds in hotels they have commandeered for their own use." There are, he said emphatically, two types of soldiers, first, you have the frontline infantrymen "who fight and endure great hardship. This," he added, "demands stamina, knowledge, and intelligence" (an obvious dig aimed at rear echelon soldiers). These "men of action," as he called them, ". . . do what only real men can do." And then, he remarked disdainfully, "there are those who do not fight." In Walker's opinion, rear-echelon troops did not like to have combat troops around because the fighting men "give them a feeling of inferiority so they order the combat troops to stay away."

For the men of the 36th, the sights and pleasures of Rome would have to wait another day. On the following day (June 6), VI Corps ordered the division to continue its pursuit of the Germans.

The capture of the first Axis city came at a high price. Since the beginning of Operation Diadem on May 11, the Allies suffered 43,560 casualties: totals for the American Fifth Army included 3,145 killed, 13,704 wounded, and 1,082 missing; French and British Fifth Army casualties numbered 10,635 and 3,355 respectively; and British Eighth Army dead and wounded totaled 11,639. Military historians have estimated German losses (Tenth and Fourteenth Armies) at more than 38,000, not including 15,606 POWs (Laurie).

Chapter Thirteen

Pursuit of the Germans North of Rome

The primary mission of the Fifth U.S. Army in its drive north of Rome was twofold: to capture the port city of Civitavecchia, and to seize the enemy airfields at Viterbo. Civitavecchia, with extensive harbor facilities, served as the major port for the Italian capital. A deep harbor was essential for the supply of goods and materials to keep pace with the rapid advance of Fifth Army units. The nearest port in operation at this time was at Naples, 100 miles to the south. Civitavecchia is located forty miles north of Rome on Highway 1. Viterbo is approximately the same distance away, about thirty miles inland from the Tyrrhenian Sea on Highway 2.

The Fifth Army, greatly reduced in size by the withdrawal of units needed to take part in the invasion of Normandy, included the II and VI Corps. The II Corps consisted of the U.S. 85th "Custer" and 88th "Blue Devils" Infantry Divisions. The VI Corps included the U.S. 34th "Red Bull" and 36th Infantry Divisions, and the 1st Armored "Old Ironsides" Division. Fifth Army's zone of military responsibility extended forty-five miles eastward from the Tyrrhenian coast, to the boundary of the British Eighth Army sector on the northeast.

The landscape of the region north of Rome is similar to that found along the coast south of the city. Both areas are part of the "Western Uplands and Plains" described in the Monte Artemisio chapter. Traversing the length of the (Fifth Army) zone are two main thoroughfares: Highway 1 (Via Aurelia), which runs along the coast, connects Rome and Civitavecchia, and then continues north to Pisa and beyond; and Highway 2 (Via Cassia) roughly paralleling the coast about thirty to forty miles inland.

The initial plan of attack adopted by the VI Corps called for the 1st Armored Division to attack up the coast along Highway 1, followed closely by the 34th

Division. The 36th Division was to advance along the inner half of the VI Corps zone over Highway 2 to its junction with the Bracciano-Manziana Road (Via Claudia), a secondary route that branched toward the northwest, approximately seven miles beyond of the city of Rome. The II Corps, on the extreme right, was to continue northward along Highway 2 in a pursuit action and to secure the area between VI Corps and the British Eighth Army boundary.

On the night of June 5, the 36th Division bivouacked near Sant'Onofrio, a suburb of Rome, and the men were able to enjoy a much-needed night's rest. At 9 A.M., the following morning, units of the division, partially motorized, continued the pursuit of fleeing German forces to the northwest along Highway 2. At the junction of the main highway and the Bracciano-Manziana Road, the division turned left toward the town of Bracciano, just west of Lake Bracciano. Destroyed and abandoned German vehicles and armor, strafed and bombed by Allied planes, lined both sides of the road for miles. In some places, a bulldozer had to go ahead and clear the wreckage-strewn road before the column was able to continue. Lead units of the division covered a distance of approximately twenty miles before stopping south of Lake Bracciano, to bivouac for the night (June 6–7). Foot elements continued to close into the area for several hours, the last arriving near midnight.

Rosaire "Ross" Rajotte (A-141) recalled that at "a small town about five miles outside of Rome" (possibly a suburb of the city) sniper fire held up the 1st Battalion advance. "Several Fascist women," he said, "had positioned themselves at the windows on the upper floors of a "four- or five-story building" located near the center of the town and were firing on the convoy. To save time, the CO brought up a tank destroyer, and the turret gunner took aim and fired a High Explosive (HE) shell through a top floor window. The explosion rocked the entire building, forcefully ejecting one of the women out the window from which she was firing, and she fell headlong to her death on the sidewalk below. She lay there in a heap, in full view, surrounded by an ever-expanding pool of blood as battalion troops marched past. A few of the men, showing little respect for the dead, spat on, or directed unkind remarks at, the crumpled body. Some men gave the dead woman a kick as they passed.

On June 7, units of the 141st Infantry began moving out during the late afternoon (5:55 P.M.) along the Bracciano-Manziana Road. After capturing the towns of Bracciano and Manziana against slight opposition, the division turned west toward the coast on the Tolfa-Allumiere Road, a lateral road that connects with Highway 1 just north of Civitavecchia. Covering a distance of twenty-three miles, the head of the regimental column closed into a bivouac area west of Tolfa at 4:30 A.M. During the long movement, division forces made no contact with the enemy.

It was on this day that 36th Division troops learned of the long-awaited cross-channel assault on Hitler's "Fortress Europe" (code-named Overlord). First Lieutenant Julian "Duney" Philips (G-143) of Houston, Texas, wrote in "Rome-Plus Twenty Days," that his company "hadn't been on the road but a couple of miles when a cheer went up at the head of the column." He heard someone up ahead shout, "They have crossed the channel into France." A sergeant from the *Stars and Stripes* was passing out the June 6, 1944, edition of the paper with bold headlines declaring the start of the Normandy invasion. For the troops in the Italian theater, this was most welcome news. The Germans would have to divert units to France, thus relieving some of the pressure on the Italian front. No longer would the German High Command be able to concentrate all of its defensive efforts in Italy.

Just west of Bracciano (June 7), the 1st Battalion, 142nd Infantry ran into what 36th Division historian Robert L. Wagner called "one of the most curious combat units ever devised." The force, which had left Denmark only ten days earlier, consisted of 200 Luftwaffe ground support personnel equipped with bicycles. To the men of the 36th, the Germans looked strangely out of place in their light blue Air Force uniforms. The unit was originally part of the 39th Luftwaffe Regiment of the 20th German Air Force (GAF) Field Division. The German High Command assigned the regiment to one of the four fresh divisions recently rushed to Italy from other theaters to bolster the depleted and disorganized Fourteenth Army.

No sooner had the Luftwaffe troops arrived, when commanders pressed some of their numbers into immediate service as infantrymen in a rearguard delaying action. Equipped with small arms and a few machine guns, the unit was without "artillery, mortars or anti-tank support." The 2nd Battalion forces easily overran the unit at a hastily prepared roadblock. Following the engagement, a group of GIs found their abandoned bicycles parked in nearby woods. When Major General Fred L. Walker arrived at the 142nd CP later in the day, he noticed that many of the men were pedaling about the area on bicycles, which piqued his curiosity. Lieutenant Colonel George E. Lynch, CO of the 142nd, explained the circumstances.

Major Roswell K. Doughty, regimental Intelligence Officer for the 141st Infantry, went to a POW enclosure near Rome to interrogate some of the Luftwaffe prisoners. He found that the airmen suffered from a "universal phobia," the fear of artillery, to which they apparently had not been previously subjected. Many among the group stated that when the unit arrived at the front, the troops continued walking toward the American lines, hoping to surrender at the first available opportunity. They obviously had no desire to fight and die for the Fuhrer. Doughty wrote that this "was one of the first signs of weakening among the German Armed Forces that had come to my attention directly."

In an article titled "A Combat Engineer's Experience," Tech/5 B.G. Pullen of Shelbyville, Texas, a member of Company B, 111th Engineer Battalion, wrote that his company had just pulled its heavy equipment off the road and tried to conceal the vehicles in the trees as best they could. The engineers found several bicycles lying about, left behind by the captured Luftwaffe unit, and some of the men began riding them up and down the road for amusement. Pullen described what happened next:

> A short distance away four of our planes came across the highway, out to the coast and turned back toward the highway. By this time, I told the [company radio] operator I didn't like the looks of this much, as they were getting in formation to strafe the road. I had seen our marking on them, but sometimes that didn't mean they were ours. We made a dive for a stone fence that ran parallel to the road. By the time I made it over the fence and hit the ground, red bullets hit all around me. I almost pushed the stone fence over trying to get closer. The first and second plane strafed the road and the third made his dive and just bumped his machine guns and pulled back up. The fourth flew on across. They were our old [Curtis Wright] P40s [Hawks]. They thought our men on the bicycles were Germans.

Pullen said that it "wasn't long before orders came in to get rid of the bicycles as they were what drew the fire from the planes."

Wagner wrote that the move forward by division units had been so swift that mistakes in identification of troops by Allied pilots were common, and that a "close liaison between ground and air seldom had been very effective." Pullen claims that Corps quickly put "recognition signals" into effect to prevent incidents such as this from happening in the future. When radio contact failed, Corps instructed officers to use yellow signal flares to warn off Allied fighters. Because of the high number of friendly casualties from strafing and bombings by Allied aircraft at Normandy, ground troops referred to the U.S. 9th Tactical Air Force as the "American Luftwaffe."

Pfc. Allen Stern (B-142) from Brooklyn, New York, related another incident involving an attack on American units by Allied planes, which took place near Civitavecchia. When the regiment stopped for a rest break, some of the men took off their boots to soothe their tired and aching feet. Several RAF Spitfires flew over and the men waved to be friendly. Without warning, Stern says, they "swished down and started to strafe us." Once again ground troops had advanced too quickly and the Allied Air Corps had not been apprised of the situation, due, he claims, "to a snafu" (situation normal all f——- up). "In less time than it takes to write about this," quipped Stern, "I ran almost a mile in bare feet to a series of caves in a nearby cliff." Radio communications were eventually established, he said, and the Brits were "signaled off."

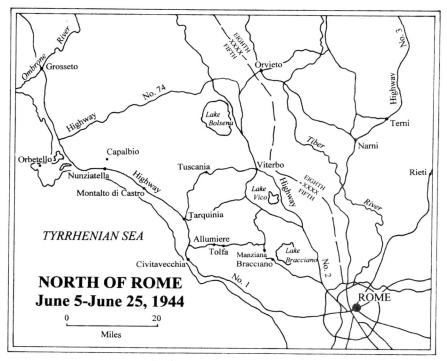

North of Rome, June 5-June 25, 1944.

B.G. Pullen's engineer battalion made a brief stop "in one town above Rome" shortly after the front had passed. Pullen heard several shots coming from the town cemetery next to the church and he decided to go over and investigate. The "Italian underground [partisans] working with the Allies," Pullen discovered, had rounded up a number of known German sympathizers and collaborators from the village and marched them off to the graveyard for summary execution. There was no trial. The guerrillas ignored pleas by weeping and wailing relatives to spare the lives of their loved ones. The partisans, accompanied by a group of angry townspeople, had dragged the men from their homes, sometimes kicking and screaming. After the local priest recited the last rites, partisans blindfolded the condemned men and stood them up against a stone wall. A makeshift firing squad carried out the executions and dumped the bodies in fresh graves.

For the loyal Italians who had so long waited for the day of liberation to come, justice was swift and for some revenge was sweet. This scenario no doubt played out in many of the towns after the Americans had moved through the area and the partisans gained political control.

The Fifth Army historian says that north of Rome, troops encountered partisans, or "anti-German guerrilla bands," in "large numbers for the first time." Some of the partisans "joined Army units and fought alongside our soldiers." These resistance units performed a number of valuable services for the Allies: they "rounded up notorious Fascists . . . brought in German stragglers bypassed by [American] forces," and "ferreted out numbers of German soldiers who had donned civilian clothes." Where the partisans "proved themselves of most value," the historian wrote, was to serve "as internal police in areas occupied by our troops before the Allied Military Government (AMG) could be set up and Carabinieri [military police] brought in to enforce laws."

During the first few days of the drive, German resistance along Highways 1 and 2 was scattered and unorganized. Toward the middle of June, resistance began to stiffen. The Fifth Army historian says that "delaying actions" by the German Fourteenth Army "both along the coast and in the mountain areas, began to show more evidence of advance planning." Enemy formations along the coast "were slowly becoming more cohesive," as well as "more aggressive." Demolitions "were the principal weapons" used until Field Marshal Albert Kesselring, "was able to bring together more troops into his order of battle." Enemy action continued to be of the rearguard type, with hit and run tactics by small groups of infantry supported by tanks and 150mm self-propelled (SP) guns, the most often encountered. Increased resistance, together with the lengthening lines of communication and supply, slowed the drive of the Fifth Army considerably.

First Lieutenant Julian "Duney" Philips (G-143) in "Rome-Plus 20 Days, Part II," says that German rearguard units consisted mostly of conscripted foreign troops. "On the drive north from Rome," he wrote, "we captured Mongolians and other non-Germans who would throw down their weapons as soon as they saw we were going to take their positions." Many enemy soldiers stood up waving white flags. The experiences of Tech/5 George A. Benton (A-143), another member of the 143rd Infantry, were similar to those of Philips. Most of the enemy soldiers captured by his unit, he wrote, were Poles "who had been forced to stay behind and hold us." Usually, Benton related, they would throw their hands up and surrender when the Americans approached their positions. Wagner noted that approximately seventy percent of the 200 troops captured by the 36th near the coastal town of Follonica, northwest of Grosetto on June 14, were non-Germans—Poles, Russians, Ukrainians (Turkomans), Mongolians, and Alsatians. Armed with small arms and infantry howitzers, the Germans had left them behind to defend the town.

According to the *Fifth Army History*, Lt. General Joachim Lemelsen, who replaced Kesselring as commander of the Fourteenth Army, considered units composed of foreign conscripts "second-class troops," and deemed them expendable. The commander regularly "sacrificed" units of this type in rearguard actions to allow his "better divisions" to make good their escape to the Gothic Line. One such unit, the 162nd Grenadier Division, consisted "primarily of Russian ex-prisoners of war . . . who 'volunteered' to fight." German commanders gave the POWs a choice of starving in a concentration camp or serving with frontline units. German forces on the eastern front had captured the Russians near Kharkov in May and June of 1942. The 162nd was typical of several of its type formed by the Germans. These men "chose to serve but took advantage of every opportunity to desert."

The Fifth Army historian reported that the Corps Intelligence Section (G-2) "estimated that 75 percent either allowed themselves to be captured without a struggle or were outright deserters." Conscripted units "were amply chaperoned by German officers and non-commissioned officers." Commanders in charge of these units had explicit orders to fight to the last man in an attempt to delay the Allied advance.

Allen Stern (B-142) wrote of the advance north of Rome, "It was mostly a matter of picking up prisoners of all kinds, though mostly Russian and Turkoman who claimed to have killed their officers and guards and who were merely waiting for us to pick them up." During a counterattack by the Germans near Nunziatella on June 11 (see next chapter), Jack Wilson (D-141), a native of Newburgh, Indiana, said that as enemy troops approached the American lines he could not believe his eyes. "I thought we were fighting the Japanese. We found out later they were Mongols captured on the Russian front and forced to fight for the Germans."

In another town north of Rome, Company K, 141st Infantry had captured four Polish prisoners. One of the officers brought the group to Pvt. Michael Stubinski, who spoke Polish, for interrogation. He located Stubinski and the other members of his squad in a nearby house sitting around the kitchen table sharing a bottle of "Dago red wine" they had found in the wine cellar. The Poles, fearing the American might shoot them, were extremely nervous. When the prisoners discovered that Stubinski could speak Polish, they were much relieved and broke out in broad smiles. They became so emotional that they could not contain themselves and showered the American with hugs and kisses. Slightly embarrassed by the outward display of affection, a backpeddling Stubinski tried to pull their arms from around his neck.

During the afternoon of June 7 (5 P.M.), troops of the 36th learned that the fast-moving 34th Division had taken Civitavecchia. At the marshaling yards in the city, the Americans captured "Anzio Anne," a.k.a. the "Anzio Express," and discovered for the first time that there were two guns, not one (Morris). These massive 280mm long-range railway guns had shelled the Anzio Beachhead throughout the winter. The gun weighed 230 tons and had a 70-foot-long barrel that fired a 550-pound projectile approximately 38 miles. The shrieking shells, which could blow a hole in the earth the size of a two-story building, evoked sheer terror in the hearts and minds of the soldiers penned up on the beachhead.

Destruction of the railroad bridges by Allied aircraft prevented the Germans from taking the big guns with them. Before pulling out, German ordnance personnel had "spiked" the weapons (inserted explosives in the barrel), rendering them inoperable. Within four days after the city fell, engineers cleared the harbor, and ships were unloading their cargoes at a rate of more than 3,000 tons daily.

The After Action Report (June 1944) for Company B, 141st Infantry noted that on this day (June 7) the troops received the first hot meal and the first mail since leaving Anzio on May 25. The historian for Company K stated in his report that the company mess served a hot breakfast on June 10, the first hot meal "in about ten days." On June 8, the 141st and 143rd Infantry Regiments stopped at the town of Allumiere and "the troops were given an opportunity to rest and clean up." They remained at the town most of the day awaiting orders from division to resume the advance.

While advancing north along the Braccino-Manziana Road, (Sgt.) Jack Wilson's machine gun squad was attached to Company A, the lead element on this particular day. The lieutenant needed someone to take a jeep and scout the road ahead in an attempt to make contact with the Germans. Rather than put one of his own men in harm's way, he chose Jack and another Company D man for the mission. The lieutenant's idea of "contact" meant, "until we were shot at," Wilson said. Jack related that this was a frequent occurrence. Whenever a "lousy detail" came up it would automatically go to someone from one of the attached heavy weapons crews. Jack was assigned a Company A vehicle and driver. The lieutenant told Wilson to lower the windshield, mount one light, air-cooled machine gun with tripod on the hood, and another on the pedestal in the rear, and then proceed up the highway. Jack said, "It didn't sound like too good a plan to me, but I had no choice—I was a buck sergeant and he was a 1st Lieutenant."

Three "very nervous" GIs drove slowly along the road ahead of the company, cautiously scanning the countryside for any sign of the enemy. Suddenly, they saw a "bright flash" up ahead at the crest of a forward hill and "heard a loud boom." At the same instant, the half-full, five-gallon metal water can attached to the side of the jeep next to Wilson's leg disappeared. The can, still in its attachment, went tumbling down the highway and landed in a ditch by the side of the road. Wilson says, "We got the hell out of there as fast as we could."

The driver completed a quick U-turn and the gunner in the back swung around and opened up. He continued firing until the jeep went around a sharp bend in the road, making the turn on two wheels. Wilson wrote, "Whether it was a tank or anti-tank gun that fired at us we didn't know, but we were lucky that he fired an armor piercing shell at us instead of an HE round (high explosive) which would have knocked out the jeep and probably killed the three of us."

The three shaken patrol members reported back to the lieutenant and showed him the damage to the side of the jeep. The officer "just shook his head and told us that we were really lucky! But we already knew that," Wilson said.

From June 6 to 9, the transportation shortage forced the troops of the division to make several long, grueling marches, a total distance of approximately fifty-five miles. Many "long marches, with little rest at night began to weary the troops," wrote 1st. Lt. William V. Church, of Lenoir, North Carolina, 81mm mortar platoon leader, Company D, 141st Infantry. "Men slept from exhaustion, rather than [as] a normal function." Michael Stubinski (K-141) recalled that during this period his feet developed blisters "the size of half dollars." The toll that the long night marches north of Rome had taken on the infantry troops is made clear in the following brief passage dictated by George E. Bennett (I-142) of Gorman, Texas, to his daughter Sharon Jones: "Marched for 5 days—55 miles on foot without stopping. Marched holding on to the man in front, never breaking the hold. There were guards walking beside us to be sure no one turned loose or they would get lost—the men marched in their sleep."

The "campaign above Rome," Allen Stern (B-142) wrote, "was a matter of daily walking 20 miles or so for a long while, principally over bramble-covered mountains." During one period, Stern says, "the regiment walked for 70 consecutive hours with only occasional 10–20 minute breaks." It was not uncommon for men to "fall asleep walking." Stern's own platoon, chosen to undertake a lengthy out-of-the-way patrol, walked for an additional twenty hours. Stern claimed this "as an American marching record."

Due to the rapid advance, supply lines became overextended, resulting in severe shortages of water, rations, and other vital supplies. Each soldier carried a quart of water in his canteen, and had to make it last all day. Wagner says, "The intense heat and dust made water the first priority of the marching columns." Lieutenant Julian Philips (G-143) wrote, "The Italian sun was murder on 7 June 1944 and the dust got into our mouths and nose each step we took." The same day, Col. Paul Adams, Regimental Commander of the 143rd Infantry, issued orders that his Supply Section (S-4) give water a priority for troops over ammunition. Division instructed drivers from the regimental Service Company, transporting ammunition, to drop their load and go back for water for the troops. The increasingly high number of men dropping by the wayside suffering from dehydration and heatstroke under the blazing Mediterranean sun necessitated the action.

Jack Wilson related the following incident:

> We had been without water for two days when we came to a farmhouse with a well nearby. There was no rope or bucket and we were trying to figure out how to get some water. Just then, an elderly man came out of the house to greet us. He smiled, then reached down into the well and pulled up a string. Attached to the other end was a bottle of home-made whiskey. I took a big swig and that stuff nearly burned my insides out. I fell to one knee clutching my throat gasping for air. The guys in the squad thought I had been poisoned and leveled their guns at the old man. I choked out, "No, no, don't shoot."

The Italian spoke no English. One of the guys held his empty canteen upside down and shook it. "The old man went back inside the house and came back out with a rope and a bucket and we got water from the well," Wilson said.

There were no Army supply dumps in the immediate rear to keep pace with advancing units. Gasoline was in especially short supply at the front. Vehicles from division had to travel all the way to the port of Naples for needed stores—a round trip of better than 200 miles. General Walker had all available transportation, including a large number of captured German vehicles, repaired by division motor pool personnel, going back and forth to Naples day and night. He ordered the dispatcher to assign two drivers to each vehicle to relieve one another at the wheel.

At 3 P.M., on June 9, the 36th Division received orders to continue west on the Tolfa-Allumiere Road in the direction of Highway 1, then turn north and continue up the coastal highway until making contact with the 34th Division. Division moved troops using a combination of foot marches and vehicle shuttles. The 142nd Regiment, in the lead, linked up with units of the 34th at 9 P.M., that night (June 9–10) near the ancient town of Tarquinia. At 11:45 p. m., the division went into bivouac on the outskirts of Montalto di Castro, about ten miles farther north.

On June 10, the 36th Division passed through the 34th, completing the move at 11:30 p.m, to become the lead division and continued the advance up the coast road. Just prior to relieving the 34th, the 36th was strongly reinforced by the following attachments: the 361st Regimental Combat Team (91st "Wild West" Infantry Division), 753rd Tank Battalion and the 636th Tank Destroyer Battalion. The immediate objective of the division was to capture the airport facilities at Grosetto, just north of the Ombrone River. Walker placed the 361st Infantry at the head of the column as attack echelon.

Chapter Fourteen

The Battle of Nunziatella, June 10–12, 1944

General Walker met with his regimental commanders at 9:30 P.M., on June 10, to outline plans for the division during the current phase of the operation. During the night, the 141st Infantry would relieve the 361st Infantry, 91st Division (attached to the 36th) in the forward positions along Highway 1, and take over as lead element. The 142nd Infantry would advance on Capalbio, a small village three miles inland, and clear the town of Germans. The 143rd would initially be in division reserve. Walker ordered the 141st Infantry to carry out the advance "as rapidly as possible, the rate depending on the ability of artillery to displace forward to cover the foot troops" (*Fifth Army History*).

At midnight, Lt. Col. James G. Balluff of Manhattan, Kansas, 1st Battalion Commander, received orders from the 141st Regimental Commander, Lt. Col. Austin F. Gilmartin, to advance along Highway 1 in the direction of the city of Orbetello. Gilmartin, a native of Cheyenne, Wyoming, scheduled the push to begin about 1 A.M., June 11.

Company A, designated as the forward echelon, left the Line of Departure (LD), "near the north edge of Nunziatella," in a column of files on each side of the road. Company B followed with Company C in the rear supporting both. First Lieutenant James L. McNeil of Austin, Texas, the CO of Company A, placed patrols to the right and left sides of the road to provide flank security. It was a very dark night, making it necessary to keep the files closed up to maintain contact. Two tanks and two tank destroyers (TDs), attached to the battalion for support, followed next in line.

First Lieutenant William A. Hawkins of Mebane, North Carolina, the CO of D Company, attached two sections (one platoon) of heavy machine guns to Company A, and the other two sections, one each to B and C Companies. The 81mm mortar platoon was to follow B Company, with the weapons left on the carriers (1/4-ton trailers). Trucks transported the remainder of the company.

The 3rd Battalion, supporting the 1st Battalion, was next in line, followed by the 2nd Battalion in reserve. Located at the end of the regimental column was the 131st Field Artillery (FA) Battalion "supporting the attack."

Approximately one mile beyond Nunziatella, a squad of Company A, acting as point, encountered fire from an enemy machine gun nest. Platoon leaders passed orders down the line for the men to get well off the highway into the surrounding fields and dig in.

A reconnaissance patrol, sent forward to ascertain the strength of the enemy force, was fired on and two men killed by an enemy machine pistol. The patrol determined that the enemy strongpoint was located approximately 800 yards up the highway, protected by a machine gun and at least one tank. In addition, German engineers had strung barbed wire entanglements across the road and heavily mined the area to the front for some distance right and left.

First Lieutenant William V. Church of Lenoir, North Carolina, 81mm mortar platoon leader, Company D, 141st Infantry, remembers that Lt. Col. Balluff called for a meeting of his company commanders to determine a plan of action. The colonel ordered McNeil to send out a sufficient force to knock out the roadblock and resume the advance. Church later commented, "If these patrols were ever sent out, it was never reported to the battalion."

Meanwhile, Balluff ordered what remained of Company A to dig in along the right side of the road while the CO of Company B deployed his troops to the left of the road, its frontage extending south to the railroad line running parallel to the highway. Company C spread out to the right of the road behind Company A. According to Church's account, "The units spent the remainder of the night digging in and establishing communications."

About seventy-five yards to the left of the highway was a large two-story school building of heavy stone masonry, surrounded by "three or four lesser buildings." Col. Balluff located his command post (CP) in the school and ordered the tanks and TDs to park adjacent to the main building and select good firing positions. Battalion transport vehicles pulled into the field behind the CP. Some drivers positioned vehicles at the back of the buildings out of sight, but a lack of space forced many to remain out in the open. Church remembered that all were "combat loaded, with ammunition, rations, etc."

Two sections of Company D's 81mm mortar platoon set up the guns (four) between two smaller buildings to the right rear (south) of the command post. Crewmembers dug pits for the guns and stacked bales of straw, found in one of the buildings, around the sites for added protection. Company D men occupied parts of both buildings. The forward observer for the mortar platoon established an Observation Post (OP) just behind the 1st platoon of Company A in the forward position. "At this period of the war," Church noted, "the only means of communication between the observer and the gun positions" was by "sound powered telephones."

Corporal Arlis D. Sizemore of Wooten, Kentucky, a mortar gunner with Company D, says that his squad, led by Lieutenant Church, set up the gun forward of the school building along the railroad tracks. The bed of the rail line ran along a high berm, which protected the crew from direct fire. It remained relatively quiet for the remainder of the night except for an occasional burst of automatic weapons fire from both sides.

Rosaire "Ross" Rajotte (A-141) of Northbridge, Massachusetts, recalled an incident that occurred during the predawn hours of June 11, 1944. One of the replacements in his company heard a noise coming from the area in front of his position. The inexperienced soldier lifted himself up out of his foxhole, exposing his head and upper torso in the process, and shouted, "Halt! Who goes there?" Rajotte said. "It was as if he was on guard duty back in the states. A German patrol opened up and cut him to pieces." He paused briefly, reflecting on this senseless death and remarked, "That is something you just never do at the front."

Sergeant Jack Wilson, the leader of a machine gun squad, 2nd Platoon, Company D, attached to Company A for additional firepower, was near the head of the column when the enemy gunner opened fire. At first light, he looked around and realized he and the other six men in his squad were all alone. He told one of his men "to crawl back and check on the situation." Apparently, at some point during the early morning hours, "orders had been given for our group [Company A] to withdraw and reorganize, but I did not get the word on it," Wilson said, "so my gun crew stayed and fired off and on all night long." During that time, "I noticed that we were the only ones firing."

A short while later, the squad member returned and told Wilson that everyone had pulled out. The squad members broke down the machine gun, packed up their gear, and headed for the rear. "We did not go far," Wilson said, "when we came to a place where some of our mortars and jeeps had been abandoned."

The squad piled into one of the jeeps and one of the men, "who had been a taxi driver in the Bronx before the war," jumped behind the wheel and they took off down the highway. "Not far ahead, we met our people coming back," Wilson said. He inquired of the lieutenant why no one had ever given them the order to pull back. The officer replied "that someone had screwed up with the withdrawal order."

As temperatures dropped during the night, a mist drifted inland off the Tyrrhenian Sea and settled over the area. At dawn on June 11, Church. wrote, "All was quiet." It was "a little hazy, but observation was still good." There was no sign of the enemy and everyone had a chance to survey the area around the battalion's position.

To the right side of the highway, the terrain rose gradually for about 800 to 900 yards to a series of low hills, generally running southwesterly to the Tyrrhenian Sea near Orbetello. This chain of hills forms a ridgeline. Dominating the ridge is Mt. Capalbiaccio (Hill 234), at 759 feet (234 meters), located approximately one mile north of Nunziatella, which enemy forward observers were using as an OP.

Highway 1, which had been fairly level, began to rise gradually, passing through a defile, or cut in the hills, as it continues toward the northwest. The enemy position that the patrol from Company A had stumbled into was, in fact, a heavily defended roadblock on the forward slope of the ridge at a point where a cart path intersected with the main highway. Heavy brush and trees along the highway and to the right and left along the dirt crossroad effectively camouflaged enemy positions.

Covering the slopes leading to the top of the ridgeline were broad rolling fields of mature wheat, or wheat stubble, where farmers had recently harvested the crop. Bisecting the area to the far right of the battalion's position, approximately 200 yards north of the road, was a "wide draw." Beyond the draw was a small ridge atop which sat a large farmhouse. The area to the regiment's front afforded little cover and concealment. Off to the right front, on the sides of the hills, were "several large stacks of wheat." Unbeknownst to the T-Patchers, several of the stacks concealed German tanks waiting to rain deadly fire on the advancing column.

South of the highway, low trees and scrub brush extended for several hundred feet to the railroad line. For a distance of about two hundred yards beyond the railroad tracks was a series of "boggy salt marshes" spread along the flat coastal plain bordering the Tyrrhenian Sea.

At about 6 A.M., Col. Balluff issued orders for Company A to continue the advance along Highway 1. Before jumping off, Lt. McNeil asked the 81mm mortar forward observer to fire a few rounds in the general direction from which the machine gun fire had come during the night and along the ridge to the right of the road. During the shelling, troops observed a lone German soldier, possibly an FO, run from the farmhouse and disappear over the ridge. When enemy gunners did not respond, McNeil assumed that the German force had pulled out under cover of darkness and ordered his men to proceed. The officer, for whatever reason, ignored the presence of the German soldier.

Balluff was at the head of the motorized column in his jeep behind the infantrymen. The column had only moved about seventy-five yards when the Germans opened up with a machine gun located near a small house by the edge of the road. Bullets, the bright tracers clearly visible, skimmed the surface of the highway, kicking up pieces of macadam.

A split second later, a tank or self-propelled gun fired a high-explosive shell directly down the highway. The shell passed over Col. Balluff's jeep, striking the windshield of the three-quarter-ton truck directly behind, killing the driver and his front seat passenger. There was a mad scramble to get off the vehicles in the column and find cover by the sides of the road. The riflemen fanned out and began digging foxholes.

Church said, "It was as if the first burst of machine gun fire was a signal," because in the next several minutes "all hell broke loose." Enemy mortar and artillery shells began exploding all around A Company's position while machine gun and small arms fire raked the area. Clusters of dirt geysers rose high into the air from the explosions. Four enemy tanks emerged from concealment behind the wheat stacks and opened fire. Two other tanks, covering the approach from the area occupied by Company B to the left of the highway, began blasting away. One veteran, John Paul Jones of Dallas, Texas, the Supply Sergeant of Company D, 141st Infantry, described the ensuing onslaught: "We experienced what we called a 'shit storm,' the Germans threw everything they had at us."

The din of battle reverberated through the surrounding hills and vales. Incoming fire from tanks, towed 88mm guns, and self-propelled (SP) artillery screeched overhead. The crash of artillery explosions was interspersed by the crump, crump, crump of mortar rounds. The shell bursts assaulted the men's ears and clouds of thick black smoke and dust obscured the battle zone. Deadly shrapnel whined through the air like angry hornets from a disturbed nest.

Off to their front, the men could hear the rattle of enemy machine guns, the burp, burp, burp of machine pistols, and individual rifle fire. Bullets cracked and snapped overhead and were striking the ground all around the battalion's position. The fire was so intense men had to scrape at the surface with their entrenching tools from the prone position to get underground. To rise up meant instant death.

Mt. Capalbiaccio, the key terrain feature of the German defenses, afforded enemy observers a commanding view of the surrounding area. The Germans concealed and protected the supporting artillery batteries from observation behind the crest of the ridge. Escaped Russian prisoners interrogated later that morning by Major R.K. Doughty of Walpole, Massachusetts, Intelligence Officer (S-2), for the 141st Infantry, stated that the Germans had been working on gun positions for three days prior to the regiment's arrival in the Orbetello sector. Doughty secured information "as to the positions of four artillery pieces, one anti-tank gun, four 88mm guns, and two self-propelled guns."

The Germans directed heavy combined fire against forward elements of the 1st Battalion from the roadblock and from riflemen and machine gunners entrenched along the ridge to the right of the road. Direct fire from enemy tanks and artillery immediately silenced all return fire by battalion machine gun and mortar crews. The Germans had chosen the perfect defensive location for a last stand before Grosseto.

"Everyone was hugging the bottom of their hole at this time," wrote Church. The lieutenant, who was with the 36th for the duration of the war, claimed that at no time in the past had the 1st Battalion been subject to enemy opposition of such intensity, nor did it ever again experience "such direct and concentrated fire." "It seemed as if," he stressed, "the enemy was determined to wipe out the entire battalion by fire." An expected counterattack never materialized and, he opined, had the enemy tried to mount an assault with a force of any size, "it would probably have succeeded."

Company A, at the head of the column, was taking a real beating. Casualties began to mount as enemy troops continued to pour deadly fire on their position. David "Rosie" Rosenbluth (A-141) of the Bronx, New York, like my father, joined the 36th at Maddaloni as a replacement in March 1944. Rosenbluth, corresponding through his son Terry, provided his memories of the events of June 11, 1944. His account began, "The situation was fairly fluid, and a jeep-mounted recon unit from the division [361st Regiment, 91st Division] the 141st was passing through, said that the way was clear for the next five miles or so." The company had only traveled a short distance, he said, when the Germans opened up with machine gun and small arms fire from entrenched positions on the forward slopes of the hills, while artillery, mortars, and self-propelled guns pounded the company from positions on the far side of the ridge.

"There wasn't much to do except lie in the ditches by the side of the road and hope," the elder Rosenbluth related. "It was the only situation he was in where you could reach over and mark the spot where the shells were going to land and you couldn't do a damn thing about it," his son said. The men "pretty much lay there and absorbed casualties until battalion could bring additional units forward to pressure the enemy, which would enable the company to pull back."

The fire was so intense that "the men couldn't go either forward or back," Terry Rosenbluth continued. "All the men could do was just fire up the slopes of the hill and hope that this would interfere with the [enemy] small arms fire as they had no real targets." Rosenbluth says his dad "managed to burn out the barrel on a carbine doing this on semi-automatic." Rosie Rosenbluth was a member of the 60mm mortar platoon. Enemy fire had the squad pinned down, preventing the crew from raising themselves high enough to set up the gun to bring fire on enemy positions. Members of the squad used personal firearms to return the fire. Rosenbluth "remembers this battle as being one of the worst fire fights he was in during the entire war." He described the shelling as "the heaviest German fire he ever experienced." His son Terry added, "To tell you how rough it must have been, he said it was the only time in the war he thought he was going to crack." "This is a man," his son wrote, "who was wounded at the roadblock at Montelimar and fought in the Vosges so it must have been bad."

Hoping to deny the infantrymen what little support they had available, the Germans were quick to concentrate on the 81mm mortars of Company D. The enemy pinpointed the position of the mortars next to the battalion CP while they were firing for Company A just prior to the move and these were among the first targets knocked out by tank and artillery fire. Church stated in his account of the battle that shrapnel knocked out all four of the guns, either puncturing the tubes or distorting the bipods. The intense shelling destroyed a large number of mortar rounds and rendered the sound-powered telephone inoperable. Church noted, that "Quite a number of rounds of mortar ammunition were lost from fire that spread from adjacent areas." The initial barrage killed one man and wounded several others from Company D.

In the confusion that followed, mortar crews, carrying and dragging the wounded, took refuge inside one of the masonry outbuildings adjacent to the CP. "Ignoring intense hostile fire," as his subsequent Silver Star citation explained, 2nd Lt. Ralph J. Eastberg (D-141) of Iron Wood, Michigan, "moved forward about 1000 yards" to the mortar position. Eastberg "assisted in loading wounded men into vehicles which removed them to a place of safety." He found an undamaged deuce-and-a-half (2 1/2-ton truck) and towed four company jeeps out of the area. In the process, the citation continued, the lieutenant received "a painful shrapnel wound," yet "he courageously continued removing vehicles, guns, and ammunition from the impact area." Despite the seriousness of his wounds, Eastberg then assisted in reorganizing the mortar platoon, "working efficiently and fearlessly, until, weak from loss of blood, he was forced to be evacuated."

Corporal Royal B. Light of San Antonio, Texas, a member of the mortar platoon of Company D, left the relative safety of the Battalion CP to help two wounded mortarmen back to the building. He returned to an unoccupied mortar position and, "in spite of direct small arms fire and continuous fire from tanks, he succeeded in putting the mortar into action against the enemy, firing it with unusual effectiveness." Light's "heroic action" on this day earned him the Silver Star.

Enemy artillery and tanks zeroed in on the battalion CP, causing heavy damage to the structure. The observation post (OP) and communications center, located on the second floor of the building, took several direct hits. Part of the roof collapsed, burying the radio equipment under a pile of rubble and debris. The initial barrage seriously wounded two officers and three enlisted men. Artillery and mortar fire continued to blast the CP "at short intervals throughout the entire morning." Shrapnel cut the telephone wires forward and to the rear, knocking out all communications. Balluff sent a wire crew out to make repairs to the lines. No sooner would a cut in the lines be located and spliced, when a new break or breaks would occur elsewhere by the constant shelling.

Staff Sergeant Paul Duffey of Lancaster, Pennsylvania, was with Company C, 141st Infantry on the right side of the road about fifty yards forward of the school building. He described the attack in a 1993 article in *The Fighting 36h Historical Quarterly*:

> Soon after we dug in, the shelling started, and it was very accurate. They hammered us relentlessly throughout the afternoon. I tried crawling up into my helmet, but my head was in the way. The shells kept coming. I'd [lie] on my back, then on my belly, then one side, then the other, waiting for the big one—mine. While lying on my back, I could see the C.P. getting hit. That is, the building the C.P. was in. The shells hit one side and the C.P. was on the far side. As I watched, I could "pick up" the shells coming in that would hit the building. They looked like a hornet—just a black dot and then, WHAM!

Duffey remembered that trees were spaced here and there along the road and one of the men in his company made the mistake of digging his foxhole under one. This "was a bad thing to do," he said, "and it cost him his life." A shell hit the top of the tree and sprayed shrapnel down into his hole.

During the barrage, Church says, the intense shelling drove the tanks and TDs from their firing positions near the CP to the rear of the school building for protection. Commanders refused to move out from the relative safety of the structure to bring fire upon the enemy, severely reducing the overall effectiveness of the regimental combat team. Tanks and TDs were responsible for most of the heavy gun work during the pursuit and it was imperative that infantry commanders bring armor, attached to their units, to the fore to engage targets. Numerous incidents had occurred in the past in Italy, whereby platoon leaders of tank and TD units had refused to obey the command of infantry officers.

Exposed battalion vehicles, located in the area just to the rear of the CP, came under intense artillery and mortar fire as well as fire from tanks and heavy machine guns. Combined fire completely destroyed seven of the vehicles and a number of others were badly damaged. Braving the shellfire, drivers scrambled to retrieve trucks and jeeps and move them a safe distance from the hot zone.

At 8 A.M., a German force, estimated at two companies, launched a counterattack against both the 1st and 2nd Battalion positions. Artillery and mortar fire "of unusual intensity" preceded the action, "which created numerous casualties." Enemy troops drove back part of the line between A and B Companies. Company C, which had moved to the regiment's right flank, managed to hold its position. German troops infiltrating through the wheat fields cut off several elements of the 2nd Battalion. The Germans captured several men, later reported missing in action (MIA).

An account of the incident found in the 141st Infantry "History of Operations" (also referred to as "Report of Operations" and "After Action Reports") reads: "The second Battalion Communications Officer, 2nd Lt. Joseph Tyrell, of Annandale, New Jersey, tapped in on a phone line to Regiment and said that he and some of his platoon had been surrounded and must surrender." Under intense pressure, Companies A and B retreated to a point approximately 200 yards behind their original positions, where they hastily reorganized and formed a new defense line.

Regiment ordered the 3rd Battalion forward to relieve the pressure on Balluff's men. The CO of the 3rd Battalion radioed for artillery fire to help stem the counterattack. Batteries "placed heavy concentrations on the German positions." With Company C holding its section of the line, the battalion managed to stop the counterattack and the enemy force began to withdraw. The report does not reveal the source of the artillery fire; possibly, it came from division or corps batteries.

As bullets cracked overhead and shell fragments whirred noisily through the air, Ross Rajotte (A-141) and his "foxhole buddy," Joseph V. "Joe" Aloie of Grant City (Staten Island), New York, burrowed into the ground like a couple of badgers in search of prey. Rajotte wrote, "The dirt was like loose sugar, very granular, made more so by the lack of rain, which made for easy digging." Ross was twenty-four years old and Joe, at age thirty-five, was the "old man" of the platoon. The two men became very close. Rajotte related, "Joe was always homesick. He was married with a young son and missed his family very much." If Joe was not telling Ross about his wife and child, he was talking about his mother and father. When Joe joined the company as a replacement after Cassino, the captain paired him up with Rajotte. "He told me to look out for him." Ross says, "I trained him and taught him what he had to do to stay alive."

The two men were huddled at the bottom of their hastily dug foxhole when the Germans mounted an attack. Shouts of, "pull back, pull back, tanks are coming," could be heard up and down the line. Rajotte could see a German Mark IV tank bearing down on their position. Joe jumped up to run and Ross yelled for him to stay down. He tried to keep his friend from leaving the hole, but Aloie pulled away from his grasp and made a dash for the rear. The machine gunner on the tank cut him down.

Rajotte remained in the foxhole as the tank passed directly overhead. The edges collapsed and dirt poured down the neck of his shirt and into the hole, trapping him, but otherwise he was unhurt. The tank made a ninety-degree turn and headed back up the ridge. Two men heard Rajotte's cries for help and came forward to pull him out. Medics took Aloie to an aid station and rushed him to an evac hospital. Rajotte heard later that Joe had succumbed to his wounds.

On June 11, Pfc. Edward J. Slavinsky (D-141) of Toronto, Canada, a gunner in a heavy machine gun squad, 1st Platoon, attached to Company A, received the Silver Star for "gallantry in action." When the counterattack began, the Germans had Abel Company "pinned down by heavy, accurate fire." The citation reads in part: "Private First Class Slavinsky's weapon was the only one returning the hostile fire. Although he became the target for heavy artillery and mortar shelling and machine gun fire, he continued operating his weapon, successfully delaying the enemy force." Seriously wounded, Slavinsky "refused medical aid and steadfastly maintained his position." The Pfc. was "one of the last to withdraw." He "would not cease firing" and had to be "dragged from his battered gun and taken to a hospital."

I was curious as to how someone from Toronto, Ontario, ended up in the U.S. Army. When a search of telephone information (I called the four Slavinskys in the Toronto area—none were related) and the Internet in March 2002 resulted in a dead end, I wrote a letter to the editor of the *Toronto Star* and provided my e-mail address. Shortly thereafter, I received a reply from Tony Mancinone, Edward Slavinsky's nephew-in-law. He said that according to Ed's sister Rene, the family was originally from the Detroit, Michigan, area. At various times during the 1930s and early 1940s, they lived in Michigan, Toronto, Windsor, and Peterborough, Ontario. Mancinone said that the family had not heard from Ed in six or seven years and that at the time he was living in Detroit.

Slavinsky was born in Port Huron, Michigan, in 1923; a sister was born in Redford, Michigan; and his other four siblings were born in Canada. When the war broke out, the family was living in Toronto. Slavinsky and a brother-in-law traveled to Detroit and enlisted in the U.S. Army. The sister says that while in Detroit he lived at the YMCA. Ed was an American citizen; his brother-in-law was not. Before 1973, anyone from a foreign country could join the U.S. military, and many Canadians volunteered during the early part of the war. Slavinsky's older brother Steve joined the Canadian Army and served with a British Army tank division (part of the U.S. Fifth Army) at Salerno and later at Anzio.

The U.S. Army sent all enlistees and draftees from Michigan to boot camp in Texas, which may have been how he ended up in the 36th Division. The brother-in-law served in another division. During the time Slavinsky was with the 36th, the sister says he was wounded several times, the last at Nunziatella. The "injuries to his legs were most severe with many shrapnel wounds." After a brief stay in a Naples hospital, the Army shipped Slavinsky back to the United States, where he entered Billings General Hospital at Fort Benjamin Harrison, Indiana, for a lengthy rehabilitation period. In all, "he spent about 1 1/2 years in various hospitals." According to his sister, Slavinsky received "the Purple Heart with clusters." Following Slavinsky's discharge, the Veterans Administration awarded him a full disability pension. Attempts to contact Slavinsky through the VA proved fruitless. The agency replied that they had "delivered" my letter to him, but he did not contact me.

About an hour after the German attack began, Col. Balluff sent a messenger to the rear with a map showing probable enemy positions and a request that the attached 131st FA Battalion bring all available fire to bear against the delaying force. The forward artillery observer with Company A made repeated attempts to radio the 131st with a request for supporting fire as well. While the artillery battalion was setting up the guns somewhere to the rear of the schoolhouse, the Germans opened up on the position with tank and artillery fire. A direct hit destroyed one of the battery's howitzers. Intense fire forced the battalion to pull back and relocate to a safe area southeast of Nunziatella. The guns were operational shortly after noon, but the lack of radio and telephone communications prevented batteries from firing a mission until about 2 P.M. "The loss of this support seriously affected the outcome of the battle," wrote Church. "With its help the battalion possibly could have reentered the fire fight," he concluded.

Meanwhile, Balluff ordered the 1st Battalion to move to the right of the roadblock in a flanking maneuver. In its attempt to encircle the position, advancing troops ran into mines. Next, the CO sent the 2nd Battalion to flank the 1st Battalion on the east and ordered the 3rd Battalion to follow close behind, ready to move up in support if the situation required.

With his company pinned down in minefields, McNeil tried to contact battalion by radio at 9:30 A.M., with a request for smoke from mortars to cover

A Company's withdrawal to the previous night's positions. When the lieu-tenant realized that radio communications were still out, he dispatched a run-ner to the battalion CP. After receiving the message, Balluff instructed 1st Lt. William A. Hawkins to carry out the mission as soon as possible.

Hawkins left the building and went to the nearby mortar position, where he found 2nd Lt. Edward W. LeValley, of Rochester, New York, and Sgt. Ralph Materra of Troy, New York, trying to reset the tubes of two mortars using parts from the four damaged guns in the face of galling enemy fire. Within a few minutes, the guns were operational.

Hawkins made his way to the second floor of the CP amid the debris to di-rect the laying of the smoke screen between A Company's forward line and the German positions. Moving from a window opening with a view of the for-ward area to a south side window facing the mortar position, he shouted the fire commands to Materra and LeValley. After adjusting the mortar fire for distance, he called for traversing fire at intervals of twenty-five yards. Hawkins observed white plumes of smoke rising skyward from the shell bursts. The slanting columns, becoming wider as they lifted into the air, coa-lesced to form a dense curtain that drifted slowly across the landscape, effec-tively screening the withdrawing troops from enemy gunners and observers.

Church wrote, "This withdrawal could hardly have been executed in a more disorderly manner. The troops jumped up and as a herd ran back down the road." Instead of stopping at their original positions, many of the men in A Company continued through the areas of Companies B and C, yelling for the others to pull back. The officers from Companies B and C stood in the road with their hands up and blocked the path of the retreating riflemen. They shouted for the men to stop and ordered them to get back into position.

About this time, the tanks and TDs located behind the school building be-gan to withdraw without permission. Col. Balluff shouted for the commanders to remain in position, but they ignored his orders. The tank platoon leader told Balluff to "Go to hell" and hightailed it for the rear with his tanks. According to Church, the sight of the armored vehicles withdrawing "really shocked the riflemen," and "probably accounted for some of A Company's men to keep moving towards the rear." He overheard one of the men of A Company, rounded up later, remark, "If it's too hot for tanks, it's too hot for me."

Many of the infantrymen went as far back as Nunziatella, approximately one mile behind the forward positions. Company A, Church says, was "com-pletely disorganized and of little use to the battalion." Officers and noncoms spent the "greater part of the afternoon" rounding up the scattered members of the company and herding them back to their positions.

With communications knocked out, Lt. Hawkins proceeded to the regi-mental CP, farther to the rear, to inform headquarters of the current situation.

After making his report, he ordered three men to assist in the loading of a truck with urgently needed ammunition. Along the way back to the 1st Battalion CP, he collected a group of stragglers. Upon reaching the frontline positions, Hawkins organized the distribution of the ammunition among the forward units, "in the face of heavy enemy fire." About this time, wiremen restored communications with artillery units and within a few minutes, batteries were saturating the ridgeline.

For "gallantry in action" on June 11, 1944, division awarded both 1st Lt. William A. Hawkins and Sgt. Ralph Materra the Silver Star. Lt. Edward LeValley received a Bronze Star Medal. A number of other men from Company D also received commendations and awards for bravery under fire during the period June 11 through 12 (See Sources—"Awards, Decorations, Citations, 1943–1944" and "Bronze Star Awards").

At 11 A.M., June 11, Col. Balluff sent the 2nd Battalion, followed by the 3rd Battalion to attack and seize Mt. Capalbiaccio and envelop the German left flank. Units moved toward the summit against concentrated enemy small arms, mortar, artillery, and automatic weapons fire. The battalion succeeded in occupying the hill by 7:30 P.M., and went into defensive positions to hold against an expected counterattack, which failed to materialize. The CO positioned one company around the perimeter to guard against infiltration through the draws.

This account of the outcome of the fight for Mt. Capalbiaccio, from the 141st Infantry, History of Operations, differs somewhat from that found in the *History of the Fifth Army*, which reads: "The battle seesawed fiercely most of the night until a final push at 0545 [5:45 A.M.], 12 June, drove the Germans off Mt. Capalbiaccio." The loss of this key terrain feature forced the enemy to begin to withdraw from the area.

The 1st Battalion held the line along Highway 1 until late in the afternoon of June 12, when Company K, 361st Infantry, supported by tanks and TDs, moved through the battalion's positions and went into the attack. The 1st Battalion pulled back and went into bivouac along Route 1 between Nunziatella and Montalto di Castro to reorganize. At this time, the 141st Infantry received 251 enlisted men to replace casualties incurred since June 1, 1944, as well as new equipment and weapons to replace those lost or damaged.

Casualties to the 1st Battalion between June 10 and 12, compiled from After Action Reports and Morning Reports (M/Rs), are as follows: Company A, one officer and eight enlisted men killed, thirty-three wounded; Company B, one man killed, one officer and fourteen enlisted men wounded; Company C, one officer and eleven enlisted men killed, eleven enlisted men wounded; and Company D, three enlisted men killed and one officer and eleven enlisted men wounded. The total was twenty-five killed and seventy-one wounded.

According to the Company D Morning Reports, Pvt. Joe Connole was wounded on June 12, 1944. Medics treated him for shrapnel wounds to the left shoulder and sent him to an evacuation hospital in the rear. The casualty report for June 12 contains the names of three other men wounded on the same day: S/Sgt. Leonard Woodall of Acorn, Kentucky; Sgt. Earl J. Martin of Saugerties, New York; and Pfc. Guadalupe J. Vargas of Houston, Texas. The back of the report reads, "Company still in combat with enemy, moving forward with some casualties." The M/R for June 11, 1944, is blank. The company clerk did not list the names of the eleven enlisted men and one officer wounded, three men killed in action (KIA), and three men missing in action (MIA) on that date until June 13, 1944. This is understandable given the heavy fighting on June 11th. It states on the back of this report, "As of 12 June 44 vicinity of Talfa [Tolfa], Italy. Company engaged with enemy."

Church wrote, "The enemy continued to harass, by [artillery?] fire, during the night" (June 11–12). The only combat activity mentioned in the 141st Infantry After Action Reports for the twelfth, took place at 0210 hours (2:10 A.M.) when the Germans counterattacked the 2nd Battalion positions, cutting off Company G. The company repelled the attack, killing five and wounding twenty-three of the enemy. These accounts lead me to believe that my father received his wound during the early morning hours of June 12, or possibly late on the night of the June 11. Joe Connole spent twenty-two days recovering at an Army hospital in Naples.

During the night of June 12, the 36th Division continued its pursuit of the German Fourteenth Army to the north. On this date, the 2nd Battalion of the 141st Infantry became "the nucleus of Task Force Ramey," a provisional force led by Brigadier General Rufus S. Ramey. Corps committed this force to the right flank of the 36th Division. Division held the 1st and 3rd Battalions of the 141st infantry in reserve until the 14th, at which time they were also attached to Task Force Ramey.

On June 13, the 143rd Infantry, acting as lead element, proceeded along coastal Highway 1 in the direction of Grosseto. A battalion of the enemy, estimated at 50 percent Russian troops (conscripted by the Germans), tried to make a last stand before the Albegna River and lateral Highway 74. Units of the 143rd easily overpowered the force and the action ended in a rout.

During the afternoon of June 13, the 142nd Infantry took the town of Magliano "after a 10-hour battle." A large German force remained entrenched in the hills to the west and north of the town, holding up the advance. The regiment made a sweep of the area capturing "two important elevations," and the chase continued. On the fifteenth, the 143rd crossed the Ombrone River and moved into the provincial city of Grosseto, abandoned by the Germans earlier in the day. The 141st Infantry, with Task Force Ramey, captured Campagnatico on June 19, followed by Paganico on the following day.

The push continued for thirteen more days, with some elements of the division advancing to a point about forty miles north of Grosseto. The 141st Infantry captured the town of Roccastrata during the early morning hours of June 23, encountering only light opposition. By June 25, the 142nd took the towns of Belvedere and Sassetta. Later in the day, the 1st Armored Division passed through the 36th, and division forces "assumed a strictly defense posture." This date marked the last day of the Italian Campaign for the T-Patchers. Fifth Army ordered the 34th Division to take over the mission of the 36th on June 26, and the division was withdrawn from the line. After being relieved, units of the division moved by truck to a rest area eight miles northwest of Rome.

In twenty-nine days of fighting (May 28–June 25), the 36th covered a distance of 240 miles and took more than 5,000 prisoners. Robert L. Wagner listed the division's losses for the operation at 322 officers and enlisted men killed ("including those who later died of wounds"); 1,325 wounded in action (WIA); and 75 missing in action (MIA).

The Morning Report for D Company, June 27, 1944, reads: "bivouaced [sic] in rest area near Rome, Italy; no training; passes to Rome for entire personnel." Shower points were set up and everyone received a clean set of clothes. During their five days of rest and recreation (R&R), the soldiers of the 36th Division enjoyed the many attractions and pleasures of the Eternal City. After the first week of liberation, Rome had changed drastically. The jubilant populace that had greeted the division on June 5, had become "cynical" and was "no longer so free with its favors," wrote British historian Eric Morris. "The Americans were to find that Rome was no different from anywhere else. Everything had a price." Joe Connole rejoined his outfit at Paestum on July 4, 1944, in time to prepare for the invasion of Southern France.

Chapter Fifteen

Preparation and Planning for the Invasion of Southern France

The Allied invasion of southern France, first code-named "Anvil" (to Overlord's "Hammer"), and later changed to "Dragoon," occurred on August 15, 1944, more than two months after Overlord, the cross-channel invasion of Normandy. Originally scheduled to coincide with Overlord, Allied military planners considered Anvil-Dragoon "a complement" to the Normandy invasion and "essential" to its success. Military leaders conceived of the operation as "a small scale diversion" to tie up available enemy divisions in the south that the German High Command might otherwise send north to bolster the Normandy defenses once the invasion began. Postponement of Dragoon came toward the end of the final planning stages for two principal reasons: first, Allied logistical needs in northern France, primarily amphibious vessels, "especially LSTs" (Landing Ship Tanks), and second, the stalled Italian campaign tying up divisions needed to participate in the secondary operation.

"After Eisenhower's Overlord forces had bogged down in the hedgerows of Normandy, the possibility and even the need for Anvil again became evident," wrote historian Jeffrey J. Clarke. Once landing craft became available in sufficient numbers and Allied forces had captured Rome, Allied command "officially resurrected" the operation. On June 24, 1944, when Seventh Army Headquarters received "a tentative green light" to proceed, planners hastily began preparations to assemble the necessary forces. Final approval did not come until August 11, just four days before the scheduled landing date, "over the strenuous objections" of Sir Winston Churchill, who proposed scrapping Anvil. The Prime Minister argued that the invasion of southern France was "an unnecessary duplication of effort" and would do "little more than sap the strength of the main Allied campaign in the Mediterranean," wrote Clarke. Churchill favored an advance on Austria from the Adriatic Sea north through the Balkans.

Shortly before the target date, the combined Chiefs of Staff decided to change the code name of the operation to Dragoon, "as a precaution against possible compromise." One possible explanation for the choice of names, which may or may not have some basis in fact, is provided by Samuel Eliot Morison who wrote, "Churchill, it is said, made the humorous suggestion that the name Dragoon be substituted, because he had been 'dragooned' into accepting it. And that it became."

Planners chose the VI Corps, consisting of the veteran U.S. 3rd, 36th, and 45th Infantry Divisions, as the main "assault team." Commanded by Lieutenant General Lucian K. Truscott, VI Corps was part of the U.S. Seventh Army under Major General Alexander M. "Sandy" Patch, the "over-all commander" for the invasion. Other major elements included the French First Army (seven divisions); the British-American 1st Airborne Task Force, "of division size"; the Canadian-American 1st Special Service Force, a "regiment-size commando force"; "and various French special assault detachments."

General Patch and his staff "were new to the European Theater," having previously "served in the Pacific," and "this was to be their first assault landing operation," wrote Truscott. Patch came to prominence on Guadalcanal, where he led a contingent of U.S. Army and Marine troops over the Japanese. This achievement earned Patch a promotion and the coveted assignment as commander of the southern France invasion force.

Patch allowed Truscott, who would command the assault, to select the divisions constituting his corps. His choice of the 3rd and 45th Infantry divisions "was an obvious one," he wrote, "since they were the most experienced of his American divisions and both of them had training and experience in landing operations." General Truscott explained his reasons for making the 36th Division, commanded by Maj. General John E. Dahlquist of St. Paul, Minnesota, his final selection:

> I designated the 36th Division as the third element because of its outstanding performance during the action following the breakout from the [Anzio] beachhead. I believed this recent success [at Velletri] would erase in large measure the setbacks of Salerno and the Rapido. Having tasted the bitter cup on two occasions, and having more recently eaten of the fruits of victory, the division could be expected to equal and keep pace with its more experienced teammates.

Following the successful performance by the 36th at Velletri, Truscott's low opinion of the division had taken a 180-degree turn.

"Logistical considerations were critical for both Anvil and the ensuing campaign," wrote Clarke. General Patch "had three principal objectives." First, and most importantly, was to "establish a suitable beachhead." The timetable called for the invasion force to push inland to a minimum depth of fifteen to twenty miles by D-Day plus 2. This, it was felt, "would provide adequate security for the ensuing troops and supply." The outer perimeter of the objective, in the shape of a "semi-circle," was designated the "blue line."

The second objective was to capture the two great ports of Toulon and Marseille, the latter being the largest in France, which would serve as major depots for the crucial buildup of supplies needed to sustain the drive inland. The honor of liberating the two port cities would go to the French First Army (French Army B). The expanded beachhead would also serve as a base for French divisions to move on the objectives. The final, and most important objective, was for Patch's divisions to "drive north," up the Rhone Valley, to link up with Eisenhower's Normandy forces for the push into Germany.

Naval Task Force planners assembled a massive amphibious assault fleet consisting of 897 American, French and British ships and landing vessels. Allied Naval forces had at their disposal approximately 1,375 smaller landing craft to carry 94,000 troops (367,000 troops would go ashore within one month), 12,000 vehicles, and 46,000 tons of stores and supplies to the landing sites on the day of the invasion. The proposed beachhead for the Anvil-Dragoon landings along the French Riviera, between St. Raphael and southernmost beaches of the St. Tropez peninsula, "included about 30 miles of coastline (and 50 miles of shoreline)."

The 3rd Division would go ashore on the left flank in Alpha sector of the VI Corps assault landing zone near St. Tropez, the 36th was to land on the right flank east of St. Raphael in Camel sector, and the 45th Division at the center in Delta sector east of St. Maxime. After the American forces secured the beaches, the French forces would come in behind the American 45th Division and turn west toward Toulon and Marseille.

General Patch scheduled the airborne assault, code-named "Operation Rugby," to begin shortly before dawn. The mission of the British-American airborne task force was to drop paratroopers, glider infantry troops, and engineers into the Argens River Valley near the town of Le Muy, thirteen miles inland, behind the coastal defenses. At Le Muy, "two vital highways converged"—Route 85, the Route Napoleon, "ran northward to Grenoble," and National Highway 7 "branched west from the Route Napoleon to Avignon and thence north up the Rhone Valley." Patch charged the airborne force with three major objectives critical to the success of the invasion, to seize and hold this vital road junction as well as a number of key crossroads, to isolate German defenders, and to prevent German reinforcements from reaching the beachhead. The "10,000-man airborne contingent," made up of "combat-hardened paratroopers," was the largest force of its kind ever to participate in an invasion.

General Friedrich Wiese, commander of the German Nineteenth Army, head-quartered at Avignon, was responsible for the defense of France's southern coast. The Nineteenth Army was part of Army Group G (First and Nineteenth Armies), under the command of Generaloberst Johannes von Blaskowitz, Wiese's immediate supervisor. By this time, the German High Command had moved most of the reserves from the south to oppose the Allies in northern France, reducing the strength of the Nineteenth Army from thirteen to ten divisions. Of the ten divisions, Blumenson says, four were "highly rated formations." Wiese also had at his disposal the "powerful 11th Panzer Division" ("14,000 top quality troops and 200 tanks").

Several of the divisions, according to Blumenson, "were of poor quality; their troops were young and inexperienced" and "heavily diluted" by Eastern European conscripts. "The abilities and loyalties of the foreign troops," he wrote, "were dubious at best."

Wiese did not have sufficient forces to defend the entire Riviera coastline. Unsure of the exact landing site, the commander deployed his divisions at strategic locations along the coast and in the interior, ready to move at a moment's notice. Four of the divisions "were located between the mouth of the Rhone and the Spanish border"; two others "were garrisoned at Marseille and Toulon; and one, a reserve division, was charged with the coast defense east of Toulon." Another division "was totally occupied in the French Alps" fighting FFI resistance units and the remaining two were otherwise committed elsewhere. Spread thin, German defenders along the coast would be able to muster only token resistance against the invasion forces until reserve units could be brought up to reinforce.

The Mediterranean Allied Air Forces ruled the sky and the German Navy had been "practically eliminated" from the area. General von Blaskowitz was without any real hope of defeating the invasion force. The best he could hope for would be to move his reserve forces, including the 11th Panzer Division, east of the Rhone River and mount an effective defense to delay what he knew to be the inevitable. Clarke wrote, "By 14 August, anticipating that an Allied assault was imminent and that the blow might well fall in the Marseille-Toulon region, the German commanders had begun to move both the 11th Panzer and two infantry divisions east across the Rhone." The 11th, under the command of Major General Wend von Wietersheim, was "stationed at Bordeaux, approximately 400 miles west of the attack zone."

On June 26, 1944, Allied Command pulled the 3rd, 36th, and 45th Divisions out of the front lines in Italy in anticipation of the proposed invasion. After approximately one week of rest and recreation (R&R) near Rome, the 36th Division "returned to its first battlefield on the Paestum beaches at Salerno" for four weeks of extensive training at the Seventh Army's Invasion Training Center (ITC). The 36th and 45th Divisions bivouacked about twenty-five miles southeast of Salerno and trained at the center between June 27 and July 22. During this period, the two divisions conducted individual and unit training; carried out joint landing exercises "with their corresponding Naval attack forces"; and coordinated fire control between Navy forward observers and Army shore parties. Because of time and space constraints, the 3rd Division, which was "far more experienced in amphibious operations, conducted their own exercises at Pozzuoli" (Truscott).

A description of the typical living conditions for the troops of the 36th Division is provided by the historian of the 141st Infantry Regiment: "Just off the beach at Salerno we lived under shelter halves, washed in helmets, took Atabrine [an anti-malarial drug], cursed mosquitoes and powdered gray dust and wondered 'when and where.'" Mosquitoes were a plague along the coastal plains of western Italy. The insects thrived in the saltwater marshes, where they proliferated. Despite the use of Atabrine, many of the GIs contracted malaria, an intermittent and recurring disease characterized by severe chills and fever. The usual incubation period is one to three weeks; however, the use of preventive medicine delayed the onset of symptoms.

Arlis Sizemore (D-141), one of the disease's many victims wrote, "We slept in tents which had mosquito nets, but the mosquitoes came in anyway." On August 29, during the waning hours of the Battle of Montelimar, Sizemore suffered from a bout of malaria severe enough to require hospitalization. His temperature was 104 degrees.

First Sergeant Morris L. Courington (K-142) of Fairfield, Alabama, stricken with malaria at about the same time, had an experience similar to Sizemore's. Courington says that the men "were given a supply of 'Atabrine' pills" and he took "one every day . . . faithfully for many months." A few weeks after landing in France, he came down with "a very high fever, and now and then a chill." Courington says, "I thought I was going to die, immediately." One of the men in the company took him to an aid station and from there to the coast where he boarded a hospital ship bound for Naples.

Courington expressed his views regarding the pesky Italian mosquito:

> They do not like all people and therefore do not bite everyone. Those little suckers only like those with fair skin and a very sunny disposition—sweet and loving guys . . . whose blood tastes just right to them. They can tell just by flying by and therefore can save all their attention for those special people. They passed up many of our guys and concentrated on me and a few others.

The mosquito, he says, is "one of the few creatures that loved Italy and thrived there in the summertime."

In his book, *Command Missions*, Lt. Gen. Lucian K. Truscott outlined the program at the Invasion Training Center (ITC) near Naples. ITC personnel conducted classes and workshops "to teach the art of waterproofing vehicles to permit landings in water much deeper than wading depth," to familiarize troops "with all types of shipping, landing craft and special vehicles," and in the "techniques of loading and unloading personnel and vehicles." Units "were drilled in mock-ups on dry land, witnessed demonstrations by experienced troops, and then participated in actual landing exercises by platoon, company and battalion."

The training staff instructed the troops "in the tactics of beach assaults." This included blasting beach fortifications with demolitions and clearing paths through barbed wire entanglements with bangalore torpedoes. Instructors also trained specialized "armored 'gapping' teams" in the various methods of breeching walls, bridging antitank ditches, and knocking out tank traps.

The amphibious phase of the training went on for twelve to thirteen hours most days. This included the loading of men and equipment onto transport ships, offloading into LCVPs (Landing Craft Vehicle and Personnel), followed by practice landings and assault drills. The center conducted the slate of exercises under the brutally hot Italian sun throughout July and into early August.

The LCVPs, known as "Higgins boats," after the craft's inventor, New Orleans shipbuilder Andrew Jackson Higgins, had a cargo capacity of 8,000 pounds. Each LCVP could carry thirty-six combat-equipped infantrymen or twelve men and a jeep. A 225-horsepower engine powered the thirty-six-foot long craft. Slung from davits on the deck of an LST, Navy deck crews lowered the LCVPs into the water by means of hand winches. The key feature of the boat was its retractable steel bow, which doubled as an off-ramp. The heavy steel plate also protected the men from enemy fire as they headed for the beaches. During the war years, Higgins Industries and other licensed companies built more than 20,000 LCVPs that saw action in both the European and Pacific Theaters. Eisenhower called Higgins "the man who won the war for us."

The operator, a U.S. Navy coxswain, steered the LCVP alongside the troop carrier to pick up the disembarking troops. The coxswain was in command, fully responsible for making all decisions until the boat hit the beach and unloaded its passengers and cargo.

To enter the LCVPs, men had to climb down a twenty-foot wide by forty-foot long piece of rope netting (nets varied in size) normally used to haul cargo aboard, that were draped over the sides of the transport vessels. As the ships rose and fell with the running sea, sailors boarded the LCVPs and held the rope ladder taut. This served a dual purpose; it kept the LCVP as close to ship as possible, while at the same time making the tricky task of climbing down to the bobbing landing craft somewhat easier. The descent proved much more difficult in choppy water. As the ship pitched and rolled, climbers hanging precariously from the net slammed against the side of the vessel. When the LCVP moved away from the side of the ship, the seamen held on to the rope ladder until the next vessel came alongside.

The average load per individual soldier was approximately sixty pounds, with extra equipment and ammunition, it could be as much as eighty pounds and more. GIs complained of straps digging into their shoulders, cutting off the circulation, eventually causing their arms to go numb. Some climbers lost their grip and fell the rest of the way into the landing craft, sustaining serious injuries.

Morris Courington recalled what the unwieldy process of climbing down the rope ladder was like:

> One of the most frightening things that I faced during the training was going down that ten-foot wide cargo net which served as a rope ladder. Several GIs would go down at the same time from the big ship to the landing craft. You had to climb down 20 or 30 feet or more, with your field pack, your ammo, your gas mask, and your weapon slung over your shoulder. We were LOADED. The hull of the big ship curved inward, so that you were just suspended out there on this moving cargo net, which was not a very comfortable position, especially when the water below us was rough.

Courington concluded that there "was only one good aspect" of the training, "when nobody's shooting at you, you're supposed to be happy, and we were."

Other vessels used by the Navy to deliver personnel and equipment directly to the landing site included Landing Craft Infantry (LCIs), Landing Craft Tanks (LCTs), and Landing Ship Tanks (LSTs). LCIs, having flat-bottom hulls designed for beaching, could transport 188 assault troops and land them directly onto the beach—in most cases. Troops exited the LCIs from two ramps or gangways, lowered on each side of the bow, which had rope railings that were very unsteady and could be precarious at times. Each LCI had a crew of twenty-four to sixty sailors.

The LSTs had two large vertical doors in the bow that opened upon landing to allow tanks and heavy equipment to roll right up onto the beach. Each LST had a capacity of 29 tanks or 350 troops, and carried eight to ten Landing Craft Vehicles and Personnel (LCVPs) on its deck. LCTs, with a capacity of five tanks, had a forward ramp similar to an LCVP.

When not practicing boat drills, infantrymen were forced to participate in long, grueling marches—15 to 20 miles or more per day. Combat troops had to suffer through the oppressive heat and dust in cold weather wool trousers and shirts, while rear echelon soldiers were sporting the cooler, light-tan cotton khaki uniforms. This only fueled the existing resentment aimed at support troops. The men tramping under the hot, broiling sun in those woolen ODs were soon soaked with sweat. Moreover, they had to contend with the uncomfortable itchy feeling caused by the cloth's coarse wool fibers.

While the infantry marched, and marched some more, the heavy weapons companies trained as a unit with crew-served heavy machine guns or 81mm mortars. Platoons conducted range firing with the weapons to sharpen their skills. NCOs schooled the replacements, who had just joined the heavy weapons companies, in the nomenclature of the weapon and in every phase of the guns' operation and modes of firing. Many had little or no prior training.

Following the Italian Campaign, the division received a large number of new men from the pool of replacements to bring its numbers up to full strength. First Lieutenant Julian H. "Duney" Philips (G-143) of Houston, Texas, says that replacements were usually from one of two sources, either they "had been in Divisions in the states," or were "just out of basic training," and had never been in combat. Smaller numbers were men returning to their units from hospitals after recovering from sickness or wounds. A number of these men left the hospital early, before their wounds had a chance to heal completely. The Medical Corps reported many of the men AWOL. When army officials discovered they had returned directly to their units, they rescinded the charges.

Philips explained the reason for the GIs' haste to return to their units up at the front, "They heard that the Division was moving and they did not want to be left behind. They knew there was a possibility they would be sent to another division if they did not rejoin the 36th." Philips emphasized, that this "type of loyalty was not uncommon in combat units." If a man had to go back up on the line, he would much rather do so with friends he knew and trusted.

After falling ill with malaria in France on August 29, 1944, Arlis Sizemore (D-141) spent sixteen days convalescing in the hospital (see above). Doctors released Sizemore on September 13 (Company D "Morning Report"), with orders to report to a replacement center, which generally meant reassignment to another outfit. "I told them that I wanted to go back to my old company," he wrote. The hospital clerk handed over his medical records and informed him he was on his own. Instead of reporting to the replacement depot as ordered, he hitchhiked back north for several days until he finally located his company.

When Sizemore arrived at the CP, he reported to Capt. William Church, the platoon leader, who welcomed him back. "He was sure surprised to see me. I could have been AWOL but I wasn't," Sizemore said. Church told Sizemore that his old job as mortar gunner was still open and had him report to his unit. "The rest of the guys in my squad were sure glad to see me," he said.

Philips said that the job of the officers and NCOs was to get the new replacements "ready to go ashore someplace in Europe against the Germans." Time was short. The training staff, made up of seasoned veterans, tried to impart whatever knowledge and survival skills they had acquired in combat to give the rookies the benefit of their combined experience. Philips wrote:

> We taught them what to expect from the Germans, how to act when they came upon a man who was there to kill them and what it was like to be in a barrage that did not let up. We also taught them how they should act on their first attack and, last but not least, they had to learn to kill—or be killed.

All the training staff could hope for was that when the time finally came to face the enemy, the replacements might have a slightly better-than-average chance of surviving the upcoming ordeal. Philips wrote, "We had trained our men well, with rifles, B.A.R.'s, mortars, machine guns, bazookas, bangalore torpedoes and explosives." The lieutenant expressed confidence that following the course of training the new men in the company "were ready to meet the Germans."

Some T-Patchers, like my father, although veterans of combat, had never been through an amphibious invasion and were just as willing and eager to learn as the new replacements. Tech/5 George A. Benton (A-143) of Bensenville, Illinois, wrote, "The veterans of the Division had been through one before at Salerno, but it was to be our first and we wanted to know all the ropes." He explained his reasoning for taking the training seriously, "The harder you trained and the more you learned the better your chances of living through the coming invasion, so we trained hard."

During "the second week in August," wrote Benton, "we went through an actual invasion—all that was missing was the enemy. This was called a Dry Run. The next one would be a Wet Run, or the real thing." The "dry run," Truscott explained, served as a "graduation exercise in the training of each division." It "was a full scale rehearsal planned to simulate actual conditions in every possible instance." The staff at the Invasion Training Center, Truscott wrote:

> constructed obstacles similar to those which intelligence indicated we could expect, and used every aid to reproduce battle conditions and to make the rehearsals entirely realistic: live ammunition, naval gunfire with reduced charges, rockets, bangalore torpedoes, mines with simulated charges, smoke and the like.

Truscott closed, "Few divisions have ever been better prepared for the task which lay ahead when we had done with our invasion training." The 36th Division participated in the final exercise on August 7, 1944. Two days later, the T-Patchers boarded the boats for the trip to southern France.

The historian for the 141st Infantry provides a description of that "last training exercise." The "regiment landed in a dry run just south of Guagliano [sic], and we climbed our last mountain in Italy with the base plate of an 81mm mortar, a [SCR] 300 radio or a tripod for a 'heavy' on our backs." Michael Stubinski noted in his memoirs that during this final practice landing, the men of K Company (141st) ascended "an ocean front hill that climbed up almost 1500 feet," no doubt the same "mountain." Stubinski's final comment is an indication of just how tough the training was. "A young recruit replacement along side of me started cursing his mother for bringing him into this world." With sadness, he noted the eventual fate of the young man, "When we landed in France this boy was killed." Right after the final training phase was completed, the men of the 36th Division were issued American flag patches to sew on the sleeves of their right arm. Some Texans wore the flag of the Lone Star state.

If the men "had free time from training," they went to Pompeii "to see the great ornate church and the ruins of old Pompeii," or to the city of Paestum, where they ate "ice cream at the Red Cross Club," wrote the 141st Infantry historian. Others took in the sights, and pleasures, of Salerno. Jack L. Scott, a 2nd Lt. with Company B, 111th Combat Engineer Battalion, says that in the evening the men in his outfit would head for Salerno, "where there were about twenty or thirty bars and restaurants and girls everywhere."

Most nights, however, the GIs just did not have the energy to clean up, get dressed, and go to town for a night of hard drinking and carousing. George Benton commented, "After a day at the beaches you were ready to crawl into the tent and hit the hay." But many men were full of youthful energy and figured their days could very well be numbered, so their philosophy was to enjoy life to the fullest while they still could. The GIs were just being realistic rather than morbid or having a fatalistic attitude. For their night of revelry, some not returning until just before morning roll call, the men suffered mightily during the following day's exercises.

Men lucky enough to receive a weekend pass traveled to the "Sorrento rest camp," seventeen miles southeast of Naples on the mountainous Cape of Sorrento Peninsula, where Seventh Army officials reserved several grand hotels for officers and enlisted men. Situated on high perpendicular limestone cliffs overlooking the Bay of Naples, the hotels offered beautiful scenery and continually changing panoramic vistas of sea and sky.

In the town of Sorrento, built on the northern slope of the peninsula, men visited the medieval cathedral and palace and toured nearby Roman ruins. Others traveled to the Isle of Capri, located in the Bay of Naples off the tip of the Sorrento Peninsula, a place of exceptional beauty and a favorite resort of wealthy Romans for more than 2,000 years.

GIs hung out in bars and cafes. They got drunk, got rowdy, and were prone to provoke fights with rear echelon types, for whom there was a universal dislike. Arguments often erupted into brawls, resulting in considerable damage to many establishments. Unruly, sometimes riotous, behavior resulted in military officials declaring certain clubs and bars off-limits to enlisted personnel.

During their visits into town, 36th Division troops mingled with those of the 3rd and 45th, often sharing a drink or a friendly argument with one other. There "is an indescribable feeling of camaraderie that exists in the infantry among men who have fought in the mud, sweated out the 88's and the burp guns together and eaten K-rations day in and day out up at the front," wrote the 141st Regiment historian. The author described this comradeship as "a feeling of solidarity" among men who had "the same tough job" ahead of them. In Naples "saluting wasn't required of combat troops," however, "[o]nce in a while," he wrote, "you would see some GI wearing combat boots, wool and a combat infantryman badge turn out a highball to a Lieutenant wearing wool and a Purple Heart with three or four clusters." It all boiled down to a matter of the high degree of mutual respect and esteem these men held for their comrades in arms.

When the training exercises were completed, the 36th Division loaded personnel and equipment on trucks and other transport vehicles for the move to a staging area near Pozzuoli, fifty miles north of Naples. On August 9, troops began boarding for the invasion and by the following day, all personnel had embarked. Ships and other craft taking part in the operation crammed the harbors of Pozzuoli, Bagnoli, and Naples. Jack Scott (B-111) remembered, "There must have been over 1,000 ships scattered all around Naples Harbor."

Charles A. Golub (K-143), of Worcester, Massachusetts, recalled many years later that while sitting in the harbor at Pozzuoli waiting to get underway, "a beautiful young blonde girl" (he could not remember her name) went down the line and came aboard each of the ships to sing for the GIs. This "lovely American girl had a wonderful voice and knew all the popular songs of the day. It was a great feeling and lifted our spirits tremendously," he said. "When she sang a patriotic song, men stood with tears streaming down their face." Golub wrote, "The memory of the young lady singing for the troops, lingers on as it will for me and those men who survived the dangers we were soon to face."

In the book *I Knew Your Soldier*, the author, Eleanor "Bumpy" Stevenson, mentions a girl named Ann Goplerud whom she described as "One of our favorite Red Cross girls." Eleanor's husband Bill was the director of the American Red Cross in England and later in North Africa and Italy. Bumpy Stevenson wrote:

She [Ann] is just about the sweetest thing you ever saw. She sings like a lark and is blonde and blue-eyed, and when she walked into a hospital, she looked like a fairy princess to the boys lying there. She was especially effective in the front-line hospitals. The wounded there just couldn't believe their eyes when they saw her. The only trouble with her was that she had to be kept under wraps, for otherwise she would sing and sing until her voice was all gone and she was dead

"SIGNAL CORPS PHOTO FROM 'YANK.' Veterans of the Italian campaign prepare to invade France as they climb up a gangplank of an Army transport. The 36th Division men are weighted down with gear. August 15, 1944" (111-SC-293243).

from exhaustion. She was equally good at both sweet and torch stuff. She sang to nearly every unit in the 36th Division during one of their rest periods. She meant so much to the boys in one regiment [143rd] that they had a scroll engraved to express their appreciation. It was presented by the colonel at a special ceremony.

Colonel Vincent M. Lockhart of Amarillo, Texas, Assistant Adjutant General for the 36th Division wrote, one "Red Cross girl who visited often and sang for the troops [of the 36th Division] . . . was Ann Goplerud, sweet, lovely, talented, and the men adored her. She was to every man his sister." There is little doubt that this was the same young woman Golub remembered.

"AUG 44, PUZZUOLI, ITALY, 36th DIV. TROOPS BOARDING LCI'S
[Landing Craft Infantry] ENROUTE TO SOUTHERN FRANCE" (111-SC-192912).

"12 Aug 1944, SEVENTH ARMY, SALERNO AREA, ITALY, 143RD INF., 36TH DIV. G.I.'S RELAX ABOARD L.C.I.[S] IN PORT AWAITING DEPARTURE." The photograph shows three LCIs docked side by side (111-SC-192915).

"World Events" envelope "ALLIES INVADE SOUTHERN FRANCE." Postmarked Louisville, Kentucky, Aug. 15, 1944.

On August 12, the ships left their moorings and moved to an at-sea assembly area just offshore from Naples to wait until the convoy was ready to depart. U.S. Navy personnel treated the men of the 36th Division exceptionally well while aboard the transport vessels and went "out of their way" to make the brief stay as comfortable, "and as enjoyable," as possible. In later accounts of the voyage, many of the T-Patchers commented on the quality of the Navy food, something GIs were unaccustomed to in the field, or anywhere else in the U.S. Army for that matter. Following dinner each evening, Navy stewards treated the men to all the ice cream they could eat. Jack Scott says that the captain of the ship he sailed on "told his personnel that if the soldiers requested anything within reason to be sure they got it."

While waiting for the convoy to depart, soldiers not assigned to shipboard duties sat around "writing letters, playing poker, shooting dice and trying to get our orders out of their minds," wrote 1st Lt. Duney Philips. Many of the men spent time up on deck, sleeping or sunning themselves. Weather conditions were fair and warm and the sea air invigorating after the dust and heat of Italy. Commanders granted permission for the men to swim to other vessels anchored in the bay. The young officer stripped to his trousers, dove over the side and swam to a nearby ship to visit two buddies in the Cannon Company, 143rd Infantry, C.L. "Tiny" Thompson and Phil Strom, who, like himself, hailed from Houston, Texas. The beautiful Mediterranean water he described as being "a deep blue and clear as crystal." Philip's final remark, "The water was warm and war seemed so far away—but oh, so near."

George Benton wrote, "Our orders were to undergo tough amphibious training and that meant only one thing to us, an Invasion! Where would we land, that was the question to be answered." Michael Stubinski (K-141) says that before the division left Naples everyone in his company "guessed we were heading for Greece and the Russian Front." Paul H. Duffey (C-141) claims that up until the official word was received, it "was a guessing game."

Morris Courington says that there were a lot of rumors floating about at the time as to the exact destination of the invasion force. Speculation included Yugoslavia, Greece, two or three of the nearby islands, and "of course, one of the rumors was southern France." Courington wrote, "In every platoon there is at least one who starts rumors just for fun and just to see how they sound when they come back to him." Anyone "with half a brain," Courington says, "knew the logical destination was the invasion of southern France, but we couldn't be told. Top Secret stuff." Still, the rumors and uncertainty persisted.

On August 13, "when they thought it was too far for us to swim back," Courington said jokingly, orders were opened and it became official—southern France—D-Day was August 15, 1944.

At 8:30 A.M., on August 12, the assembly began moving up the west coast of the Italian boot, sailed past the Pontine Islands, and then turned west toward Corsica. Positioned on the outside of the convoy were Allied warships ranging up to cruiser in size to provide protection. After passing through the straits between Sardinia and Corsica, the convoy proceeded along the west side of the island to anchor in the harbor of Ajaccio at 5:30 P.M., on August 13, 1944.

Duffey says that once units were informed of the destination, officers passed out "small booklets" containing words and phrases in French, "to learn (if you could) to help you get along with the new people you would meet." Comment allez-vous, mon cher?, as well as a few other apt phrases, were committed to memory, just in case. Thomas H. Sherman, a sergeant with the Recon platoon, Company A, 636th Tank Destroyer Battalion, says that the "guide books dealt more with general information about the French people than anything else." What the pamphlets lacked, he said, "were decent maps of any kind."

En route, "troops were oriented as to the location of the invasion site, known enemy defenses, nature of terrain, and probable enemy strength in the invasion area." A picture in *The Fighting 36th Pictorial History*, taken aboard one of the troop carriers, shows a group of officers and enlisted men intently studying the details of the French coast on an aerial photograph. The group scrutinized charts and maps and carefully examined "scale models of the approaches and beaches." Officers projected slides of the coast onto a large screen to give an added perspective. "The months of planning and the weeks of filling in every detail were brought down to the final phase, with every squad learning its mission, every man discovering the smallest part of his participation," the caption states.

In the 36th Division zone (Camel), there were three possible landing spots initially under consideration, Beaches Red, Green, and Blue, in that order, from west to east (see map).

Situated just west of the resort town of St. Raphael, at the head of the Gulf of Frejus, where the Argens River flows into the sea, was Red Beach, described by the division historian as the "most important" landing site "in the entire Seventh Army sector." Red Beach, "typically sandy," was the largest site and therefore deemed the most preferable of the three for a landing, as it would be "essential," once the invasion was underway, "for the necessary rapid build-up of supply." Another consideration was a small airfield and seaplane base located behind the beach.

Set back about one hundred feet from the shoreline was a retaining wall about five feet high and two feet thick, running from St. Raphael on the east to a wooded area on the west, a distance of several hundred yards (see photograph of Red Beach in *The Fighting 36th Pictorial History*). Jack Scott's engineer platoon, had the job of blowing out several sections of the wall using a "special saddle type explosive, much like the saddle packs that go on a horse." Scott helped design and develop the explosive device for just this specific purpose.

Anticipating that Red Beach would be a prime landing spot for the Allies, the Germans heavily defended the area with artillery batteries, concrete pillboxes, gun emplacements, and casements (armored enclosures). Just offshore, German engineers constructed cement structures, buttresses, and underwater obstacles to impede the approach of landing craft. Morison wrote, "As the Argens valley is a natural invasion route to the interior—and had been so used for at least 1500 years—the Germans guessed that we would land there if anywhere on this part of the coast, and had prepared a hot reception."

Green Beach, which extended for "a mere 250 yards," was located to the west of Cap(e) Drammont, a high mass of rock projecting out into the sea. An "abrupt cliff" flanked Green Beach on the left, atop which there were three known pillboxes in close proximity to each other, and a "jutting barren rock formation on the right" with two additional pillboxes. Invasion planners considered this site "a potential trap." The beach area, "a strip of rocky shale," had an average depth of ten to twenty yards extending to the base of the embankment on the backside. A "large quarry of graystone" was located to the

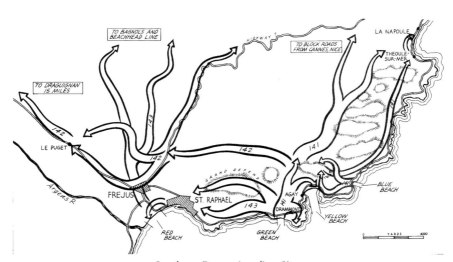

Southern France Landing Sites
(*Source:* The Fighting 36th, A Pictorial History,
see "The Invasion of Southern France." N.p.).

right rear of the beach, at the top of the embankment. Planners nicknamed the landing site "Quarry Beach."

A single narrow dirt road, the sole exit from the beach, led up a sharp incline to the coastal (Cannes-St. Raphael) highway. Green Beach was the only landing site that could immediately accommodate heavy vehicles. Division considered the site "too small for the landing of a large force, but here a surprise might be possible and a foothold gained."

Blue Beach, eighty yards long, was located a few miles east of Green Beach. Leading to the landing point, described as a "pebbly beach," was an inlet, or deep cove, having rocky sandstone cliffs jutting out on both sides. This site was considerably smaller and could only accommodate "two or three" small landing craft at a time. Blue also had an exit route leading to the top of the embankment, but engineers would have to widen and grade the road before it could accommodate traffic by heavy vehicles and armor. There were three known pillboxes atop the cliff to the right and one on the left, at advantageous positions. Antiaircraft and antitank guns comprised the remainder of the enemy's defenses in the area.

The "coastal road skirted Blue Beach and just inland was a high railroad viaduct that," Breuer says, "Allied pilots had done their best to destroy." Directly behind Blue Beach "rose the Rastel d'Agay [280m], razor-edged and formidable, a precipitous [reddish-purple rock] formation which commanded the entire division landing area" (Hyman).

The top of the embankment along the coast in the area of Blue and Green beaches levels off to form a narrow plateau or shelf over which the parallel railroad line and main coastal highway runs. Beyond the railroad tracks and road, the terrain ascends in elevation to a series of high hills. These coastal elevations were the foothills of a more mountainous sector, the Maritime Alps, situated a few miles inland.

Extending east from St. Raphael to Monaco is the Côte d'Azur, the French portion of the Riviera. This resort region and fashionable playground is dotted with beautiful "golden" sandy beaches. Elaborate stone and stucco villas, hotels, and resorts, painted in bright pastel shades of orange, green, pink, and other colors lined the seashore. The Germans converted a number of the homes and other buildings along the coast, many directly overlooking the landing sites, into heavily fortified strongholds or strongpoints.

The invasion plan "finally adopted" by the division called for the 141st Infantry Regiment to spearhead the landing simultaneously on both Green and Blue beaches. Division split the Regimental Combat Team (RCT) into two groups, 2nd and 3rd Battalions, which would land abreast on Green Beach, on the right and left respectively, while the 1st Battalion would come ashore on Blue Beach, beginning at H-hour, 8 A.M. The initial objective of the 1st

Battalion was to secure the beach, capture the town of Agay, and protect the division's right flank.

As soon as the 2nd and 3rd Battalions cleared all defensive positions surrounding Green Beach, the 143rd Infantry would come in and land. The mission of the 143rd was to drive to the west, and seize the heights overlooking St. Raphael and Red Beach prior to the scheduled landing there by the 142nd Infantry.

Division deferred the landing by the 142nd Infantry Regiment on Red Beach until H plus six hours (4 P.M.) to allow for the capture of flanking shore defenses near St. Raphael-Frejus, and for the removal of mines and underwater obstacles obstructing the approach (Hewitt). Once ashore, the 142nd would link up with the 143rd and capture St. Raphael, the nearby airfield, and the Port of Frejus.

Chapter Sixteen

D-Day–August 15, 1944, Southern France

The morning of Tuesday, August 15, 1944, dawned with "a murky overcast sky and a slight fog on the water near the coast." GIs unable to sleep went up on deck where they caught a glimpse of the great Allied invasion fleet assembled for the first time. Pvt. William F. Hartung, Sr. (E-143) of Pittsburgh, Pennsylvania, recorded his memories of that morning in a 1979 article, "Company E's D-Day": "What a shock it was to see hundreds of ships of all kinds in all directions when the night before you were there alone in just the vessel you were going to hit the beach in. It was unbelievable." The great armada sat at anchor about ten to twelve miles off the coast, waiting for the huge naval guns and Allied Air Forces bombers to pound the coastline and soften enemy defenses before the landings.

At 4:45 A.M., the men were treated to the "traditional 'last breakfast' of fresh eggs and steak" served invasion troops by the Quartermaster. First Lieutenant Jack L. Scott (B-111), called it "fattening us for the kill." Uppermost in every GI's mind was the thought that he might not survive the day. The Germans, he says, had "bitterly contested all previous Allied assaults on the Continent"—at Salerno, Anzio, and Normandy—and there was no reason to believe this landing would be any different. After the meal the ship's speakers announced, "Now hear this. All Army personnel assemble on deck and report to your stations." In the semidarkness of the breaking day, the troops quietly lined up in formation. The only noise the men heard was the sound of creaking winches as members of the deck crew lowered the LCVPs to the water.

For the climb down to the beaching craft, individuals were burdened with only the "bare essentials": personal weapons, combat pack, canteen, a couple of bandoliers of ammunition slung around their necks, and a few hand grenades clipped to web belts. Heavier gear, parts of mortars, machine guns, radios, as well as bulky mortar rounds and boxes of ammunition, had already been loaded onto the boats the previous afternoon. Rifles, carbines, BARs, and pistols had been "carefully inserted into cellophane containers" ("invasion case waterproof for rifle M1 Garand or Carbine") to protect them from the corrosive salt water in the event the landing craft could not make it all the way in to the beach. Historian Lee B. Kennett described the waterproof cases:

> The hazards of surf and sand encountered in amphibious operations posed such serious problems that the Army developed a special bag for soldiers to put their M1s into. Once closed, the bag was watertight; if the soldier blew into it to inflate it before closing, the bag had enough buoyancy to keep the rifle afloat.

In an emergency, infantrymen could fire the weapon without removing it from the bag.

Paul Duffey (C-141) wrote that before disembarking, "we were checked over by our lieutenants to make sure we were 'rigged' properly." This he defined as having "the long strap of our helmet . . . held in our teeth—our pack, rifle belt and rifle were rigged so that you could slip your right hand under the shoulder strap of your pack and rid yourself of all three articles—open your mouth and the helmet would fall free—if you fell into the sea." In the event you happened to step out into deep water, or into a shell hole over your head, and were unable to free yourself, there was a good chance you might be dragged to the bottom and drown. It was as simple as that.

During the training period, officers issued each man a specially designed "life belt," to prevent accidental drowning, and instructed the group on its proper use. Duffey provided a description of the flotation devices: "These belts, worn around the waist, were two tubes with a CO_2 cartridge in each tube. If you fell in the water and went under, you squeezed a trigger [mechanism] to puncture the CO_2 cartridge to inflate the belt." This apparatus was supposed to keep a man from drowning, at least in theory. The problem was that the safety device had a specific maximum capacity. Many of the men, fully loaded, exceeded the weight restriction of the belt. With most of the weight above the waist, there was an distinct possibility they might stumble and topple over, making it that much more difficult to free themselves from their equipment, as some invasion troops later discovered. Because of the perceived need, it is possible the manufacturer rushed the belt into service before completing adequate testing.

When all of the troops were topside, naval officers assigned to direct the transfer operation announced over the ship's P.A. system that all Army personnel should begin off-loading into the assault boats. GIs went over the rail in the semidarkness of the morning and climbed down the nets, three and four at a time. As soon as the troops filled one boat, it pulled away and another slid into position. The loaded boats assembled about seven miles offshore, out of range of German shore batteries, forming ever-widening series of circles as landing craft from other ships joined up.

U.S. Army Lt. Francis S. Quinn, Jr., was a member of a Naval Shore Fire Control Party (NSFCP) assigned to "a company from the 2nd Battalion, 142nd RCT" (Regimental Combat Team). The Navy assigned three teams to the 36th Division, one with each regiment, and one team member with each rifle company. The mission of the NSFCPs was to "bring in Naval Fire on appropriate enemy targets."

A Naval Liaison Officer was in charge of each NSFCP team. Quinn says each man was equipped with "a 45 pound back-pack for our radios, telephones, wire and related equipment as well as small arms, ammunition and three days of K-Rations." The NSFCPs were in the initial assault waves to hit the beaches. When the regiment received the "signal" to load on the landing craft (LCVPs), Quinn wrote: "We climbed down the thick stranded rope netting feet first, hands grasping the thick ropes tightly. I remembered thinking, 'Be careful now, one slip and you're into the water and, with that load on your back, you'll sink right to the bottom of the Mediterranean!'" Many GIs were still in the process of climbing down as one boat pulled away, and the next one moved into place to be loaded, and the men were left hanging out over open water. Quinn later served with A and B Companies of the 636th Tank Destroyer Battalion attached to the 36th Division.

The historian for the 141st Infantry provides an account of the series of events leading up to the launching of the amphibian assault force:

> Wave after wave of bombers came in low and began to saturate the beach with their loads. At 0650 hours the naval preparation started with the battlewagons *Texas* and *Arkansas* rumbling into action. Then the famed cruiser *Marblehead* opened up and was joined by half a dozen destroyers immediately in back of us, all spewing tons of shells on the concrete emplacements, the coastal guns and the wire entanglements along the beach.

Paul Duffey remembered distinctly his impression of this incredible spectacle, "Some of us thought, 'Hey, there will be nobody alive to meet us.' Then you thought back to the Rapido River in Italy and maybe a few other bombardments. They would be there—they always were."

By the time all the LCVPs were loaded, it was broad daylight. The haze, created by moisture in the air, combined with the dust from the aerial bombing and shelling by naval craft, dissipated and, by 7:15 A.M., the French coast was clearly visible. Finally, when the Navy commanders gave the order to proceed to the landing sites, the circles split and the boats straightened out to form a line of Vs made up of five vessels each, called a wave.

In a letter to Michael Stubinski, Tech Sergeant Henry L. Ford (K-141) of Belmont, North Carolina, told of an incident that occurred while the LCVPs were being held up by the Navy about 1,500 yards off the coast until minesweepers could finish clearing a path through the minefields to the beach. "Almost everyone was down in the bottom of the boats and not saying a word as everyone was dreading the landings." Sergeant Ford was up in the front observing all that was going on, when one of the GIs aboard yelled to him that he "had to go real bad, and that he couldn't hold it any longer." The sergeant told him to "hold on to the gunwale [or gunnel] and shit in the sea," which the man proceeded to do.

One of the guys in a nearby LCVP spotted the GI with his backside hanging precariously over the edge of the boat and yelled for everyone to look. "All at once all the men were off the bottoms of the invasion barges to see the action." Everyone started whooping and hollering and talking back and forth. The sight resulted in a good laugh at the expense of the embarrassed GI. "For a few moments," Ford wrote, "the serious tension of the invasion was lifted off everyone's minds." The incident provided "just the diversion needed in that circumstance. It was great!!" wrote Ford. Shortly thereafter, "the Navy men on the minesweepers announced over their speakers, 'You all are now on your own. Good luck and good shooting!'"

Francis S. Quinn, Jr., provides a description of what it was like for the men aboard the landing craft while the coxswain waited for the signal to proceed through his headphones:

> Timewise, I really don't know how long we circled under that hot sun waiting further orders. It probably seemed longer than it actually was. What made it so uncomfortable was that we were all in woolen ODs! Yep, the middle of August . . . the hottest time of the year . . . and we were all in ODs! That went for every soldier in the invasion and was an order from Army headquarters. We envied the navy men who were in cotton. Our lined helmets protected us somewhat from the sun. But after a while the steel helmets became too hot to touch with your hand.

Quinn's final comment, "We must have sweated away 5–10 pounds just sitting in that assault craft."

Specially modified Landing Craft Tanks (LCTs) equipped with banks or tiers of "up to 1,000" rocket launchers (Multiple Launch Rocket Systems) sped ahead of the assault boats. The 7.2-inch rockets "could be fired in salvos or discharged simultaneously." The GIs called the boats "Whoofus," mimicking the sound made by the projectiles as they left the cylinders. As the rocket-bearing craft drew within range of the beach, approximately 2,000 yards, they turned parallel to shore and directed their destructive missiles at the beaches and upper defenses (Truscott). Morison wrote, the "cr-a-a-ck of the rockets" as they exploded "sounds as if the beaches were being lashed by a mighty whip."

Immediately in the wake of the rocket concentrations, idling engines roared to life and assault craft, their square prows rising high out of the water, plunged toward the landing sites at full speed. The first of the LCVPs ground ashore at 8 A.M., exactly on schedule.

At full speed, the Higgins boats kicked up a spray, giving the men in front a good soaking. Shore batteries not knocked out by naval and air bombardments opened up on the waves of incoming landing boats as they plowed through the calm blue waters toward the beaches. The scream of artillery shells increased in pitch as they neared the speeding craft. The screeching sound ended abruptly in scattered explosions, sending geysers high into the air. Soldiers, packed shoulder-to-shoulder, crouched low inside the boat praying silently. As the LCVPs came closer to shore, machine gun rounds thudded into the metal ramp and splintered the wooden gunnels, approximately six-inches wide, that lined the upper edges of the boats. The air inside the craft reeked of diesel fuel, body odor, and vomit.

The Germans blasted a number of boats out of the water before they made it all the way in to the beach, others as they landed or were backing up. At Blue Beach, three LCVPs had released their passengers and were pulling from the shore when shells from antitank guns sank them before they could turn around and be off. The Germans deflected their antitank guns to fire directly upon the assault craft.

Mike Stubinski witnessed a "lone German plane" fly low overhead and release "a rocket which cut one of the landing ships in half." His friend, Joe Kamertz of Phoenixville, Pennsylvania, survived the attack and described the details of the harrowing experience to Stubinski after the war. In a letter dated March 29, 2002, Stubinski says, "Kamertz was a Navy man with the LSTs." He was referring to LST-282 sunk off Cap(e) Dramont, just to the east of Beach Green, by "a glider bomb" from a Ju-88. Military historian Jeffrey J. Clarke reported that on D-Day "the Luftwaffe limited itself to a few radio-controlled missile attacks."

Sixth Corps scheduled the 143rd Infantry to come in behind the 141st Infantry in the eighth wave at 9:15 A.M. The entire regiment was aboard Landing Craft Infantry (LCI). Years later, Tech/5 George A. Benton (A-143) recorded what he was feeling as the boat closed in on the landing point:

> Judging by my own thoughts I would say that everyone was thinking of home, in those last few moments, and wondering if we would ever see our loved ones again. Finally, the word came for us to get ready. We would hit the shore in 10 minutes. We lined up and waited for almost anything to happen. Maybe we would hit a mine, maybe the artillery would get us, in Army terms, we were "sweating it out."

As the ships landed, the men ran down the ramps and "scurried across the beach amid machine gun fire and a few shells," wrote Benton.

Corps scheduled the 142nd Infantry to land on Red Beach at 2 P.M., but mitigating circumstances forced a change in plans. Minesweepers sent in to clear a channel leading to the beach took on heavy fire from shore emplacements and had to turn back without completing the task. German gunners reportedly sank several of the craft. Navy demolition crews sent in specially designed radio-controlled robot demolition craft called "drones," which were released by "Apex boats," to explode submerged obstacles just prior to the scheduled landing by the first wave. Each Apex boat towed two drones "at an angle behind them." The drones, "loaded with ten tons or more of high explosives," were moved into position by radio control over an underwater obstacle "and detonated with tremendous explosions and huge clouds of black smoke" (Truscott).

Upon release of the drones by the Apex boats, German technicians successfully jammed the frequency of the robot craft's guidance systems. U.S. Navy operators stood by watching helplessly, as "all but one" careened out of control and "dashed wildly up and down the beach." The other headed back out to sea, causing naval personnel much consternation, before it turned back to shore. Earlier in the morning, one "runaway" drone in the Alpha sector (west of St. Tropez) detonated near an Allied subchaser, causing considerable damage (Hewitt).

Murderous flanking fires from enemy positions near St. Raphael and the hills beyond Frejus covered the approach to Red Beach "with unabated intensity." The big guns of the fleet pounded the beach defenses throughout the morning and into the afternoon. At 1 P.M., "nearly a hundred B-24's in close formation blasted the beach defenses in a magnificent exhibition of precision bombing," reported Col. Vincent M. Lockhart. When the smoke and debris began to settle, the guns of the fleet once more pounded away at the surrounding defenses. Lockhart asked himself, "Could anything live under such a bombardment?" All efforts "to soften" enemy defenses surrounding the beach by air and naval bombardment were "defiantly rebuked," wrote the 36th Division historian.

Rear Admiral Spencer S. Lewis, commander of the Naval Task Force transporting the 36th Division, on the U.S.S. *Bayfield*, directed the landings on Beach Red. Lewis was "a veteran of the great Pacific sea battle at Midway." At approximately 1:45 P.M., Admiral Lewis signaled the landing craft to proceed.

The following two accounts indicate the flotilla made at least two unsuccessful attempts to land before the intense fire forced the boats to turn back. Reconnaissance Sergeant Thomas M. Sherman, of Company A, 636th Tank Destroyer Battalion, was on an LST with the 142nd Infantry preparing to land on Red Beach. The LST carried Sherman's "jeep, a half track and four tank

destroyers and their crews." Sherman wrote: "As the assault boats started towards the shore, a terrific artillery barrage greeted us and there seemed to be
a solid wall of water thrown up by the artillery and the underwater demolitions being set off in front of our landing craft." Sherman says that at one
point the LCTs "circled back" and then "made another run for the shore
again," but once again the heavy shelling forced the boats to abort the landing attempt.

First Lieutenant Jack Scott (B-111) was in an LCVP with his platoon proceeding slowly toward Red Beach. The flotilla was out of range of the shore
batteries. As the waves of LCVPs "approached and got closer to the shore, the
German artillery began a continuous barrage." Scott described the scene to
the front of the boats:

> As we got nearer to it, we could see the explosions blowing holes in the water
> right in front of us. At first the splashes were about a half of a mile in front of
> us, and then they narrowed down and they were three or four hundred yards in
> front of us. Finally, they were a couple of hundred yards in front of us. We were
> getting closer, and we could see all the time exactly what was going on and what
> we were going into.

At this point, Scott, who was in the back of the craft, crawled along the gunnel
to get to the front so he could be with his men when they first exited the boat.
Suddenly the landing craft slowed, turned toward the east and headed back.

Owing to the determined enemy resistance, combined with the Navy's failure to destroy all mines and underwater obstacles, Admiral Lewis's "professional expertise," Breuer wrote, "told him that the Texas [regiment] would be
heading into a bloody disaster at Red Beach." Lewis reportedly said, "No. I
am not going to watch these men being blown to bits for no good reason"
(Scott). To order the boats in at this time would most certainly have resulted
in heavy loss of life. At this critical juncture, Lewis tried to consult with Maj.
Gen. John E. Dahlquist by radio, but the 36th Division commander had gone
ashore to observe the scheduled landing and was out of reach.

Admiral Lewis, "acting on his own responsibility . . . made the decision to
change the point of assault of the 142nd Infantry" from Red to Green Beach,
"in accordance with an alternate plan which had been previously prepared,"
the 36th Division historian wrote. The LCVPs carrying the 142nd turned east
and landed on Green at 3:30 P.M. All units made it ashore without a single casualty. "His courageous and timely action probably saved hundreds of men
from death." General Truscott was furious at the change because it set back
his timetable. Dahlquist later sent a message congratulating Lewis on his
prompt and decisive action.

After landing on Green Beach, the 142nd Infantry "swung in an arc north and west over the mountains between the 143rd and 141st to attack Frejus from the rear." The 143rd Infantry seized St. Raphael, then moved west and secured Red Beach while U.S. Navy demolition teams cleared anti-invasion defenses from the shallow water, allowing supply craft to come ashore. Nine hours after the first landing, all beaches were secure. As it turned out, Green and Blue beaches ended up being the only division landing sites. In less than ten hours, 20,000 troops waded ashore.

The 1st Battalion, 141st Infantry, encountered heavy resistance as they stormed ashore on Beach Blue. In the absence of armored vehicles, prevented from coming ashore because of the nature of the terrain, securing "the high rocky cliffs" surrounding the beach was "strictly a job for the doughboy with his rifle," wrote the historian of the 141st Infantry.

Resistance on the beach "was rapidly overcome and the battalion pushed in to drive the Germans from the craggy dominating heights." He credited the "effective gun fire" delivered by the Navy and saturation bombing by the Air Corps during the preinvasion preparations with softening the shore defenses. Without their valuable assistance, "we probably never would have been able to land a whole battalion on that little strip of rocky land," the historian added. Morison says that the defenses on the heights surrounding the beach "were manned mostly by discouraged Poles, some 60 of whom surrendered on D-Day."

After a "scramble landing" (described as one that takes place on a beach surrounded by high cliffs, which does not permit the landing of armor or other vehicles), 1st Battalion faced "the most determined resistance" encountered by the division. Enemy antitank gunners opened up on incoming landing craft with "heavy fire," sinking three boats "when retracting" (mentioned earlier). Morison wrote, "Several German machine guns and two anti-tank guns on Point d'Antheor [to the right of the beach] became active as soon as they got the assault craft in their sights."

Major R.K. Doughty of Walpole, Massachusetts, Intelligence Officer (S-2) with the 141st Infantry, landed at Green Beach with the 2nd and 3rd Battalions. He pointed out that the landing "had been made relatively easily due in great measure to the bold tactics employed by General John E. Dahlquist." The commander's plan called for "a single assault Battalion," the 1st Battalion, (141st), to make the initial landing on Blue Beach, clearing the way for the rest of the regiment. The primary objective of the unit was to ascend the Rastel d'Agay, knock out the German guns as well as deny observation by artillery FOs.

At noon, 1st Battalion made contact with the 2nd Battalion on its left and picked up its attached armor, which had come in over Green Beach. The 1st Battalion's immediate objective was to establish a roadblock on the main highway and seize "Grand Defend," the high ground to the northwest.

The success of the operation earned the 1st Battalion a Presidential Unit Citation for "heroism, gallantry, and esprit de corps during the period 15–16 August 1944 in France." The citation, written by Capt. William A. Hawkins, the CO of Company D, 141st Infantry, reads in part:

> During the 2 days of this action, the 1st Battalion successfully assaulted the most difficult beach in the 36th Division sector in a hazardous amphibious operation. Overwhelming the strongly fortified enemy beach defenses, the battalion moved rapidly forward in the face of concentrated machine-gun and mortar fire to seize the high ground dominating the beach. Killing or capturing all Germans in their path, the men of this battalion pressed on to seize immediate objectives with such speed and aggressiveness that the enemy soon became completely disorganized. Then moving east along the coastline, the 1st Battalion assaulted and captured numerous strongly manned German pillboxes, casements, and entrenchments. Capturing over 1,299 prisoners and killing 150 of the enemy, the 1st Battalion, 141st Infantry Regiment seized the bridges on the coastal highway, which were the final objective of this assault, and broke the enemy's power within the sector so effectively that the Germans were never able to reorganize their forces for a counterattack.

The above citation, which provides a detailed portrayal of the action, was submitted through channels to the Department of the Army by Lt. Col. William A. Bird, CO of the 1st Battalion.

Michael Stubinski (K-141) who was among the first to wade ashore on Green Beach, wrote, "I had my pack on my back, ammunition belt on my waist, four grenades hanging from my chest, my gun, binoculars, and I carried 60 lbs. of TNT on a ten foot pole that weighed another ten pounds" (a "pole charge"). The dynamite on the pole was to be used to destroy a known pillbox on a seaside cliff. Later Stubinski wrote, "I was the first one up that hill with the 60 lbs. of TNT, but thank God, the Navy guns blew up the pill box, or I probably wouldn't be writing this account."

Shells from the big sixteen-inch Navy guns were hitting on both sides and in front of Company K's position. Stubinski says that "the mountain shook like an earthquake." Company K paid a high price for seizing the objective. On the way up the hill, "my lieutenant got killed along with about a dozen more of my friends," he recalled sadly.

Paul D. Hinkle (L-141) says, "There was a Navy FO with each Battalion," and that "during the first couple of days the Navy provided great artillery support." On the afternoon of August 16 (D-Day plus 1), the 3rd Battalion passed through the 1st Battalion, to become the attack echelon, and began advancing inland from La Napoule "into a mountainous sector" (the Maritime Alps). The battalion traveled over "winding, narrow mountain roads," increasing the overall distance to the objective by "numerous miles."

Hinkle wrote that at one point his platoon ran into "some Germans to the left front in a wooded area." The platoon sergeant ordered a patrol, including Hinkle and several other men, "to check it out." They were slowly working their way toward the position, when the big Navy guns fired a couple of shells into the area. Hinkle said they "heard what sounded like an incoming freight train and took cover." One "round hit close by at a very low angle and did not explode." He recalled his immediate reaction, "I just thought 'thank God for that.'" After the round hit, "it went spinning end over end." Even though "it landed as a dud round, it still shook the ground," he said. One of the other men asked if they should continue on to the wooded area. Hinkle, thinking the Navy just might fire a few more shells, said, "Hell no, let's go." When they caught up with the company, the sergeant said he "did not know who called for fire."

At Blue Beach, the Higgins boat Arlis Sizemore (D-141) came ashore in, crunched up on the sand short of the shoreline and the ramp slammed down with a thud. The 81mm mortar platoon was in the seventh wave, behind the infantry platoons. It was 8:30 A.M. Sizemore recalled, "Just as the boat landed, we heard gunfire." Machine gun rounds tore into the gunnel on the left side of the boat, sending a spray of wood chips and splinters into the air. One of the ammo bearers, he said, "raised up to put ammunition on his shoulders, when a bullet hit him in the neck." Arlis could not recall the man's name, but remembers that he always used to sit around endlessly singing or whistling the catchy tune "Mairzy Doats," a recording made popular by the Merry Macs in 1944. A medic rushed to his side and administered first aid. "We found out later that he died," Arlis said. A check of the Morning Report (M/R) for August 15, lists Pfc. William C. Benter of Bellaire, New York, KIA. Machine gun fire also wounded the coxswain.

Sizemore stepped off the ramp into knee-deep water. Staying low, he proceeded across the beach toward the far embankment "dragging the mortar barrel." Suddenly, a German machine gun opened up from a rocky area to his left front, probably the same one that had fired on the landing craft. He quickly jumped into a nearby bomb crater. Several medics from his boat piled in on top, nearly crushing him. Infantrymen succeeded in knocking out the machine gun emplacement and the men proceeded inland.

Sizemore "headed up the narrow road leading from the beach area and went underneath the railroad bridge that was partially bombed." Here, he ran into Capt. William Church, who was trying to reassemble his mortar platoon, and reported the casualty on his LSVP. Once the platoon leader accounted for everyone, the unit moved north of the railroad trestle to a nearby hilltop having a commanding view of the surrounding area. The mortar platoon stayed at this location for about four hours waiting for orders to proceed. "When the jeeps, trucks, and heavy equipment arrived, we went on down the coast" (to the east toward Cannes), Sizemore said.

S-Sgt. Jack Wilson (D-141) and his machine gun squad was also part of the seventh wave landing on Blue Beach. In addition to his personal gear, he carried a bangalore torpedo. During invasion training, Jack attended demolition school where he "qualified" in the use of the device and was designated as a "bangalore torpedo man" for the LCVP he was riding in, "which meant" he said, "I would be the first one off the boat."

The bangalore torpedo M1A1 was a two and one half-inch diameter metal pipe, five feet in length, with threaded ends. The torpedo weighed thirteen pounds and contained eight pounds of TNT. To extend the length of the torpedo, the operator spliced two or more pipes together using "5-inch connecting sleeves." The device was capable of blasting a ten- to twenty-foot-wide path through a section of barbed wire, or a minefield. A blasting cap, inserted into the "recessed end cap well," was set off, using a time-delayed fuse. To prevent snagging when pushing the tube through obstacles, the torpedo man placed a rounded nose sleeve on the leading end.

As the Higgins boat approached the beach, machine gun bullets smacked into the wooden gunnels on both sides. The boat "hit something and ground to a sudden stop." The navy crewman up front lowered the ramp and "was immediately hit and killed by a burst of machine gun fire." Wilson had to jump over the body to get out of the boat. He stepped off the ramp into waist-deep water as bullets were hitting all around. "I really thought that this was it and I'd never get to the beach," he wrote. Wilson described his close brush with death, one of many, as he rushed to get through the surf onto dry land:

> Holding my rifle over my head with my left hand, and the bangalore over my head with my right, I felt a slight sting in the hand holding the bangalore, and noticed blood running down my arm. If that bullet had hit the torpedo instead of my hand, it would have been over for me and several of the fellows behind me.

After several tense minutes, he made it safely to shore and found safe cover among the rocks.

Wilson says he heard "the motor of a slow, low-flying airplane" overhead. He looked up and saw a "Kingfisher pontoon plane" (Vought-Sikorsky 0S2U), "launched from the deck of [one of] our destroyer ships." The ship-based scout and observation plane had a crew of two, an officer pilot and an enlisted man as gunner. Armament included a fixed .30 caliber machine gun mounted in front, and a second .30 caliber on a flexible mount operated by the gunner in the cockpit behind the pilot. The plane spotted the machine gun emplacement and opened up on the position. Whether he "took it out or not I don't know," Wilson said, "but most of the men made it onto the beach."

When the firing finally stopped, Wilson and his squad headed for the back side of the beach where they encountered "five or six strands" of concertina wire blocking their passage. He "slid" the bangalore torpedo under the coils of wire, "lit the fuse," and "rolled back toward the beach." The torpedo exploded with a tremendous roar, clearing a lane through the entanglement. The Germans usually laid mines beneath wire, Wilson says, but this time they had not. The group moved up the far embankment toward the main road paralleling the coast.

At the 2003 reunion of the 36th Division Association Midwest Chapter in Fort Mitchell, Kentucky, Rex B. Hoon (F-141) of New Concord, Ohio, related an experience he had during the landing on Green Beach. The LVCP he rode in made it all the way to the beach and ground up on the rocks, possibly damaging the front end of the craft. The sailor in the front tried desperately to lower the ramp, without success. It refused to budge. After a few seconds, the coxswain started to panic. He shouted, "Get the Hell out. I'm backing up." There was a lot of yelling and confusion as men hurriedly bailed out of the craft. "We scrambled over the sides into knee-deep water and headed for the beach," Hoon said.

Rosaire "Ross" Rajotte's (A-141) most vivid memory of the landing was of his platoon leader 1st Lt. Joseph "San Antone" Sanchez (nicknamed for his home town), standing stoically at the front of the landing craft near the ramp. Just before the boat hit the beach, Sanchez "turned around facing us, and said 'join me in a silent prayer.' When the ramp went down," Rajotte said, the officer "was the first man off." Rajotte reported sadly that "Lt. Sanchez later suffered from a bad case of battle fatigue."

Among Ross Rajotte's possessions relating to the war, is a copy of the "Northbridge Service Men's Album," produced by the town's "News From Home Committee" in 1947. The booklet lists the names of more than 1,400 "sons and daughters of Northbridge, Massachusetts," who had served in the armed services. The "In Memoriam" section of the publication contains "fifty names and faces" of members of the military who died while in the service of their country. In *God is Our Co-Pilot*, Ross Rajotte's biographer, Rod Lee, wrote that in "the 'NOTES' section in the back of the book, in Ross's own handwriting, are five inscriptions . . . personal reflections about several of his

Army buddies. These men he holds in obvious high regard"—one of the in-
scription reads, "Never to forget, Lt. Sanchez."

Pfc. William F. Hartung, Jr. was a member of Company E, 143rd Infantry
Regiment. He spent the day before the landings celebrating his twenty-first
birthday. "Some celebration," he said facetiously. Hartung wrote, "We were
told the night before we were to go ashore that because of the reputation we
made in Italy, our company was given the job of clearing the beach [Red],
while the others [2nd and 3rd Battalions, 141st Infantry?] went directly inland." He emphasized, "This is a very dangerous mission."

Company E was in "the second wave and waded ashore at H-hour plus 15
minutes which was 8:15." Hartung wrote:

> We were all loaded down with extra ammunition and bangalore torpedoes—
> long poles with dynamite on the end [?]—to blow up any barbed wire. You were
> lucky you didn't drown, because the landing craft only got in so far and we must
> have weighed 300 pounds. We waded into water up to our necks.

"The main thing they tell you," he said, "is to get off the beach, because that
is where they can really chew you up."

Sixth Corps planners had not scheduled the 2nd Battalion, 143rd Infantry,
of which E Company was a part, to land on Green Beach until 10:30 A.M., after the landings by the 141st Infantry, beginning at 8 A.M. Division detached
Company E from the 2nd Battalion and assigned it the job "of clearing the
beach from Frejus to St. Raphael" before the initial landings by the 142nd,
described by Hartung as "a suicide assignment."

Easy Company suffered a high number of casualties in Italy, and at this
time was comprised almost entirely of new replacements. "On top of that,"
Hartung added, "we had a 'green' company commander." Hartung was the
company runner, whose job it was to get messages from the commanding officer to the platoon leaders by walkie-talkie (SCR-300 radio). He had two of
the portable backpacks, but these proved useless, as all he could pick up was
the chatter of RAF fighter pilots high overhead. Shortly after going ashore,
Hartung said he "threw both away." After that, he had to deliver each message between the CO and the forward units in person.

Captain James H. Blake of Kingstree, South Carolina, was the new CO, assigned to the company after the Italian campaign. Hartung described Blake "as
a quiet, deep thinking man." He was "a swell guy and well liked, right out of
West Point, and it showed. He could kick a football 50 yards in his bare feet."
The captain "wanted someone with him that knew the score. He knew I had
been through Italy. I was made company runner for this," Hartung wrote. "I
was his right hand man, in more ways than one." Captain Blake "knew what
he was up against." Then he added, "Not quite."

Like many of the men in the 36th, it was Hartung's first invasion. "I had been through hell in Italy"—the Rapido, Monte Cassino, the breakout at Anzio, and the liberation of Rome—"but still it bothered me. It was new. I was scared," Hartung admitted. "You put on a [brave] front when they ask you questions, but try not to show it. I even had to do it with Capt. Blake." He was not alone.

After landing on Green Beach, Company E moved west along the coastline in the direction of St. Raphael. The company continued to advance without opposition until it came to a stone wall, "about four feet high and about three feet thick," which "ran all the way down to the water." The wall increased in height (as it continued up to the main road) "to about ten feet with a huge iron gate" which enclosed a large waterfront villa with "a huge courtyard." The Germans had set up several machine gun emplacements on the near side of the main house, described by Hartung as a "mansion." Due to a number of large trees and thick foliage in the garden, "visibility was bad." German troops opened with small arms and machine gun fire from several emplacements. "Men were falling everywhere. We couldn't dig in."

"The machine gun fire pinned us down, and the mortars started coming in," wrote Hartung. Shells began exploding all around. German mortar crews were close enough that he could hear the distinct ping and cough of the mortar rounds as they left the barrel. Some of the shells "hit the trees and burst above the ground, making them twice as effective." "The first attempt to go over the wall was really costly, almost all who tried were killed or wounded." Several additional attempts to get over the wall were likewise unsuccessful. Hartung described the scene: "They were picking us off like flies and we couldn't see them to do anything about it . . . It was really a very sad sight to see. Bodies and parts of bodies were everywhere. On our side, and on the German side. Wounded were screaming for medics."

Hartung relayed instructions from Blake to the platoon leaders throughout the morning amid heavy machine gun and mortar fire. Each time he returned to the CP he would assist a couple of walking wounded to the rear area. "I was going through minefields all day and I didn't know it. I was so exhausted I did not care any more . . . The good Lord must have been guiding me." Two nearby buildings, used as an aid station, "were full of wounded and I don't know how many dead," he wrote. Because of the situation, medical personnel could not evacuate the casualties.

The author (anonymous) of "From the Riviera to the Rhine," edited by Pfc. John A. Hyman, provides some additional details of the engagement:

Easy Company found the Germans barricaded in a large courtyard. They had machine gun nests all over. Behind these were heavy concertinas of barbed wire fronting a house, which sheltered mortar positions. It was impossible to get at them without presenting a silhouetted target. Pfc. Lewis H. Rose, Conneaut, Ohio,

climbed the high stone wall in front of the courtyard and fired twelve boxes of ammunition at the enemy, thirty yards away. Cradling his machine gun in his arms,
he fired until his gun barrel burned out and his heavy leather gloves caught fire.

Hartung said Rose "was standing in full view, and firing his machine gun
from the hip. I thought it was a John Wayne movie."

Blake called up a Sherman tank and the driver made several unsuccessful
attempts to ram his way through a big metal gate leading into the compound.
A "trap" (possibly a concrete barrier), halted the tank's forward progress. Taking on heavy fire, the crew bailed out and headed for the rear and safety. "I
don't blame them," Hartung commented.

Hartung's "best buddy, a Puerto Rican named [Pfc. John] Neves [of
Fairhaven, Mass.]," who, he says, "was a wireman and knew nothing about
tanks, climbed in, somehow got it started, and kept trying to ram the gate. But
the tank finally stalled and he had to get out fast." Neves returned later with
"twelve pounds of TNT" and "blew out the obstacle," thereby allowing the
tank to proceed into the compound.

Neves "had been with the company ever since the Salerno landing and
thought he should be sent home on rotation." He told Hartung "that the only
way out was the Congressional Medal of Honor" and that was his goal. "He
was always where he wasn't supposed to be," Hartung added. "I don't know
how many times I told him he was crazy, the things he did." About six weeks
later, a sniper's bullet found its mark, killing him instantly.

Captain Blake, "who was new to all this," wrote Hartung, "had that 'thousand yard stare' already" (usually used to describe men in combat for extended periods). "He asked me, 'What do we do?' I told him we stay right
where we are. I had been there before, and knew what was happening." The
captain, he says, "had already made up his mind . . . Finally, we sat down up
against the wall and did nothing but wait. This was about one o'clock."

At about 2 P.M., Col. William H. Martin, Commanding Officer of the 143rd
Infantry, arrived on the scene. He confronted Capt. Blake and demanded to
know what was causing the holdup. The captain explained the situation to
him ("He was barely able to speak."), but it was not what the colonel wanted
to hear. Martin ordered Blake to lead the rest of the company ("35 men left of
more than 200") over the wall and take the position, "no matter what." The
captain refused. "Thank God," wrote Hartung. Martin relieved Blake of his
command, placed him under arrest, and sent him to the rear. "We never saw
him again," he said. We all felt bad as he was well liked and doing the right
thing." Reading Hartung's account, written thirty-five years later, one can feel
the emotion and experience the enormous sense of relief conveyed by his
words. Time has not dulled the pain of having seen good friends struck down.

At this point, Martin took over command of the unit. He ordered the remaining men to follow him and was "shot off the wall on his first try, almost cut in half by machine gun fire." *Stars and Stripes* reported that Martin "was hit in the chest while reconnoitering the situation."

The battle raged for more than six hours. Late in the afternoon Company E was relieved and "the wall was taken that night." When the final body count was completed, only twenty-seven men remained out of a company of approximately 200. Hartung's final comment, "We lost a hell of a lot of good men that day. What a waste."

After coming ashore on D-Day, regiments of the 36th Division regrouped then began to fan out and move inland to take assigned objectives. By nightfall, the 141st Infantry had advanced inland about six miles, cut the Cannes-Frejus highway and set up roadblocks on all roads leading to the coastal city of Cannes. On the night of August 16, D-Day plus 1, the 142nd broke the last German strongpoint before Le Muy, twelve miles north of Frejus in the Argens Valley. On the following day, the regiment linked up with British and American paratroopers who had jumped nearby, and moved into Draguignan.

The 1st Battalion, 141st Infantry, swung east and began driving up the coast over the main highway leading to Cannes and Nice, clearing defenses not blasted by the Navy. Units of the battalion were walking along the highway in two files, one on each side of the road with vehicles in the center. Jack Wilson's machine gun squad, attached to one of the line companies, was near the head of the column. "Other than sporadic sniper fire," he says, the company "encountered little resistance."

At one point, the company began taking heavy fire from up in the hills. Everyone scattered, seeking cover in the road ditches or behind vehicles, and trained their rifles on the hillside, trying to detect the source of the firing. The platoon leader had Jack set up his machine gun and spray the thick brush where they suspected the Germans might be hiding. The machine gun chattered away, echoing throughout the surrounding hills. Branches and leaves flew and little puffs of dust rose as the rounds hit rocks and earth. The sound of ricocheting bullets rang through the still summer air. Wilson expended a full belt of ammunition. The gun ceased firing, but the reverberation continued for a few seconds, seeming far longer. Then complete silence. The lieutenant sent a three-man patrol up the hill to investigate. The men returned and reported finding eight riddled German bodies.

Farther down the highway, Wilson says, "I was walking beside a fellow when someone in back of us spoke to him." The man turned around and was about to answer when a shot rang out from somewhere up on the hillside to the left of the road. The bullet hit the man between the shoulder blades. "His hands went up in the air and he fell to the ground." He lay there in a lot of pain, screaming. Wilson says, the "wound looked like he had been hit with a shotgun at close range." The sniper "had used a wooden bullet that explodes on impact." This practice was against the Geneva Convention, and considered a war crime. The wooden projectile had apparently hit the man's spine and splintered into many tiny pieces.

Normally, a wooden bullet would not kill a man unless it struck him in a vital spot. The rounds did a lot of damage to flesh and bone and the resulting wound took longer to clean. The concept behind the use of this type of ordnance, which became more common toward the end of the war, was to tie up hospital personnel and place a drain on medical resources. Doctors had to be sure not to leave any fragments behind, or infection quickly set in.

A squadmate dragged the wounded man off to one side of the road, out of the line of fire, and a medic rushed over to administer first aid. The aid man called for stretcher bearers, who placed the GI on a jeep ambulance and rushed him off to the battalion aid station located on Green Beach.

One of the riflemen came over to the CO and reported that he thought he saw movement up on the hillside, and pointed to the approximate area. He offered to go after the sniper. Wilson and another man volunteered to go with him. They "zigzagged up the hill leapfrog fashion," converging on the spot where they thought he might be located. When they "were about half way up the hill, a German jumped up from his hiding place and yelled 'Comrade.'"

One GI covered the man while the second kept a lookout in case there happened to be any other Germans nearby. Wilson "shook him down" for concealed weapons. In the breast pocket of the man's jacket, he found several cartridges with wooden bullets. The Germans painted the tips purple to distinguish them from other types of ammunition. When Jack scraped off some of the paint, he discovered the damning evidence. All three men opened up at once, as if on cue, emptying their clips. They left the man's corpse to rot in the hot Mediterranean sun and headed back down the hillside without even the slightest bit of remorse. In their eyes, the man deserved to die.

The three men finally caught up with the company down the road and reported the incident to the lieutenant. He commented that "he would have shot him too if he had been there." Jack says he "often wondered" about the wounded man "throughout the years and if he survived." Wilson kept one of the bullets for many years as a souvenir. When the Texas Military Forces Museum opened at Camp Mabry ("Home of the 36th Division"), Austin, Texas, in 1993, he donated the unusual trophy to the collection.

Enemy resistance, in the form of artillery fire from self-propelled guns and tanks continued to increase, reaching an unusual intensity at times. The Germans attempted to infiltrate the thinly spaced lines of the division in several places, but enemy forces were never able to do so in large numbers. Due to the extent of the sector assigned to the division, approximately eighteen and one half miles, troop coverage along the rapidly advancing front was spotty.

Advancing units experienced shelling of unusually heavy caliber, believed to be from German coastal guns on the Ile Sainte-Marguerite, located off the coast from Cannes and the nearby Cap de la Croisette. Division requested naval counterfire on the afternoon of August 17, and the shelling slackened considerably. History of Operations, 141st Infantry, reported that fire from the big guns created more casualties than the number recorded during the landings.

Jack Wilson said that the big coastal guns were "firing mostly white phosphorus at us." White phosphorus ("WP or Willy Peter") is a highly volatile chemical. When exposed to the air, it bursts into flames and produces a dense white smoke. Phosphorus is luminous and used by munitions manufacturers in tracer bullets. The particles can cause serious, painful burns to the skin, and damage to flesh continues until the chemical burns itself out.

Immediate first aid measures are called for to prevent oxygen from reaching the embedded particles. Medical personnel must flush the wound continuously with water from their canteens and remove the particles with tweezers or forceps. In the field, this is not always practical. "We used mud to smother the wound," Wilson noted.

When the heavy shelling started, Wilson's squad was walking along some railroad tracks in the direction of Callian. Members of the unit raced toward the mouth of a railroad tunnel a short distance up ahead, seeking safety. They remained inside until the firing ceased. When the group emerged, Wilson says, "We looked like we had slept in a coal bin, all train engines used coal then, and the tunnels were loaded with coal dust and soot."

Edward Langdon related a story told by his late father, Ernest, a member of Company D and later Company B, 141st Infantry, who entered the service from Baldwin, New York. His dad was traveling down a dirt road in southern France with his squad when suddenly they heard strange noises coming from a nearby stand of scrub oak trees and tangle of brush. Moving cautiously toward the wood line, with rifles at the ready, the men went in to investigate. It turned out to be an old swayback horse, frightened by the nearby shelling. The men calmed the shaking horse and led the nervous animal safely out of the thick woods to a nearby field.

One of the guys in the group was a big strapping boy from Texas, who had been a champion rodeo rider before the war. The horse was a bit skittish and one of the men bet the Texan that he could not ride him. Not one to back down from a challenge, even one so absurd, the man grabbed the horse by the mane and jumped on. The old horse started bucking and rearing, throwing the Texan about twenty feet through the air, whereupon he landed flat on his back. The guys in the squad were just about rolling on the ground in a fit of laughter. Needless to say, when the story got around, the embarrassed Texan was the subject of severe ribbing for some time thereafter. Langdon says his dad "used to laugh like hell when he told that story."

When Ed related this incident to me during a telephone conversation in 2003, I had the strangest feeling that I had heard the story before. As I mentioned earlier, when I was younger, my father would, on rare occasions, tell a brief story about the war, usually a humorous one.

On the night of August 17, D-Day plus 2, Ross Rajotte's platoon sergeant picked him to go out on a four-man patrol to scout enemy positions. Able Company, 141st Infantry, was fighting somewhere in the hills north of St. Raphael. As the patrol worked its way behind enemy lines, Rajotte described what happened. "It was about 2 o'clock in the morning. We could see the silhouettes of Germans a short distance away and opened up on them." The German troops dove for cover and returned the fire. A bullet ricocheted off an outcropping behind Rajotte's position, striking him in the back of the neck, lodging near his spine. This was the second of four wounds Rajotte was to receive during the war. The last wound, which occurred during the Rhineland Campaign, was severe enough to get him out of combat for the rest of the war. He was "reclassified limited assignment non-combat," and transferred to a desk job in an engineer supply depot.

Medics evacuated Rajotte to an aid station somewhere in the rear. In the morning, medical personnel put him aboard a hospital ship. That night the ship sailed for Naples, Italy. "It was all white with a large red cross painted port and starboard side and was lit up like a Christmas tree. The nurses and doctors were from Switzerland," wrote Rajotte.

At the hospital in Naples, here was a separate wing for German wounded. During his recuperation period, Rajotte met and spoke with several of the German patients. One young man was from Alsace-Lorraine, part of Germany near the French border, and the two conversed in French. Ross's family immigrated to the United States from French Canada in the early 1900s, and he spoke the language fluently. The German said he "was glad the war was over" for him. He told Ross how he had been fighting since 1938, and had not seen his family for many years and missed them terribly. Others, who spoke French or English, had similar stories to tell.

Aboard ship, Ross ran into 1st Lt. Charles R. Mattis of Chicago, Illinois, an officer with Company A, whom doctors were treating for malaria. Rajotte says fondly, "he was the nicest officer in our company." A smiling Mattis came rushing over to Rajotte, gave him "a big bear hug and said, 'Let's have a drink.'" Both men later returned to the company and the fighting. Ross closed, "Then I got hit again. And he got killed." Two months after doctors removed the bullet from Rajotte's neck, he rejoined his old outfit.

Following the Riviera invasion, Allied Headquarters issued a communiqué boasting that the southern France campaign was a "model of effective organization, cooperation of all services, and vigor of action—one of the best coordinated efforts in all of military history." Because the landings succeeded on a grandiose scale, some writers and historians have downplayed the cost of the overall operation in terms of lives lost. Accounts of the invasion report that troops coming ashore met "minimal resistance," and that the number of casualties had been "exceedingly light." Statements to this effect do not reflect an accurate assessment and tend to promote the impression, wrongfully, that the invasion was a "piece of cake." While this may have been true of the initial landings, as the Americans pushed inland, resistance stiffened and casualties increased dramatically. The total number of Allied casualties on D-Day was 597—198 KIA and 399 WIA.

Two members of the 36th Division take umbrage with the general consensus and have expressed almost identical sentiments. Wendell C. Phillippi (Hq., 2nd and 3rd Bns.-143), originally from Indianapolis, Indiana, wrote, "Our landings in southern France were a great success and some historians have written that the opposition was a near pushover." He added disdainfully, "They failed to read the casualty lists." After the war, Phillippi rose to the rank of Major General in the 38th Infantry Division, Indiana National Guard.

Fellow T-Patcher 1st Sgt. Morris L. Courington (K-142) provided this assessment: "Compared to Salerno, Normandy and some other invasions, it was not nearly as bloody on the initial landings. But it still bothers us a little to hear people say that it was nothing, that it was just an automatic deal." He elaborated, "When you go back several years later and see that there are several hundred GIs buried there in a beautiful cemetery in Draguignan," and "almost 8,000 crosses and stars of David" in the cemetery at Epinal, "it shows that a heavy price was paid." His final poignant comment, "That's what war is all about—killing. And we had some of that everywhere we went.

Chapter Seventeen

Truscott's Plan

Once VI Corps forces smashed the coastal defenses and established a suitable beachhead, "a phase of highly-mobilized warfare began." To "avoid a repetition of fateful Anzio," wrote the 36th Division historian, "troops pushed hard to exploit their initial victory with lightning speed, refusing the Germans a moment in which to regroup and strike back." The decision to delay the push inland at Anzio had ended in complete disaster, and Allied Command was determined to avoid a repeat. Relentless pursuit by American forces continued to drive defending German units farther and farther from the coast. Constant pressure by invasion forces along the entire front kept the Germans completely off balance and prevented them from reestablishing new defensive positions as they fell back.

At the same time, paratroops and glider forces (special service troops and commandos) seized and occupied several key inland villages. Units threw up blockades over the rail and road network leading to the coast, thus preventing needed reinforcements, including armored units, from coming to the aid of coastal defenders. Also at work behind the German lines were members of the Maquis or French Forces of the Interior (FFI), rural guerrilla bands of French resistance fighters, which hampered German movements over interior roadways and completely disrupted the enemy's communications capabilities. In the days immediately following the landings, the pace of the inland push far exceeded all expectations and projected time frames had to be revised downward.

On August 17, the German High Command ordered General Johannes von Blaskowitz to leave sufficient forces behind to hold the major ports of Marseille and Toulon and pull the remainder of Army Group G (First and Nineteenth Armies) back toward the Vosges Mountains in northeastern France where engineers were hastily preparing defensive fallback positions. Blaskowitz chose the north-south running Rhone Valley as the best escape route back to Germany.

Route National No. 7, the major highway from the Riviera to Lyons and points beyond, ran the entire length of the valley.

As Anvil-Dragoon progressed, various commands relayed intelligence regarding enemy troop movements to VI Corps Headquarters. By D-Day plus 4 (August 19), German forces in the south of France were in full retreat. Aerial reconnaissance units were reporting that all roads leading north out of the Marseille-Toulon area, where the bulk of von Blaskowitz's army group was concentrated during the summer of 1944, were crowded with fleeing German convoys. Once the Corps Intelligence Section (G-2) confirmed von Blaskowitz's intentions to withdraw rather than make a stand, Gen. Truscott realized that if the current situation played out as anticipated, an opportunity might present itself whereby he would be in an enviable position to cut off and annihilate the bulk of the German forces in the south of France.

The concept was a simple one: block the enemy retreat to the north and do, Truscott says, what every military leader on the offensive seeks to do, "attack in flank and rear where he is most vulnerable." In his own past campaigns, in Africa, Sicily, and Italy, Truscott explained that this had always been his intent, but two principal factors prevented him from achieving this goal. First, Truscott wrote, the Germans were "just as mobile as we were," and second, "the forces which we placed at the enemy's rear had not been strong enough" permitting "him to escape before we could close the trap."

In his 1954 book, *Command Missions*, the commander wrote, "Every military leader dreams of the battle in which he can trap the enemy without any avenues or means of escape and in which his destruction can be assured." During the preinvasion planning stages several weeks earlier at VI Corps Headquarters in the "Block House," a former Italian Army barracks near the waterfront in downtown Naples, Truscott made a careful and detailed "study of the terrain of eastern France and of the many possible ways the battle might develop." His findings led him "to dream of creating such a maneuver."

Truscott conferred with his staff in preparation for whatever eventualities might lay ahead. According to Col. Vincent M. Lockhart if in the event all objectives for the assault landing were successfully accomplished and a breakthrough by the 3rd and 36th Divisions occurred, Truscott had devised a contingency plan "for a cavalry type exploitation." He designed the stratagem to maneuver a strong contingent into position ahead of the retreating German XIX Army and block their main escape route. To effect this, the commander conceived the formation of "an independent mobile task force." Truscott, himself a cavalryman, "stipulated that the group would be built around the Corps [Cavalry] Reconnaissance Squadron—the 117th," commanded by Lt. Colonel Charles J. Hodge, and he formulated tentative plans for its subsequent deployment.

Like a chess master seeking to finish off his opponent, the general began thinking of several possible moves in advance. Time was critical. Truscott knew he had to strike quickly to exploit the advantage, or the opportunity for a major victory would be lost.

The move was an attempt by Truscott "to set the stage for a classic—a 'Cannae,' in which we would encircle the enemy against an impassable barrier or obstacle and destroy him." Students of military history named the stratagem after an ancient town of southeast Italy near the coast of the Adriatic Sea where the Carthaginians under Hannibal defeated a superior Roman Army in 216 B.C. The Battle of Cannae took place during the Second Punic War fought between Rome and Carthage for mastery of the ancient world. Military strategists and tacticians consider Hannibal's victory to be the "perfect example in the history of warfare of the double envelopment of an opposing army" (Creasy and Mitchell, Blumeson).

Greatly outnumbered, Hannibal positioned his weakest troops at the center of the main battle formation so as to make it appear vulnerable, inviting attack. The Romans fell for the ploy and charged deep into the Carthaginian lines, as Hannibal had anticipated. Both flanks closed in around the Roman legions while Hannibal's cavalry, after defeating the inferior Roman horse, attacked from the rear. Out of a total force of 86,000 (80,000 infantry and 6,000 mounted), only 15,000 Romans escaped death or capture. The Carthaginian army numbered 50,000 (40,000 infantry and 10,000 horse). Roman forces killed an estimated 6,000 Carthaginian warriors. The Battle of Cannae was the greatest defeat in the history of the Roman Empire (Creasy and Mitchell, Blumenson).

The geography of the Rhone Valley in the Montelimar area figured prominently in Truscott's bid to stop the German withdrawal. One of the vital components of the general's proposed strategy was a "narrow defile"—known as the "Cruas Gorge"—just east of the town of Cruas. The City of Montelimar sits astride Highway 7, the main valley thoroughfare, approximately six miles south of Cruas (125 miles from St. Raphael). Just north of the city, the high ground on the east bank of the Rhone, "a sharp north-south ridgeline," slopes practically to the river's edge, leaving "barely room" for Highway 7 and the adjacent railroad line to squeeze through. Truscott referred to this narrow pass as the "Montelimar Gap" and the high ground to the east as the "Montelimar Ridge."

Truscott considered the "high ground immediately north of Montelimar" to be "a vital factor for blocking any German retreat up the east bank of the Rhone." South of the east-west flowing Drome River, the foothills of the Lower Alps extend westward to the Rhone Valley "terminating in ridges that parallel the Rhone closely for a distance of about fifteen miles." The ridges average 1,000 to 1,500 feet in elevation, "with precipitous western slopes" that dominate Highway 7. The most significant of these is the aforementioned ridge comprising the east side of the Montelimar Gap.

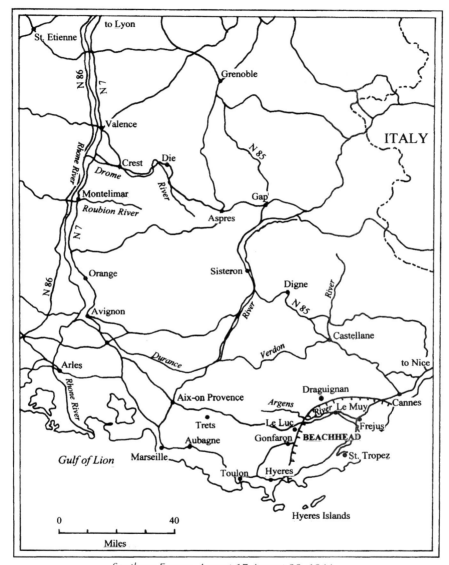

Southern France, August 17-August 28, 1944.

This "key terrain" feature began approximately three miles north of Montelimar and extended "in a long ridge" for a distance of two and three-quarter miles to the "river village" of La Coucourde. The average elevation of the "Montelimar Ridge," as referred to hereafter, is about 900 feet. The highest point on the ridge, designated "Hill 300" (984 feet) by military planners, was located at the very northern end. There was a second major prominence, located "in the middle," known as Hill 294 (967 feet).

Truscott also designated several other strategic elevations as being critical to the success of the plan. A second parallel ridge, situated just to the northeast of Montelimar, "dominated the valley of the Roubion [River] and the secondary roads leading north to the east of Crest," possible avenues of escape. The city of Crest is located seventeen miles northeast of Montelimar, on the north bank of the Drome River. Next in importance were the foothills of the Lower Alps south of Crest. "If the fortunes of war permitted us to seize this terrain," the general wrote, "we could block the retreat of enemy forces to the north along the east bank of the Rhone."

Truscott formulated a preliminary master plan that entailed three distinct phases. For the scheme to end in success, VI Corps commanders had to carry out each stage in concert. First, he had to maneuver a sizable force into position ahead of the retreating Germans to "plug the bottleneck" in the German's main line of retreat north of Montelimar. For this to occur, Truscott's forces had to seize and hold the high ground on the east side of the Rhone Valley. Should the enemy gain control of this terrain, Truscott warned, "we would be confronted by an enormously strong position which would be difficult to turn, and which the enemy could hold long enough to make good his escape."

Second, Allied forces had to destroy all bridges over the Rhone, as well as those over the tributaries entering the west bank of the river. This, Truscott says, "was well within the capabilities of our Air Forces," and would effectively close the German's left flank. The FFI was also responsible for the destruction of a number of the spans. This tactic would also isolate the enemy forces to the east and west of the Rhone from coming to each other's aid. The Germans on the east side of the river, left with no other means of exiting the valley and therefore bypassing the block, would be forced to continue their escape north over Route 7 toward the Montelimar Gap and into the waiting trap.

The "impassable barrier or obstacle" envisioned by Truscott in his equation for a decisive victory, consisted of the Rhone River, "a broad, deep river with an unusually swift current," on the west; the dominant elevations of the foothills that are the terminus, or western edge, of the French Alps, to the east; and a major roadblock or blocks to be positioned across Highway 7, which would in effect seal off the main escape route. The barrier would create a pocket in which Truscott's waiting forces would trap and destroy the German XIX Army.

The final phase of the operation involved sending a second, division-sized force to press the enemy from the rear. Force B would drive the Germans north up the Rhone Valley into the waiting block at Montelimar, while at the same time prevent them from reversing direction to seek alternate escape routes when they realized what was about to happen. Truscott eventually entrusted this important mission to the 3rd Infantry Division on August 24.

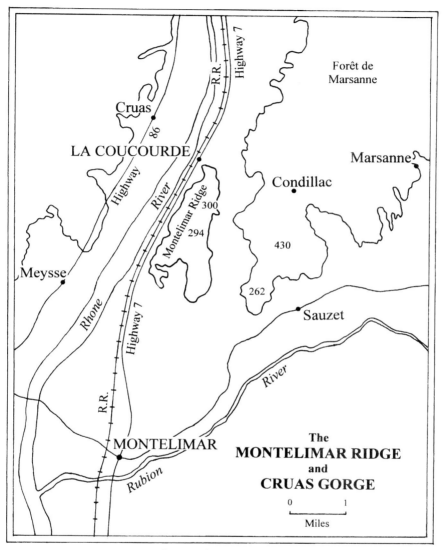

Montelimar Ridge and Cruas Gorge.

Once the German commanders discovered that American forces had cut off all avenues of escape to the north and west, they would be faced with one of two choices: smash the blocking positions, or break out of the cordon to the east by finding an alternate route or routes that would enable German convoys to bypass the defensive barrier. Only one possibility existed: exit the

Rhone Valley by turning east along the Roubion River, and then north again near the town of Bonlieu. Plans formulated by Dahlquist to deal with the latter are discussed in the next chapter. German commanders were reluctant to enter the vast mountainous region east of the Rhone Valley proper because it was under the control of the dreaded Maquis (FFI).

Truscott's first priority was to create a "highly mobile striking force" with the express purpose of cutting off the German's retreat by encirclement. The flanking maneuver was designed to outdistance the German XIX Army by racing north over secondary routes on a course parallel with the Rhone Valley on the east, placing itself ahead of the fleeing Germans columns. Truscott assigned responsibility for the formation of the special task force to his Deputy Corps commander, Brig. Gen. Frederick B. Butler. Designated components, which included the 117th Cavalry Reconnaissance Squadron; 59th Armored FA Battalion; 2nd Battalion, 143rd Infantry, 36th Division; elements of the 636th TD Battalion; 753rd Tank Battalion; 111th Medical Battalion; along with engineers and ordnance, assembled at Le Muy on August 17. Correspondents promptly dubbed the unit "Task Force Butler" (TFB), after its leader.

Truscott also created a second, smaller task force to include the remainder of the 143rd Infantry and attached units, with orders to proceed north along secondary roads to the east of TFB. This force, led by Brig. Gen. Robert I. Stack, the Assistant 36th Division Commander, was designated "Task Force Stack" (TFS). Stack's orders were to proceed to Grenoble, occupy the city, and block reinforcements from the north. The city fell on August 22, seven days after D-Day (see below).

A third "element," made up of the 142nd Infantry, raced eastward from Gap to block passes through the High Alps at the Italian border near Briancon and Guillestre, to prevent the Germans from sending reinforcements from that direction.

TFB jumped off from Le Muy on the morning of August 18, and sped northward toward the French Alps over secondary roads "from Draguignan to Salernes, Riez, north to Oraison and Sisteron." Butler decided against using the main highway north, Route Nationale 85, the Route Napoleon, a mountain road to the east connecting Cannes with Grenoble. The commander reasoned that the terrain along Route 85 was so mountainous, that "a small enemy force with a single self-propelled gun could have made this 'cavalry sweep' just another crawling Italian campaign." The motorized force made a temporary stop at Sisteron, sixty-five miles northwest on the Durance River, to await further orders. En route, Butler "had dispersed several enemy detachments," capturing more than 1,000 prisoners in the process.

Truscott would be forced to deal with the overall strength of the retreating German XIX Army east of the Rhone, at this time an unknown factor that could only be estimated. In addition to the "crack" 11th Panzer Division, "one of the German's best," he said, it "seemed likely that at least three full divisions with parts of four or five others as well as numerous Corps, Army, and coastal defense troops, were still south of Montelimar." This being the situation, Truscott decided on August 19 to increase troop strength in the Montelimar sector by sending the remaining units of the 36th Infantry Division north behind Butler.

On the evening of August 20, Truscott sent an urgent message to Butler: "You will move at first light 21 August with all possible speed to Montelimar. Block enemy routes of withdrawal up the Rhone Valley in that vicinity. 36th Division follows you." He ordered Butler to remain in place (at Sisteron) to wait for lead elements of the 36th to arrive. In his "letter of instructions," Truscott told his second-in-command that the "essential task" of his force was "to seize the high ground north of Montelimar." The directive was hand delivered by Lt. Col. Theodore J. Conway, one of Truscott's top aides, who had sped north for almost 100 miles over narrow mountain roads under blackout conditions.

Major General John E. Dahlquist, the 36th Division Commander, received orders from Truscott to rush one regimental combat team (RCT), "Corps Artillery Long Toms" [155mm] and the 155th [FA] Battalion north to support Butler. All remaining units of the 36th Division "would follow as rapidly as conditions permitted," wrote Truscott. Upon arriving in the area, Dahlquist would "assume control" of the sector, and take over the command of TFB.

Truscott, in his written orders to Dahlquist, left no doubt as to the mission's priority. The VI Corps commander summarized the substance of this communiqué in his book *Command Missions*:

> He was to join Butler at Montelimar and employ the bulk of his forces for blocking there, with lesser blockades east of the Durance River and north of Aspres to prevent interference from those directions. He would have to decide upon his troop dispositions when he had familiarized himself with existing conditions; but blocking the Montelimar Gap was to be the important mission.

Truscott ordered Dahlquist to capture the town of Montelimar, calling it "the most important piece of ground in Southern France." While Truscott gave his commanders "specific missions to execute," he "left it up to their own discretion" on the means to complete the task.

Stack, meanwhile, advanced northward by way of Castellane, Digne, Sisteron, and through Gap before pressing on to Grenoble, a university city nestled at the foot of the French Alps. In one fourteen-hour period, TFS advanced more than ninety miles. Stack's group arrived at Grenoble on August 22, D-Day plus 7, capturing the city on the same day. Under the original timetable, planners tentatively scheduled Grenoble to fall in November, nearly three months later (D-Day plus 90).

In the south, the First French Army surrounded the ports of Marseille and Toulon and attacked simultaneously "from all sides" beginning on August 20. "Between 21 and 23 August," wrote Jeffrey J. Clarke, "the French slowly squeezed the Germans back into the inner city in a series of almost continuous street fights." Battling "from street to street and house to house," French units isolated and then neutralized groups of defenders. The Germans also had to contend with French resistance fighters within the city, most often at their backs. Ordinary citizens assisted as well, directing troops to strongpoints blocking the French advance. Except for a few isolated pockets of stubborn resistance, the heaviest fighting was over by the twenty-sixth.

Both cities formally surrendered on the same day, August 28, Toulon "a week ahead of schedule" and Marseille "nearly a month before the target date." The French claimed 17,000 prisoners at Toulon and another 7,000 at Marseille, "indicating that few Germans had followed the Fuehrer's 'stand and die order,'" Clarke wrote. French forces suffered 4,500 casualties.

In every town and hamlet along the route of march, French citizens massed by the side of the road to greet the advancing Americans. The reception by the civilian population was intensely emotional and joyous. People stood cheering and waving an assortment of French, American, and British flags, and white handkerchiefs. Children held up tiny fingers giving the "V" for victory sign. Smiling women came out of their homes and presented the troops with fresh fruit, bread, wine, and small gifts. For the young GIs, there were plenty of kisses and adoring hugs from the pretty young mademoiselles. Cries of "VIVA LA FRANCE . . . VIVA L'AMERIQUE!" rose above the noise of the crowds. The tolling of church bells echoed through the hills and down the valleys to announce the long-awaited day of liberation.

Groups of Maquis, identified by their FFI brassards, stood guard at various points to give assurance to American units that the road ahead was clear and to direct traffic. They wore "every kind of uniform imaginable" and carried an array of assorted firearms. Units of the FFI protected flanks and effectively cleared the area of German snipers and pockets of resistance.

Richard E. Talley, a member of Company K, 143rd Infantry, wrote, "I have a strange and vivid recollection of the town of Grenoble, a very beautiful place in the French Alps. The people there welcomed us wildly." It was the French people, Talley says, he remembered most of all. "They were just great. They gave us some good things to eat (real cheese). They supplied us with wine. We were their liberators but kindly liberators as we dispensed chewing gum, cigarettes, candy bars, and K-rations."

TFB continued to Aspres, seventy-five kilometers north, then turned west in the direction of Montelimar over Route 93, exiting onto secondary roads leading to the objective. Butler arrived in the Marsanne area, twelve miles east of Montelimar, at 5 P.M., on August 21, and established his CP. Troop B, 117th Reconnaissance Squadron, leading the advance, traveled via the road through Condillac to the town of La Coucourde to scout the high ground overlooking the Rhone Valley. Some vanguard units of the German Nineteenth Army had already passed through the area but the main body was still somewhere south of Montelimar. Lieutenant Colonel Hodge, CO of the 117th, quoted in Lockhart, says that at this time the Germans had no idea the Americans were in the area.

Chapter Eighteen

Setting the Trap

Immediately upon arrival in the Marsanne area, General Butler began to deploy his limited force. The 2nd Battalion, 143rd Infantry, was placed at La Coucourde, "just west of Condillac, in the narrowest defile of the Rhone River" with orders to block Highway 7. Butler apportioned tanks and TDs to support the infantry companies accordingly and sent a "small company" (see Stubinski below) west to Montelimar and then south on Highway 7 until contact was made with the Germans. Troop C, 117th Recon, "pushed straight through Crest along the north bank of the Drome to the mouth of the river," near Loriol. Just before nightfall, Butler reassigned the troop to "outpost duty" in protecting his right flank.

The "first night" (August 21), "patrols" from the 2nd Battalion, 143rd, managed to establish a roadblock at La Coucoudre, "but were driven out by superior forces" (infantry and tanks) and the German columns resumed their flight to the north.

General Butler placed his artillery, the 59th Armored FA Battalion, in the foothills east of the Rhone Valley, west of Marsanne, in position to fire on Highway 7. An encouraged Butler stated, "Although we did not hold the main east bank highway along the Rhone during the daylight hours of the 22nd, little lived to escape on that road." Artillery, combined with "tanks, TDs, armored cars," and the "ground mounted 57's [57mm antitank guns] of the infantry were pouring aimed fire at the dense traffic." Even the "flak wagons" of the 443rd AAA AW (SP) "got in on the shooting," wrote Butler. "As the main highway became blocked with wreckage and death, the Germans took to the paths and lanes between the highway and the river," he wrote. Interdicting fire from Butler's combined forces "took an appalling toll."

In a letter dated August 23, 1944, Butler informed Truscott, "We have improved position today. Have gained more high ground north of Montelimar and are getting into position to clean up the latter place this afternoon." The TDs and tanks had moved into position on the heights and were firing directly on convoys moving up the highway north of the city. He reported, "Jerry is hurt plenty. Yesterday over 100 vehicles destroyed and two trains were hit and badly messed up."

Interdicting artillery fire successfully blocked the rail line east of the Rhone, stopping all traffic. Butler, obviously elated, concluded, "and what a show these trains put on as cars burned and ammunition blew up." Butler noted, "2 B[attalio]ns 141st now in. Third reported en route . . . 131st Artillery is here."

Michael Stubinski (K-141) says that on D-Day plus 4 (August 19), he and two other members of his company, 2nd Lt. Eugene Saffold of Rosebud, Texas, and Corporal Gatha W. Norton of Sulligant, Alabama, were sent to Le Muy to join Task Force Butler (TFB). The force was being "hastily assembled," he said, and he sensed a great urgency on the part of the officers for the group to be on its way. None of the enlisted men had any idea as to the purpose of the group or its intended destination, which was the norm. Stubinski wrote, that as ordinary soldiers, "We never knew where we were going or how far we were going. The only thing we were ever sure of was that when we met the enemy we were going to fight."

The average GI had no inkling of the big picture or the long haul. Most of the time, he knew no more than what was going on a few feet to the left and right of his position. A soldier's job was to go where he was told and carry out orders without question. Paul D. Hinkle (L-141) of Frackville, Pennsylvania, said he did not know what he or his outfit was doing at Montelimar until many years later.

Stubinski rode in a weapons carrier at the point leading the convoy "along with about six other men," including Saffold and Norton. Saffold, Stubinski says, had been the 1st Sgt. of Company K until he received a battlefield commission "for bravery." The going was slow as the FFI had taken down or changed the direction signs to confuse the Germans. "Great!" Stubinski wrote with a bit of sarcasm, "But it confused us also. All we knew was that we were heading north. We kept asking the very few people we came in contact with where we were on the map, and where the Germans were." The convoy went through Digne, Sisteron, and then headed west along the Roubion River to the Marsanne area, arriving on August 21.

On August 22, the "branch of TFB I was with," Stubinski wrote, "splintered off from the main force and went down along the Roubion River toward Montelimar." The unit traveled west along the railroad tracks until it reached the marshaling yards at Montelimar and then turned south on Highway 7 through the center of the town in an attempt to make contact with the Germans. Truscott's memoirs indicate that Butler ordered this group to capture and hold the town. Stubinski says that "the rest of the force [TFB] remained north of Montelimar." "Our T-F-B group was less than a company," approximately "200 soldiers," including "tanks about 3 or 4 and no linemen . . . The only officer I remember was Lieutenant Saffold," he said.

As they passed through the seemingly deserted town, the GIs could see American and French flags flying from poles attached to the buildings or draped over window ledges. "It was beautiful to see the Stars and Stripes," Stubinski said proudly. The only movement observed "was the shades being raised in the windows enough to peek through, it had to be children," Stubinski recorded in his memoirs.

Just south of the town the column stopped for a rest break. Up to this time, Stubinski says, the force had made no contact with the enemy or the FFI. His squad of twelve men sat in a circle brewing coffee when they heard the drone of a small aircraft overhead. They looked skyward and observed "a small piper cub size plane with an open cockpit flying real low, and real slow." The German pilot, "wearing large flying glasses," was clearly visible. Within seconds, an artillery shell came whistling overhead and scored a direct hit on the group's position. "That shell missed my head by inches," he said incredulously, "and got the man opposite me and his parts were on either side all over the others, had I moved my head it would have been blown off." The group scattered and headed for cover as more shells began striking the area.

When the shelling eased up, Stubinski's section headed south for about 100 to 150 yards "to a small knoll that had a farmhouse and a stone barn on it." Most of the men, including one of the tanks, moved to the south side of the barn and took up positions. Saffold ordered the men to dig in. Stubinski, Norton, and a couple of other men took shelter on the north side. "Next," Stubinski says, "all Hell broke loose." Artillery shells fell like hail on and around the barn. "One shell exploded a few yards away and raised me about six inches off the ground." The barrage killed or seriously wounded all of the men on the south side of the barn.

Right around dusk, members of the platoon spotted German infantrymen advancing up the highway in their direction. An American machine gun crew, located about seventy-five yards to the right, opened fire, causing the Germans to disperse along the side of the road and begin digging in. A lone Sherman tank, in the meantime, moved to the north side of the barn and began firing down the road. The Germans, having no idea as to the strength of the opposing force, immediately took up a defensive posture and opened with small arms and machine gun fire. About fifty yards away, Stubinski could see the helmets of two German FOs directing mortar and artillery fire through field glasses. As darkness fell, the action quieted down. Sporadic firing took place throughout the night as both sides let loose at the slightest noise or movement, both real and imagined.

The next morning (August 23), the Germans "sent one gun, an 88 or anti-tank gun, around our flank to knock out our tank." A truck was towing the weapon, followed closely by an "ammunition carrier." As the crew began moving the gun into position to fire, the American tank commander fired a single round, scoring a direct hit. The gun and the truck pulling it "blew up together." Stubinski remarked, "What a beautiful shot. Now who would give that gunner a medal?"

After taking the gun out, the tanker turned and headed for the rear with Stubinski and Norton close behind. They eventually made contact with Lt. Saffold and what was left of the rest of the company. Saffold figured it would only be a matter of time before the Germans attacked in force, so he decided to move to the high ground northeast of Montelimar. Crouching low and taking advantage of the terrain and natural cover as much as possible, the men made the long, arduous climb to the top of the adjacent hill (262?) undetected. Once on the summit, Stubinski says, "we had the most beautiful view of the Rhone Valley." On both sides of the river, crop fields, mostly grain, and pastureland checkerboarded the gently sloping valley floor, with farmhouses, barns, and outbuildings clustered here and there. "The first thought that entered my mind, and I was sure the others were all thinking the same thing, was how the Germans were looking down at us on the beaches of Anzio."

Saffold set up his defenses on the highest part of the mountain. He positioned his machine gun crew about twenty yards below the crest of the ridge in front of Stubinski's foxhole. At first light (August 24), a German patrol of about fifteen men "followed by two rows of tanks side by side" began advancing up the side of the hill. Stubinski estimated that "there was at least a dozen of their largest tanks" (Mark VI—Tiger tanks). Lieutenant Colonel James H. Critchfield, CO of the 2nd Battalion, 141st Infantry, says that Montelimar was the first time he encountered the Mark VI tank. The Germans were still some distance away, but for some unknown reason, Stubinski says, "our machine gunner opens fire on them to our disgust. It gave away our position. We could have fired mortars at them, and they wouldn't know where it was coming from." The tanks sped up in a race to the top, firing as they went.

The sight of the Mark VIs with the devastating fire from their 88mm guns unnerved some of the GIs and they began to retreat down the back side of the ridge to the east. Stubinski was sharing a foxhole with Lt. Saffold. "The lieutenant says to me 'UH-OH here they come,' and he started to run. I always looked up to him as a fearless man and there was my answer. Everybody is scared, and everybody, including myself was retreating from the mountain to another mountain on the side of us." That is the last time Stubinski saw Saffold until he returned to Company K.

The men ran headlong down the steep slope and spent most of the night (August 24–25) climbing to the top of the adjacent hill. By the time the tanks reached the crest of the first hill, it was dark. The second elevation was much higher with a more commanding view. The German tanks tried to move up the face, but it proved too steep. An artillery observer with the group radioed for supporting fire. Stubinski says they were "sitting ducks." The group watched as two of the tanks exploded in flames. The rest fled up the draw toward the north, out of sight of the observer.

As Stubinski and Norton were going down the first mountain to the next during the night of August 24 to 25, they stumbled upon a footbridge that crossed a small, stagnant pool of water, part of a dried up streambed. The little pond was full of ducks and the two men chased them off. Choked with rotting vegetation, algae, and weeds, the water gave off a foul odor. A thick scum, mixed with molted feathers, coated the surface. Clearing a small opening with his hands, Stubinski stuck his face in the tepid water and forced it down his parched throat until he quenched his thirst. "I got sick for an hour or two, then I was OK," he said.

By August 25, Saffold's men had been without fresh water for more than two days, having long ago emptied their canteens. It was brick oven hot, the sun blazing down unmercifully from a cloudless sky, sending temperatures soaring into the nineties. A search of the mountain for water was unsuccessful. Stubinski's lips were cracked and his throat parched. "I was dying of thirst," he related. "I tried urinating in my canteen and mixing it with the lemon extract we got in our K-rations . . . One taste of the urine turned my stomach." Stubinski put a "fig bar" in his mouth hoping the small amount of moisture would provide some measure of relief, but it only made matters worse and he had to spit it out.

The following morning the artillery FO "was having a field day" calling strikes against the enemy columns retreating north on Highway 7. The Germans "were running in all different directions trying to avoid mortars and [artillery] shells," Stubinski wrote. That night the Germans sent screaming meemies at the division from the floor of the valley. "They made a terrible noise," he said, and "killed many Americans."

"After that," Stubinski says, "we lost track of time." Finally, the company came down off the mountain to the road running southwest to Montelimar (parallel with the Roubion River), where they made contact with elements of the 3rd Division coming up from the south on Highway 7. They hitched a ride on trucks with personnel from Graves Registration who were picking up the dead, both German and American, and stacking them in the back.

On their way north, they passed back through Montelimar which artillery fire had "completely destroyed." He learned later that Lt. Col. Critchfield's 2nd Battalion (141st) tried unsuccessfully to capture the town (see next chapter). Montelimar, he says, "was a shambles." Stubinski wrote that he often thinks of the people, "especially the little children peeking under those window shades," and the terrible ordeal they must surely have endured. There is "no way they could have survived," he said sadly. About a mile or two north of the city, they ran into several members of Company K, who escorted them to the regimental bivouac area.

On August 20 (D-Day plus 5), the 1st Airborne Task Force relieved the 141st Infantry. Division Headquarters ordered the regiment and supporting units to move, first to Castellane and then farther north to Digne (closing in at 10:30 P.M., on August 21). Lockhart noted that "most of the moves made by the 36th Division during the highly fluid period were made by shuttling or on foot, or both." Later he added, "the 141st Infantry was moving mostly on foot." Martin Blumenson provides a description of the pace set by foot troops not fortunate enough to be provided with transportation: "At some times and places, the infantrymen did not march; they rushed ahead at what they called the 'Truscott trot,' a pace just slightly short of double time." When the regiment arrived at Digne, orders were waiting to proceed to Aspres. By the late morning of August 22, all units had arrived at the assembly area.

At the time orders were received from VI Corps to converge on Montelimar (August 22), elements of the 36th Division were dispersed over three widely separated sectors of southern France. The 141st Infantry, on the south, proceeded from Draguignan; the 142nd was at Guillestre, near the French-Italian border in the east; and the 143rd (minus the 2nd Battalion, with TFB) was at Grenoble to the north. The 36th Division Command Post was located at Aspres (until displaced to Marsanne on August 23). It was not until late in the day, on the twenty-fourth, that the entire division arrived in the Montelimar sector.

The 1st and 2nd Battalions (141st) received orders on the twenty-second to proceed to Crest and then turn southwest until contact was made with friendly troops for the location of the regimental assembly area, but a shortage of gasoline halted all operations. The situation forced Truscott to take 10,000 gallons of gasoline from the 45th Division and turn it over it to the 36th. It was not until 3:30 A.M., the following morning that the Service Company made a fuel delivery and the march resumed. Later that morning (August 23), Col. John W. "Jazz" Harmony, Commanding Officer of the 141st Infantry, established his CP in the small town of Condillac, three miles east of the Rhone River and six miles northeast of Montelimar.

The mountainous region through which the regiment traveled "was a stronghold of the FFI." The historian for the 141st Infantry stated, "The information and assistance furnished by this force was invaluable." Furthermore, he added, the "Allied thrust so far north in a few days could not have been accomplished without their aid." The 36th Division historian reiterated, "French Forces of the Interior, well-organized patriots harassing the enemy from the rear and controlling vast stretches of territory, greatly contributed to the success of the Allied invasion of Southern France." Lockhart wrote, "Nearly every unit of the 36th had a Maquis officer, and frequently a platoon of men from the Maquis, anxious to rid their land of the hated 'Boche.'"

Tech/4 Glenn C. Raithel of Jefferson, Wisconsin, was an aide with 36th Division Headquarters in the Inspector General's section. During the advance inland, Major Richard A. Nott of Long Island City, New York, the division Inspector General, asked Raithel to accompany him to a forward echelon. Nott replaced Lt. Col. Harold Reese, killed during the assault on Velletri, Italy, in May. The I.G. was heading north in a jeep with Lt. Col. Herbert E. MacCombie of Lynn, Massachusetts, the Division Chaplain, to conduct an investigation into an alleged incident involving the kicking of a captured German general by a sergeant of the 141st Infantry, after the officer stubbornly refused to surrender his weapon.

Some additional details concerning the incident are provided by MacCombie's memoirs under the section "Advancing Through Southern France." McCombie's version, written fourteen years earlier in 1977, differs slightly from that of Rathiel's account ("copyright 1991"):

> About this time one of our units captured several prisoners, including a German general. The sergeant in command ordered the general to line up with the other prisoners. The general refused, claiming the privileges of his rank. The sergeant kicked him where it would do the most good. Each protest was met with a good kick to the general's backside.

It was a humiliating experience for the senior officer in the presence of the men formerly under his command. "When he arrived at the Corps P.O.W. cage, the general lodged a protest at such inhumane treatment," wrote McCombie. "An investigating officer [Nott] was sent by the division to look into the charges."

It had been raining intermittently all day and the weather was cold and miserable, as it can get in the higher elevations of the mountains at any time of the year. The rainfall increased to a steady downpour, with occasional thunder and lightning strikes, and the members of Nott's party, riding in an open jeep, were soon soaked through to the skin. They passed truckload after truckload of infantrymen on the road.

After driving for several hours over narrow, congested roads, the group finally reached the head of the column, which had come to a halt. Off to one side, there were five or six Sherman tanks parked with their motors running, awaiting orders to move out. The 1st Battalion (141st) Command Post was billeted in a nearby house. Some of the men were huddled together in the rain, collars up and shoulders hunched forward trying to keep the chills at bay, while others a little farther on were busy digging foxholes. The troops were wet and miserable. Nott's driver parked the jeep behind a small building for cover and the I.G. proceeded to the battalion CP on foot.

Unbeknown to Major Nott at the time, this happened to be on the front lines. A colonel informed Nott that when he passed the tanks and the troops digging foxholes he was at the head of the advancing column. Raithel says that the I.G. "seemed surprised, and I don't think he would have driven in front of them had he known."

Nott "contacted the officer [possibly the sergeant's CO?] to be interrogated," and brought him to a nearby shed, where it was "fairly dry," for questioning. Raithel recorded the officer's testimony for Nott's final report. "My fingers were so cold and numb from the weather," Raithel recalled, "I hoped it would be possible later to read what I had written." Raithel said he "felt aggravation wondering what they would do to the boys if they had kicked him [the German general] all over the lot." It appears, from MacCombie's version of the account, that the sergeant had done just that.

Capt. R.K Doughty, Intelligence officer (S-2) for the 141st Infantry, was at the division CP (August 20) at Sisteron when the order came down from Corps Headquarters for the 36th to proceed to Montelimar posthaste and establish a roadblock on Highway 7. "Since the other two regiments of the Division were well to the north," he wrote, "there was little hope that they could be brought into the situation quickly." The mission fell to the 141st Infantry. Commanders put every possible means of transportation to use.

At one point, a "hospital column that just happened to be passing was grounded and its vehicles taken to provide transportation." Critchfield's 2nd Battalion, at the head of the regimental column, was the first to arrive at Sisteron. Col. Harmony ordered Critchfield to move out immediately. There would be no time to rest. The 2nd Battalion had been on the go since D-Day and the men were tired and hungry. Harmony rode in the lead vehicle at the head of the convoy. The 1st and 3rd Battalions were still en route.

Doughty "alerted" the regimental XO "by radio about the sudden new mission and the need to get cracking tactically and started for Montelimar with the I and R Platoon" (Intelligence and Reconnaissance). Doughty wrote, "The route from Sisteron to Montelimar was an unknown factor to the troops of the 141st Infantry." Doughty knew the units "would be driving at night and under pressures of time," so he "posted I and R guides at critical junctures." He later noted, "*The 36th Division History* does not describe the tangled terrain and maze of roads of the area that baffled both our own troops and the Germans."

Traveling in advance of the main column, over winding country back roads through German-held territory, was extremely dangerous, especially at night. As the I and R Platoon was nearing the town of Liveron, Doughty spotted a group of Maquis "squatting around a small fire near the road" and stopped to ask "about German troop dispositions." The Maquis leader informed him "that a German anti-tank gun was located around the next bend about a half a mile from where [they] stood." Doughty gives no indication as to how he was able to eliminate the obstacle before proceeding and before the following 141st Infantry column arrived. We can only assume that he called up attached armor or radioed for artillery fire. Having placed guides all along the route of advance, Doughty arrived at Marsanne during the early morning hours and waited for units of the regiment to arrive.

Major Marcel F. Pincetl of Kansas City, Missouri, a member of Headquarters and Headquarters Company, 1st Battalion, 141st Infantry, was present during the rush to Montelimar to block Highway 7. Shortly before his death, Pincetl related the following story of an unusual incident that took place during the advance to his friend John Coyne:

> It was night and we were moving forward under blackout conditions. We followed the noise of the tank treads ahead as it was too dark to see. When dawn came we found to our surprise that our jeep had been following a German tank. The tank noticed us also and stopped. We were lightly armed so we turned off the road and the jeep turned over on its side. (I hurt my back there.) We ran for cover. The tank backed up, the hatch opened, and the gunner took aim. Then one German soldier got out of the tank and walked to our jeep, took out his knife and cut the rope holding the wheel of cheese that we had liberated, and took it to the tank and left.

The tank "never fired a shot," Pincetl said. "They must have been real hungry, and we were sure glad." Paul D. Hinkle (L-141) wrote, "The Rhone-Drome valleys were wide open territory during that time. Fleeing German units and U.S. units were running the same roads. Sometimes the locals did not know the difference."

During the push north, units of the 36th Division had captured more than 1,700 prisoners. Opposite the road from the 1st Battalion (141st) CP, visited by Major Richard Nott, there were several POW cages containing large numbers of German prisoners. Nott's aide, Glenn Raithel, accompanied by one of the guards who happened to be from his old unit, interviewed several captured Wehrmacht soldiers. He said he was surprised to find that the prisoners were not "the least bit arrogant but quite satisfied and content." Most "talked freely" and were of the opinion that the war was lost and estimated that it "would be over in six weeks to six months."

Raithel learned that the average German soldier had a great fear of American artillery, "which they called 'whistling death.'" The massive displays of devastating firepower by Allied ground and air forces had a demoralizing effect on the battle weary German troops. This fact was clearly evident as indicated by his conversation with one young soldier. "It's no use," the prisoner said dejectedly. "If you live through the strafing by the American planes you have to sweat out the American artillery; if you are lucky enough to get through that deadly fire, the infantry comes up—it's just no use!"

What the Germans feared the most, Raithel discovered, was the French Maquis, "who had no mercy whatsoever on them." He related, "The Germans knew the French wouldn't hesitate to shoot them immediately if they didn't come out of their hiding places." At the first opportunity to surrender to the Americans, enemy soldiers, many of them conscripts, would rush out of the woods with their hands on top of their heads. Truscott claims that more than 4,000 Germans surrendered to American forces rather than risk capture by the Maquis.

As the remaining units of the 36th arrived in the Marsanne sector, first Butler, and then Dahlquist, after taking command of the operation, began to deploy the troops where the two commanders thought they would be the most effective. Advance elements of the 141st Infantry joined TFB late in the afternoon of August 23. Dahlquist dispatched the cannon and antitank companies to reinforce the Drome River force; he ordered the 1st Battalion, 141st Infantry to seize and hold the high ground south of Condillac and physically block Highway 7. The 2nd Battalion would move southwest of Marsanne and attack Montelimar; while the 3rd Battalion, which arrived later, was held in reserve. As soon as the rest of the 36th arrived, Dahlquist intermingled the units with TFB forces wherever needed.

Dahlquist positioned the 36th Division field artillery battalions, the 131st, 132nd, 133rd, and the 155th with attached battalions, which included the 141st and 977th FA, and the 59th and 93rd Armored FA (self-propelled), high up in the foothills northeast of Montelimar between Condillac and Puy-St. Martin (for the location of artillery batteries, see Montelimar Situation Map, No. 2–"GERMAN ATTACKS," from *The Fighting 36th, A Pictorial History*). Artillery FOs established observation points on the high ground overlooking the Rhone River to call in coordinates. From positions in the mountains, artillery and armored units "began to fire missions in a great arc south, west and north." The battle of Montelimar had begun.

Chapter Nineteen

The Battle of Montelimar Begins

According to Colonel (then Major) Vincent M. Lockhart, Assistant Adjutant General, 36th Division Headquarters, the Battle of Montelimar, France, began on the afternoon of August 23, 1944, with "the highest crescendo of the battle" taking place on August 26. The confrontation, which pitted elements of the German XIX Army, commanded by General Friedrich Wiese, against Major General John E. Dahlquist's 36th Division, with attached supporting elements, lasted approximately seven to nine days, depending on the source. August 23, 1944, marked the ninth day of continuous action for the troops of the division and the men were already beginning to show the effects of the strain.

The primary mission of division forces was to occupy and hold the vital high ground on the east bank of the Rhone River north of Montelimar and to interdict Highway 7, the German's primary escape route to the north.

Presented in the next two chapters is a highly detailed account of the initial phase of the battle, beginning on August 23, the day the 141st Infantry arrived in the sector, through the night of August 24 to 25. General Dahlquist charged the 141st Infantry Regiment with occupying and holding the Montelimar Ridge. Over the next two days, units of the regiment, supported by division and corps artillery batteries, directed a relentless shower of fire from every available weapon at its disposal, wreaking havoc on the long columns of vehicles and equipment of the German XIX Army heading north over Highway 7.

Beginning on the afternoon of the twenty-fourth, General Wiese mounted a major offensive operation to dislodge American forces from the heights in an attempt to relieve the mounting pressure. German commanders concentrated every available fighting unit, spearheaded by the tanks of the crack 11th Panzer Division, against the drawn out lines of the 141st Infantry holding the ridgeline. Following a series of fierce engagements, superior enemy forces succeeded in driving units of the 141st Infantry Regiment down off the ridge. Chapter 20 details the loss of this vital high ground.

To piece together a comprehensive narrative of the events that occurred over this critical forty-eight hour period, I have relied almost exclusively on primary source material (see "Sources" for the respective chapters). Of extreme value in the study were the 141st Infantry History of Operations reports, which clearly illustrate the seesaw action of battle, with both sides vying for possession of the heights overlooking the Montelimar Gap. These documents provide information on the movement and location of units, details of operations, major engagements with opposing forces, as well as an assessment of the outcome of each, and casualty lists. What is missing are German sources.

Other primary sources include first-person accounts of the battle by veterans of the 36th Division published in books, journals, periodicals, and gathered from personal interviews and correspondence. Used in combination, these present the reader with a picture of what battle conditions were like as seen from the perspective of the individual combat soldier.

On August 23, Lieutenant General Lucian K. Truscott, VI Corps Commander, issued orders for General Dahlquist to assume command of the battle from Brig. Gen. Frederick B. Butler, commander of Task Force Butler (TFB), as soon as possible. Dahlquist's headquarters contingent arrived in the Marsanne area, nine miles northeast of Montelimar, at approximately 3:30 A.M., and established a CP. Lockhart says the division commander requested that General Butler remain in control of the sector until he "could get acquainted with the area and the troop dispositions." Butler wrote that Dahlquist asked him "to continue direction of the action until later in the day while he was absorbing the situation and getting organized." The task force commander explained the battle plan he had been following to the general, "and Dahlquist asked for no changes."

Dahlquist ordered Col. John W. Harmony, CO of the 141st Infantry, the first regiment to arrive in the area, to relieve TFB as soon as all units were in position. Elements of the 36th, critically short of transportation, continued to arrive throughout the day and into the night.

Dahlquist dissolved TFB the following morning and all units reverted to division control. When Truscott visited Dahlquist's headquarters later that day, the division commander asked for permission to divert the 143rd Infantry, his reserve regiment, to occupy Valence, "in order to avoid trouble in capturing the place later." Truscott agreed, but directed Dahlquist to "reassemble Task Force Butler by dark so as to have [a] strong striking force in

Division reserve." The "reconstituted" TFB force, made up primarily of new units, carried out a number of key missions assigned to it over the next several days that the battle raged. Lockhart noted that the "records do not reflect what units were serving under Butler" at this time. General Butler wrote that the "original units did not come back, nor could it be anticipated from day to day what units would constitute the force." Butler concluded that the new group under his command saw "plenty of action," and during the span of its brief existence, conducted "some effective fighting."

No sooner had the 1st Battalion (141st) Commander, Lt. Col. William A. Bird of Barberton, Ohio, and his staff arrived in the sector when orders came down from regiment to "prepare for an attack on Hill 300," located at the north end of the "long ridge," overlooking the Rhone Valley north of Montelimar. This elevation was the highest point on the ridge. Company A drew the assignment. At Bird's request, 1st Lt. William A. Hawkins, the CO of Company D, attached a machine gun platoon and 81mm mortar section to Company A for support. Eight tank destroyers and three tanks would provide armored support for the mission. Once the battalion had taken and secured the

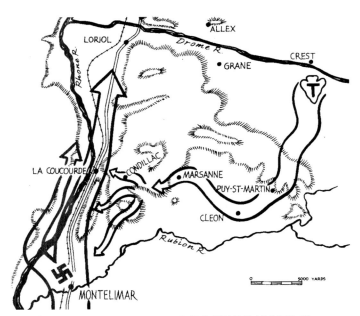

Montelimar Situation Map No. 1–"THE BATTLE IS JOINED. Elements of the 141st [Inf.] arrive to join Butler Task Force and attempt to enter Montelimar. German traffic pours up both sides of the Rhone valley" (Source: The Fighting 36th, A Pictorial History, see "Montelimar." N.p.).

initial objective, orders called for Bird to send a sufficient force down to the valley floor to cut Highway 7.

By noon (August 23), Company A had reached the top of Hill 300 without opposition and set up defensive positions. Company C moved onto the hill during the late afternoon hours, passed through Company A, and dug in to the south. Bird requested a second machine gun platoon from Company D to support Company C.

Toward evening, elements of Able Company made their way down the western slope of the ridge to the floodplain. The force proceeded to a point on Highway 7 southwest of Condillac near the town of La Coucourde, situated at the base of the ridge on the north, and established a roadblock.

According to the 141st Infantry History of Operations, the Germans launched an attack against the block at approximately 1 A.M. It appears that the purpose of the initial phase of the attack was the destruction of Able Company's attached supporting armor, as the force was successful in destroying six of the eight TDs and all three tanks. Eyewitness testimony (see below) indicates that a special antitank squad or platoon may possibly have carried out the mission. Later that night, a second, stronger enemy force, including infantry and tanks, made an assault against the roadblock successfully opening the highway, which allowed the convoys to continue their exodus out of the valley.

Sgt. David "Rosie" Rosenbluth, of the Bronx, New York, a "squad leader of the weapons platoon" (light machine guns and 60mm mortars) of Company A, related his recollections of the roadblock assignment (August 23) through his son Terry. According to Rosenbluth's account, a four-man patrol, led by 1st. Lt. Joe "San Antone" Sanchez, worked its way down the steep western slope to determine the safest and easiest route to the valley floor. Sanchez sent one man back to lead the rest of the company to the rendezvous point.

Upon reaching the highway, Rosenbluth says that before the sun went down the officers and NCOs carried out some "minor reconnaissance work," to determine the best possible defensive location for the block. Commanders moved tanks and TDs into position to bring fire on advancing enemy armor. Platoon leaders were in the process of deploying infantry squads for maximum combat effectiveness, but darkness fell before they could complete the necessary preparations, and the company, Rosenbluth says, "was in a state of disorganization."

Rosenbluth maintains that coordination and communications with attached armored units was nonexistent. Later that night, he said, "some of the tankers came over to the infantry positions and asked for support as they could hear German infiltrators and were worried." The infantry lieutenant answered curtly,

"You've got machine guns and personal weapons. You cover yourselves." The reply was not to their liking, and harsh words and threats passed between the two parties. No sooner had the bitter exchange taken place when "all hell broke loose with one of the TDs going up in flames and the other tanks and TDs getting hit." Rosenbluth said he heard no German armor approaching, so it is his belief that "German infantry with Panzerfaust [handheld antitank weapons] and magnetic antitank mines" had carried out the initial attack. "From that point on," Rosenbluth says, "the situation was one giant screw up with no one knowing where anyone else was, German infantry and tanks all over the place and general confusion."

Francis S. Quinn, Jr., a lieutenant with B Company, 636th Tank Destroyer Battalion, was attached to Headquarters, 143rd Regiment, as a liaison during the Battle of Montelimar. Quinn explained the strategy used by German panzers against American tanks and TDs:

> Our task force tried to stop the German Nineteenth Army, but there were too many Germans and they overran many of our positions. In the process, "B" Company lost 10 tank destroyers. The story I got was that when "B" Company's tanks pulled into position in camouflage in daylight, the German tanks were waiting for them. Already hidden, they zeroed in on the TDs and, when darkness came, opened fire.

This may very well have been the situation at the roadblock established by Company A near La Coucourde.

At this time, the Executive Officer of Company A was in charge. Rosenbluth remembered that the Commanding Officer had been wounded earlier, but was uncertain as to exactly when this occurred. The XO, he says, "was a battle fatigue case and should not have been there." Rosenbluth described him as "a good man but one who had seen too much and been pushed beyond his limits even before this battle, and at the road block he came apart and couldn't make any decisions." To the best of Rosenbluth's recollection, "the lieutenant died of wounds received during the attack, or possibly within the next several days." Recalling the engagement some sixty plus years later, Rosenbluth says that the details were "a bit hazy."

Later that night, Rosenbluth could hear the distinct clank-clank-clank and diesel whine of an enemy panzer approaching his position (most American tanks were gasoline-powered). Armed only with a carbine, he "figured it was an uneven fight" and decided to seek safety elsewhere. Just as he got up out of his hole and turned to flee, the machine gun on the tank opened up and Rosenbluth "took a bullet through both thighs and the scrotum." He "promptly" jumped back into "his nice safe ditch and waited for the tank to go somewhere else." Fortunately for Rosenbluth, the bullet hit only flesh and produced little bleeding. "A short while later," he said, "the platoon sergeant came by and told everyone to pull back."

Rosenbluth informed the sergeant he had been hit and asked for help getting to his feet. As incredible as it may seem, he managed to walk unassisted back to the aid station, set up in a small farmhouse some distance to the rear. Medics bandaged Rosenbluth's wounds and advised that he report to the battalion aid station in the morning so a doctor could stitch him up. He "spent the rest of the night sleeping in a nearby pigsty."

When the company received orders to pull out, Rosenbluth walked back with everyone else. At the battalion CP, he reported to the aid station where the doctor checked his wounds and tagged him for immediate evacuation to a field hospital. "My father was pretty much surprised by the decision," Terry says, "because he didn't think he had been hurt that bad" and "just wanted to be stitched up so he could get back to his unit." Medical personnel strapped Rosenbluth to a canvas stretcher and placed him in an ambulance headed for the 111th Field Hospital.

The trip, over bumpy, crater pocked back roads with many detours and stops, took more than eight hours. By the time Rosenbluth arrived, he says he "was really hurting." Rosenbluth was "quickly checked out by the surgeons" and transferred to a hospital farther behind the lines. The young sergeant finally ended up on a ship back to the main hospital in Naples, where he remained for more than three months. Doctors discharged Rosenbluth near the end of November and he rejoined his outfit on December 6, 1944.

His son Terry wrote that in his father's "own words," the situation at the roadblock "was a confused mess." With regard to his personal involvement, Rosenbluth concluded that he was "mainly concentrating on staying alive" so that his "view was pretty much limited to a few yards on either side of him."

The next unit to arrive at the 141st Regimental assembly area near Marsanne was the 2nd Battalion, commanded by Lt. Col. James M. Critchfield of Fargo, North Dakota. The battalion "set up in a grove of trees" just outside the town. Critchfield went to the regimental CP and reported to Lt. Col. John W. Harmony. The colonel directed Critchfield to make the necessary preparations "to attack and take the town of Montelimar," as soon as was possible.

The 3rd Battalion, commanded by Col. Paul D. Adams, was the last unit to arrive. Adams received orders to occupy the high ground four miles south of Livron (15.5 miles or 25 kilometers north of Montelimar), in the vicinity of Loriol, to prevent the Germans from sending reinforcements from the north.

Critchfield coordinated the attack against Montelimar "in conjunction with a platoon of tank destroyers and some tanks." The CO also had Troop B of the 117th Cavalry Reconnaissance Squadron and two companies of the French

Maquis at his disposal. The 59th Armored FA Battalion would provide artillery support.

At 3 P.M., the 2nd Battalion and attached units closed into the designated assembly area in the vicinity of the tiny hamlet of Sauzet, approximately five miles northeast of Montelimar. The CO scheduled the force to cross the Initial Point (IP) at 4:30 P.M., on the afternoon of the twenty-third. Much to the commander's dismay, the tanks and TDs failed to arrive at the appointed time, forcing him to launch the drive without the support of armor.

Company F, the 2nd Battalion "advance guard," closed in on the town from the northeast. Critchfield used Company G "as a diversionary and blocking force on both sides of the main road running [in a southwesterly direction] into central Montelimar." This byway, which connects Montelimar with Sauzet and Marsanne, runs north of and "parallel with the Roubion River," and served as the battalion's main supply route. Company E was in reserve.

Critchfield provided an account of the battle in a 1995 article in *The Fighting Historical 36th Quarterly*, titled "Setting the Record Straight on the Battle of Montelimar." Colonel Vincent M. Lockhart's book, *T-Patch to Victory*, contains a second account of the battle based on an interview with Critchfield in 1980. Critchfield began, "We [Company F] reached a point a little more than a kilometer from Montelimar, when we got into a heavy firefight with the Germans." Small-scale counterattacks occurred along the company's flanks as well.

The 2nd Battalion set up defensive positions on a "low hill with limited cover provided by a scattering of old stone buildings." Critchfield chose the strongest structure to establish his CP. German infantry, behind the protection of a staggered row of between eight to ten Mark V panzers, began advancing toward Critchfield's position. The beleaguered battalion managed to hold its ground against a far superior force, but continued taking heavy casualties throughout the afternoon.

During the heated exchange of fire, tracer bullets from the machine guns, both American and German, ignited the dry grass and brush over the entire front sending up a wall of flames that crept across the valley floor, flaring to great heights where the vegetation was thickest. It was a calm day, causing billowing clouds of gray-black smoke to hang like a pall over the battlefield. The dense haze, plus the onset of darkness near twilight, cut visibility almost to zero, stopping the action. It remained quiet for the remainder of the day and night, allowing Critchfield to resupply his units. As the morning dew descended, the remaining hot spots eventually petered out and died.

The attack resumed at dawn on the twenty-fourth and continued unabated throughout the morning hours. Company F, again in the lead, succeeded in cutting Highway 7 at a point just north of Montelimar. "I think our success astonished the Germans," commented Critchfield. At this particular time, vehicular traffic on the highway was sporadic. The bulk of the German XIX Army was still some distance to the south.

In an attempt to smash the block, German forces, "accompanied by a small number of Mark V tanks," launched a series of attacks from out of the town. At one point, Critchfield says, German tanks "ran right over our position," forcing the company to pull back. Casualties continued to mount steadily. Critchfield described the situation: "Gradually, we were forced back into a perimeter defense. Our connections to the rear were very tenuous—we really didn't have a rear area except for those up at Marsanne. There were no stable lines at this time."

Over the next six or seven hours the battle continued to mount in intensity. Fortunately, at about 11 A.M., Major Herbert E. Eitt of San Antonio, Texas, Critchfield's Executive Officer, came to the battalion's rescue with "four tanks and some infantry." The combined force managed to stem the attack, preventing a complete rout.

Initially, medical personnel evacuated the wounded by jeep ambulances to an aid station near the regimental CP at Marsanne. At noon, the Germans succeeded in closing the route, cutting the company off from the rest of the battalion. The medical officer set up operations in a "little hut" located just to the rear of the CP adjacent to a "deep cut road," and "began accumulating the wounded." When the hut could hold no more, medics placed the overflow along the edge of the sunken road, "which provided some shelter" from the intense fire.

About 1 P.M., Critchfield was observing the battle through his field glasses, when he picked up the movement of two German Mark VI tanks. "These were the first Mark VI 'Tiger' tanks that any of us had encountered," he noted. Critchfield provided a brief but vivid account of the ensuing, clearly one-sided, clash between the American and German armor:

> The battle between our medium tanks with 75mm guns and our tank destroyers with the larger 90mm guns did not last long. Hits on the forward armor of the German tanks seemed to be doing no damage; within a few minutes six plainly visible Mark VI tanks were firing on us. I could call up neither artillery nor air support. Within minutes[,] all of our tanks and tank destroyers were out of action—most in flames resulting from direct hits by the German 88mm guns on the Mark VI.

At 3 P.M., Critchfield received orders by radio from regiment to cancel the attack and withdraw.

Critchfield sent word down the line for his men to begin pulling out of the area at 9 P.M., and to take up positions on the high ground north of the Roubion River northeast of the town. The CO began making arrangements for a "sequence of artillery fires" by the 59th FA beginning at 8 P.M., to cover the withdrawal from, what he described as "our increasingly vulnerable position." At the appointed time, batteries of the 59th laid down a sixty-minute barrage of 155mm artillery fire after which the withdrawal commenced. Critchfield wrote, "we had experienced devastating casualties" and the "medical evacuation route [to Marsanne] had been closed since noon." The wounded were loaded on two vehicles, a TD that had its turret shot off, "dragging behind it a small disabled truck towing a 57mm antitank gun—all casualties of those formidable 88mm guns on the German tanks."

The history of the 141st Infantry Regiment, *Five Years, Five Countries, Five Campaigns*, provides the following summation of the battle:

> For us in the 2nd Battalion, Montelimar means a barren hill with German tanks and infantry surrounding us for six unforgettable hours; thousands of rounds of our own artillery thudding into the waves of Germans that were flung at our position from every side; Mark V tanks so close that you could feel the heat from the motor[s]; a withdrawal at night from a hill covered with burning, exploding tanks, knocked out guns and dead men. We will never forget the eery [sic] sight of a TD pulling a knocked out ton-and-a-half and a 57mm AT gun loaded down with 50 men swathed in blood soaked bandages and a handful of Medicos with their white and red helmets gleaming in the moonlight. We were all too dazed to think much; just surprised and thankful that we were still alive and free; thanking God for having the kind of Medicos we had; thanking God for the 131st Field Artillery [?] which was throwing hundreds of rounds of shells over our heads keeping the Krauts pinned down.

Lockhart attributes this passage to Critchfield who contributed material to the 141st regimental history regarding the 2nd Battalion's participation in the fighting at Montelimar.

What remained of the 2nd battalion moved east to the town of Marsanne, arriving at 1 A.M., on August 25. Here, Critchfield found the regimental commander, Col. Harmony, lying wounded upon a stretcher. Harmony, whose XO had become a casualty earlier, turned over temporary command of the 141st Infantry to Critchfield. The "situation of the regiment," Critchfield says, "was a shambles." Critchfield spent the next several hours assessing the damage and effecting a reorganization.

Years later, after touring the site of the engagement and retracing his steps on the battlefield, at which time he had a chance to "examine the area from the viewpoint of German commanders," Critchfield says he "came away convinced it probably had been a tactical error to send us into Montelimar." General Truscott later confirmed his assessment. The former VI Corps Commander told Critchfield "he had been astonished to learn that the 36th had sent a single isolated battalion out into the open plains of the Roubion to attack Montelimar itself instead of sticking to the high ground on the north of the Roubion to simply reinforce Task Force Butler."

On Hill 300 (August 23), the Germans launched a strong counterattack against 1st Battalion positions from the south with tanks and infantry in an attempt to dislodge the Americans and take possession of the commanding heights. The battalion came under intense enemy artillery fire, but managed to hold the line throughout the evening and into the night. Small German patrols, under cover of darkness, began to infiltrate through and around 1st and 2nd Battalion positions.

The slopes of the ridge were mostly barren with waist-high scrub oak here and there and scattered stands of trees, which was typical of the foothills region. The maze of trails and farm roads crisscrossing the countryside facilitated enemy movement. Because of the extensive area covered by the regiment, insufficient troop strength made it impossible to maintain close contact between units along the line to adequately block enemy infiltrations. Instead of one continuous front, the defense line was a lightly held network of outposts and strong points. Consequently, enemy patrols managed to get behind some units and cut off their routes of supply and reinforcement. German artillery was active throughout the 141st regimental area, subjecting units to continuous harassing fire.

It became increasingly clear to Harmony that in order to hold the Montelimar Ridge, as well as maintain an effective block on Highway 7, he would have to bring up additional troops. The urgent need for reinforcements prompted the Assistant Division Commander, Brig. Gen. Robert I. Stack, to recall several units tied up at roadblocks north of the Montelimar battlefield. On the morning of August 23, regiment ordered the 3rd Battalion, 141st Infantry, one of the units recalled, to "take over the positions" of Companies A and C on Hills 300 and 294, the two highest points on the Montelimar Ridge.

The night of August 23 to 24 ended on a quiet note. At 1 A.M., all battalions of the 141st Infantry Regiment reported no fighting in their respective sectors. Regiment alerted 1st and 2nd Battalions to expect a counterattack early the next morning. Enemy activity was evident across the entire regimental front as troops massed for another attempt at a breakthrough. The history of the 141st Regiment reported that the men in the forward positions could hear the constant hum of German motor transports moving along the roads, the clanking of tanks and TDs ("Jagdpanzers") maneuvering into position, and the muffled sounds of men shouting instructions. Throughout the hours of darkness, the entire regimental area was subject to sporadic artillery and mortar fire.

Lockhart described August 24 as the day that the battle of Montelimar "burst forth in all its fury." Beginning on this day, he wrote: "Elements of three German Divisions began pounding the 36th Division's lines—these were the 198th, the 338th, both infantry divisions, and the mighty 11th Panzer Division," commanded by Major General Wend von Wietersheim, "the best unit

Hitler had in southern France." Historian Jeffrey J. Clarke says that Wiese had received word on August 21 that American combat forces, including armor and artillery, had begun interdicting traffic a few miles above Montelimar, between the Drome and Rubion Rivers." The destruction of the bridges over the Rhone had trapped the 11th Panzer Division on the west side of the river. General Wiese's "immediate response was to urge" von Wietersheim "to hasten efforts to ferry his heavy vehicles across the Rhone and move north as quickly as possible to secure the German route of withdrawal."

German engineers constructed barges to transport tanks and heavy support vehicles to the opposite bank of the river, no mean feat. Consider that the German Mark V Panther weighed in at forty-five tons while the larger Mark VI Tigers tipped the scales at fifty-five tons (the King Tiger weighed between sixty-eight and seventy-five tons), making the crossing a monumental task for the engineers. By comparison, the standard American tank, the M4 Sherman, weighed only thirty-three tons.

The Germans were desperate to capture the strategic high ground east of the Rhone River highway. By this time, fleeing elements of the German XIX Army were arriving in the Montelimar area in greater and greater numbers. The sheer volume of vehicular traffic attempting to shoot the gap and continue their escape to the north, combined with stoppages caused by roadblocks, created a massive backup, three and four columns abreast that extended for miles.

As traffic continued to stack up behind the bottleneck, division and corps artillery "ranged up and down the highway delivering a steady stream of fire on the completely disorganized, bumper to bumper column of vehicles which included armor and horse drawn guns [artillery] and equipment." The main highway was under observation for a distance of sixteen miles. Hour after hour throughout the day and night, batteries hammered away at the "motionless enemy vehicles" trapped in the ever-narrowing pocket (VI Corps "After Action Report").

First Lieutenant Remus L. Jones of Corsicana, Texas, XO, Battery B, 132nd FA, provided the following account of the situation: "When our artillery destroyed a truck and the column stopped, another column would pull up beside them in an effort to pass. When the artillery stopped that column, another would try to pass and soon there were masses of burning vehicles and dead or wounded troops."

Paul D. Hinkle (L-141), a native of Frackville, Pennsylvania, who witnessed an artillery barrage on the fleeing German columns, wrote, "the artillery covered the Drome valley just north of Montelimar with the most devastating fire I have ever been close to! It looked like a thunderstorm rolling through the valley from a/o 0330 thru 0530, flashing and exploding rounds continued for almost 2 hours. Nothing moved in that place after dawn. Dead

"Road of ruin and retreat. This German convoy of approximately 400 vehicles was destroyed by cannon, mortar, and small arms fire on the outskirts of Montelimar, France. August 28, 1944" (111-SC-193586-S).

"6 Sept 44, Seventh Army, Montelimar Vicinity, So. France. American forces knocked out this horse-drawn German artillery piece. Supply truck and equipment are strewn over the ground." 163rd Signal Corps Photo Company. Photograph purchased on ebay. The NARA Special Media Archives Services Division was unable to locate the image.

men and horses, wrecked vehicles and wagons, all over the road." In a second account of the same incident Hinkle told how the Germans "that were alive and could walk, raised their hands and lined up to surrender."

Add to this Allied fighter-bombers, in direct support of VI Corps, which swept down out of the sky to pound away at the escape routes of the northward retreating Germans. One 36th Division historian described German losses, in terms of both men and materials, as "prodigious."

At the 36th Division reunion in Dayton, Ohio, in June 2002, John M. Hockenbury (F-142) who entered the Army from Bedford, Pennsylvania, related that the one thing about the battle of Montelimar that he remembers most vividly was the destruction of the German columns by U.S. Army Air Corps P-47 Thunderbolts. "From our position on the ridge overlooking the Rhone Valley, we could see the German convoys proceeding north up Highway 7." Hockenbury was very animated as he related his recollections of the action. "We watched as a formation of big bodied P-47s, with their huge

"An American tank [actually a self propelled gun–"M8 75mm Howitzer Motor Carriage"] rolls past destroyed German Vehicles on Highway #7 leading to Montelimar, France. Seventh Army. 8/29/44" (111-SC-193797).

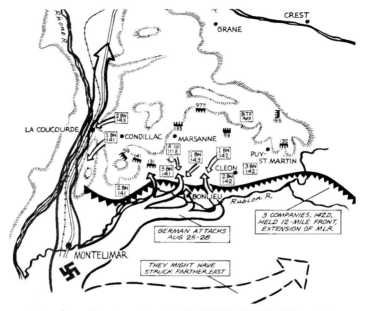

*Montelimar Situation Map No. 2–"GERMAN ATTACKS against
the Division main line, established along the Rubion creekbed,
were driven off. Eight Battalions of artillery raked enemy
forces streaming up Rhone valley" (Source: The Fighting 36th,
A Pictorial History, see "Montelimar." N.p.).*

cowls, came sweeping up the valley from the south. We were actually looking down on the planes from above." One ship "peeled off and knocked out
the lead vehicle. Another hit the vehicle in the rear, forcing the entire column
to come to a halt. The formation zoomed back around and made several strafing and bombing runs. They tore the convoy to pieces. We could actually see
the cannons flashing and the bullets exploding," he said excitedly.

During the afternoon of August 24, 1st Battalion received orders from regiment to retake the town of La Coucourde, six miles north of Montelimar, and
then, to reestablish the roadblock on Highway 7. Colonel William A. Bird,
scheduled the attack to begin at 1 P.M. German forces had forced the Americans out of La Coucourde on the previous day. The battalion commander designated Company B as the attack echelon, with Company A to follow. If need
be, assistance would be provided by the 3rd Battalion, which was being held
in reserve. To soften fortified enemy positions, combined fire from artillery
and tanks, as well as from the heavy mortars of Company D preceded the attack. By 2:30 P.M., units had entered the town in force and proceeded to clear

out the enemy. The sweep met with very little resistance. After securing the perimeter, defensive positions were set up.

As Company A was digging in, the Germans opened up with a heavy concentration of artillery and mortar fire, followed almost immediately by an unexpected counterattack with a strong force of infantry and panzers. The brief "Record of Events," attached to the Company A Morning Report for August 24, noted, "In afternoon enemy attacked company position with hand grenades." Headquarters reported seven casualties, including two killed. The defenders were about to be encircled, and the ammunition supply was getting dangerously low, when orders came down from battalion to pull back.

As more and more armor, artillery, and transport vehicles of the German XIX Army became penned up in the ever-narrowing neck of the Rhone Valley north of Montelimar, remnants of the massive force began to probe the "tenuous 36th Division line" for an alternate escape route to the east along the division's left flank, where the line was weakest. With an "end around" run to the east expected to come at any time, Dahlquist "elected" to set up a second major defense line north of the east-west running Roubion River, a tributary of the Rhone. The Roubion enters the Rhone just south of Montelimar. As more and more units of the 36th "hastily arrived," Dahlquist strategically deployed the troops "along [north of] the little Roubion streambed (in front of a vital supply road) on a flat, bowl-shaped plain backed by a wall of hills." It was not until late in the day on August 24, that the last units of the 36th Division finally arrived in the Montelimar area.

Dahlquist arranged his defenses along this second blocking line as follows: the 142nd Infantry "rushed over from Gap and Guillestri" to defend a twelve-mile front west of Cleon; three companies of the 142nd (battalion unknown) "HELD [a] 12-MILE FRONT, EXTENSION OF [the] MLR" east of Puy St. Martin on the far left flank; and the 1st Battalion 143rd Infantry, brought down from Valence, covered the middle portion of the line just north of Bonlieu, with assistance from two platoons of Company A, 111th Engineer Battalion (see next chapter). Dahlquist considered the Bonlieu sector to be the weakest point in the division's defenses.

Initially, the 117th Cavalry Reconnaissance Squadron was assigned the right flank, but could only do so using roving motor patrols, as the area of responsibility was much too large for such a small force. On the twenty-fourth, division ordered the 2nd Battalion, 141st Infantry to move to the area south of Sauzet to reinforce the 117th. The 1st and 2nd Battalions, 141st Infantry, remained in position on Hill 294.

Over the previous thirty-six hours, the division established several major roadblocks at key points on Highway 7, which commanders determined could be more easily defended, but German forces soon knocked them out. This allowed a number of enemy units to escape the trap. Lockhart wrote, "under the intense pressure aimed at the 36th Division, none of [the blocks] could remain effective for more than a few hours." There was nothing in the division's offensive arsenal that could stop the mighty tanks of the 11th Panzer Division. The behemoths, followed by infantry in superior numbers, would drive straight through, practically unimpeded, successfully smashing the block and scattering defenders. Supporting American medium M4 Sherman tanks and TDs, thin-skinned and outgunned, proved no match for the Panzer's 88mm high velocity guns. Once the way was open, German engineers would clear the road of debris and the columns would run the gap and continue the retreat to the north.

Chapter Twenty

German Forces Succeed in Driving Units of the 36th Division from the Montelimar Ridge (August 24–25, 1944)

Back on the ridge north of Montelimar, dawn (August 24) broke with an intense enemy artillery and mortar barrage across the entire regimental front of the 141st Infantry. Elements of the 3rd Battalion moved to the top of Hill 300 during the morning and took up "new positions," in an attempt to consolidate the line. Division ordered the remainder of the battalion to secure Hill 294 farther down the ridge. History of Operations reported that "constant enemy infiltrations kept all units occupied in beating off piecemeal counterattacks."

Following the aborted attempt to take Montelimar on the previous day, the 2nd Battalion moved to the high ground to the northeast, on the north side of the Roubion River. The ridge running from 2nd Battalion's position south to the Roubion "was heavily fortified by the Germans." At 7:30 A.M., a strong force of the enemy launched an attack, which was repelled. Second Battalion forces counterattacked with infantry, tanks, and tank destroyers "and gained the upper hand." German forces withdrew to their previous positions, reorganized, and attacked again. The battle raged back and forth with twenty enemy soldiers killed and another twenty taken prisoner. A three-man reconnaissance patrol, sent out by the 2nd Battalion, failed to return.

Enemy patrols managed to infiltrate around the right flank of the battalion, cutting the only supply line to the rear. "Every movement to the rear for supplies necessitated forcing a route." Lieutenant Colonel Critchfield, the battalion CO, sent out combat patrols to keep the supply line open. At one point, enemy tanks infiltrated through Company L and to the rear of Company M. Both companies reported heavy casualties. Harassing artillery and tank fire continued almost nonstop throughout the morning.

About noon, the 2nd Battalion, coming under intense pressure, had to abandon its positions on the high ground and fight its way to Le Martinet

(?), described as a "a tiny village one mile northwest of Montelimar." Upon reaching the objective, the battalion "organized a defensive position."

During the morning (August 24), 1st and 3rd Battalions, defending the Montelimar Ridge, had to fend off persistent enemy attacks to keep supply lines open and maintain positions overlooking the main highway. Enemy patrols and armored vehicles breached the line in several places, cutting off and isolating units from the main body of the 1st battalion. At noon, a large force of enemy infantry launched an assault against Company A. Colonel Harmony, CO of the 141st Infantry, advised Division Headquarters at 2:15 P.M., "that the regiment was so spread out that it was virtually impossible to keep the Germans from infiltrating through to the rear."

First Lieutenant Robert W. Brickman of Holstein, Iowa, a machine gun platoon leader (2nd Platoon) with Company D, 141st Infantry, received an assignment from his CO, 1st Lt. William A. Hawkins, to hold a section of the line on the Montelimar Ridge near La Coucourde. Brickman spaced out his machine gun squads to provide overlapping fields of fire across the entire forward area. One of the rifle companies assigned a 60mm mortar squad to Brickman's sector. Sgt. Jack Wilson, a member of the 2nd platoon, says that the mortar squad was located in a wooded area about fifty yards away, to his rear. On a trail running parallel with the crest of the ridge, just below Wilson's position, was a 57mm antitank gun and crew. A short distance to his right, a blacktop road ascended the hill.

Late in the afternoon of August 24, a German armored half-track, equipped with twin, heavy machine guns, pulled out of the retreating column of vehicles speeding north on Highway 7, and began advancing up the paved road toward Wilson's position, intent on putting a stop to the harassing fire from the American units. The half-track had a crew of three—the driver, a gunner, and his assistant.

Brickman could see a "squad of infantrymen," astride the advancing vehicle. He estimated that the unit consisted of "approximately 15–20 riflemen," but admitted he had "no time to count." The lieutenant realized that if the enemy force succeeded in breaching the line, they would discover how thinly spaced the troops of the regiment protecting that section of the ridge and possibly attempt a major breakthrough.

The half-track's heavy armor plate made it impervious to the fire from the platoon's .30-caliber machine guns and the vehicle continued to make steady progress on unit's position. The 60mm mortar squad fired several rounds at the approaching vehicle, but lacked accuracy. While attempting to adjust their fire, one round hit the branches of a tree above the position, causing the shell to burst overhead. Luckily, no injuries resulted from the blast. Wilson was leery of the mortar squad's position from the start. "I knew they were going to have trouble," he said.

Direct fire from the half-track had forced the crew of the 57mm antitank gun "to abandon their weapon and withdraw to a place of cover." As the Germans moved closer, Lt. Brickman called out to his men to see if anyone had any experience firing the gun, when Sgt. Frank A. Golwitzer of Flint, Michigan, answered in the affirmative. He told the lieutenant that he fired the weapon during basic training back in the states. Wilson says, he "had taken his basic training in an antitank company."

Leaving the safety of his foxhole, Golwitzer "crawled across the exposed terrain" under intense enemy fire to reach the antitank gun's position. He managed to load the weapon, aim it, and fire a round in the general direction of the half-track. The shell missed, but caught the German's attention. The enemy gunner spun his turret around and began concentrating fire against the antitank gun. With Brickman directing fire from his vantage point, Golwitzer closed the range. On his third shot (Wilson claims it was the second shot), he scored a direct hit on the engine compartment, effectively halting the enemy advance. As the crippled half-track sat burning by the side of the road, the infantry unit fled back down the hill.

Jack Wilson says that the German crew bailed out of the disabled vehicle and jumped into a large concrete drainage culvert that ran under the road for protection. Wilson wrote, "I let go about a half a belt of ammunition into the culvert. I was just at the right angle so that the bullets ricocheted around, killing all three men." Later, when the situation quieted down, a couple of men from his squad went down the hill to investigate. They returned and told Wilson that, in addition to the three Germans, they found six dead French citizens in the channel. The group had apparently taken refuge from the fighting and was hiding in the culvert.

Wilson wrote, "None of us had any idea there were civilians in there, and this bothered me for a long time to come. But it could not be helped. I had no knowledge of them being in the culvert."

Brickman recommended Frank Golwitzer for the Silver Star for "gallantry in action" on August 24, 1944, and submitted the request through channels for processing. Division approved the award, but the paperwork got lost and did not catch up with Golwitzer until after the war ended. Years later, the two men began to correspond and in one of Golwitzer's letters the topic of the Silver Star came up. Golwitzer wondered who had put him in for the award, and Brickman wrote to him that he had.

Brickman mailed me a copy of the citation that Golwitzer's son sent him after his father died. It stated that, instead of a half-track, "four enemy tanks charged the company's flank." Brickman later explained the discrepancy in a letter:

> As you can see, the official version differs considerably from the story I gave you and which was somewhat verified by Jack Wilson. In their zeal to obtain as many decorations as possible for the division, the higher-ups, if your write-up was considered lacking, would embellish considerably on the original. My story, related to you is the true story as it happened.

Golwitzer was supposed to attend the 2002 Midwest Chapter of the 36th Division Association reunion in Dayton, Ohio, and I was looking forward to meeting another veteran of Company D. He did not attend, and several members reported that he was in bad health and had entered the hospital. Frank Golwitzer passed away shortly thereafter.

While on the ridge, Sgt. Jack Wilson's machine gun squad was running low on ammunition so he sent a two-man detail back to the supply area. "I never saw them again," he said. Wilson later "heard that the two men had run into a German patrol and had been killed," but company records reveal otherwise. One of the men, Wilson says, was Pvt. Louis McCarter, "a full-blooded Cherokee from [Tahleqah] Oklahoma," the other was Marvin Castor of Guernsey, Wyoming. According to the Company D Morning Report for August 28, 1944, McCarter was wounded on August 24—"SFW [superficial wound?] l[ef]t hand." Marvin Castor is listed as "LWA [light wound in action] as of August 25." The discrepancy in the dates was probably due to inaccuracies in the M/Rs that occasionally occurred under battle conditions. The official 1946 division roster lists Castor as "MIA." Why McCarter never returned to the unit is a mystery.

According to several news articles provided by Castor's son, Charles, his father encountered a German patrol and received a bullet wound in the foot. Taken prisoner, he spent the remainder of the war in a German prison camp. McCarter "was a good man," Wilson says, "and could always be relied upon to do what was asked of him." He described Castor as "a damn good soldier."

Ernest Smeltzer (D-141), another member of Wilson's squad, remembered that McCarter, for whatever reason, never wrote home to his family. His concerned parents eventually contacted the Red Cross, who in turn went through channels to notify their son's company commander. Hawkins told Lt. Brickman to remedy the situation. Brickman says he "handed McCarter pen and paper and ordered him to get a letter off to his family immediately."

Jack Wilson related the following story to me during a chat at one of the 36th Division Midwest Chapter reunions. He later included it in his memoirs. Robert Brickman also provided me with his version in a letter. Sometime during the morning of August 23, in anticipation of a move to Hill 300, Lt. Brickman and Wilson went up to the summit to determine the best place to set up the machine guns. As they "were walking along the forward slope, a German machine gun emplacement, concealed by a patch of brush about fifty yards away, opened fire with a long burst." Both men hit the ground. The gunner fired a second burst. Wilson carried with him "a long handled shovel," which he had "picked up at a farm house nearby." The shovel, he said, "made digging in the hard, rocky ground a Hell of a lot easier than with an entrenching tool." A round struck the shovel, splintering the wooden handle. There was a third burst and several rounds slammed into Wilson's backpack.

Brickman called out, "Are you all right, Jack?", and rushed to his side. Wilson described the next series of events:

> I said, "I guess I am, I can feel blood running down my back, but I don't feel any pain." He said, "can you move your legs?" I told him I could. We knew that we had to get out of there real fast for our luck would not hold out for much longer. We both jumped up and ran back to the [far] side of the ridge, and were surprised when we didn't catch another burst of fire.

Once safely on the opposite side of the hill, Brickman told Wilson to pull off the pack so he could check his wound. It was then that the lieutenant realized what had happened. "What color is blood?", Brickman asked. Wilson, puzzled by the question, replied, "What do you mean?" One bullet passed through a can of warm beer that Wilson had stashed in his pack, "for a special occasion," and was running down his back and leg. He was much relieved, and the story later resulted in a good laugh.

The machine gun fire had badly damaged the pack and it was no longer usable. Later, Wilson took the pack and turned it in to the company supply sergeant, S/Sgt. John Paul Jones of Dallas, Texas, for a replacement. "John Paul was a good supply sergeant," Wilson acknowledged, but he "acted like the torn up [piece of] equipment was his own personal stuff."

Corporal Arlis D. Sizemore, another member of Company D, 3rd Platoon (mortars) was also in position on the ridge. "We drove the jeeps as close to the top as possible and carried the mortars and ammunition the rest of the way up," he recalled. "Lt. [William] Church, our platoon leader, showed us where to set up the guns in our sector." Sizemore says, "He chose a large gully just below the top of the ridge where we were protected from direct fire. We could not see the highway or the targets from where we were. Our FO moved to a position down the slope and called in our fire missions. We fired pretty much non-stop."

Throughout the battle for possession of the Montelimar Ridge, the lines of the 141st Infantry remained in a constant state of flux. Both sides attacked and counterattacked. Enemy units, using infantry-tank teams, would charge the line in an attempt to drive defenders back and off the high ground. The attackers would take up positions where their forward progress was stopped, dig in, and gird for an expected counterattack. Both sides repeated the process, the Germans seeking to advance, the Americans trying to hold the line, or to take back lost ground.

As had been mentioned earlier, the main line of resistance (MLR) was not continuous. It consisted of a series of independent strongpoints or strongholds spread across the defended frontage. The greater the distance to be covered, the larger the undefended gaps in the line. Each sector, manned by platoon or company strength, consisted of four, five, or more positions concentrated at possible access routes, such as, in this case, roads and trails, defiles, or areas of dense vegetation. One position was usually in sight of the next, but not always. Because of the shortage of personnel, platoon leaders usually left unlikely avenues of approach undefended. It was more like being on outpost, than part of an MLR. Communication between the CO and the forward elements was by runner from the platoon leader, who had the only means of communicating with the rear, by either radio or telephone.

German infantry, using the natural cover and terrain features to conceal their approach, or operating under cover of darkness, struck suddenly and without warning. Enemy attack forces would overrun the American positions, forcing defenders to beat a hasty retreat, resulting in a state of complete disorganization. Men often abandoned weapons and equipment, which needed replacing. Commanders called upon reserve units to launch an immediate counterattack against enemy penetrations. This option, however, was often limited because of the shortage of troops and the area to be covered.

Small enemy patrols, probing the line for any weakness, managed to slip undetected through one of the many gaps where the troops were thinly spaced. Once into rear areas, the Germans would cut off routes of supply and attack unsuspecting units from behind or flanks. At night, patrols searched for communication wires and followed them back to the source. The Germans, being particularly stealthy in their approach, would often catch the GIs unawares and take them prisoner or cut them down before they had a chance to react.

Company C (141st), in position on Hill 300, was subjected to a fierce frontal attack by a large force of the enemy infantry and armor. The CO urgently requested artillery fire from supporting batteries to assist in repelling the seemingly endless human wave of attackers. The barrage commenced with a deafening roar as artillery fires blanketed the slope below the forward positions. Hot shrapnel buzzed and whirred as it careened through the air in search of human flesh. Exploding shells chewed up the earth, causing the ground to tremble and quake. The staccato of explosive sounds caused by the different caliber guns blended into a syncopated rhythm that continued nonstop for thirty minutes.

The bombardment stopped as suddenly as it began, followed by an eerie stillness. Peering ahead, the men of Charlie Company could see the ghostlike silhouettes of enemy soldiers advancing through the haze and smoke. It seemed incredible that anyone could have made it through the wall of exploding shells that left not a square inch of ground untouched. As the smoke dissipated, a pockmarked landscape, void of all vegetation, came into focus. It was as they imagined the cratered surface of the moon to look. Mangled corpses and wounded Germans dotted the area to the company's front.

Units responded with withering fire in an attempt to beat back the charge, but enemy soldiers continued onward in a ragged line. Forward observers from Company D called for supporting fire from 81mm mortars to help stem the advance.

German infantry surged forward, dropped, and fired, using the bodies of their dead comrades for cover, then sprang to their feet and sprinted ahead a few more yards. When they got in close, the T-Patchers tried desperately to stop them with a fusillade of grenades. By sheer weight of superior numbers, the Germans managed to continue their advance all the way to the objective and the MLR began to deteriorate. History of Operations reported that during the engagement, the attacking force "drove the company back with heavy losses."

Late in the day of the twenty-fourth, enemy forces managed to capture "the two top peaks [Hills 300 and 294] at the northern end of the ridge," while elements of the 1st and 3rd Battalions, 141st Infantry, maintained a "tenacious hold" on "the lower northern slopes."

Just before last light, officers and NCOs went from foxhole to foxhole warning the men to be on the alert for enemy patrols attempting to infiltrate the line. Routine harassing artillery and mortar fire continued across the regimental sector, while off in the distance men could hear spasmodic fire from German machine guns, small arms, and the distinctive sound of burp guns.

As darkness descended over the area, the diminishing light played tricks on the eyes and minds of the American infantrymen in the forward positions. Visions and imaginary perceptions, hallucinogenic in nature, intensified near dusk. Men's imaginations started to work, causing bushes and trees to take on human form. Men perceived sounds from leaves rustling on the ground, or twigs and acorns dropping, as the footsteps of German scouts sneaking up on their position. Branches swaying ever so gently from the slightest breeze caused reflected light to flicker and shadows to dance.

All during the dark hours of night, men on watch searched the area to the front and sides with eyes and ears for any telltale sign that might give the enemy away. Eyeballs ached from staring intensely into the black void all around them. An occasional artillery or mortar shell bursting nearby, or the sudden appearance of the moon as it popped in and out of the thick clouds hampered night vision. Ears strained to separate natural night noises from possible movements by enemy soldiers. Sounds, which carried great distances in the still night air, seemed only an arm's length away. Any strange noise or movement sent hearts beating wildly.

GIs were under strict orders not to open fire unless under direct attack, lest they reveal their positions. As mentioned in an earlier chapter, officers and NCOs instead instructed the men to use a hand grenade, for the explosion would not pinpoint their location. Nevertheless, the safety on individual weapons remained in the off position and nervous fingers caressed the trigger. Riflemen had to fight off the compelling urge to empty a full clip into the darkness, especially if they believed that enemy soldiers were approaching, or they suspected activity nearby. Tension continued to mount as the seemingly endless nighttime hours dragged on. With everyone's nerves on edge, some men could not restrain themselves and opened up, firing blindly at any perceived danger.

Any noise or movement on the part of the GIs would likewise result in detection. Remaining perfectly still hour after hour put a severe strain on body and nerves. While sitting or lying motionless for hours at a time, bones ached and muscles stiffened and cramped. The hard, rocky ground cut off circulation, causing legs and buttocks to go to sleep. A shift in position brought needles and pins, adding to the overall discomfort. An itch, usually in an inconvenient place, from an insect bite, or a rash or cracked skin that developed on unwashed bodies, was a major source of annoyance. If a man had to leave his hole to urinate or defecate, it greatly increased the possibility of detection. Most went in their all-purpose helmets and tossed the contents off to the side.

Being on full alert twenty-four hours a day afforded the GIs no appreciable rest and the lack of sleep began to take its toll on mind and body. Restful sleep was all but impossible, owing to the constant buildup of tension in anticipation of a sudden surprise attack that could come at any time and from any direction. If one did nod off, he would awaken with a start and break out in a cold sweat. Jumpy GIs anxiously awaited the break of dawn.

General Frederick Butler, the Assistant Corps Commander, mentions an incident that occurred during the night of August 23, which will give the reader some indication as to what it must have been like for jittery line troops in anticipation of a surprise attack or discovery by a patrol. The lack of uncommitted troops forced Butler to attach two platoons from Company A, 111th Combat Engineers, to serve as rifleman with the 1st Battalion, 143rd Infantry, along the Rubion River defense line (see earlier). Engineers usually operated in rear areas, well behind the front lines. They had no previous experience "near or under fire," Butler wrote, and on this occasion, "it was their first exposure to enemy contact." The company was, he explained, "unemployed" at the time, there "being no engineer work in hand other than road demolitions which the riflemen themselves would handle."

It turned out to be a "sad night" for the company, wrote Butler, as men in the foxholes mistook each other for the enemy and engaged in a wild shootout. Butler described it as a case of "buck fever," which resulted in the unit suffering "more casualties than the infantry." The general added that with experience, the unit went on "to eventually accomplish first rate work as infantrymen." Unfortunately, the lesson proved to be a costly one.

There was no rest for the other side. Finding their progress impeded by the blocks, the German XIX Army faced slaughter and annihilation. Commanders tried to instill in regular Army units charged with breaking out of the cordon a sense of urgency with regard to the utter gravity of the situation. Units responsible for protecting the escaping columns stepped up the number of attacks and infiltrations, especially at night, to beat the Americans back from the rim of the Rhone Valley to provide a respite from the murderous artillery and heavy mortar fire.

German infantry and supporting armor were at a distinct disadvantage, having to continually attack uphill against an entrenched force. Units of the division drove the Germans back time and again, inflicting heavy losses. Assaults against the American forces continued without letup throughout the day and night. Only under cover of darkness did the advantage swing in favor of the Germans. Urged on by their officers, fighting by German units was fierce, becoming almost fanatical at times.

During the night of August 24 to 25, 1944, chaos and confusion reigned among the units of the 141st Infantry who were trying desperately to defend the Montelimar Ridge. The Germans attacked in force in an attempt to drive the Americans off the hill mass. Enemy patrols infiltrated the lines, cutting units off, and in some instances, as noted above, surrounded or captured small units defending their positions. As the Germans were about to overrun the lines, men abandoned their positions and headed for the safety of rear areas.

Panic often ensued. Men ran so far back they became separated from their outfits and scattered over a wide area.

Second Lieutenant John T. Scoggins of Dallas, Texas, leader of the 1st Platoon, Company D, 141st Infantry, positioned his machine gun squads in his assigned sector along the Montelimar Ridge and, it is assumed, returned to the company CP. Pvt. Harley R. Grotzke of Portage, Wisconsin, a member of the 1st Platoon, was an ammunition bearer for a machine gun squad. Grotzke was on the ridge overlooking the Rhone Valley during the night of August 24 to 25. The Germans overran, or infiltrated the position, and captured Grotzke, possibly along with other members of his squad. The August 28, 1944, company Morning Report lists Grotzke as missing in action "as of 26 Aug 44." The August 28 M/R also lists six other men from Company D as MIA on the 26th. Grotzke spent the rest of the war in a German POW camp.

In an article published in *The Fighting 36th Historical Quarterly* (Spring 1986), "Lost in the Rhone Valley," Cpl. John H. Lindsey, Jr. of Victoria, Texas, Company A, 111th Engineer Combat Battalion, provides an account of his ordeal after the Germans overran his position on the Roubion River defense line. Lindsey explained that the "infantry was too scattered to cover the front so the engineers were called up to help hold the line" (see above).

Lindsey and his buddy, Pfc. Daniel J. Ryan of Astoria, Long Island, New York, "were dug in a brushy area with a [.]30 caliber water cooled machine gun with several belts of ammo." The emplacement was positioned forward of the main defense line to afford the gun better fields of fire. Just prior to the attack, platoon Sgt. Donald D. Barnett of Texas City, Texas, sent word by runner for the two men to pull back to strengthen the MLR, but the order came too late. Lindsey and Ryan observed enemy tanks followed by infantry troops bearing down on their position. The Germans were mounting a full-scale attack.

Ryan swung the gun back and forth as far as it would go; spraying bullets across as much of the forward area as possible in an attempt to beat back the frenzied onslaught. Lindsey was feeding the ammunition belt and trying his best not to interfere with the motion of the gun so Ryan could maintain a steady stream of fire. Dead enemy soldiers began piling up in front of their position, but still they came. Eventually, the barrel got so hot from the almost-continuous fire that the gun jammed. Ryan had difficulty removing the breech so he could toss it away before withdrawing, a standard procedure that rendered the weapon inoperable.

Cut off, the two men headed for cover in a "cement and brick two-story building" about 100 yards away. Bullets were cracking all around their heads and kicking up the ground as they raced for safe cover. An eight-foot-high gated wall surrounded the courtyard. As they entered the compound, machine gun bullets splattered against the fieldstone wall. Lindsey says he "felt the heat from the bullets and froze for a few seconds." Upon reaching the house, they entered the doorway and charged up the stairs. Enemy tanks and mortar crews opened fire, filling the structure with smoke, dust, and flying debris from well-directed blasts. They huddled in a corner of the room and instinctively covered their helmeted heads with their arms, as if that might protect them.

The intensity of the shelling forced Ryan and Lindsey to bail out of a second-floor window, narrowly escaping death from a direct hit on the room they had just vacated. Lindsey, the first to jump, made it to a clump of bushes where he lay hidden, feeling that his heart would pound out of his chest. His friend Ryan was not so fortunate. Two Wehrmacht soldiers came darting around the corner just as he hit the ground. Without a word from the Germans, he automatically dropped his weapon and put his hands on top of his head.

The two Germans stood between Lindsey and Ryan's position, blocking the line of sight. "I couldn't fire at them for it would have endangered Danny's life," Lindsey wrote. The two Germans took Ryan prisoner and led him away. When it appeared safe to do so, Lindsey headed back in the general direction of the American lines. At one point, he came to a large area of swampland interspersed with tall reeds and thick low brush. The landscape was broken here and there by an occasional hillock or raised mound, covered by a stand of tall trees choked with thick, hanging vines.

For several hours, Lindsey continued to slog along in the wetland area with water knee-deep in some places. The thick vegetation and uneven ground hindered his progress and the going was slow. High overhead, the hot Mediterranean sun beat down unmercifully. The stifling, oppressive heat, combined with the high humidity of the swamp air, caused him to sweat profusely. Clouds of pesky insects surrounded his head and face. The exposed parts of his body soon became a mass of welts from insect bites. To gain some measure of relief from the itching, he slapped and scratched until the sores oozed blood.

During the afternoon, Lindsey happened upon a small party of enemy soldiers who had stopped to rest and eat. He was almost upon them before he realized it and quickly slunk down in the murky water, keeping very still. "I didn't move or even breathe loud," Lindsey related. As the soldiers were finishing their lunch, they tossed uneaten scraps of food into the foul-smelling, algae-choked swamp water. It had been many hours since Lindsey had eaten anything, and he had gnawing pangs of hunger from the hard going through the muck and mire. After the Germans went on their way, he greedily plucked the scraps out of the slime and devoured them. The leftovers made tasty morsels, for which he was thankful, and provided him with energy to keep going. Lindsey had emptied his canteen long ago, and the thought of a cool drink of water occupied his every thought.

Corporal Lindsey continued trudging through the swamp until dusk, as it afforded him greater cover and concealment among the patches of brush and high grass. As night fell, the temperature dropped precipitously. "I was very cold" and "every bone in my body ached," he wrote. Traveling by moonlight, Lindsey continued until he could no longer go on. Just after dawn, he found a patch of dry ground and concealed himself among some bushes. Despite his physical discomfort and the ever-present insects, he fell fast asleep.

Lindsey is not sure how long he slept. When he finally awoke, he was very weak and unable to get to his feet. "I just felt limp, couldn't keep my eyes open," he wrote. The last thing he remembered before blacking out was the outline of two shadowy figures coming toward him. Luckily for Lindsey, they turned out to be members of the FFI. Sometime later, he awoke and found himself in a "French underground headquarters" surrounded by a group of resistance fighters carrying an assortment of weapons. On the table in front of him were two glasses, a large one containing French wine and smaller one with water. He grabbed the larger glass and gulped it down. "I thought it was going to burn my insides out," he recalled. The men offered him a little bread and some cheese, which he greedily consumed. Because of the language barrier, he had difficulty trying to explain that he "wanted to get back to the American lines," which was probably not necessary.

Next, two armed Frenchmen put him in the back of a black Citroën sedan and, with a third man at the wheel, drove him to an abandoned, partially bombed-out stone building where twelve other GIs from the 36th Division were hiding. Lindsey thanked the Frenchmen and waved as the car drove back along the valley road in the direction from which it had just come. He watched in horror as the vehicle struck a mine in the road, flipped on its side, and burst into flames. This, he said, "drew fire" from enemy soldiers positioned in the surrounding hills. The "car was demolished and all the Frenchmen killed," he remembered sadly.

The T-Patchers, it turned out, "were from the infantry, artillery, and other parts of the division," men who "had also been cut off from their units." A Tech Sergeant, the highest-ranking member of the group, took charge. What little food and water they had, the group shared among them. When darkness fell, half the men slept while the rest stood guard, alternating every two hours. During the night, a mortar round, apparently intended for the building, landed close by without exploding. At daybreak, the men set out in an attempt to get back to the division, walking for "two days and nights" before finally making contact.

Upon reaching the division lines, the men said their goodbyes and split up, each to locate his own unit. After Lindsey finally tracked down his outfit, the men gave him a hearty welcome. His First Sergeant told him, "I knew you would make it back." Rumors of his death had been circulating since his disappearance, as Lindsey had been away for more than four days. The company clerk was "getting ready to place me missing in action," he said. Lindsey learned that his entire platoon "had a rough time getting back also."

At war's end, his buddy Danny Ryan, recently liberated from a POW camp, returned to the company. It was a joyful reunion. Lindsey was surprised that Ryan looked none the worse for his ordeal. He told Lindsey that he had "worked on a potato farm and so ate a lot of potatoes." Lindsey says, "We rejoiced that we both lived through the war."

Fierce enemy counterattacks all across the 1st Battalion, 141st Infantry Regiment's front during the night of August 24 to 25, eventually succeeded in pushing the American troops down the back slope and off the ridge. At 10 P.M., Colonel Harmony, the Regimental CO, ordered the battalion to abandon its positions and move to the high ground to the east and occupy Hills 430 and 262 to reorganize and dig in, in anticipation of a continued push by the Germans. Located northwest of Sauzet, the two prominences, dominated the valley of the Roubion River. The 141st Regimental CP, located at Condillac, came under attack, forcing headquarters personnel to move their operations farther east to the vicinity of Marsanne. At 2:30 A.M. (August 25), the 3rd Battalion received orders to abandon its position on the ridge and join the 1st Battalion on the high ground northwest of Sauzet.

By 3 A.M., on the May 25, the Germans were in possession of the entire ridge. With the heights cleared of American forces, the German XIX Army resumed its flight to the north over the Rhone Valley highway practically unimpeded.

Later that day (August 25), Major General Wend von Wietersheim, commander of the 11th Panzer Division, received orders from General Wiese to clear the Americans from the entire area. General von Wietersheim massed his armor together with the bulk of the 198th Infantry Division and remnants of several surviving infantry divisions, two Luftwaffe air defense regiments, and several other smaller units, along the southern bank of the Roubion River. With added support from "several railway guns," von Wietersheim "launched five separate attacks" against 36th Division forces, "while his armor struck deep into both flanks" in an attempt to surround the American positions, wrote Jeffrey J. Clarke. "But lack of coordination hampered the complicated series of attacks, which met strengthened American resistance." The 36th Division historian wrote, "On two successive days, regiments of the German 198th Division bolted against the center of the Roubion line at Bonlieu and were thrown back in a fury of fighting by battalions of the 143rd and 142nd."

As mentioned at the beginning of this chapter, General Truscott chose the 36th Division to be part of the southern France invasion force on the strength of its recent successes in Italy. The question is, did the division live up to the VI Corps commander's expectations? Brig. Gen. Carl A. Baehr, the Corps Artillery officer, and Brig. Gen. Frederick B. Butler, the leader of TFB, were highly critical of Maj. Gen. John E. Dahlquist's handling of the situation, both on the drive inland and after taking over as battlefield commander from Butler in the Montelimar sector. Truscott himself, in his initial assessment, had expressed "disappointment" with the division's overall performance. Was this criticism justified?

Colonel Vincent M. Lockhart, in his book *T-Patch to Victory*, has, in my opinion, adequately refuted all criticism leveled at General Dahlquist and the 36th Division concerning two major controversies: first, the lack of speed in moving troops into blocking positions at Montelimar following the orders to proceed inland with all due haste and, second, the failure to halt the drive of the retreating German XIX Army (see Lockhart, Chapter 4, "Controversies").

Lockhart, in his highly detailed analysis of the battle, cites numerous logistical problems, primarily the lack of sufficient organic transportation, a shortage of precious gasoline, as well as a critical manpower shortage in covering such a large area of French countryside encompassing the battlefield, as the leading causes of the purported "deficiencies and outcomes." Colonel Lockhart's critique is supported by statements and observations made by several staff officers of the 36th Division, who later attested to the many problems encountered. At the time Baehr and Butler leveled their criticism at Dahlquist and the division, they may not have been aware of the scope and magnitude of these problems, and so did not consider these factors.

Truscott later admitted that although the division had been unable to stop the German retreat entirely, it managed to inflict considerable damage in terms of men and equipment. Lockhart also pointed out that, while a portion of the enemy force "escaped to fight another day . . . the cost of reequipping and remanning must have been a terrible burden." Upon touring the battle site by air shortly after its conclusion, Truscott could not deny that the losses to the German XIX Army were far greater than his staff had initially led him to believe.

In his final assessment of this engagements, one of the great battles of World War II, Truscott commented, "I know of no place where more damage was inflicted upon troops in the field." He added, "Even if Montelimar had not been a perfect battle, we could still view the record [of the 36th Division] with some degree of satisfaction." Lockhart, in his closing comments, described the Battle of Montelimar as "a great victory for the Americans, and, especially for the great 36th Infantry Division."

Chapter Twenty-One

The Night of August 24–25, 1944

At some point during the night or early morning hours of August 24 to 25, members of Company D found Joe Connole huddled in a depression, confused and disoriented, and escorted him to a medical aid station for evaluation. The preliminary diagnosis was "battle fatigue," which medical personnel later confirmed. When questioned about his breakdown by a Veteran's Administration (VA)-appointed psychiatrist at a later date, he stated that on the night in question, "two buddies of his were shot" (doctor's report).

The Company D Morning Reports (M/Rs) between August 15 and 30, list only one man killed during this period, and that occurred on August 15, 1944 (the day of the landings), a clear indication that his buddies were wounded and evacuated or possibly captured. The brief VA record of this incident contains no other details.

Copies of military records contained in Joe Connole's VA file also reveal that, in addition to the loss of his two combat buddies, there were a number of other extenuating circumstances, that occurred over the preceding four to six weeks, which had a direct bearing on his mental stability and likely contributed to his eventual breakdown. I discuss these below. Also contained in my father's VA file is information regarding his subsequent recovery and return to duty.

The trauma of losing close comrades in combat, possibly seeing them gunned down in battle, was the culminating event that sent Joe Connole over the edge. Finding himself on the battlefield, at night, alone and scared following the loss of his squad mates, caused him to reach his "breaking point," to succumb to combat exhaustion. His buddies were his strength; they had sustained him through difficult times. Without the close support of friends, he could no longer hold up under the strain of combat.

This chapter will reconstruct the series of events that preceded my father's temporary breakdown on the night of August 24 to 25, 1944, and to piece together what happened on that fateful night. The complete story, unfortunately, my father took to his grave. Unless someone who was present that night happens to turn up, which is highly unlikely, but not entirely out of the realm of possibility, all of the facts will remain unknown. I have presented here several possible scenarios based on the few facts available in his VA File, accounts contained in the division and unit histories, information provided by family members, and, because of the incomplete evidence, by the use of conjecture in an attempt to fill in some of the blanks. I have posed numerous questions for consideration, as they arise, for the reader to ponder. I have also presented several possible answers and outcomes as well. For some questions, of course, there are no answers.

On the evening of August 24, the 1st Battalion, 141st Infantry, was defending positions somewhere on the southern end of the Montelimar Ridge. Joe Connole's mortar section was, as standard procedure dictated, set up some distance behind the infantry platoons manning the forward positions. One distinct possibility is that at some point during the night, a strong German force may have breached the Main Line of Resistance (MLR), driving the defenders back.

When the initial attack on the MLR began, the rifle company holding the line would have radioed for fire support from mortars and artillery to help stem the enemy advance. If a sudden breach of the line did occur, the mortar FO would likely have alerted the mortar section by radio or telephone. The mortar crews would have had to pick up fast, or abandon the position, and get out of the area. It is also possible, that the mortar section was unable to withdraw in time and enemy troops overran the position.

Yet another possibility is that a German patrol infiltrated behind the lines and stumbled upon or surprised the mortar position. There is a high probability that this is what had occurred, as an assault on the frontline would most definitely have alerted the mortarmen as to the presence of enemy troops in the area, and if combined fire could not stem the attack, it would have afforded the group time to prepare a defense or to pull back.

In the case of an infiltration, the first indication that the position was under attack would have come when guards, outposted to secure the mortar section's perimeter (standard procedure), detected the presence of the enemy. This, of course, depended entirely upon whether the guards were in place at the time. Security may have been lax, especially to the rear of the MLR, and German troops may have taken the mortar position completely by surprise.

Generally, the area behind the front lines was relatively secure, but during the battle of Montelimar, an attack could have come from any direction, as indicated in the previous chapter. Knowing this, the likelihood is that the platoon leader or platoon sergeant posted a guard detail around the entire perimeter. Because my father was an ammo bearer, the platoon sergeant may have assigned him to guard duty.

At Montelimar, commanders had to spread the defenses out due to the coverage of so large an area with such a small force. Had a German patrol made it through and past the spread-out infantry squads of the 1st Battalion and penetrated into a rear area, there would have been little or no early warning.

The standard mode of attack for enemy troops would have been to rush the mortar platoon's position, running and shooting as they moved forward in leapfrog fashion. Upon detection of the position, members of the enemy attack force most likely would have opened with an intense concentration of small arms and automatic weapons fire. The Germans may have used 50mm light mortars (comparable to the U.S. 60mm) in the attack as well. Once in close, enemy soldiers probably lobbed potato-mashers. A surprise attack in the dark would have created a tremendous amount of confusion.

Mortar personnel, equipped with standard issue M-1 carbines or .45 caliber side arms, would have been no match for the greater firepower of German infantry armed with an array of automatic weapons. While muzzle flashes would have given the presence of the enemy force away, hitting a moving, crouching target with small arms carried by members of the mortar platoon would have been nearly impossible in the dark. Zigzagging as they advanced and then dropping to the ground, the forward element would have provided intense covering fire as those behind moved up.

It is entirely possible, as mentioned above, that the mortar section was, at the time the attack occurred, executing missions. If so, exposed crews would have been extremely vulnerable to weapons fire. The noise of firing mortars would have led a German patrol directly to the platoon's position and would also have masked its approach until they were almost on top of them. When the firing started, everyone would have scattered for nearby foxholes or the nearest cover. For the men subject to a sudden, surprise attack at night, pandemonium reigns.

Complete surprise could possibly have forced the mortarmen to hurriedly abandon their positions, heading in the opposite direction from which the attack was coming. The clatter of rifle and automatic weapons fire in close, interspersed with the explosion of grenades and mortar rounds, must have unnerved the men of the platoon, who did not normally come under direct attack by enemy forces. Panic must have ensued, scattering members of the platoon.

During the noise and confusion of the battle, men suddenly found themselves separated from their units and from each other. It is possible that some men received wounds during the initial attack and were taken captive after the engagement and went missing in action (MIA). German troops may have cut a number of others down as they fled. The mortarmen likely did not stop running until well after the firing ended. With the company widely dispersed, many would have lost their way in the dark (see previous chapter).

As stated above, at some point during the night of August 24 to 25, two of Joe Connole's buddies were wounded, either during an initial surprise encounter or at an earlier time. If not firing missions, this may have occurred as they rose up out of their foxholes to locate the source of the weapons fire directed at their position or as they tried to get to safe cover.

The VA doctor's report reveals, "In spite of orders not to fire at all, he fired his gun aimlessly into the night." Orders dictated that men on the front lines hold their fire at night to prevent the muzzle flashes from giving their position away, as discussed in an earlier chapter. Standard procedure called for the men to use a grenade if they suspect enemy activity in their forward sector. This might have occurred right after German small arms or machine gun fire wounded his buddies. This is the only information provided by Connole's VA file concerning the incident.

If an all out attack against the mortar position did in fact occur, the men, Joe Connole among them, might have panicked and run. We can only surmise what it must have been like for the individual soldier under fire fleeing for his life, alone in the dark, his night vision hampered by flashes of light. Running away at top speed, he probably dodged and weaved as he ran through the thick growth of scrub brush and trees. To slow his descent and prevent himself from falling headlong down the steeper slopes and precipitous rocky ravines that characterized the region's rugged, hilly terrain, he grabbed at tree branches and held on to large rocks. Branches snagged at his clothing and snapped in his face. Bullets clipped twigs and leaves and whistled past his ears as he ran. Tripping over rocks, fallen limbs, and brush, he fell, got up, and continued running.

The massive rush of pure adrenaline coursing through a man's veins would have carried him far beyond his physical capacity. As shells landed nearby, the flash of the explosions lit up the night sky. He continued to run until his legs could no longer carry him and, when his strength finally gave out, collapsed exhausted in a heap on the ground. He lay there gasping for every breath, his chest heaving as he fought to get air into his lungs.

Finding himself alone in the dark, the fleeing GI feared that enemy soldiers were close behind and closing in. To prevent detection, he probably moved to a nearby clump of dense underbrush or other place of concealment. Possibly, he crawled into a depression or behind a large rock or tree for protection. He could hear his heart thumping, like a big kettledrum, positive it was going to explode inside his chest. German soldiers could be anywhere. So sure that the sound of his heavy panting and pounding heart would give his position away, he cowered in his hiding place, concealed by thick foliage.

After a while, the man's breathing slowed and he began to detect strange noises in the dark. Small critters lurking in the underbrush scurried about, emitting faint calls and cries. Insects buzzed noisily around his head. Every little sound became magnified, causing his chest to tighten from the heightened anxiety. His mind raced, conjuring up the worst possible fate that could befall him. Were German soldiers creeping up on his position? He was sure they were coming to hunt him down. Would they discover his hiding place?

Occasional flashes of varying intensity, coming from beyond the distant horizon, lit up the sky with a glow and silhouetted the crest of the ridge. The muffled sounds of explosions and small weapons fire coming from some far-off encounter reverberated across the hills and down the valley behind him. The flickering light made the bushes and scattered trees appear to move and take on strange and haunting shapes. He strained his ears and eyes for some telltale sign of enemy soldiers approaching and imagined he could hear foot-steps and see movement. The combination of noises and light spooked him. In his heightened state of agitation, he may have panicked and run some more.

Could this have been what happened to Joe Connole? Filled with terror and fear of detection, it may have been at this time that he fired his rifle against orders.

The difficult question for me, which I will attempt to address, is whether my father panicked and left his seriously wounded buddies behind? As painful and disturbing (but understandable as well) as the possibility might be, it is just too important an issue to ignore. If he did indeed run away, what were the circumstances? Was the instinct for self-preservation, or the fear of dying, so inherently strong that it caused him to flee? Was it a situation where he felt nothing more could be done for his buddy or buddies? I would like to think that he would not, and did not desert his close friends in their time of need.

Another possibility is that the two men received their wounds a short time earlier in the night or during the day, and medics evacuated them to an aid station. Thereafter, the support he had come to rely on to get him through the difficult times in battle was lacking and his mental stability probably began to deteriorate rapidly. When Joe Connole realized the enormity of the loss of his comrades, he eventually broke down.

If he was overcome by fear and fled, which is purely conjecture, was he haunted by guilt feelings? Did he carry these feelings with him for the rest of the war and forever thereafter? Unfortunately, the truth will forever remain a mystery.

One of the first things I did was to check the Company Morning Reports (M/Rs) for the dates August 15 through August 28, 1944, in an attempt to identify my father's two buddies who were shot. On August 25, the M/R has Connole listed as "Fr[om] duty s[ic]k to abs[ent]." The company clerk posted all casualties from August 15, the day of the landings, through August 28, 1944, on the latter date. Two men were listed as wounded on August 25, Pvt. Marvin E. Castor (spelled Caster on the 36th Division 1945 roster) of Guernsey, Wyoming, and Pvt. James J. Greene (no hometown listed on the 1945 roster). The 1945 roster has Castor listed as MIA. Greene entered the service at Camp Croft, Spartanburg, South Carolina. Soldiers usually reported to the Army base nearest their hometown.

For a long time I believed these were my father's two buddies. Castor, I discovered later, was a member of a machine gun platoon. Greene is still a possibility. I spoke with Castor's son Charles, who sent me several articles from the local Guernsey newspaper, indicating that on the day of his father's capture he received a bullet wound in the foot. He spent the rest of the war as a POW in a German prison camp (see previous chapter). Castor was one of the two men Sgt. Jack Wilson (D-141) sent to a supply dump on August 24, to replenish the squad's dwindling ammunition supply and never returned.

As shown, the M/Rs were not always accurate. A man may have been un-accounted for but not listed as MIA for several days, as in the case of Cpl. John H. Lindsey (A-111). Reports from August 15 to the 27, reported "NO CHANGE." With Company D scattered in all directions, some lost or other-wise unaccounted for, others taken captive by the Germans, compiling an ac-curate report of the missing or wounded would have been difficult for the company clerk. Under battle conditions or rapid pursuit of the enemy, mis-takes in the M/Rs were a common and understandable occurrence.

Company D reported no one as MIA until August 28, 1944, when the names of seven men appeared on the M/R—all went missing between August 24 and 27. Six others, who received light wounds in action (LWA) between August 24 to 27, were also listed on the report of August 28. Any of these men could conceivably have been my father's buddies.

On the morning of August 25, 1944, Joe Connole was "taken to an aid sta-tion" ("Clearing Station 111 Med Bn"), where medical personnel diagnosed his condition as "Battle Exhaustion." Two days later, on the twenty-seventh, doctors transferred him to the 51st Evac Hospital for further evaluation. Clearly, what caused his breakdown was the loss of his two combat buddies, most probably the result of intense fire from small arms and automatic weapons fire during an enemy attack on his mortar position earlier that morning or during the previous night.

Next, is an analysis of Joe Connole's VA medical records, which indicate that, several weeks prior to the event, he received some rather disturbing news from relatives at home that his wife Mary was suffering from tuberculosis, and the family physician had her admitted to a long-term care facility.

On September 5, while at the Evac Hospital, Connole was examined by a doctor, one "G.M. Beels, Maj.," possibly a psychiatrist. His brief report, portions of which are indecipherable (because of poor handwriting), reads in part: "This is an emotional reaction. Is concerned about wife who is in T.B. Sanitarium for a [illegible] after having had two children in rapid sequence." Further on, he wrote, "[Connole] thinks there is a personality change in past 6 weeks—became more reclusive." Apparently, the news about his wife had been uppermost in his mind during that time. This, plus his reentry into combat, must have affected his mental state.

Overcome by feelings of hopelessness and inadequacy because of his inability to do anything about the situation at home, he probably became deeply despondent, which no doubt eventually caused him to sink into a state of severe depression. My father was normally a quiet and introverted person. Major Beels was somehow able to gain his confidence and get him to open up about what was troubling him.

The constant worry and concern for the welfare of his wife and young children, combined with the anxiety and fear of battle, probably lowered his resistance to stress, thereby increasing his vulnerability to psychological collapse. His sister Helen, in the meantime, had taken temporary custody of his two young sons, which, no doubt, eased his mind somewhat.

In all probability, the disturbing news lowered his resistance to disease as well (see below). These combined factors evidently proved too much for him to handle. Over time, the situation at home, plus the strain of battle, eventually caused him to reach his limit and were, without a doubt, major factors in his eventual breakdown.

According to Joe Connole's clearing station medical records (August 25), "he slept for two days, cried a great deal, and then felt better." Most likely, medical personnel sedated him, which was standard procedure.

Shortly before his death in 1990, he mentioned to my sister Kathleen that during the war he had suffered from "shell shock," of which I learned only recently. Not being familiar with the term, she had absolutely no idea what he meant. Shell shock was a medical term used to denote psychological casualties in World War I. "Battle fatigue" or "battle exhaustion," was the terminology commonly used during the Second World War. If the Germans had preplanned an attack on this part of the line, an intense artillery and mortar barrage would have preceded the operation. Thus, his use of the term "shell shock" in reference to his condition, as he later may have associated this to be one of the causes of his breakdown. A combination of the barrage and the wounding of his buddies would have been the final straw that triggered the collapse.

The U.S. Army Medical Corps recognized two major classifications of battle exhaustion, or battle fatigue: acute and simple. At a medical aid station, personnel carried out psychiatric screenings to sort out the more serious cases. After a preliminary evaluation, the medical staff would have conferred with a psychiatrist to evaluate the degree of trauma and determine the type of treatment and disposition of the patient. The majority of those deemed acute were unable to return to combat.

Doctors found that the most severe of the acute cases generally suffered from disabling mental problems caused by severe trauma and would have little chance of a complete recovery. The medical staff processed these individuals and shipped them directly back to the United States for discharge, or if necessary, further treatment in a mental facility. Standard procedure was to take those cases of acute battle exhaustion, considered less severe, off the line and reassign them to a noncombat job—communications, food service, driver, etc.—behind the lines.

Simple or "common" combat fatigue, considered a temporary and treatable condition, made up about two-thirds of all psychological casualties. Following a period of combined treatment and rest, the majority of these men were able to return to combat duty, most of the time without further incident. Doctors diagnosed Joe Connole's condition as a case of simple combat fatigue.

When a combat fatigue case arrived at the aid station, standard practice called for medical personnel to sedate the individual. To induce sleep, historian John C. McManus says, many patients "were given a concoction called a 'Blue 88,' which was made up of various calming drugs, mostly barbiturates," such as sodium amytal and sodium pentothol. One veteran quoted by McManus said medics gave him a "blue bomber" (identified by McManus as "sodium pentothol"). The use of drugs resulted in a deep, "almost trance-like sleep" for anywhere from twenty-four to seventy-two hours. Once the patient was up and about, doctors conducted a more extensive evaluation.

The "best treatment," in a majority of the cases, McManus wrote, "was time off the front lines." After a period of supervised rest and recuperation, anywhere from a few days to several weeks, depending upon the severity of the trauma, the patient was ready to return to his unit. Doctors and staff monitored patients daily for signs of improvement. A doctor, usually a psychiatrist, made the final determination as to whether or not the patient was fit for duty. If the patient had not as yet made sufficient progress, doctors kept him for further treatment. Military policy was to return battle fatigue cases to duty as soon as possible. The longer they were away from their unit and the farther behind the lines, the more difficult this became.

A small percentage of psychiatric casualties deemed common by medical personnel failed to respond to treatment. Some individuals balked at orders to return to combat, telling doctors, "I just can't take it any more." Some reached a point, where they had simply "given up." Most, however, went back to the line as ordered, albeit reluctantly.

During the period of recuperation, doctors placed combat fatigue patients in an atmosphere of quiet and total relaxation and saw to it they received plenty of rest. Hospital staff provided the men with a new set of clothes, daily showers, and hot nourishing meals, something they had not had for some time. Doctors found that these measures alone went a long way in restoring a man's sense of balance. The men could lounge about and relax, talk to others with similar experiences, play games or cards, and listen to the radio to pass the time. The medical staff arranged to have some type of evening entertainment or group recreational activities. Therapists were available to lend a "sympathetic ear," so patients could discuss what it was that was bothering them and to have someone to confide in about their fears and anxieties. Many patients found these sessions to be extremely therapeutic.

Toward the end of 1943, during the long-drawn-out Italian campaign, the number of battle fatigue cases began to rise dramatically. Troops became battle weary and exhausted from being on the line for extended periods, sometimes as long as four to six weeks and longer. This forced military leaders to take a close, hard look at the overall problem. As psychiatrists and psychologists with the U.S. Army Medical Corps expanded their knowledge on the subject, attitudes concerning the best methods of treatment, as well as views on how to deal with the overall situation, began to change.

Medical Corps personnel began to switch their management policy from an emphasis on treatment to one of prevention. The question doctors began to ask was, What measures could be taken by the military, under the circumstances, to maintain a soldier's mental health and well-being? The implementation of prevention measures, they believed, would sharply reduce the number of psychiatric cases. Doctors knew that extended periods of combat wore men down, both physically and mentally. McManus wrote:

> By 1943, many Army psychiatrists began to emphasize the "fatigue" in the phrase combat fatigue, in so doing removing the damaging stigma of mental illness. After

treating numerous cases, they realized that combat exhaustion most always occurred not because a man was psychologically unfit but because he was physically or mentally exhausted. The exhaustion had lowered his resistance to stress, the same way it would to disease.

The physical and emotional toll caused by the mental strain or anxiety of prolonged combat proved too much for some men to bear and as a result they could no longer function effectively. No man was exempt. Entire units suffered collectively from the fatigue factor as well.

With not even a rumor of relief off the line to look forward to, men despaired, often falling into a state of depression. The future of the individual soldier at the front for extended periods looked bleak at best. This proved one of the biggest aspects of the problem, and resulted in men going on sick call for minor ailments and injuries to get a break from combat. It was also one of the major causes for the mounting number of battle fatigue cases. The longer a man spent in a combat situation, the greater his chances of ending up dead or seriously wounded. Men knew that the prospects for survival diminished with each passing day. Many began to believe strongly that a "million dollar wound" was all that might save them. Some GIs have admitted to secretly wishing, sometimes praying, for this to occur.

Doctors investigating the problem recommended "planned rest periods" or "rest breaks" for, at the very least, two or three days' duration. This would allow men time away from combat and give them a chance to recuperate. It also gave them something to look forward to, a glimmer of hope in an otherwise gloomy outlook. The situation seemed a little less desperate knowing they would eventually be relieved, even if it were only for a short period.

A respite from the fighting would allow the troops to clean up, get some good hot chow, and catch up on much needed sleep. The winter months were especially hard on the men. Heated tents were set up with cots, which enabled them to dry out and get the blood circulating in cold feet and limbs. These simple measures kept the number of cold weather illnesses and injuries from skyrocketing.

When the troops arrived at the designated rest area, they were weary and exhausted. Many looked dazed and listless and had to be helped along by buddies. When II Corps removed the 36th Division from the line at Monte Cassino in February 1944, Ross Rajotte (A-141) reported that many of the men were so stiff from crouching in their foxholes for such long periods without relief, squad-mates literally had to lift them up and out and provide support. "They couldn't bend their legs, though they were willing to hold their positions against the Germans," Rajotte said with a note of pride. Combat correspondent Ralph G. Martin wrote, that of "the final fifty GI's" in the 36th

Division to be relieved at that time many "were so numbed from exposure" they "had to be carried out on stretchers. The stretchers were ripe targets, and many of them never made it."

The men's uniforms were filthy, smeared with grime and mud, and stained by sweat from going without proper hygiene for weeks on end. Months of marching and climbing through rugged terrain left boots falling apart and soles worn thin. Upon arrival, they received a reissue of clothing. The men stripped and took hot showers without time restrictions (shower time was usually limited because of the number of men and the shortage of hot water). Next, the cooks prepared them a hot nourishing meal, all they could eat. After filling their stomachs, most of the men slept for an extended period, 24 hours straight or longer.

Most evenings, the staff scheduled a movie or other form of entertainment. The division or regimental bands and small combos played on a regular basis, presenting all the latest numbers. In some of the larger rest centers, the USO frequently provided shows providing professional entertainment, which included many Hollywood celebrities. "Soldier Shows" were also tremendously popular with the boys. These variety shows, "made by soldiers for soldiers," were produced under the direction of the Entertainment Section of the Army Special Services Division. "A wide range of talent was employed in creating soldier shows—including singers, dancers, actors . . . costume and scenery [designers] . . .and artists."

Entertainers in the troupe sang, played a wide variety of musical instruments, performed dance numbers, acted in skits, and performed comedy routines. These "shows were remarkably effective in boosting morale," especially that "of hospitalized soldiers." They had high degree of "therapeutic value" as well, playing "an important role in the physical and mental rehabilitation of injured soldiers" (John C. Becher Playscript Collection).

After only a short time away from the front, a remarkable change took place—the planned periods of rest and recuperation rejuvenated the men. The rest breaks did wonders for the morale of the troops. Unfortunately, the time passed all too quickly and before they knew it, they were on their way back to the front.

Previously, rotation of units off the line was not always possible because of the limited number of committed divisions in each theater and a shortage of men caused by the high number of casualties and other losses. Beginning in early 1944, the army shipped hundreds of thousands of replacement troops from the states to bring undermanned units up to strength. This enabled commanders to institute a program of rotating units off the line for short periods. Companies, regiments, and even entire divisions were relieved and placed in reserve. Sometimes, when entire units could not be spared, it might only be small groups of soldiers.

Before commanders scheduled units to undergo training or retraining and refitting for a new mission or operation, troops were given a much-deserved rest period. Training areas were most often located near a large metropolis. The 36th Division trained at Naples prior to the Anzio breakout, and at Salerno before the southern France invasion. Men received passes to go to the city or a nearby town—to eat in a restaurant, take in some entertainment, do some sightseeing, relax in one of the many cafés and bars—and do whatever else it was that soldiers have been known to do while on pass.

At the clearing station, doctors also discovered that Joe Connole was suffering from "Enteritis, acute, simple, undetermined, catarrhal." Enteritis, also known as "Crohn's disease," is an autoimmune disorder that causes severe gastrointestinal problems. The mucous membrane lining of the small intestine, usually the lower part, called the ileum, becomes inflamed. All parts of the intestinal tract, including the stomach may be affected. A bacterial or a viral infection is the cause of the disease, usually from ingesting contaminated food or water.

Common symptoms of the disease include abdominal pain, often in the lower right area (the condition can mimic appendicitis), diarrhea, and severe weight loss. Fever and rectal bleeding may also occur. My father told medical personnel he had been suffering from "stomach [pains?], diarrhea, and vomiting for [the] last 4 days" (prior to his breakdown). The daily medical log also noted that he complained of "anorexia [loss of appetite] and dizziness." On September 5, the Army doctor noted that Connole was "concerned about loss of weight."

On August 27, the on duty physician wrote in his report, "Diarrhea has ceased but pt. [patient] continues to complain of abdominal pains, weakness, general malaise." He ordered that Connole "be evacuated for adequate study," and transferred him to the 51st Evac Hospital. The doctor's final notation reads, "Symptoms may all be secondary to anxiety state."

Doctors at the hospital prescribed a regimen of medication to treat the enteritis. Over the next several days, his condition improved steadily. The daily report for September 2, reads, "P.E. [physical examination] negative believe able to go on duty in a few days."

Two days later, on September 4, Connole told a doctor that about two weeks earlier, on August 15, the day of the invasion, he "fainted twice." Connole stated, "that on 14 Aug he slept well in the Boat. The morning of D-Day, carrying ammunition, tho[ugh] not particularly hot, he fainted—thinks he was unconscious about 10 min. Brought to with water, [Connole indicated] that he could make it. Pnt.[patient] had a similar attack a few hours later."

Mental or emotional problems brought on by stress can interfere with the normal functioning of the body's autoimmune system. Often, this can result in the onset of a host of physical ailments, particularly infectious diseases. Researchers have linked stress to a weakening of immune responses—white blood cells (macrophages), molecules, and chemical messengers—produced by the lymph organs, which defend against pathogens that manage to make it past the body's natural barriers. These defenders work together as an internal defense mechanism to identify and overcome pathogenic microorganisms, which, if allowed to multiply to excessive levels, could result in a person contracting a particular disease. Immune responses weakened or rendered ineffective by stress can also delay or impede the healing process.

My father's physical problems and subsequent breakdown were, most likely, a result of the emotional stress brought about by the news of my mother's hospitalization and his concern for her, as well as for his children's welfare. Stress does not cause Crohn's disease, although medical research has shown that the condition worsens under emotional tension, pressure, or other strain.

The final medical report, signed by Major Beels, confirmed the earlier diagnosis of combat fatigue. Beels' entry reads: "Diag[nosis]: Battle Exhaustion. Recom[mend]: Duty." Apparently, the doctor felt he had recovered sufficiently to go back to his unit. According to the medical records, Dr. Beels ordered Connole to return to duty on September 8, 1944.

At the time my mother, "Mary" or "Mickey" (her given name was Michelina) Connole, contracted tuberculosis, she lived with her mother, Lucia "Lucy" Palumbo, at 17 Shamrock Street, on Worcester's East Side. My mother worked days while my grandmother took care of my brother Rick and me. She must have entered the hospital shortly after my brother Rick was born on April 8, 1944. According to my Aunt, Helen Palumbo, the son of the family living in the apartment downstairs had the disease. My grandmother, who was friendly with the boy's mother, used to go down to the apartment on a daily basis to visit and help with the son's care.

Helen said that before feeding us, my grandmother would check the temperature of the milk in the bottle and taste the food to make sure it was not too hot. Family members feared that she might contract the disease, if in fact she had not already done so, although she showed no outward symptoms, and transmit it to me or my brother. It is very likely that she was already a carrier, showing no apparent symptoms, an "asymptomatic carrier." Somehow, the infected person's body manages to control the disease and they do not become ill. Most carriers are "not contagious," but, at the time, the family apparently had no knowledge of this. They were concerned for our safety, and soon after my mother entered the sanitarium, Rick and I were removed from my grandmother's home and placed in my Aunt Helen's care. At the time, my Uncle Mitt was in the service somewhere in the states, playing in an Army band.

The couple had lost a baby girl due to a late-term miscarriage just a few months earlier (April 13, 1944). This was my aunt's first pregnancy and the termination must have been devastating. With her husband away most of the time, she was probably filled with a sense of isolation. Many women who lose a child, especially their first, go through a long period of grief and suffer from bouts of depression. Helen was more than happy for the chance to take us in and care for us in my mother's absence, which no doubt eased my father's worry somewhat.

Because of the circumstances of my mother's illness, my aunt contacted local Red Cross officials in an attempt to obtain my father's early release from the service on a hardship basis. The Department of Defense did not view my mother's hospitalization as a valid enough reason to have him sent home, and denied the request. Military officials stated in the letter of refusal that he was a frontline soldier, "essential to the war effort." My aunt said she remembered that phrase being used, and therefore the Army could not spare him. As an alternative, the Red Cross did manage to obtain my Uncle Mitt's early discharge instead.

Curiously enough, one of the causes of death listed on my grandfather Antonio Palumbo's death certificate is "pulmonary tuberculosis." He passed away at age sixty-four on March 15, 1941. In a conversation with my Aunt Helen about my mother's illness, she made no mention of this. It is possible, but highly unlikely, she had no knowledge of his condition.

After the war, in 1948, the family physician hospitalized my mother once again after she suffered a relapse of the disease. She spent approximately one year and eight months in the Worcester County Sanatorium in West Boylston, Massachusetts, recuperating. My brother Rick and I, approximately five and six years of age respectively, went to stay at St. Anne's Orphanage on Granite Street in Worcester, operated by the "Gray Nuns," so called because of the color of their robes, also known as the "Sisters of Charity of Montreal," a world renowned Catholic order that originated in Canada. We remained at the orphanage from January 8, 1949, through September 1, 1950. My father placed my sister Maureen Deborah, "Debbie," born in 1946, at St. Gabriel's, an orphanage for girls on High Street in Worcester, run by the Sisters of Mercy, under the auspices of the Worcester Diocese.

Doctors finally released my mother from the hospital in the late summer of 1950, and we returned home to 10 Peace Avenue in a veterans' housing complex called Lincolnwood (see next chapter). At the time, I was in the third grade. I remember distinctly the day my father arrived at the orphanage to take us home for the reunion with my mother. It was a very happy day in my life.

Joe Connole received word of his wife's illness approximately six to seven weeks before his breakdown, which would have been some time in early July 1944. The troubling news from home, it is obvious, was a source of worry and concern and probably marked the beginning of his eventual collapse. Today, I wonder why the family told him at all, given his circumstances, as the disease was not life threatening. He had to contend with the upcoming invasion and his return to combat. There would be fierce fighting during the landings and on the beaches and the drive inland as the Germans tried to prevent the Allies from gaining a foothold in the south of France. Most invasions resulted in high casualties.

My father experienced feelings of helplessness and inadequacy regarding his wife's situation at home in the states. He tried to carry on as best he could. His anxiety level began to build and he no doubt sank into a state of deep depression. Gradually, his mental as well as physical health began to disintegrate. Joe Connole had the comfort of his close buddies to help stabilize his deteriorating condition. They tried to console him and gave assurances that everything would work out. At least his children had the benefit of good care from loving relatives.

Chapter Twenty-Two

Buddies

Men who fought together during wartime became extremely close, in many cases closer than the relationship that existed among family members, a spouse, or sweetheart. Because these men had suffered so much together, they developed strong emotional bonds of loyalty and trust. A good buddy was a special friend with whom a person could share his innermost thoughts—his hopes and dreams, his plans for the future—and swap stories of family and home. It was someone he could confide in about his deepest fears and anxieties—the fear of dying, the fear of never seeing loved ones again, or even the fear that his wife or girlfriend was being unfaithful. It was someone to whom he could bare his soul. Loyalty among friends in combat was unconditional.

A GIs entire world extended no further than his squad or section. His small circle of friends generally consisted of one to four men, usually within the squad. Men found a common bond in their squad mates. Among this coterie of companions, a man developed a close association, an interdependent relationship. The group made up what historian John C. McManus referred to as a man's "frontline family."

Buddies relied on each other for mutual support. The relationship was such that, when need be, they could calm each other's fears, allay anxiety, and restore lost confidence. Sometimes it would be nothing more than a few soothing words of encouragement, the gentle touch of a hand on the shoulder, or a reassuring smile, which provided some small measure of comfort and solace. When down—when at his lowest point—a buddy would be there to bolster a man's sagging spirits. Such was the case when my father learned of my mother's illness and hospitalization—his close friends tried their best to comfort him.

In an article published in *The Fighting 36th Historical Quarterly* titled, "Good Buddy," Morris Courington (K-142), described the "relationship that is formed between foxhole buddies" as "unique." So unusual, he went so far as to say, "There is no other human relationship that it can be compared with." Courington expressed it this way:

> You eat together, fight together, sleep together, pray together, etc., etc. Being of different religions is not a problem. You cover for each other, you share whatever there is to share, as little as it may be. You might even save each other's life. There is a total trust in each other. You don't need to talk about it, but you know that he will be there for you and you will be close by on patrols, attacks, counterattacks and invasions. He does not judge you and you do not criticize him. You know that neither one of you will screw up, but if by any chance one of you does, you know you'll get another and another "second chance." Because you're his good buddy.

Courington was writing about the relationship he had with his wartime buddy, Gerald "Jerry" Creehan, whom he described as "my 'twin brother' through thick and thin." The two men, he says, "were almost inseparable."

The intimate relationship, the strong emotional ties, which existed between a combat soldier and his buddies has been the subject of numerous discussions by authors, historians, and frontline veterans. During an interview conducted by historian John C. McManus with a WWII combat officer, "a former rifle company commander," the veteran "expressed amazement at how well his men, most of whom were ordinary Americans, held up under the stress of combat." When McManus asked what "he thought was the most significant single factor," the former officer stated without hesitation, "Brotherhood. Everybody sharing the same dangers, the same joy and the same sorrow."

McManus further defined the brotherhood as:

> the bond . . . that developed among those at the front lines, who did the bulk of the fighting. This brotherhood motivated American soldiers to fight and at the same time provided them with a small, tight-knit "family" in which they could feel secure and needed. Along the way, soldiers became as close as brothers, forging a unique friendship.

McManus referred to this powerful bond as the "deadly brotherhood—a man's immediate comrades."

Every day on the line, these men lived with the constant threat of being killed or maimed. Their buddies helped them get through the bad times—under fire, in the face of an enemy advance on their position, during the endless shelling, or at night, surrounded by the enemy. "With their lives on the line," McManus goes on to say, close friends "learned that they could depend on one another." In a critical situation, a man could always count on his buddies—they would always be there, no matter what. Knowing this helped to keep men going when they had nothing else; for example, when they were facing a particularly tough combat situation in which the chances for survival seemed almost hopeless.

Historian Gerald F. Linderman referred to this close bond as "comradeship—the connection between a soldier and his fellows." Linderman presented his perspective on this subject: "In very utilitarian ways, comradeship strengthened the individual for participation in battle. It provided a powerful motivation to fight, helped to overcome fear, enhanced safety, strengthened perseverance, provided against disintegration, and offered a basis for reconciliation with death." Comradeship served to promote a man's well-being and stability. Among other things, it "heightened the soldier's determination to overcome his fear of battle." Most importantly, he stressed, "It could by itself make some feel more secure." In essence, men derived an inner strength from their comrades in battle.

"Comradeship," Linderman says, "also served to divert the combat soldier from self absorption, from obsession with his own cares and fears." Linderman followed with numerous statements by veterans of every rank who had fought in both the European and Pacific theaters, attesting to the importance of friendship in helping a man to survive the terrible ordeal of combat.

"As the soldier's span in combat lengthened," Linderman wrote, "comradeship also served to protect him against, or at least to retard, psychological disintegration." A man's buddy or buddies helped to stabilize him and provide much needed support, which helped keep him on an even keel. Friendship, as one GI quoted by Linderman emphasized, "kept [men] sane." Another stated, it was "the main thing that keeps a guy from going haywire."

British military historian John Ellis wrote, "American observers" (military psychiatrists, L.H. Bartemeier, et al.), who conducted countless interviews with veterans after the war, noted that "the vital precipitating factor in most breakdowns was not so much a particular military encounter," but more often, "some event which necessitated a sudden change" in the man's "pattern" of life within the combat family. If the integrity of a man's family was "shattered" by "a precipitating event," or otherwise interrupted for any reason, the status quo of the "group relationship" would be "lost," and the soldier "forfeited all the strengths and comforts with which it had sustained him." Investigators concluded that as "a member of the team he would have been able to take it; alone he was overwhelmed and became disorganized." Men in combat were "able to carry on" only if the group relationship was maintained.

Combat veterans readily acknowledged the deep and abiding friendships that developed among squad mates in personal memoirs and other accounts of war. It is quite clear the intense feelings these men had for one another ran much deeper than most ordinary relationships, even those among family members. Linderman states, "It should surprise no one then that, under the pressures of the battlefield, feelings of friendship intensified—and sometimes moved to love." John Ellis agrees. He talks of "the selflessness, pride," and "mutual respect" among combat soldiers; yet he says, "These are not adequate concepts to fully describe the front-line soldiers' feelings toward one another. In the final analysis one is speaking of an identification with and a concern for one's fellows so all consuming that one can only speak in terms of love." He concluded, "In the midst of seeming chaos it was the love of individuals, one for another, that enabled them to carry on."

Veterans themselves stopped short of describing these close personal relationships in terms of the affection or love that indeed existed, lest it be misinterpreted by someone in civilian life who had never experienced it. Rarely, Linderman wrote, did soldiers "employ the word 'love' in descriptions of their feelings for one another in combat." The word love, he says, "was so powerfully and indissolubly bound to heterosexual relationships that its application to comrades was almost always hidden behind a curtain of reticence." Ellis also wrote of the hesitancy on the part of veterans when "expressing their feelings fully, yet," he says, "a deep love was there and for all those who shared it the memory will never fail." Linderman wrote in the concluding remarks of his chapter on comradeship, "Love between men did sometimes move some to sacrifice their lives for others" (see below).

On the subject of special friendships and the influence these relationships had on motivation, Linderman wrote, "No force urged [a soldier] forward more powerfully than comradeship." Men did not fight for God or country, nor out of a sense of duty or loyalty to one's unit—division, regiment, battalion—they did it for one purpose, to support their combat brothers. Former General S.L.A. Marshall, who, Ellis noted, "devoted himself to a study of the ordinary soldier's reactions to modern combat," concluded: "I hold it to be one of the simplest truths of war that the thing which enables an infantry soldier to keep moving with his weapon is the near presence of a comrade." "Military psychiatrists" as well, according to Ellis, "were not slow to recognize the importance of small-group solidarity" as a critical factor "in enabling soldiers to keep going."

There was, in some outfits, the occasional loner, usually, but not always, an antisocial type, who seemed to get along fine without any friends. This was, however, a highly unusual situation. Bill Mauldin referred to these men as "misfits." These were men "who can't make friends or who are just plain ornery." Without close companionship—alone—there would be no one to provide a man with the motivation to go on—to urge him to continue, especially when, in the heat of battle, fear limited his ability to function as a soldier. What was probably saddest of all, when that person died on the battlefield, there would be no one to mourn him.

Among this small group, some were men who had lost a close buddy earlier and did not want to commit to another relationship and risk being hurt again. William F. Hartung (E-143) wrote about "the first real friend" he made in the Army, a young Puerto Rican in his squad named John C. Neves of Fairhaven, Massachusetts. Neves died at the hands of a German sniper in France, "who shot him through the heart." They found the German, "a kid about seventeen, hiding in a drain pipe." Hartung described his reaction:

> I was on a hillside when it happened, so I went down to see him. He was covered with a blanket. I moved it down some and saw the small hole. He didn't feel a thing when it hit him. His eyes were still open, so I closed them and covered him up again. I looked at the German who shot him. He was a prisoner sitting in the back of a jeep laughing and smoking. I don't know where I got the strength but I picked him up bodily and threw him to the ground. I pointed my rifle at his forehead and he was whimpering and begging as I walked away.

After Neves was killed, Hartung explained, "I didn't want to make any close friends as it would hurt more if they were killed or wounded. I saw so many who were there one day and gone the next."

All the men shared everything they had, "as little as it may be," Courington said. A man would take his last cigarette, light it, and pass it around, and he would do the same with a bottle of wine or liquor. If a man in the squad received a gift package from home, he immediately tore open the parcel and all shared equally in the batch of goodies, usually specialty food items such as canned and preserved meats, cheeses, or candy. The recipient doled out any leftovers, if there happened to be any. Never would a man think of hoarding anything. When rations were low or ran out, if a man had a single scrap of food, no matter how small, he would not hesitate to divide it equally among fellow squad members. It did nothing at all to relieve the hunger—it was a symbolic gesture of the friendship, of the close bond that existed between comrades.

It was the same for the contents of personal mail from wives, sweethearts, and family members. Men read aloud excerpts from letters containing good news from home for all to hear. The men took turns sharing the latest happenings. Other members of the squad would be happy for the recipient and just as excited. They were no less sad about bad tidings. Even when a man was silent, the men in the squad could tell immediately when the news from home was not good. Unmarried guys in the group celebrated the birth of a squad mate's baby as if it were their own. Everyone followed the progress of a child's growth and development from one letter to the next. Men greeted the word of a youngster's first steps, or a toddler's first words and phrases, with cheers and congratulatory remarks. The men of the squad stopped what they were doing and hung on every word as the proud father related the momentous event. Many of these men, including my father, had never seen some of their children.

Accounts of comrades giving of themselves unselfishly to help an ailing or troubled friend are legion. Up at the front, many men were sick or suffered from a chronic, nagging ailment or injury—a bad cold or the flu, a mild case of trench foot, a sore back—but one not severe enough to get them out of combat. A man had to persevere under all types of conditions and rarely was anyone excused because of illness or fatigue, unless medical personnel deemed his condition critical. Medical personnel regularly sent men who went on sick call back to the front unless incapacitated. A close buddy would feed, bathe, and sponge a sick man down to lower his fever, or even help him to defecate—do whatever was necessary to nurse him back to health or to ease his pain and suffering.

In September 2002, I attended a reunion of Company H, 181st Infantry, 26th Infantry Division, my father's old outfit before joining the 36th. I happened to be present among a small group of Company H veterans, when I heard one particularly moving story that typifies the way a man looked after another's welfare in wartime. Sulo Ruuska said to the group, "Did I ever tell you about the time Nick," who was standing beside him at the time, "saved my life." His friend Nick Renzetti stood with lips pursed, seeming ill at ease and a bit embarrassed as his friend spoke, but also, I sensed, with a great deal of pride. I also got the feeling from Renzetti's demeanor at that very moment that he did not consider what he had done for his friend to be of any significance. He could not have acted in any other way. The incident took place at a "repple depple" in Italy in February 1944, while the two replacements were awaiting reassignment to a combat outfit.

Billeted in pyramidal tents, the GIs slept fully clothed on a bedding of dry straw, covered by a single, standard-issue, wool Army blanket. The unheated tents were extremely drafty and the ground cold and damp. The Italian winter of 1943 to 1944, as it turned out, was one of the worst on record.

One cold, raw day, Ruuska was laid up, his body racked by chills, fever, and a painful cough that emanated from deep within his chest. His congested lungs ached as he fought for every breath. After roll that morning, Sulo had made his way to the battalion aid station, "located about two miles away," to report for sick call. About 200 GIs had arrived ahead of him, and the long line wound down at a snail's pace. After standing out in the bitter cold and wind for what seemed like hours, Ruuska, barely able to hold himself up, could bear it no longer. He left his place in the line and made the exhausting trek back to his tent, where he collapsed in a heap. "Most of the guys in line," Sulo said, "were goldbricks."

Ruuska lay on the cold ground in the fetal position coughing and shaking, while clutching the corners of the thin Army blanket to his chest. "I couldn't stop shivering," Sulo remembered. Nick, greatly concerned for his friend's welfare, brought him a little food and something to drink from the mess hall and tended to his needs as best he could.

Late that night, when the camp was asleep, Renzetti somehow made his way past the perimeter guards and managed to slip out of the "barbed wire encirclement." Ruuska wrote in a later letter, "To this day I still don't know how he did it." Nick walked to a nearby hillside town, where he traded some cigarettes with one of the villagers for a heavy quilted blanket, tattered and torn and smelling as though it had been used as bedding for the family dog. Renzetti returned and, after covering his friend, crawled under the blanket with him. He put his arms around Sulo and pulled him close to keep him warm. "Today, we would have been looked upon as being kinda strange," Ruuska said with a laugh.

Early the next morning, Nick practically had to carry his sick friend to the aid station. While waiting in the stalled line, a doctor happened by, and upon seeing Ruuska's condition, "yelled for an ambulance." Diagnosed with a severe case of pneumonia, the medical staff had him evacuated to a hospital for treatment. Ruuska remembers nothing of the trip. He awoke several hours later and, to his surprise, found himself "in a hospital room full of men in straitjackets." As it turned out the facility was so overcrowded, the only available bed was in the "psych ward," he said. Renzetti visited Sulo at the hospital a few days later to check on his friend's condition.

While Ruuska was recovering, Renzetti went to the 45th Division and so the two friends separated. They had been together ever since arriving at Camp Edwards as recruits in the spring of 1941. "I met him when we were drafted, both on the same day," Ruuska wrote. "He and I are only a few days apart in age." Nick was from Boston and Sulo from nearby Quincy. After Sulo recovered, he was sent to the 85th Division. Both men ended up seeing plenty of action. Ruuska never forgot the kindness shown him by Renzetti. He contacted Nick after the war and the two ended up becoming lifelong friends.

Other selfless acts were commonplace and stories of such incidents abound in veteran's memoirs and historical accounts of every war. Men would volunteer for night reconnaissance patrol, a dangerous assignment dreaded by every GI up at the front, just to spare a good buddy from having to cross enemy lines. A friend would not wake an exhausted foxhole buddy, but would allow him to sleep through his watch just to let him get some extra shut-eye, even though he himself was in no better condition, and then shrug it off by saying "I wasn't at all tired."

Buddies put their lives on the line for each other on countless occasions. One example of this among the men of my father's company occurred on May 31, 1944, near Velletri, Italy. An article in the Newark, New Jersey *Star Ledger* (c. June-July, 1944), titled "Artillery Fire? Phooey!", described how Pfc. Phillip M. DeRiggi (D-141) of Newark, New Jersey, "second gunner in a machine gun squad," received the Bronze Star Medal for "saving the life of a wounded comrade." While under heavy artillery and machine gun fire "which caused his company to withdraw 100 yards," DeRiggi "left the comparatively secure position he had acquired in the withdrawal when he saw that the last man to leave the forward position was severely wounded and unable to move." According to the citation, DeRiggi "calmly and swiftly picked up the rifleman and carried him back to [a] rear position then returned to his squad and continued the fight." The only possible explanation for this type of behavior, in many of these instances, was the intense love and devotion these men had for one another.

On October 6, 1944, Phillip DeRiggi died of wounds received near Herpelmont, France, in the Vosges Mountains. DeRiggi is buried in the World War II American Cemetery in Epinal, France.

DeRiggi's nephew Greg wrote on September 23, 2003, "I never knew my uncle Phil but have seen some pictures and with some discussions with my father [his brother Louis, a Merchant Seaman in World War II] and others, found that he was a tall, 'strong as an ox' tough young man who feared nothing—he was funny and well respected." Ernest Smeltzer, a member of Company D, who knew DeRiggi "very well" said, "he was always upbeat and everyone who knew him liked him."

There were "two things that were unthinkable to combat men," wrote McManus, "letting your buddies down and appearing cowardly in front of others." Historian John Ellis wrote that there existed among combat men a "mutual sense of pride," which he says, "helps to explain the selflessness of the front-line soldier in that, as a man looked at what his comrades seemed to endure, he set for himself enormously high standards and became almost obsessed with the fear of letting them down."

After the war, Army researchers conducted a survey in an attempt to determine how much the fear of "letting buddies down" influenced a soldier's motivation. Samuel Stouffer and colleagues, as stated in *The American Soldier*, reported that this concern ranked second, after "prayer," as to what "most helped 'when the going got tough.'" Researchers posed the following question to combat veterans of both the Pacific and European Theaters, "When the going got tough . . . how much did it help to think that you couldn't let the other man down?" The results of the survey, as interpreted by McManus, showed that "nearly nine out of ten American combat soldiers in World War II found the strength to endure even the worst combat and continue fighting because they could not bear the thought of letting their buddies down. For most, the threat of death was preferable to betraying one's combat brothers." This is a powerful testament to the closeness of combat buddies—that they would do everything within their power to be there for a friend when he needed him the most.

On one occasion, after having spent a "few days" off the line and then being ordered to go back up, Morris Courington (K-142) expressed his thoughts on what it was like for veterans of combat: "There is no way to describe the awful feelings of dread, fear, hopelessness, etc., when you go back for more. Now you know what it's like and that some will not make it this time. But you go, of course, because its your job, your duty, and you cannot let your buddies down." In a later chapter, Courington reiterated this view, "It was unthinkable that you would not do your part, not do your duty, that you would let your buddies down."

First Lieutenant Robert J. Gans of Chicago, Illinois, a platoon leader in Company I, 142nd Infantry, expressed similar sentiments. Wounded in southern France, Gans spent a lengthy recovery period in a hospital in Marseille. He rejoined his outfit in the "tiny town" of Rehaupal. The former officer recounted what happened next: "I was immediately surrounded by '40 to 50 of my guys' all hugging, yelling and screaming, 'Gans is back!' The shout went up and down the line." He later contemplated the reason for this unusual display of emotion, his and theirs, and suddenly "realized that it was an act of love." Gans expounded on the reasons for the powerful feelings men on the line had for one another: "These men were my family—my home. They were closer to me than anybody had been in my life. Through two solid years we had fought together, and they had never let me down, and I knew I would never let them down." In September 1944, Gans was wounded a second time in the Vosges Mountains and "withdrawn" from combat.

Men had a difficult time dealing with the loss of a buddy or buddies from either death or wounds. The death of a comrade was like losing a brother or other family member and could have a devastating effect on a man's stability in combat. One statement, made by a combat veteran and quoted by McManus, illustrates just how much a man depended on his buddies—"The dog soldier feared separation from his squad more than he feared the enemy."

The following accounts written by two members of the 36th Division, give testimony to the overwhelming effect the loss of a close companion could have on an individual. These passages show the powerful emotional strain, as well as the pain and hurt experienced because of such a tragic event.

During the first week in January 1945, somewhere in the Colmar-Vosges area of north central France, T-Sgt. Ben Palmer of Holland, New York, learned that his close friend David Arvizu had become a casualty while leading a patrol behind enemy lines. This troubling news proved more than Palmer could handle. Palmer was a squad leader with Company B, 143rd Infantry Regiment. David Arvizu, who hailed from Pigeon, Michigan (see below), had been Ben's first scout before receiving a promotion to staff sergeant and assigned his own squad.

Over the previous several weeks, Palmer's platoon had been involved in "a holding and probing action." He described the surrounding Colmar-Vosges region as "rolling country with very heavy pine forest," making combat "a real challenge." The company sent patrols out on a regular basis to "scout enemy positions" and bring back prisoners for interrogation. The Germans, who were "masters of camouflage," would allow American forces to advance and "then spring a trap on them." This, he surmised, must have been how his close friend Dave got hit.

"Dave was one hell of a soldier and the third squad would surely miss him and naturally we all prayed that he would be OK," Palmer wrote. "Dave's getting wounded really got to me since we had been each other's strength since Italy." Arvizu would eventually recover from his wounds and return to the company.

Palmer had been through a particularly difficult time of it during this period. "Some of the toughest fighting we encountered," he wrote, "was in north central France." Combat seemed to be "never ending." Harassing artillery barrages occurred at any time of the day or night and there was the continuous threat of infiltration by German patrols.

Suffering from weather conditions that Palmer described as "vicious," the troops could only survive out in the cold and freezing rain or snow for a few days at a time. It "seemed like our teeth never stopped chattering," he recalled.

At night, members of the platoon huddled together next to foxholes, wool caps pulled low over their ears and standard issue Army blankets wrapped around their shoulders for warmth. The bottom of the holes quickly filled with several inches of icy groundwater. They were "only used," Palmer said, "if we thought that a round of artillery might be dead on us." Direct exposure to wind and freezing rain or blowing snow made conditions even more unbearable. When darkness fell, temperatures at higher elevations plummeted. As wind speeds increased, wind-chill temperatures dropped, causing the body to lose heat rapidly

Freezing and thawing conditions created muddy, slippery conditions on roads and trails making all movement especially difficult and sometimes hazardous. There were many swollen rivers and streams to cross and the men's feet never had a chance to dry out. Day after day, the company's "active numbers" continued to drop because of casualties and men reporting to sick call for weather related ailments—colds, pneumonia, frostbite, and trench foot—which put a greater burden on those left behind. The number of trench foot cases alone was almost as high as the figure for battle casualties.

Later that day, Palmer received more bad news. The platoon leader had picked his squad to go on routine patrol that night. The job of the patrol was to seek prisoners and scout the German forward positions, "which," he says, "generally meant drawing enemy fire." His state of mind was so low that he decided against going, in direct disobedience of an order. In his words, he "lost it." Palmer wrote, "I hadn't cried in a long time, but I did that night in HELL on that mountain." The platoon sergeant came by at three o'clock the next afternoon and told Palmer to prepare his squad for an attack the following morning. Much to his surprise and relief, the sergeant never asked him to submit a report about the previous night's patrol. "Maybe our captain knew we were at the breaking point," was the only explanation he could give.

Just a few days later (the second week in January), Palmer, still hurting from the news about Arvizu, suffered the loss of yet another "combat buddy" (not named), whom he described as "a very close friend." The squad had dug in along the crest of a ridge and the Germans began pounding the American positions with an intense artillery and mortar barrage. A shell, most probably an 88mm, burst in the trees overhead, sending a shower of deadly shrapnel, broken and shattered branches, and wood splinters earthward. Palmer commented, it was "the loudest blast that I ever heard and God knows I had heard many loud noises." The explosion left Palmer dazed and disoriented. His ears would not stop ringing. Days later, in the hospital, he informed medical personnel that he still "couldn't hear a damn thing."

Not more than "an arm's length away," next to the foxhole they shared, his friend lay mortally wounded. After the shelling ceased, the platoon sergeant, Richard K. Hupman of Oakland, California, and the company medic, Pfc. Charles F. "Doc" Everest of Battle Creek, Michigan, came along and checked the two men for injuries. Everest had to break the sad news to Palmer that his friend "had died of a concussion." Strange as it may seem, a large metal fragment from the blast had shattered the stock of Palmer's rifle, yet neither man received a single cut.

"We were very close and this event pushed me to the limit," wrote Palmer. The last thing he remembered was waking up in "a very large hospital." Medical personnel questioned him, but his "memory drew a blank on dates and other things that happened during those few days of hell." Doctors were certain that he had "received a severe concussion." During Palmer's lengthy rehabilitation period, the events leading up to his head injury gradually returned.

The "scene" of his friend's death, combined with the fact that "I had escaped the 'Grim Reaper' once again . . . never left my mind," he wrote.

Doctors evaluated his condition and mutually concluded that he "had been near too many bursting artillery shells." Palmer thought, "They might have been right." He had, up to this point in the war, "endured about 300 days of combat," and was of the opinion that this "might qualify" him "for a 'Section Eight,' or what they referred to as 'shell shock,'" two terms used to describe psychological combat trauma. Palmer returned to his company the first week in February somewhere near Drusenheim, France.

In an article written for *The Fighting 36th Historical Quarterly* (Spring 1990), Ben Palmer's friend, David Arvizu, tells of his reaction to the death of "two of his best friends" on November 27, 1944. The engagement, which claimed the lives of the two men, took place "at a point near the highest crest of the Vosges Mountains" in "the vicinity of Sur le Haute and Eschery." Arvizu wrote, "For me, that day will remain in my memory as the most terrible experience of WWII as long as I live."

The death of Arvizu's two buddies happened as Company B, 143rd Infantry, was attacking uphill across an open hillside pasture to the top of a commanding ridgeline about 500 yards away. Reconnaissance indicated that "the enemy had defenses along the tree line near the top of the ridge; however, exactly where and in what strength was not known." A dense, swirling fog shrouded the area, limiting visibility to between twenty and thirty yards. The thick fog, Arvizu says, "initially favored the attack." Then suddenly, the company broke through the heavy mist, which extended to a certain elevation, into bright, clear sunshine, exposing the advancing infantrymen. The fog had no sooner dissipated, than enemy machine gun and small arms fire opened from the tree line just below the crest of the ridge.

At the top of the ridge was a large ski lodge, "the center of the enemy's defense line," with defensive emplacements extending to the left and right of the building. Squad leader S-Sgt. Bob Cassidy (spelled Cassady on the 1945 roster) of Blackstone, Illinois, rushed a machine gun firing from inside the building. Arvizu, watching the action from about fifty yards away, saw his friend stumble and fall about ten yards to the front of the lodge. He learned later that Cassidy had succumbed to his wounds.

Arvizu and his assistant squad leader, Sgt. Joseph Brocato of Baltimore, Maryland, took refuge from the unrelenting fire behind the trunk of a very large pine tree. The men took turns firing at enemy positions from their respective sides of the tree. One man would empty a clip, go behind the tree to reload, and then the other would peer out and open fire. Squad leader Arvizu was shouting instructions, when suddenly Joe slumped to the ground.

Arvizu "pulled him behind cover of the tree." Not seeing any visible wounds, he turned Joe over and discovered a small bullet entrance hole "just below his left nipple." The round had pierced his heart and exited the body "just below the left shoulder blade." Arvizu observed very little bleeding and immediately screamed for a medic.

Upon checking his friend's vital signs, Arvizu realized he was gone. Overcome by grief and sorrow, he sat there stunned. "By this time, the rest of the company had routed the enemy," he said, and all shooting had stopped. The men disarmed the defenders and lined them up for escort back to POW cages in the rear.

Arvizu says that an "unbelievable anger" came over him. Suddenly, he went "completely berserk" and rushed toward a group of prisoners, intent on killing the German soldier he believed responsible for Joe's death. Several members of the platoon restrained him, took his weapon away, and sat him down next to a tree. Some time later, when he finally came to his senses, he found himself alone. In his dazed condition, he got up and headed in the direction the company had traveled. Arvizu had only gone a short distance, when the grief again became too much for him to bear and he sat down on a tree stump. He expressed his feelings at that particular moment: "I was still in a state of mental shock. I thought about what had happened to Bob and Joe, then started crying. Joe and Bob had been closer to me than anyone since I joined the company in Italy. They had patiently taught me all those little details that keep an infantryman alive in combat." Arvizu was so distraught over the loss, he said he felt like giving up.

Mortar rounds began exploding close by, yet Arvizu made no attempt to take cover. He lost all sense of time and was oblivious to the bedlam around him. It was not until a piece of hot shrapnel sliced through the top of his boot going about one-half inch into the flesh of his calf that his head began to clear. After digging the embedded shard out of his leg with a knife and applying a bandage, he once again started walking.

Several hours later, Arvizu finally caught up with the tail end of the company and rejoined his platoon. His men, realizing all he was going through, left him to grieve alone. Arvizu tells how the troubling thought, "that maybe if [he] had done something different Joe would still be alive," kept turning over in his mind; leaving him with a "sense of guilt" he could not shake. Arvizu lapsed into a severe state of depression, the depths of which left him so distraught he felt he could no longer carry out his duties. However, the more Arvizu thought about this, he realized the last thing Bob and Joe would have wanted was for him to be was a quitter. Following a night of restless sleep, he was once again ready to lead his squad.

These two accounts, more than anything else, helped me to understand what my father must have gone through after the loss of his two buddies on the night or early morning of August 24 to 25. He suddenly found himself alone on the battlefield, at night, without the support he had come to depend on to help get him through each day in combat. In the past, just knowing his friends were there, close by his side, providing encouragement and words of comfort when needed, was enough to sustain him. Even though they were all scared to death, friends gave each other the strength and the courage to carry on, to do their duty, and get the job done. With the enemy pressing in all around, Joe Connole could no longer sustain the will to continue. His inner strength, which came from the close support of his buddies, failed him.

Chapter Twenty-Three

Changes

Every American serviceman in World War II came back a different person. War brought about both physical and psychological changes in the men who served. And of course, just as one might expect, those in the military who experienced the most profound and lasting change were the men who survived the hell of combat.

Soldiers who faced the shock and horror of war day in and day out for extended periods aged rapidly, far beyond their years. The frontline soldier in World War II, described by author Paul Fussell as "half man, half boy," soon left his youth behind him. Many writers and historians, veterans included, have stated that "their youth had been stolen from them." This conclusion, of course, holds true for the young men of every army in every war, in every land, from time immemorial. As has been mentioned earlier, my mother once told me, that between the time she last saw my father just prior to his going overseas, at Christmastime in 1943, and the time he returned, about eighteen months later, he looked as though he had aged ten years.

During their time in the service, many of the men went through radical changes in personality. By virtue of their overall military experience—by all they had been exposed to in and out of battle—these men attained a far greater level of maturity and became more world wise as a result of their war service. For most, exposure to the brutality and atrocities of war resulted in a "hardening" or "coarsening" of their overall character. Men also acquired new habits and traits, some good, some not so good—a direct result of a serviceman's lifestyle and length of time served.

Infantrymen in a war zone went through a series of distinct phases—they made the initial transformation from "rookie" to "veteran"—eventually progressing to battle-wise and battle-hardened GI. In many cases, the transition to veteran occurred in a matter of just a few days, or in some instances even after only a few short hours. James Estepp (E-142) wrote, "They say, and it is true, that if you make it the first twenty-four hours in combat in an Infantry Rifle Company, you are an old veteran. What you have to look forward to after that is being killed, wounded, captured, or the war being over." Ben Palmer (B-143) probably said it best: "Combat made veterans in a hurry."

Untried and untested troops, lucky enough to survive their first encounter with the enemy, whether it be in battle, while on night patrol, or during an artillery or aerial bombardment, completed a "rite of passage" and were thereafter accepted by the veterans, the "old timers" of the unit, as one of their own. Then, and only then, did they become a member of this unique club—part of the fellowship. Historian John Ellis expressed it this way:

> The rookies only remained such for a very short time. Either they were hit or they soon acquired the instinctive caution of the other veterans. They were absorbed into the fraternity of the frontline and began increasingly to share the comradeship, the mutual respect and regard that typified the sharp end of battle.

Cartoonist and author Bill Mauldin jokingly referred to this unique group as the "Benevolent and Protective Brotherhood of Them What Has Been Shot At."

The most marked change in these young men occurred when they entered the arena of combat. It was not until many of these young adults, and in many cases mere boys, experienced their "baptism of fire" that they actually became "men." Before the transformation took place, however, all went through a very painful and humbling experience.

Following the attack perpetrated by the Japanese against the United States at Pearl Harbor, a patriotic fervor, reminiscent of the First World War, swept the country. The general feeling of America's young men was "We're not going to let those damn Japs get away with this." Now their country needed them, and they did not hesitate to answer the call. On the Monday following the surprise attack, men began joining up in droves. Many would have done so on Sunday, December 7, had recruiting offices been open. Those already in the military, like my father, fresh from maneuvers and in the best shape of their lives, declared loudly and proudly that they were ready to go. These men were saying, "Let's go over and get the job done and get back home." One popular misconception of the time was that one American soldier could whip ten of their Japanese counterparts. They imagined themselves as vengeful warriors ready to defend their country's honor.

Virile young men of every generation think of themselves as being brave and fearless, capable of performing heroic deeds. They considered it unthinkable to back down from a challenge or threat. Most men felt they could handle whatever adversity they faced. They could overcome any obstacle, or do whatever needed doing to help win the war. Like the comic book or cinematic heroes of the day, they could and would, if need be, perform superhuman feats and conquer all that was evil, in this case, the Japanese Empire. The thinking of many of these young men was that they would go off to war, come back with a chest full of medals, and return to a hero's welcome.

They believed themselves invincible. Young men of every generation experience feelings of immortality—that they are exempt from death. The thought of being killed, or even hurt in the process, simply never occurred to them—it was something that was inconceivable. Before the war, death was something far in the future—something that happened to someone else.

Men who saw combat learned a great deal about themselves. They soon discovered who they were and who they were not. Sometimes what they found was not always to their liking. My father was a tough street kid who grew up without a father. At the time Joe Connole entered military service, he was just twenty-one years old. He no doubt considered himself a man, rough and tough, as do most young men his age. Men, who suddenly found themselves in the presence or imminence of danger, soon discovered that they were not as tough or as courageous as they once thought. The stark realization that they were not the fearless warriors they envisioned themselves to be before going into the hell of war was for many a disconcerting revelation. For the first time in their young lives, they came face to face with their own mortality. That they might die before they had a chance to live was a chilling and terrifying thought.

The majority of returning American servicemen had not been home in many months, sometimes as long as two or three years or longer. The veterans who returned to their families from a war zone were, in effect, changed men. The totality of their military experience was a defining period in their young lives and they were different people after the war. One's overall military experience had a tremendous influence on personal growth and development. It was the result of several determining factors. Those factors having the greatest impact included the armed-forces lifestyle and the contact they had with men from other parts of the country—men from every conceivable background and level of the social strata. Certainly, their experiences abroad had a defining influence as well. Finally, for the impressionable young veterans of combat, the most deep-seated and lasting effect on their maturation and personality was the exposure to conditions on the battlefield.

Most had changed for the better in spite of all they had seen and done in the service. During those service years, their personal outlook on life had undergone a radical modification. For one thing, returning veterans came to view the world in a different light, with a different slant, one might say. The values and priorities of most had changed as well. First, most combat veterans were extremely grateful they had survived, and thus had a much greater sense of appreciation for every remaining day of their lives. They felt it was time given to them—a gift. Most veterans resolved to do better—to make something of themselves and provide a good life for their families.

The majority of the men coming out of World War II were highly idealistic. They vowed to strive in some small way to make the world a better place. Many veterans became more religious and attended church or synagogue regularly, to give thanks to their God for having spared them. Many became more involved in community affairs.

Most returnees were upbeat and confident about their future chances in a postwar economy. Passage of the GI Bill in 1944 was welcome news to the men serving overseas. It opened a whole new realm of possibilities that would not otherwise have been available to them. More men went on to college (on the GI Bill) in the postwar years than at any other time in the history of the nation.

Another change in the men who served at the front for extended periods was that they became a much tougher breed of individual. Not tougher physically, which most had definitely become, but in the sense that they developed an inner strength, a mental, or psychological toughness, that served them well in many situations throughout their lifetime. Call it fortitude, or personal grit, for want of a better term, a quality of character that enabled them to endure even the most difficult of situations. It was an attitude that they assumed—a powerful determination to persevere in spite of the many obstacles and disappointments they would encounter in their post-war civilian life. After all they had endured in the war, the feeling was that they could effectively deal with any situation or face any adversity thrust upon them. No matter how difficult or overburdening the situation, they would forebear, because nothing could ever be as bad as what they had experienced in battle.

These men were not afraid to stand up for themselves and for their civil rights. They would never again let anyone push them around or take advantage of them. In this regard, my father was a very tough individual. During the 1950s and early 1960s, he was active in the Brotherhood of Railroad Trainmen Union, serving as the local agent, and he fought hard for improved working conditions as well as increases in wages and better benefits.

Unfortunately, not all of the changes in behavior these GIs had undergone in the military were for the better. For example, many individuals developed drinking or gambling problems or other habits that, while in the military, were part of the everyday life of a soldier and considered normal behavior. No one gave it a second thought. Upon their return to civilian life, most men shed the bad habits acquired while in the service. Some habits, reinforced over a long period, unfortunately, were not easily given up. There were a number of other changes in personality as well, a direct result of the military lifestyle and exposure to combat, which they continued to exhibit after the war.

Combat definitely changed my father in a number of ways. Those changes were profound and indelible. While overseas, Joe Connole likely started smoking, because no one in the family can remember him smoking before he went in the service. He also acquired a drinking habit. The Army was where, as historian Lee B. Kennett says, many men "had learned to drink." I believe this was the case with my father. The late Bill Mauldin noted that, "Some guys brought the habit overseas with them," which was certainly true. My Aunt Helen, my father's sister, said to me, "Before the war your father was not a heavy drinker. He only had a drink or two socially." His sister Margaret confirmed this. This was their perception; it may not have been entirely accurate.

GIs drank for many reasons—because they were homesick or bored, but mainly for recreational purposes, a diversion from the mundane life of a soldier. It provided an escape from the tedium of a GI's daily routine both in and out of combat. Mauldin wrote in 1945, "Drinking is a big thing in a dogface's life." If one man obtained some liquor, he would share it with buddies. As the men sat around together during a lull in the fighting or at a rest area, he would pass the bottle around and each man would take a big swig. Mauldin says that even though he drank "very little," when the bottle "came around" to him, "I just naturally took a belt at it."

Some men drank to forget. Liquor could at times "dull the sharp memories of war," Mauldin said. Of course, alcohol lessened their fear and had a calming effect on the nerves. Kennett wrote, "When soldiers had taken and 'secured' a town or hamlet in France or Germany, they frequently sought out a cache of cognac or schnapps to finish the day's fighting with celebrating, relaxing, or just putting the war out of their minds for a while." One observer, quoted by Kennett, spoke of the "recuperative benefit" of alcohol, which, he noted, was used effectively to "counteract shock and fatigue." A high percentage of veterans who suffered from alcoholism after the war developed their dependency while in the service.

Memories of my father's drinking are that he rarely drank to the point where he was totally inebriated. I do not remember seeing him in that condition, ever. That is not to say it never happened. Frequently, he would come home after the family, at least the children, were asleep. He may have been a bit tipsy at times, but overall he always seemed to be in control when he drank. Joe Connole was not a hard drinker. He paced himself, and his manner of drinking was very deliberate.

I never considered my father a drunk or an alcoholic or even that he had any kind of a drinking problem. I did not think much about it until I was much older. I cannot deny that during his younger years, for some time after the war, he was a heavy drinker. By today's stricter standards, society would definitely consider him an alcoholic. In those days, however, the term carried a different connotation. An alcoholic was someone who drank all the time, who could not hold a job, or a homeless person who slept out in the park. My father never, to my knowledge, let a drinking problem interfere with his job. When I lived at home, he rarely missed a day's work. In those days, I do not believe there was any such thing as paid sick days.

I have to confess that during my growing-up years, there were many times that my father's drinking did interfere with his family obligations. When I was a youngster, and throughout my teen years as well, he spent very little time at home. On most nights off, after work, and weekends, you could find him sitting on a stool at his favorite bar, Jigger McGrail's on Green Street, or one of the other bars in his old neighborhood, the Kelley Square area in Worcester. Green, Water, Vernon, Madison, and Millbury streets all converge on the square (today, an exit from the Worcester Expressway also enters Kelley Square). In those days, there were probably thirty or more barrooms within a half-mile radius of the square. Many of these have closed over the years, including Jigger's. Today, a count reveals that there are twenty-one establishments still operating in the immediate area.

Possibly, he missed the camaraderie, the companionship, and comfort of war buddies that he had experienced in the military. While attending a reunion of the 35th Division Association, Gov. Orval E. Faubus of Arkansas, quoted by Kennett, was discussing with a war buddy the things they "missed in civilian life which we had known with our fellow soldiers." Both men had come to the same conclusion, "We were lonesome for the unequaled fellowship we had found in the ranks of our comrades. We missed the pleasure of the deep and abiding friendships." Most days or nights, when my father finished work, or on weekends, he would head for Jigger's to drink for several hours with friends, coworkers, and other acquaintances, possibly many exservicemen like himself. He was also a lifetime member of the Vernon Hill American Legion Post and would often stop there for a few drinks. After a period of time, depending on his work situation, he would usually come home for supper or go straight to bed.

In my father's defense, he was a hard worker and put in a lot of overtime whenever possible, which meant long, grueling hours, which I have mentioned in an earlier chapter. I remember him pulling double shifts and sometimes an occasional "triple" (24 hours straight). During his early years with the Boston & Maine R.R., he worked irregular shifts and workdays. For many years, he had to work 3 to 11 or the "graveyard shift," before he had finally accrued enough seniority to go on days. It was even longer before he got weekends off. As a result, there was very little social interaction with his wife and children.

My father worked outside in the rail yard during all kinds of weather. A yard conductor's job is to strike freight cars from inbound trains for distribution to local points and to direct outbound cars to the proper tracks, assembling them in the correct order for departure to distant points along the main line or a connecting track.

During a downturn in the economy, there would be slowdowns on the railroad, resulting in layoffs. When my father was laid off, I remember that the family experienced lean times. Men held bumping rights under the union contract. When cuts in the rank-and-file became necessary, a man from another yard with more seniority would bump someone from his position, and so on down the line until the low man would be out of work.

After a layoff, Connole's name went on the "spare board," which enabled him to pick up a shift or two per week. This often meant that he might have to travel some distance to a yard in another city or town. Management called men in to cover shifts on an as-needed basis—when co-workers reported in sick, went on vacation, or were out with a work injury, which was a common occurrence. Union rules required that whenever work became available, the company spread it evenly among those laid off. Some weeks my father might work only a day or two, others not at all.

Joe Connole also acquired a chronic gambling habit that plagued him throughout his postwar life. Was this something that started while in the service? More than likely he had gambled some before entering the Army, but probably only on a small scale. Nothing more than a small wager or a friendly card game. Growing up during the Depression years, it is doubtful he or any of his pals had money to waste on gambling. It was most likely in the service that he developed a compulsion for the habit, to the point of addiction.

Servicemen gambled out of sheer boredom. Like drinking, gambling was something GIs did to pass the time, to while away the many boring hours out of combat or during R&R. As a civilian, Joe Connole liked to frequent nearby horse and greyhound race tracks. He did not, that I know of, gamble to the point that it ever hurt the family financially. This assumption could be way off base, as my mother would have been the only one who could have answered that question.

One of my father's more peculiar traits, which seems to stick out in my mind for some reason, was his suspicious nature when negotiating any type of a deal—a sale, a purchase, or a trade, for example, and he would be extremely cautious during the bargaining process. At times, his behavior bordered on paranoia. Somewhere along the line, during his early years, probably in the military, he had developed a basic mistrust of other people. He was always alert to the possibility that the other person was trying to take advantage of him—in his words "trying to pull a fast one." Someone from the "big city," as he used to say, "who has been around the block a few times." He would not consummate a deal if he had any inkling that something was amiss.

Whether this attitude developed during his time in the service, I cannot say for sure. In any event, while in the Army, it probably did not take Joe Connole long to lose his prewar naiveté. On one or more occasions in the past, someone may have taken unfair advantage of him, and as a result, he was determined never to let it happen again.

It is a difficult thing to write about a parent's shortcomings, as I have discovered. My Dad had his flaws, but he also had many good points. I honestly believe he did his best to be a good father and husband. His own father died when he was only seven years old, and he had no role model in this regard—no one to emulate in raising his children.

When it came to disciplining his two oldest male children, Joe Connole was very tough and overly strict as a parent. He rarely reversed his decisions. He did not believe in sparing the rod; however, corporal punishment was never used to excess. I do not believe that this had any long-term harmful effect on me, contrary to what many child psychologists profess. The punishment hurt, but it was quick, and it was final. I much preferred this method of punishment to a period of confinement in my room for several days, especially on the weekends. The physical punishment stopped about the time I was in junior high school. I believe he thought he was doing the right thing at the time. It is possible that for the first seven years of his life this is how his father dealt with any misbehavior on his part.

During the late 1950s, I was the only teenager among my crowd of friends who had a curfew. I had to be home by nine o'clock on school nights and midnight on the weekends, "or else." This resulted in a lot of ribbing from my friends, not always good-natured, especially if we were partying or out with girls. If I came home late, my father would be waiting up, and he would be in no mood for any excuses on my part.

My father always made sure we did well in school. He checked our report cards when they came out and if we did not get good grades, there would be hell to pay. He was concerned that all of his children get a good education and urged us to go on to college. I can hear him say, "You'll never get anywhere in life, without a good education." He felt this way, I believe, because he had to work so hard all his life to get where he was. I was no Horace Mann scholar, but I always did what I had to do to pass every subject.

My father, as I remember, did not miss many family functions—birthdays, First Communions, Confirmations, graduations, and other events or celebrations. He and my mother attended all my sisters' dance recitals, school plays, and all my brother Rick and Joe's baseball games. In the late-1950s, he was working days (7-3) and had weekends off, which enabled him to spend more time at home doing things and going places with the family.

In his later years, my father mellowed. He was not as strict or harsh with my younger siblings, and they never had to endure the corporal punishment that my brother Rick and I had to go through. My brother Joe was ten years younger and my sister Kathy thirteen years younger. I was married at twenty-one and out of the house when they were eleven and eight respectively. Rick was off to college in Nebraska in 1962, and my sister Debby was married in 1964. It was as if my parents had a second family.

Chapter Twenty-Four

Home Again

When the war ended, most returning GIs, an estimated 35,000 a day, wanted only to get home and resume their normal lives. These men had a lot of catching up to do. What many wished for, was to pick up where they left off, but this of course would not be possible. As discussed in an earlier chapter, these men had undergone profound personal changes. When they arrived home, they found that the world they had left behind had changed drastically as well—it seemed to them a different place—family members, the country, the times, had also changed. After a brief readjustment period, most of them, not all, managed to ease right back into civilian life.

Married men returned from the war to wives and children. Some unmarried men came back to wed waiting sweethearts and start a family. Individuals without romantic ties when they went overseas, or those whose fiancées or girlfriends could not endure the long separation and had married others, hoped to establish new relationships. Others met and married women while in the service, many after a brief courtship.

My father's situation, which was similar to that of many other veterans at the time, had changed considerably since he entered the military. Inducted in March 1941, at age twenty-one, Joe Connole was twenty-five years old when discharged. Before being drafted, he was single with few cares and responsibilities. He married my mother in February 1942, shortly after the war began. By April 1944, the couple had two children.

While in the service, Joe Connole's involvement with his family had been minimal. Upon his return, he now had a wife and two sons to care for and support, an enormous responsibility heaped upon him all at once. His first priority was to find a decent job and then adequate housing for the family. This, he was to discover, as did many of the returning GIs, would not be an easy task.

He flew home from Europe on an "Air Transport Command C-54 Cargo carrier" to LaGuardia Field in Queens (now LaGuardia Airport) on Sunday, June 17, 1945. Historian Lee B. Kennett wrote that when the war was over, the Congress was under " 'intense pressure' to get the men back from overseas." The Army stepped up its efforts "to accelerate the movement—including bringing men home by air, several thousand each month." The flights, described as "a new system of returning veterans from the ETO," began on June 16, 1945, the day before my father arrived in the United States. The program began with three scheduled flights a day, and was expected to "ferry an estimated 30,000 . . . soldiers to the United States monthly." The first ship "took off from a field near Paris," with stops at the Azores, Newfoundland, and Presque Isle, Maine, a trip of approximately twenty-five hours. The military selected men with "a high priority rating," those having eighty-five points or more ("category four") or "medical patients" bound for hospitals in the states. The men slated for discharge would "go to reception centers near their homes for processing."

My father was one of those lucky enough to fly back to the states, sparing him the long, boring journey home, first by truck and train to the French coast and then the cross-Atlantic voyage by troop transport, a trip of at least nine to ten days, possibly longer because of delays created by the sheer numbers of returning servicemen. Found among his personal effects after he died was a small clipping from the June 19, 1944, edition of the Worcester *Evening Gazette* announcing his flight home.

My Aunt Helen said that she and my Uncle Mitt, my mother, my brother Rick, and I traveled by car to New York City, a four- to five-hour trip before the days of the superhighway, to pick up my father at the airport and make the drive back to Worcester.

A large crowd of relatives and friends waited anxiously as the C-54 carrying approximately twenty-five officers and enlisted men touched down on the runway and taxied up to the terminal. The *New York Times* weather forecast called for "hot and humid weather" with "an expected high of 90 degrees at 4 P.M.," and "possible thunder showers in the afternoon and evening." One by one, the smiling servicemen stepped out of the airplane and waved, before hurriedly descending the steps to the tarmac and into the waiting arms of loved ones. It was a joyous and tearful occasion. Joe Connole held his son, fifteen-month old Richard, whom he had never seen, in his arms for the first time. Thus began a new phase of his life.

Ten days later, on the twenty-seventh, Joe Connole traveled to the Separation Center at Fort Devens in Ayer, Massachusetts, where he received his discharge papers and officially became a civilian again. At that time, he received a bronze lapel pin decorated with an image of a spread eagle, awarded to servicemen of every branch upon discharge. GIs irreverently dubbed the pin the "ruptured duck." His "separation pay" came to $301.50, but he received only $101.50 (the discharge states "THIS PAYMENT $100"). Apparently, there were two other installments. The $1.50 was for "travel expenses."

As soon as my father mustered out, the monthly allotment checks to his wife ceased ("30 June 45"). She had been receiving $100 per month for herself and two dependent children. The wife of an enlisted man (Pfc.) with one child received a monthly family allowance of $80 and $20 for each additional child. Of that amount, the government contributed $78. The Army deducted the difference from my father's Pfc. pay which, was $110 in 1945. This left him with $88 while overseas. I obtained these figures from conversations and correspondence with veterans or their sons. For several months after my father's discharge, the family stayed at my Uncle Mitt's and Aunt Helen's apartment at 21 Carver Street in Worcester.

Demobilization, combined with a shift in the nation's economy from a wartime to a peacetime footing, resulted in a dramatic upheaval in the job market. Gone were the lucrative military contracts, which now meant massive layoffs. The media reported three million jobs lost within ten days after V-J Day. Especially hard hit were women in the workforce, primarily those employed as factory workers in heavy and light industry. The flood of returning GIs exacerbated the employment situation. For the few available jobs and careers, competition was keen.

Government and military planners wanted to carry out the demobilization process in set stages, but there was a clamor by the civilian population to have the servicemen returned home as soon as possible. Families besieged the Congress with letters and telegrams protesting the slowness of the policy. They demanded the immediate release of their loved ones from the military. As part of a planned protest, wives deluged Senators and Congressmen with thousands of "pairs of baby booties with 'I miss my daddy!' tags attached."

In the period following the war, domestic consumer goods and products were in high demand and short supply. Production of motor vehicles, household furnishings and appliances, as well as apparel and footwear ceased almost entirely during the war because of shortages of raw materials. It would take industry some months to retool from the production of war machinery to consumer goods in order to meet the purchasing demands of the postwar American public.

Shortly after the war began, newly created government regulatory agencies instituted mandatory wage-and-price controls to limit cost increases and prevent inflation. As soon as the Congress lifted these controls in 1946, the cost of goods and services, as expected, increased sharply, in some cases by as much as 100 percent and more. The overall cost of living for the average working-class American rose dramatically. Wages, however, failed to keep pace.

In an attempt to ease veterans back into civilian life, as well as to make it up to the men for the lost years fighting for their country, the federal government passed the "Serviceman's Readjustment Bill of 1944," better known as the "GI Bill of Rights." This landmark legislation, signed by President Roosevelt on June 22, 1944, provided a number of benefits, including federal aid for education and technical training, and job-finding assistance. The bill also contained a provision that guaranteed low-interest bank loans for the purchase of a home or farm or to start a business. The GI Bill was the largest government assistance program in the history of the United States.

Upon receiving his discharge, Joe Connole joined the "52-20 Club"—$20 a week unemployment compensation for fifty-two weeks, another benefit provided under the GI Bill. Six months later, during the 1946–47 Christmas Holiday season, he obtained a temporary position with the U.S. Postal Service in Worcester, as a "carrier" at $1.04 per hour. After the Christmas rush, he was again out of work.

On February 27, 1947, the Veterans Administration (VA) "Division of Vocational Rehabilitation and Education" in Worcester placed him in a position at the Messenger Printing & Publishing Company, 70 Piedmont Street, in the city, where he began "on-the-job training" as an "apprentice compositor." The company published the *Catholic Messenger*, an independent weekly newspaper. In 1950, the Catholic Diocese of Worcester purchased publication rights and changed the name of the paper to *The Catholic Free Press*. Starting wages were $28.00 per week (70 cents an hour). He quit five months later after a disagreement with a supervisor.

In July of that year, my father went to work unloading freight cars and later driving a delivery truck for the Railway Express Agency, with offices located at Union Station in Worcester. Sometime in early 1948, he landed a permanent job with the Boston & Maine Railroad as a yard conductor (his starting wage is not known). He remained with the B&M until he retired on August 1, 1983, after thirty-five years of service.

For several years after the war, there was an acute housing shortage in Worcester, as well as throughout the United States. The construction of new civilian dwellings had all but ceased during the preceding four to five years, placing the availability of housing units and apartments at a distinct premium.

At some point in 1945, our family left our temporary quarters at my Aunt Helen's and Uncle Mitt's apartment and moved into a rented apartment on the first floor of a two family house at 37 Shelby Street. In the latter part of 1947, we moved into a newly constructed "veterans' emergency housing project" called Lincolnwood on Lincoln Street, in Worcester, near Lake Quinsigamond.

On March 24, 1946, the Federal Public Housing Authority received "an appropriation of \$192,000,000." from the federal government under the "Lanham Act" to provide 2.7 million new housing units in the United States by 1948. The Worcester Housing Authority (WHA) received a contract for \$1 million to construct "25 converted Seabee barracks" that would serve as "temporary housing" for veterans and their families. Each of the two-story, flat roofed buildings contained twelve apartments, six on each floor "arranged in two rows of three[,] placed back to back," for a total of 300 units. Lincolnwood was "the largest housing development in the city's history and the largest of its type in Massachusetts. There were "over 3,000 units of similar frame construction in other Massachusetts cities and towns." "City bulldozers . . . chewed out Worcester's 13 newest streets—Victory Lane, Peace Avenue, Tolerance and Pacific Streets, Armistice Road and others." Our new address was 10 Peace Avenue.

Government officials estimated the city's share at between \$400 to \$500 per unit, which would be recovered by rents. The city voted to appropriate \$13,500 (\$450 per unit) to cover expenses. The WHA received more than 2,200 applications for the 300 available units. The first tenant moved in on October 15, 1947. The complex had a population of approximately 1,200. Rent on the apartment we occupied was thirty-five dollars per month.

It was not until 1954, that Joe Connole took advantage of the VA's home loan program, when he obtained a government-backed mortgage for \$6,500 to purchase a three-decker house (see Chapter 2) at 50–52 Paine Street, in Worcester. The property had a large barn in the back that once accommodated horses and carriages and an eight-car garage on a second attached lot. Discovered in the sealed crawl space of the barn after we moved in, were parts of leather bridles and reins and some old bales of hay, among an assortment of other junk. My mother and father lived in the house until their deaths, my mother in 1981 and my father in 1990.

Chapter Twenty-Five

Wounds of the Mind

After arriving home, most combat veterans wanted only to put the war behind them and get on with their lives. For many, thoughts or recollections of their experiences in battle evoked memories too bitter to relive. To revisit the scenes of ghastly carnage, terror, chaos, and grief was too painful for them to bear. Veterans made a conscious effort to suppress all memory of the war, but to their dismay, the majority discovered they could not easily forget. As much as they would like to have done so, they found it next to impossible to blank the war out of their minds. The memories seemed always to be there—lurking in the distant recesses of their subconscious—ready to intrude upon their thoughts and invade their dreams. It would be some time before their lives would return to any kind of normalcy. Disturbing memories and dreams of the war continued to periodically haunt them throughout their lifetimes, although the episodes tended to decrease gradually over time.

In an article titled "To Remember or Forget," published in the Fall 1996 issue of *The Fighting 36th Historical Quarterly*, Morris Courington (K-142) tried to convey just how difficult it was for combat veterans to suppress all memory of the war. The article was later incorporated into Courington's book, *Cruel Was the Way*, written with seven other T-Patchers. Courington's situation was typical of most GIs after the war.

Upon his return to the states, Courington said that he made the "decision . . . to slam the door on the past, on the war, and army life and never look back." He "did not want to relive the war or answer any questions." Courington was, as he says, an "all-out 'control freak,'" and believed he would have absolutely no trouble repressing all memory of the war, only to discover how difficult this proved to be. He believed he had a choice, "to remember or forget." There was never any doubt in his mind what he would do. Courington explained: "I would choose to forget because my experiences varied from bad to horrible. I found the war to be so abhorrent, so unacceptable, that I never even considered trying to remember. My thought was always, 'wipe it out, forget it, and never look back.'" Courington believed that "there would be no problem"; after all, he "was in complete control." For "almost fifty years" his efforts "worked pretty well," that is, he said, "90 percent of the time."

After a number of years, the protective barrier Courington had put up to block out painful memories of the war began to slowly crumble. Still he persisted in his attempts at pushing all unwanted memories from his conscious thought. "During these many years, I believe I was largely in denial—not willing to face the past or to accept the war memories as part of me. But I was not really in control," he said. Courington described the process of trying to suppress all memory of combat as, "THE WAR WITHIN." The older he got, it became "much harder" for him to avoid—or turn off—or deny what had happened, he said.

As "an all-out 'control freak,'" Courington says he had "to learn the hard way." What he discovered was, "that some details and minor events" could be cleansed from the mind, but "the most traumatic things . . . cannot simply be forgotten." In the final analysis, what Courington determined was that:

> The physical wounds healed and the pain went away, but emotional scars never heal. You can try to run away from it, push it aside, and keep yourself busy. But the hurt is never far away. You can run but you cannot hide for long. You can never forget—especially those things you thought you had refused to remember. To forget is impossible. To remember is most painful.

Courington's insightful thoughts into the mindset of many veterans has provided me with part of the answer as to why my father refused to discuss the war with me.

No one who experienced prolonged combat came through the war unscathed—some suffered more psychological damage than others did. They wanted just to forget, but this was, as Courington so eloquently explained, simply not possible, nor would it ever be. Most veterans found it difficult enough under ordinary circumstances to suppress memories of horrifying battle experiences, without someone bringing the subject up in conversation that would set their minds racing and trigger feelings of pain and depression.

During the course of my research, I interviewed and corresponded with a number of men from both the 26th and 36th Divisions. Inevitably, at some point, the subject of combat veterans' refusal to discuss their combat experiences would come up in letters or conversation. Peter Androne of Cleveland,

Ohio, a member of Company D, 141st Infantry, said in a telephone interview: "After I left France, I decided to wipe it out of my mind. Guys who were on the front lines and saw a lot of action did not want to talk about it after the war. When my kids asked what happened to me during the war, I'd reply 'nothing interesting.' It's the rear echelon guys that do all the talking."

Severely wounded on September 19, 1944, near the town of Fougerolles, France, Androne spent a lengthy recovery and recuperation period at the 300th General Hospital in Naples, Italy. His days as a combat soldier over, Androne traveled back to the United States aboard a hospital ship for further convalescence stateside.

Of my father's reluctance to discuss the war, William Claude Harrelson, originally from Ruffin, North Carolina, wrote in 1999, "I can understand why he would not talk about the war. I still have dreams about it and they are not very pleasant dreams." Harrelson was a medic with the 141st Medical Detachment assigned to the first platoon (machine guns), Company D, 141st Infantry. In the mid-1950s, Harrelson entered the ministry and later served as the pastor of a Baptist church for forty years.

Many of the veterans' wives or widows with whom I have spoken or corresponded told me that for many years their husbands never discussed the war with anyone, not even with them. Reneta Benenati, the widow of Sgt. Carl G. Benenati, a forward observer for the mortar platoon of Company D, 141st Infantry, wrote, "My husband did not talk about the war for more than forty years. It was only after he started going to reunions of the 141st that he started to open up. In the last few years of his life he would talk about his experiences." Benenati joined the regiment just before the Battle of San Pietro in Italy and remained with Company D until the Vosges Mountains in France when he was seriously wounded by a German 88mm flak gun while directing fire from the 81mm mortars on enemy positions (see Chapter 5, "Stovepipe Platoon").

Most veterans of combat refuse to discuss the war with anyone except other veterans. As one veteran quoted by historian John C. McManus put it, "Others don't know a damn thing about what you're talking about and don't care." McManus posed the question, "How does a man who has truly faced his own mortality at an early age communicate what that was like to someone who has never had to do so?" After surveying all the literature containing information on the subject, it was his expert opinion that "most combat veterans" would answer "that they do not." He concluded that the "outsider can listen to the words, but he or she can never really feel the emotions, and it is the emotion generated by combat experiences that stay with most combat soldiers forever."

In a 1988 article in *The 36th Division Historical Quarterly* titled, "Flashbacks," S-Sgt. Rex Harrison, Jr., of Shreveport, Louisiana (143rd Medical

Detachment), an aid man with Company L, 143rd Infantry, described the mind as "an accumulation of memories—pleasant ones are remembered with a smile," while the "others are stored in a dark area." The "others" in this case are horrifying battlefield memories, of which he wrote:

> An individual who hasn't experienced the trauma of witnessing sudden death, fatal wounds, extreme heat/cold or smelled gas gangrene is never initiated into that select group of warriors who, after over forty years, still "flashback" and bring these memories back in all of their ugliness and or weird humor as the occasion demands.

Harrison said, "Most of our 'war stories' are only discussed with other veterans," that is, "other associates who have gone through these experiences."

In 1991, William F. Hartung, Sr. (E-143) invited three of his former Easy Company comrades, whom he had not seen since the war, to his home in Ravenna, Ohio, for a four-day reunion. On the day of their arrival, the four men spent five hours discussing their days in the 36th Division. As each man spoke about a particular incident, it brought back a flood of memories for the others. Hartung told a reporter from the *Ravenna Record-Courier* that "it felt good to talk about the war with those who shared the same experiences. With men like that, you can talk about it and it doesn't bother you, because they understand what it's like."

After the war, many of the men joined veterans' organizations, and later began attending reunions. After having heard others express feelings that had been bottled up inside for years, they began to open up more. They discovered that they were not alone. Many of their comrades, they learned, had on occasion been unable to control their fear in combat or suffered a psychological breakdown and later felt a sense of guilt and shame. Other veterans were the only people they could discuss their experiences with—they could understand what they had been through and how they had suffered for it afterward. To my knowledge, my dad never attended any reunions. He was a member of the Vernon Hill American Legion Post 435 in Worcester where he, no doubt, had on occasion a chance to commiserate with other veterans.

In a posting on the 36th Division Message Board titled, "The Reluctant Veteran," Paul D. Hinkle (L-141) wrote:

> When [the returning veteran] tried to tell his story, his family and friends had more current things to talk about. They lived through the war at home and had their own problems. He also wanted to adjust to civilian life, so he put his stories away and started to live the life he left behind. He joined the civilians to start a new life and family. Decades went by; he retired and suddenly the 50th Anniversary of WW II battles reawakened those memories (stories) of men and

places he knew. Military music and taps caused him to choke up; tears welled in his eyes. Memories of lost buddies came back. Some vets found family friends who were interested and would listen to their stories.

But many veterans, he added, "still had trouble remembering and telling about those times," and there were others, "who took their story to their grave." Many men "who received medals had not told their family or friends."

Many of the combat veterans I spoke to or corresponded with in the past several years mentioned that they still had occasional, and in some cases frequent, nightmares, as expressed by several veterans above. One 26th Division veteran told me, "I fight the war almost every night. The dreams seem as frightening as when the actual events occurred." Bill Hartung, expressed similar feelings, "The nightmares make it seem like it all happened yesterday, not 50 years ago."

Once, at a reunion of Company H, 181st, 26th Division, I asked Dr. Romeo LeBlanc if he had seen the movie *Saving Private Ryan*. "No," he answered softly. I said it was a great movie and that he should go and see it. "I can't go to war movies," was his response. Why not? I asked, a stupid question on my part, which I realized as soon as the words left my lips, but it was too late to catch myself. "I wouldn't be able to sleep for three weeks," he said quietly. This was almost sixty years after the fact. After leaving the 26th, the Army assigned LeBlanc to the 5th Armored Division where he rose to the rank of First Sergeant. He saw extensive action in France and, because he spoke fluent French, became a liaison to FFI forces.

In a telephone conversation in 1999, Charles B. Price (Hq. Co., 3rd Bn.-142nd) said, "When I first got out of the service, I was so nervous I would not get on a trolley. When I finally got on one for the first time, I thought all the passengers were staring at me. To this day, I still have occasional nightmares." Originally from Granbury, Texas, Price met and married Ruth Stevens, a local girl, while stationed at Camp Edwards on Cape Cod. After the war, the couple settled in Worcester, Massachusetts.

Some veterans, those exposed to the grim realities of extended combat, carried the scars of war deep within their psyche. Following the war, these men suffered from a host of combat-related emotional and psychological problems. The degree of post-combat stress was directly proportional to the length of time and levels of exposure to trauma during their deployment period. Disturbing recollections of their days in combat came back to haunt them on an almost daily basis. Individuals regularly re-experience these traumatic events through recurring thoughts, vivid flashbacks, and troubling nightmares. The wounds these men suffered in the war were not of the body, but of the mind.

In 1945, professionals in the psychiatric field had very little knowledge or understanding of the psychological problems experienced by combat veterans and the detrimental effect they had on a person's overall physical and mental health. Extensive studies conducted by psychiatrists and psychologists following the Vietnam War eventually led to the classification of a new type of anxiety disorder referred to by the American Psychiatric Association (APA) as Post-traumatic Stress Disorder (PTSD). Today, the psychiatric community classifies PTSD (initially identified as "Post Vietnam Syndrome") as one of a number of anxiety disorders that include Panic Disorder, Obsessive-Compulsive Disorder, Phobias, and Generalized Anxiety Disorder.

Anxiety disorders, according to the National Institute of Mental Health (NIMH), "are illnesses that fill people's lives with overwhelming anxiety and fear that are chronic, unremitting, and can grow progressively worse." The NIMH defines PTSD as "an anxiety disorder that can develop after exposure to a terrifying event or ordeal in which grave physical harm occurred or was threatened." Traditionally, the mental health community believed the disorder applied only to men "who had been involved in heavy combat." Researchers now know that the condition can occur in survivors of rape, physical or sexual abuse, criminal assault or other violent crimes, accidents, terrorist attacks, and other disasters, both natural and manmade. The means of exposure may include, "witnessing, experiencing, or participating in a traumatic event." Experts divide Post-traumatic Stress Disorder into two broad categories, Combat PTSD and Noncombat PTSD. People of any age, male or female, including children or adolescents, can suffer from PTSD.

People with PTSD "repeatedly re-experience the ordeal in the form of flashback episodes, memories, nightmares or frightening thoughts, especially when they are exposed to events or objects reminiscent of the trauma." The American Psychiatric Association defines "flashbacks" experienced by people with PTSD as "sudden vivid memories that are accompanied by painful emotions that take over the victim's attention." During flashbacks, the recollection "may be so strong that individuals almost feel like they are actually experiencing the trauma again or seeing it unfold before their eyes and in nightmares."

Major psychosomatic symptoms of PTSD include panic attacks, emotional withdrawal, feelings of anger or irritability, and difficulty falling asleep or staying asleep. Victims may also experience emotional numbness, difficulty concentrating, and have an exaggerated startle response to any sudden noise or movement. A number of "physical symptoms" are common in people diagnosed with PTSD including "headaches, gastrointestinal distress, immune system problems, dizziness, chest pain, or discomforts of other parts of the body."

If a person survived a traumatic event and others, friends, or relatives did not, they often developed guilt feelings, sometimes called "survivors guilt." They constantly asked themselves why, and wondered if there was a reason. The guilt may be the result of "an actual or perceived mistake or error" on their part.

Any external cue can trigger these unwanted, intrusive memories—a television documentary, radio announcement, a significant date (V-E Day, V-J Day, December 7, 1941, etc.), the anniversary of a traumatic event, or even the mere mention of the war in conversation—which could result in one or more symptoms. Anything reminiscent of their days in battle, certain objects, noises such as a low flying airplane, any loud bang, the sound of a jackhammer, certain smells, for example, would send a chill down their spines, or cause a sudden, severe panic attack. Sometimes the memories could pop into a person's conscious thought unexpectedly, for no apparent reason at all—it could happen at any time, anywhere, and when least expected.

William Hartung wrote, "Memorial Day—is a day designated in the U.S. for honoring the dead members of the armed forces. It brings back a lot of memories to me, some good, some bad. I think the bad outnumber the good."

The American Psychiatric Association says that "many people with PTSD also attempt to rid themselves of their painful re-experiences, loneliness, and panic attacks by abusing alcohol or other drugs as a 'self medication' that helps them blunt their pain and forget the trauma temporarily." Alcohol and antidepressants bring about only temporary relief, as well as a host of side effects.

"In some cases," the Public Information Section of the APA writes, "the symptoms of PTSD disappear with time, whereas in others they persist for many years," and "often occurs with—or lead to—other psychiatric illnesses, such as depression." One study of Vietnam veterans, quoted by the Surgeon General's office, "found 15 percent . . . to be suffering from post-traumatic stress disorder 19 years after combat exposure."

After learning about this condition, and reviewing my father's VA medical records, there is no doubt in my mind that he suffered from PTSD. After the death of my mother in 1981, I would visit him at home in the evening and we would talk, and on occasion, have a couple of drinks. If he happened to be in a particularly good mood, I would try to steer the conversation around to the war by mentioning a great book I had recently read, or tell him about a movie I had seen that was playing locally. I tried different strategies. He was well aware of my interest in WWII and could tell immediately where I was going. If I persisted, he would get up from the table and say, "I've told you before, I don't want to discuss the war." End of conversation, it was time to leave. After a while, I stopped asking.

Looking back, I now know that whenever I asked him to tell me about his experiences during the war, it resulted in an adverse reaction. I remember the strange look on his face. He would get angry. I continued to broach the subject only because I thought that one day he might open up and relate some of his experiences, not the bad ones. I only wanted to hear about where he had been and what he had seen and done. I did not convey to him that this was my only intention, which, in hindsight, I should have done. This approach, I now believe, might have netted better results. Maybe not. I realize now, also, that the mere mention of the war triggered disturbing thoughts and memories of his days in combat.

On June 28, 1945, one day after his discharge date, Joe Connole applied for "disability compensation" for a "nervous condition" from the regional office of the Veterans Administration in Boston, Massachusetts. Following a scheduled psychological evaluation, the VA awarded Connole a 10 percent disability pension for "Anxiety Hysteria" in the amount of $11.50 monthly, retroactive to the date of the application. One of the stipulations of the judgment was that he submit to periodic examinations by a VA appointed psychiatrist. One year later, the VA increased the benefit amount to $13.80.

My father continued to collect the pension until December 25, 1947, at which time the VA reduced his compensation to zero. The VA declared him ineligible, "due to an improvement in [his] service related nervous condition." The "Opinion," found on the report submitted by the examining doctor, dated July 23, 1947, states that he was "essentially negative for physical disability or neurotic ailment."

Seven years later, on July 30, 1953, my father submitted an application to the VA in Boston, seeking "restoration of compensation" for his "service connected disability." After the Worcester tornado struck on June 9, 1953, he went to the VA office in Worcester requesting treatment for his "nervous condition," that he claimed was "aggravated" by the disaster. Veterans Administration personnel scheduled an appointment for a VA appointed psychiatrist to examine him at Worcester State Hospital. The appointment took place on January 10, 1954. At this time, Connole told the doctor that he was "very nervous, tense, and couldn't sleep" and that he was "bothered by dreams."

At this time, the doctor questioned him about his "service related nervous condition" and he answered that he had been hospitalized for battle fatigue in August 1944, and that the breakdown occurred following the loss of "two buddies," who, he related, "were shot." Following the examination, the doctor prescribed the sedative phenobarbital.

The 1953 Worcester tornado was one of the worst storms on record, killing ninety-four people, injuring thousands, and causing massive destruction to property, with damage in the millions of dollars to the city and surrounding towns. Our apartment at the 980 unit Great Brook Valley veterans' housing project was in the direct path of the tornado and sustained heavy damage. The complex's brick and steel construction, however, saved many lives. Homes constructed of wood adjacent to the complex were leveled. The National Weather Service Storm Prediction Center in Norman, Oklahoma, ranks the Worcester tornado as the twentieth most deadly recorded tornado in U.S. history and the most destructive ever to touch down in the northeast.

The funnel, with winds estimated at between 200 to 260 mph (some estimates are higher) touched down in Petersham, and cut a forty-six-mile path through eight communities in Central Massachusetts. The Great Brook Valley veterans' project where we lived was in the direct path of the tornado resulting in extensive damage. Tenants had to vacate the complex until contractors completed the necessary repairs, and the families were unable to move back for nearly four months.

At the time the twister struck, about five o'clock in the afternoon, my brother Rick and I and two other friends were playing in a nearby field. Suddenly, the sky grew ominously dark, and golf-ball-sized hailstones began to fall, completely covering the ground, an inch or two thick. They were falling with extreme velocity, and it felt like someone was pelting us with stones. We had to crouch low, protecting our heads with our arms to prevent being hurt. One of my friends, Patrick Thibaud, and I made a dash for his apartment about the length of a football field away, and barely made it inside the hallway of the building before the storm hit in all its fury. I remember a gust of wind ripping the door to the apartment building, which was very thick, out of my hand and slamming up against the side of the building. My brother made it home safely.

Members of the Thibaud family were looking out the picture window at the papers and other debris violently swirling about, when all the windows suddenly exploded inward with a loud crack, showering everyone in the apartment with broken glass. We instinctively threw our hands up to cover our faces, and several of us had tiny cuts on our forearms and hands. The family huddled behind parlor furniture or inside walls, waiting for the storm to subside.

I can only describe the noise, which lasted several minutes, as sounding like a thousand railroad locomotives. The storm ended as quickly as it began, and afterwards, it became eerily quiet, and the sun shone brightly.

I walked home cautiously, dodging downed power lines, sparking and snapping on the still wet pavement. The area looked like a battle zone, with debris strewn all about, and wrecked and overturned cars in the project's parking lots, including the family automobile. I saw a dead woman lying in the middle of nearby Tacoma Street, her head in a pool of blood. A newspaper account reported that she had been waiting at the bus stop across from our apartment when the storm hit. I heard screams coming from a bus with its front end leaning up on the side of one of the project buildings. The funnel had picked the vehicle up and carried it about thirty to forty feet from the street. The newspaper stated that two people in the bus died and several others suffered serious injuries. My father was outside looking for me and ran to my side to escort me around the live wires blocking my path to the basement where the tenants in our building had congregated.

I learned only recently from a family member that until I returned home, my parents were extremely worried that I might have been severely injured, or possibly killed. My mother and father must have gone through a very stressful time waiting for word that I was safe.

The disaster had a deep psychological effect on every member of the family. For many years thereafter, whenever the sky darkened and a thunderstorm approached, I suffered severe anxiety. It was the same for my parents and siblings. I have spoken with other victims of the tornado and their reaction to approaching summer storms after the tornado was similar.

On November 23, 1953, my father submitted a letter to the VA written by the family physician, Dr. Carl P. Benaglia of Worcester, which is printed here in full:

Dr. Carl P. Benaglia, M.D.
80 Shrewsbury Street
Worcester 4, Massachusetts

October 26, 1953

TO WHOM IT MAY CONCERN:

This is to certify that I have been treating Dennis J. Connole, 43 Great Brook Valley [Ave.], Worcester, Mass., for a nervous condition ever since his discharge from the service in June 1945.

I have been seeing him approximately every 4 to 6 months up to this date.
Chief complaints have been:

1. Nervousness
2. Inability to sleep
3. Stomach upsets

Physical exam: Well developed and nourished male. Heart, lungs and abdomen are negative.

Diagnosis: 1. Neurosis
2. Anxiety

These symptoms have all been greatly exaggerated since the tornado in June 1953. At the present time he is being treated by a Physician at the Veterans Administration office.

Very truly yours,

Carl P. Benaglia, M.D.
CPB/ges.

Upon receipt of Dr. Benaglia's letter, and after reviewing Connole's application, a VA board voted to restore his compensation on January 27, 1954, retroactive to November 5, 1953. The compensation continued until his death in 1990.

The paper trail on my father's time in the U.S. Army ends on September 8, 1944, when doctors declared him fit for duty and ordered him to return to his unit after his temporary breakdown during the battle of Montelimar on August 25, 1944. The VA file contains no other military records, an indication that he had no further psychological problems. According to his discharge papers, he remained with Company D, 141st Infantry, until the end of the war.

Dennis "Joe" Connole died of cancer on August 9, 1990, at the age of seventy. His death certificate states the cause of death as, "Metastasized Squamous Cell Laryngeal Cancer." Approximately one year earlier, at age sixty-nine, he had had several cancerous skin lesions removed from his face. Several months later, doctors discovered a tumor in his throat. After smoking his entire adult life, he finally gave up the habit. It was too late. The cancer eventually spread to his lungs.

Bibliography

SOURCES USED IN INTRODUCTION

Connole, Dennis J. U.S. Army "Enlisted Record and Report of Separation Honorable Discharge, 27 June 45." Form WD AGO 53–55, November 1944.

"Executive Order 9419, Authorizing Award of the Bronze Star Medal, February 8, 1944." <http://www.amervets.com/replacement/bs.htm#exo1> (July 4, 1988).

"Executive Order 11046, Authorizing Award of the Bronze Star Medal, August 24, 1962, Supersedes: EO 9419." <http://www.amervets.com/replacement/bs.htm#exo1> (July 4, 1988).

The Piersall Collection of Orders, Decorations, and Medals From Around the World: The Bronze Star Medal. <http://www.marksmedals.com/us_medals_files/bronze _star.html> (June 6, 2005).

SOURCES USED IN CHAPTER 1: THE WAR SOUVENIRS

Hinkle, Paul D. "Honorary Texan." 36th Division Association, *The Fighting 36th Historical Quarterly,* vol. 12, no. 1 (Spring 1992): 42–45. See also "Memories Never Forgotten." <http://www.kwanah.com/36division/ps/ps900337.htm> (2001).

Nasso, James A. "Payroll." 36th Division Association Message Board, posted December 1, 2006. <http://p081.ezboard.com/36th-InfantryDivision/btexasmilitaryforces museum> (1999–2007).

Interview

Jack W. Wilson (D-141)

SOURCES USED IN CHAPTER 2:
26TH "YANKEE" DIVISION, 1941–1943

"Army, United States, World War II (1939–1945)." *World Book Encyclopedia.* Chicago: Scott Fetzer Company, 2001, vol. 1: 730–41.

Connole, Dennis J. U.S. Army "Enlisted Record and Report of Separation, Honorable Discharge, 27 June 45." Form WD AGO 53–55, November 1944.

Dear, I.C.B., General Editor, and M.R.D. Foot, Consultant Editor. *The Oxford Companion to World War II.* Oxford: Oxford University Press, 1995.

Doubler, Lt. Col. Michael D. "Guard Century–Not So Calm, Before the Storm: 1920 to 1940" (Second in a five-part series). *National Guard Magazine*, vol. 53, issue 10 (October 1999): 32–35. Available online at <http://www.ngaus.org/content.asp?bid=2491>.

Drum, Lt. General Hugh A. "The Eastern Defense Command: A Review of Its Operations." *Army & Navy Journal.* Special edition, vol. LXXXI (Dec. 7, 1943): 57, 152.

Gabel, Christopher R. *The U.S. Army GHQ Maneuvers of 1941.* Washington, D.C.: U.S. Army Center for Military History, 1991.

Gearan, John. "Remembering Days Gone By/Forgotten St. John's Gym Sparks Memories." *Worcester Telegram & Gazette* 25 March 1994, D3.

"History of the 181st [Regiment]." Paper on file at the Massachusetts National Guard Military Museum & Archives, Worcester, Mass.: 1–9.

Kimball, Warren. "Lend-Lease." *The Oxford Companion to World War II.* I.C.B. Dear, General Editor, and M.R.D. Foot, Consultant Editor. Oxford: Oxford University Press, 1995: 677–79.

"Lend-Lease." *World Book Encyclopedia.* Chicago: Scott Fetzer Company, 2001, vol. 12: 190.

Macksey, Kenneth. "Blitzkrieg." *The Oxford Companion to World War II.* I.C.B. Dear, General Editor, and M.R.D. Foot, Consultant Editor. Oxford: Oxford University Press, 1995: 140.

Patterson, James T. "Roosevelt, Franklin Delano." *World Book Encyclopedia.* Chicago: Scott Fetzer Company, 2001, vol. 16: 452–63.

Pope, Chris. "Draft for WW II recalled: Worcester men in '158 Club.' " *Worcester Sunday Telegram* 14 October 1990, A1, 14.

Price, Alfred. "Blitz." *The Oxford Companion to World War II.* I.C.B. Dear, General Editor, and M.R.D. Foot, Consultant Editor. Oxford: Oxford University Press, 1995: 138–40.

"Selective service system." *The Oxford Companion to World War II.* I.C.B. Dear, General editor, and M.R.D. Foot, Consultant Editor. Oxford: Oxford University Press, 1995: 996.

Short, Joseph B. "First Peace-time Draft is Voted." *Worcester Telegram* 15 September 1940, 1, Sec. 2, 13.

Snyder, Louis L. "World War II." *Academic American Encyclopedia.* Granby, Connecticut: Grolier, Inc., 2002, vol. 20, 249–81.

Stokesbury, James L. "World War II." *World Book Encyclopedia.* Chicago: Scott Fetzer Company, 2001, vol. 21, 468–98.

Sword, Keith. "Poland." *The Oxford Companion to World War II*. I.C.B. Dear, General Editor, and M.R.D. Foot, Consultant Editor. Oxford: Oxford University Press, 1995: 891–903.

U.S. Army, Office of the Chief of Military History. Eastern Defense Command, G-3, New York. "History of the Eastern Defense Command, and the Defense of the Atlantic Coast of the U.S. in the Second World War," 1945. See Chapter IV, "Combat Teams and Reconnaissance Patrols," 52–55. Paper on File at the U.S. Army Military History Institute, Carlisle Barracks, Carlisle, Pennsylvania.

Yankee Division Veterans Association. *The History of the 26th Yankee Division: 1917–1919 and 1941–1945*. Salem, Mass.: Turner Publishing Company, 2000 (Reprint).

Interviews and Correspondence

John F. Judge (C-181)

Helen G. Palumbo

SOURCES USED IN CHAPTER 3: OVERSEAS

Benton, George A. "We're On Our Way." 36th Division Association, *The Fighting 36th Historical Quarterly*, vol. 11, no. 3 (Fall 1991): 36–43.

Charles, Roland W. *Troop Ships of World War II*. Washington, D.C.: Army Transportation Association, 1947.

Clover, Jack L. "The Strange Saga of Corporal Leslie." 36th Division Association, *The Fighting 36th Division Historical Quarterly*, vol. 2, no. 1 (Spring 1982): 39–42.

Connole, Dennis J. Veterans Administration (VA) File #05-075-171.

"Deck Log and War Diary." USS *General A.E. Anderson* (AP-111). National Archives and Records Administration (NARA), Modern Military Records, Textual Archives Services Division, College Park, Maryland.

Dictionary of American Naval Fighting Ships, Vol. III. Washington, D.C.: Navy Department, Office of the Chief of Naval History Division, 1968.

Kennett, Lee B. *G.I.: The American Soldier in World War II*. Norman, Oklahoma: University of Oklahoma Press, 1997.

Kibbey, Samuel F. "A Rebel Without a Coors." 36th Division Association, *The Fighting 36th Historical Quarterly*, vol. 4, no. 2 (Summer 1984): 24–31.

Lee, Rod. *God Is Our Co-Pilot: The Life and Times of Ross Rajotte–An American Patriot* Whitinsville, Mass.: Old Colony Stationery, 2002.

141st Infantry Regiment Association. *Five Years, Five Countries, Five Campaigns*. Clifford H. Peek, ed. Munich, Germany, 1945.

Stern, Allen E. "A Personal View of World War II, Part 1." 36th Division Association, *The Fighting 36th Historical Quarterly*, supplement to the *T-Patcher Newsletter*, vol. 15, no. 4 (Winter 1995): 20–21.

USS *General A.E. Anderson* Association. <http://www.ussgeneralanderson.org/>.

Wilson, Calvin R. "Air Attack, Torpedo Snatch Bullet in Head, Back Home." 36th Division Association, *The Fighting 36th Historical Quarterly*, supplement to the *T-Patcher Newsletter,* vol. 15, no. 8 (Spring 1995): 8.

Correspondence

William E. Hamelman (USS *General A.E. Anderson*)
Rosaire J. Rajotte (A-141)
Nicholas J. Renzetti (H-181)
Sulo O. Ruuska (H-181)

SOURCES USED IN CHAPTER 4:
REPLACEMENTS JOIN THE 36TH "TEXAS" DIVISION

Doughty, R. K. "Sanctuary." 36th Division Association, *The Fighting 36th Historical Quarterly*, vol. 10, no. 3 (Fall 1990): 37–41. See also 36th Division Association, "Memories Never Forgotten." <http://www.kwanah.com/36division/ps/ps900337.htm> (1999).

Etienne, Robert. *Pompeii: the day a city died*. New York: H.N. Abrams, 1992.

Grant, Michael. *Cities of Vesuvius, Pompeii and Hurculaneum*. New York: Penguin, 1976.

"History of Operations, 141st Infantry Regiment, Rifle, May 1944" (After Action Reports). Headquarters 36th Infantry Division: 1–12. National Archives and Records Administration, Modern Military Records, Textual Archives Services Division, College Park, Maryland.

Kennett, Lee B. *G.I.: The American Soldier in World War II*. Norman, Oklahoma: University of Oklahoma Press, 1997.

Lee, Rod. *God Is Our Co-Pilot: The Life and Times of Ross Rajotte–An American Patriot*. Whitinsville, Mass.: Old Colony Stationery, 2002.

"Maddaloni, Italy, March 1944" (unsigned article). 36th Division Association, *The Fighting 36th Historical Quarterly*, supplement to the *T-Patcher Newsletter,* vol. 16, no. 1 (Spring 1996): 9.

141st Infantry Regiment Association. *Five Years, Five Countries, Five Campaigns*. Clifford H. Peek, ed. Munich, Germany, 1945.

Pyle, Ernie. *Brave Men*. New York: H. Holt and Company, 1944.

Shaffer, Roger L. *Letters Home: A Soldier's Legacy*. Plano, Texas: Republic of Texas Press, 1997. A biography of William A. "Buck" Rodgers.

Sinacola, Chris. "Army Vets Recall 'T-Patcher' Days: Association Keeps Tabs on Members of the 36th Infantry." *Worcester Sunday Telegram* 22 March 1992, B1.

Taney, Warren E. "WW II Diary of an Engineer." 36th Division Association, *The Fighting 36th Historical Quarterly*, vol. 9, no. 1 (Spring 1989): 62–80.

36th Division Association. *The Fighting 36th: A Pictorial History* (reprint of the 1945 edition). Paducah, Kentucky: Turner Publishing Company, 1995. N.p.

Wagner, Robert L. *The Texas Army: A History of the 36th Division in the Italian Campaign.* Austin, Texas: State House Press, 1972.

Interviews and Correspondence

Edward A. Chrobak (E-142)
Charles A. Golub (K-143)
John Paul Jones (D-141)
Romeo C. LeBlanc (H-181)
Rosaire J. Rajotte (A-141)

SOURCES USED IN CHAPTER 5:
THE "STOVEPIPE PLATOON"

Bond, Harold L. *Return to Cassino: A Memoir of the Fight for Rome.* New York: Doubleday & Company, Inc., 1964.
Bunker, Robert D. "Memories of the 36th Texas Infantry Division." 36th Division Association, *The 36th Division Historical Quarterly*, vol. 13, no. 4 (Winter 1993): 68–71.
Doubler, Michael D. *Closing With the Enemy: How GIs Fought the War in Europe, 1944–1945.* Lawrence, Kansas: University Press of Kansas, 1994.
81mm Mortar Instructional Pamphlet ST 7-191 FY 77. Fort Benning, Georgia: United States Army Infantry School, 1977.
81–MM Mortar M1, Basic Field Manual, FM 23–90. Washington D.C.: U.S. Government Printing Office, 1942.
Ellis, John. *The Sharp End: The Fighting Man in World War II.* New York: Scribner, 1980.
Gaul, Jeffrey, et al. *Fighting 36th Infantry Division.* Paducah, Kentucky: Turner Publishing Company, 1988.
Hogg, Ian V. *The Encyclopedia of Infantry Weapons of World War II.* New York: Crowell, 1977.
———. "Mortars." *The Oxford Companion to World War II.* I.C.B. Dear, General Editor and M.R.D. Foot, Consultant Editor. Oxford: Oxford University Press, 1995: 759–60.
IRTC [Infantry Replacement Training Center]. "I am a Doughboy." See "I am a member of a Heavy Weapons Company": 14–19. Pamphlet (c. 1944).
Kelley, Charles E. "Commando," with Pete Martin. *One Man's War.* New York: A.A. Knopf, 1944.
Kirby, Wayne C. "Memories That Won't Fade." 36th Division Association, *The Fighting 36th Historical Quarter*ly, supplement to the *T-Patcher Newsletter*, vol.18, no. 2 (Summer 1998): 2–3.
McFall, John F. "An Infantryman's Concerns About Survival." 36th Division Association, *The Fighting 36th Historical Quarterly*, supplement to the *T-Patcher Newsletter,* vol. 19, no. 3 (Fall 1999): 15.

———. "First Day of Combat." 36th Division Association, *The Fighting 36th Historical Quarterly* supplement to the *T-Patcher Newsletter*, vol. 19, no. 4 (Winter 1999): 14.

Mansee, Earl A. "Hope I Did My Part." 36th Division Association, *The Fighting 36th Historical Quarterly*, vol. 9, no. 2 (Summer 1989): 36–40.

Mauldin, Bill. *Up Front*. New York: H. Holt and Company, 1945.

Mortar Gunnery, FM 23–91. Washington, D.C.: Headquarters, Department of the Army, 1971.

Sizemore, Arlis D. *Hidden Memories of World War II*. Topeka, Kansas: Learning Resources, Inc., 2002.

Spencer, Robert F. "The Big Little Artillery Piece of the Inf. WW II." 36th Division Association, *The Fighting 36th Historical Quarterly*, vol. 12, no. 4 (Winter 1992): 59–60.

"Table of Organization and Equipment [TO&E] Infantry Heavy Weapons Company, No.7-18." Washington, D.C.: U.S. War Department, 15 July 1943.

Interviews and Correspondence

Robert D. Bunker (M-143)
George L. Ferguson (M-141)
Guido J. Fratturelli (H-181)
Walter T. Loster (D-141)
David H. McKee (M-143)
George N. Morse (M-141)
Ray A. Osborne, Jr. (D-141)
James W. Robinson (A-141)
Herman G. Scott (D-141)
Arlis D. Sizemore (D-141)
Earnest R. Smeltzer (D-141)
Jack W. Wilson (D-141)

SOURCES USED IN CHAPTER 6:
THE STALLED ITALIAN CAMPAIGN RESUMES-MAY 1944

Blumenson, Martin. *Anzio: The Gamble That Failed.* Westport, Connecticut: Greenwood Press, 1978.

Chandler, David G. *A Guide to the Battlefields of Europe, vol. 2.* Philadelphia: Chilton Books, 1965. Quoted in Wagner.

"History of Operations, 141st Infantry Regiment, Rifle, May 1944" (After Action Reports). Headquarters 36th Infantry Division: 1–12. National Archives and Records Administration, Modern Military Records, Textual Archives Services Division, College Park, Maryland.

Laurie, Clayton D. *Anzio: The U.S. Army Campaigns of World War II.* Pub. 72–19, Washington, D.C.: U.S. Army Center for Military History, 1992.

141st Infantry Regiment Association. *Five Years, Five Countries, Five Campaigns.* Clifford H. Peek, ed. Munich, Germany, 1945.

"Report of Operations, 141st Infantry Regiment, Rifle, 28 May–4 June 1944" (After Action Reports). Headquarters 36th Infantry Division: 1–11. 36th Infantry Division Collection, Microfilmed Records and Reports, Archives Division, Texas State Library, Austin, Texas, Reel no. 3033.

36th Division Association. *The Fighting 36th: A Pictorial History* (reprint of the 1945 edition). Paducah, Kentucky: Turner Publishing Company, 1995. N.p.

Vaughan-Thomas, Wynford. *Anzio.* New York: Holt, Rinehart, and Winston, 1961.

Wagner, Robert L. *The Texas Army: A History of the 36th Division in the Italian Campaign.* Austin, Texas: State House Press, 1972.

Walker, Fred L. *From Texas to Rome: A General's Journal.* Dallas, Texas: Taylor Publishing Company, 1969.

Wallace, Robert. *The Italian Campaign.* Alexandria, Virginia: Time-Life Books, 1981.

SOURCES USED IN CHAPTER 7: ENTRY INTO BATTLE

Belden, Jack. *Still Time To Die.* New York: Harper & Brothers, 1944.

Courington, Morris, "and Seven Buddies From the 36th Division." *Cruel Was the Way.* Park Forest, Illinois: Velletri Books, 2000.

Dollard, John and Donald Horton. *Fear in Battle.* New Haven, Connecticut: The Institute of Human Relations, Yale University, 1943.

Ellis, John. *The Sharp End: The Fighting Man in World War II.* New York: Scribner, 1980.

Faught, Robert J. "Army Service Experiences Questionnaire." Department of the Army, U.S. Army Military History Institute, Carlisle Barracks, Carlisle, Pennsylvania. N.d.

Fussell, Paul. *Doing Battle: The Making of a Skeptic.* Boston: Little, Brown and Company, 1996.

———. *The Boy's Crusade: The American Infantryman in Northwestern Europe, 1944–1945.* New York: Modern Library, 2003.

Haddock, Philip R. "Follow Me." 36th Division website, "Personal Accounts." <http://www.kwanah.com/36division/ps/ps811131.htm> (1999).

Harlinski, Anthony. "Army Service Experiences Questionnaire." Department of the Army, U.S. Army Military History Institute, Carlisle Barracks, Carlisle, Pennsylvania. N.d.

Kennett, Lee B. *G.I.: The American Soldier in World War II.* Norman, Oklahoma: University of Oklahoma Press, 1997.

———. *For the Duration: The U.S. Goes to War, Pearl Harbor—1942.* New York: Scribner, 1985.

McFall, John. "First Day of Combat." *The Fighting 36th Historical Quarterly*, supplement to the *T-Patcher Newsletter,* vol. 19, no. 4 (Winter 1999): 14.

McManus, John C. *The Deadly Brotherhood: The American Combat Soldier in World War II.* Novato, California: Presidio Press, 1998.

Meo, Anthony O. "Army Service Experiences Questionnaire." Department of the Army, U.S. Army Military History Institute, Carlisle Barracks, Carlisle, Pennsylvania. N.d.

Pyle, Ernie. *Brave Men.* New York: H. Holt and Company, 1944.

Stern, Allen E. "A Personal View of World War II, Part 1." 36th Division Association, *The Fighting 36th Historical Quarterly*, supplement to the *T-Patcher Newsletter,* vol. 15, no. 4 (Winter 1995): 20–21.

Stouffer, Samuel A., et al. *The American Soldier: Combat and its Aftermath, vol. 2.* Princeton, New Jersey: Princeton University Press, 1949.

Stubinski, Michael. "Michael Stubinski," in *The Ordinary Infantrymen: Heroes Then, Heroes Now,* Imogene Woods, et al., Chapter 11: 129–43. Springfield, Missouri: I. Woods, 2003.

Wells, Raymond C. "Army Service Experiences Questionnaire." Department of the Army, U.S. Army Military History Institute, Carlisle Barracks, Carlisle, Pennsylvania. N.d.

———. "Memories Never Forgotten." 36th Division Association, *The Fighting 36th Historical Quarterly*, vol. 12, no. 4 (Winter 1992): 54–55.

SOURCES USED IN CHAPTER 8: BAPTISM OF FIRE

Bond, Harold L. *Return to Cassino: A Memoir of the Fight for Rome.* New York: Doubleday & Company, Inc., 1964.

Clover, Jack L. "Over the River and Through the Woods." 36th Division Association, *The Fighting 36th Historical Quarterly*, vol. 1, no. 4 (Winter 1981): 55–60.

Duffey, Paul H. "Action at Anzio." 36th Division Association, *The Fighting 36th Historical Quarterly*, vol. 13, no. 1 (Spring 1993): 4–10.

Fowler, Wick. "Wick Fowler's Dispatch." Originally published in the *Dallas Morning News* (c. May 1944). N.d., n.p. Reprinted in *The Fighting 36th: A Pictorial History*. Paducah, Kentucky: Turner Publishing Company, 1995. N.p.

Harmony, John W. "Regimental History and Conclusions from Operations," in "Report of Operations, 141st Infantry Regt., May 1944." 36th Infantry Division Collection, Microfilmed Records and Reports, Archives Division, Texas State Library, Austin, Texas, Reel no. 3029 (1 page).

———. "Regimental History and Conclusions from Operations," in "Report of Operations, 141st Infantry Regt., June 1944." 36th Infantry Division Collection, Microfilmed Records and Reports, Archives Division, Texas State Library, Austin, Texas, Reel no. 3029 (2 pages).

"History of Operations, 141st Infantry Regiment, Rifle, May 1944" (After Action Reports). Headquarters 36th Infantry Division: 1–12. National Archives and Records

Administration, Modern Military Records, Textual Archives Services Division, College Park, Maryland.

Kendall, Delbert W. Quoted in "Bull's-eye Bullets–Sharpshooters and Snipers," William E. Jary, Jr., ed. 36th Division Association, *The Fighting 36th Historical Quarterly*, vol. 6, no. 1 (Spring 1986): 46–56.

McFall, John. "First Day of Combat." 36th Division Association, *The Fighting 36th Historical Quarterly,* supplement to the *T-Patcher Newsletter,* vol. 19, no. 4 (Winter 1999): 14.

McManus, John C. *The Deadly Brotherhood: The American Combat Soldier in World War II.* Novato, California: Presidio Press, 1998.

141st Infantry, "Awards, Decorations, and Citations, 1943–1944." 36th Infantry Division Collection, Microfilmed Records and Reports, Archives Division, Texas State Library, Austin, Texas, Reel no. 3034 (28 Pages).

141st Infantry Regiment Association. *Five Years, Five Countries, Five Campaigns.* Clifford H. Peek, ed. Munich, Germany, 1945.

"Report of Operations, 141st Infantry Regiment, Rifle, 28 May-4 June 1944" (After Action Reports). Headquarters 36th Infantry Division: 1–11. 36th Infantry Division Collection, Microfilmed Records and Reports, Archives Division, Texas State Library, Austin, Texas, Reel no. 3033.

Sherman, Thomas M. *Seek, Strike, Destroy: The History of the 636th Tank Destroyer Battalion.* Marquette, Nebraska: T. Sherman, 1986.

Stern, Allen E. "A Personal View of World War II, Part 1." 36th Division Association, *The Fighting 36th Historical Quarterly*, supplement to the *T-Patcher Newsletter,* vol. 15, no. 4 (Winter 1995): 20–21.

36th Division Association. *The Fighting 36th: A Pictorial History* (reprint of the 1945 edition). Paducah, Kentucky: Turner Publishing Company, 1995. N.p.

"36th Infantry Division Artillery, Special Operations Report, Velletri-Colli Laziale Operation, May-June 1944" (After Action Reports). Headquarters 36th Infantry Division: 1–11. 36th Infantry Division Collection, Microfilmed Records and Reports, Archives Division, Texas State Library, Austin, Texas, Reel no. 3008.

36th Infantry Division, "Bronze Star Awards, March 1944–May 1944." 36th Infantry Division Collection, Microfilmed Records and Reports, Archives Division, Texas State Library, Austin Texas, Reel no. 2076. Entire reel contains lists of award recipients. Some pages numbered.

Wagner, Robert L. *The Texas Army: A History of the 36th Division in the Italian Campaign.* Austin, Texas: State House Press, 1972.

Walker, Fred L. *From Texas to Rome: A General's Journal.* Dallas, Texas: Taylor Publishing Company, 1969.

Interviews and Correspondence

Alfred Dietrick (B-141)
Arlis D. Sizemore (D-141)
Michael Stubinski (K-141)
Raymond C. Wells (F-141)

SOURCES USED IN CHAPTER 9: MONTE ARTEMISIO

Blumenson, Martin. *Anzio: The Gamble That Failed*. Westport, Conn.: Greenwood Press, 1978.

Bond, Harold L. *Return to Cassino: A Memoir of the Fight for Rome*. New York: Doubleday & Company, Inc., 1964.

Dixon, Kenneth L. "History's Greatest Jailbreak." Originally published in the *Charleston* (North Carolina) *Gazette* 1 June 1959. N.p. Reprinted in 36th Division Association, *The Fighting 36th Historical Quarterly*, vol. 3, no. 1 (Spring 1983): 36–41.

———. "The Velletri Infiltration, Five Years Ago Rome Fell and a New Story is Told." Originally published in the *Dallas Morning News*. N.p., n.d. (c. 1949). Reprinted in 36th Division Association, *The Fighting 36th Historical Quarterly*, vol. 12, no. 1 (Spring 1992): 35–38.

Ellis, John. *Cassino, the hollow victory: The Battle for Rome, January-June 1944*. New York: McGraw-Hill, 1984.

Estepp, James M. "Combat Soldier." 36th Division Association, *The Fighting 36th Historical Quarterly*, vol. 13, no. 2 (Summer 1993): 7–9.

———. "I Left My Friend on Mt. Artemisio." 36th Division Association, *The Fighting 36th Historical Quarterly*, vol. 10, no. 4 (Winter 1990): 64–69.

Fisher, Ernest F., Jr. "A Classic Stratagem on Monte Artemisio." Originally published in *Military Review Magazine*, vol. XLIII, no. 2 (February 1963): 78–90. Reprinted in *From Texas to Rome*, Fred L. Walker, Appendix D: 420–31.

———. *U.S. army in World War II, The Mediterranean Theater of Operations: Cassino to the Alps*. Washington, D.C.: Center of Military History, United States Army, Superintendent of Documents, U.S. Govt. Printing Office, 1977.

Fowler, Wick. "Wick Fowler's Dispatch." Originally published in the *Dallas Morning News*. N.d., n.p. (c. May 1944). Reprinted in *The Fighting 36th: A Pictorial History*. Paducah, Kentucky: Turner Publishing Company, 1995. N.p.

Hartung, William F., Sr. "Reflections of World War II." 36th Division Association, *The Fighting 36th Historical Quarterly*, supplement to the *T-Patcher Newsletter*, vol. 24, vol. 4 (Winter 2004): 11–12.

"History of Operations, 141st Infantry Regiment, Rifle, May 1944" (After Action Reports). Headquarters 36th Infantry Division: 1–12. National Archives and Records Administration, Modern Military Records, Textual Archives Services Division, College Park, Maryland.

Kurzman, Dan. *The Race for Rome*. Garden City, New York: Doubleday, 1975.

Laurie, Clayton D. *Rome-Arno: The U.S. Army Campaigns of World War II*. Pub. 72–20, Washington, D.C.: U.S. Army Center for Military History, 1992.

141st Infantry Regiment Association. *Five Years, Five Countries, Five Campaigns*. Clifford H. Peek, ed. Munich, Germany, 1945.

"Report of Operations, 141st Infantry Regiment, Rifle, 28 May-4 June 1944" (After Action Reports). Headquarters 36th Infantry Division: 1–11. 36th Infantry Division Collection, Microfilmed Records and Reports, Archives Division, Texas State Library, Austin, Texas, Reel no. 3033.

Sevareid, Eric. "On the Standards of the 36th Proudly Inscribe 'Velletri.' " Originally published in *The American Legion Magazine*, vol. 29, no. 10 (October 1944):13, 49–51. Reprinted in *The Fighting 36th: A Pictorial History*, Paducah, Kentucky: Turner Publishing Company, 1995. N.p.

"36th Infantry Division Artillery, Special Operations Report, Velletri-Colli Laziale Operation, May-June 1944" (After Action Reports). Headquarters 36th Infantry Division: 1–11. 36th Infantry Division Collection, Microfilmed Records and Reports, Archives Division, Texas State Library, Austin, Texas, Reel no. 3008.

36th Division Association. *The Fighting 36th: A Pictorial History* (reprint of the 1945 edition). Paducah, Kentucky: Turner Publishing Company, 1995. N.p.

Wagner, Robert L. *The Texas Army: A History of the 36th Division in the Italian Campaign*. Austin, Texas: State House Press, 1972.

Walker, Fred L. *From Texas to Rome: A General's Journal*. Dallas, Texas: Taylor Publishing Company, 1969.

SOURCES USED IN CHAPTER 10:
THE BATTLE FOR VELLETRI–WALKER'S MASTERPIECE

Dixon, Kenneth L. "History's Greatest Jailbreak." Originally published in the *Charleston* (North Carolina) *Gazette* 1 June 1959. N.p. Reprinted in 36th Division Association, *The Fighting 36th Historical Quarterly*, vol. 3, no. 1 (Spring 1983): 36–41.

———. "The Velletri Infiltration, Five Years Ago Rome Fell and a New Story is Told." Originally published in the *Dallas Morning News*. N.d., n.p. (c. 1949). Reprinted in *The Fighting 36th Historical Quarterly*, vol. 12, no. 1 (Spring 1992): 35–38.

Doubler, Michael D. *Closing With the Enemy: How GIs Fought the War in Europe, 1944–1945*. Lawrence, Kansas: University Press of Kansas, 1994.

Farmer, Sgt. James, E. "When Our Doughboys Became Men: Green and Untried One Moment, They Emerge Fast as Veterans on Italian Front." Story filed by Farmer from Italy in April 1944, originally published in the *Indianapolis Star*. N.d., n.p. Reprinted in 36th Division Association, *The Fighting 36th Historical Quarterly*, vol. 13, no. 2 (Summer 1993): 65–66.

Fowler, Wick. "Wick Fowler's Dispatch." Originally published in the *Dallas Morning News*. N.d., n.p. (c. May 1944). Reprinted in 36th Division Association, *The Fighting 36th: A Pictorial History*. Paducah, Kentucky: Turner Publishing Company, 1995. N.p.

"History of Operations, 141st Infantry Regiment, Rifle, May 1944" (After Action Reports). Headquarters 36th Infantry Division: 1–12. National Archives and Records Administration, Modern Military Records, Textual Archives Services Division, College Park, Maryland.

Lockhart, Col. Vincent M. *T-Patch to Victory: The 36th "Texas" Division, France–Germany–Austria*. Canyon, Texas: Staked Plains Press, 1981.

McManus, John C. *The Deadly Brotherhood: The American Combat Soldier in World War II*. Novato, California: Presidio Press, 1998.

141st Infantry Regiment Association. *Five Years, Five Countries, Five Campaigns.* Clifford H. Peek, ed. Munich, Germany, 1945.

"Report of Operations, 141st Infantry Regiment, Rifle, 28 May-4 June 1944" (After Action Reports). Headquarters 36th Infantry Division: 1–11. 36th Infantry Division Collection, Microfilmed Records and Reports, Archives Division, Texas State Library, Austin, Texas, Reel no. 3033.

Sevareid, Eric. "On the Standards of the 36th Proudly Inscribe 'Velletri.' " Originally published in *The American Legion Magazine*, vol. 29, no. 10 (October 1944):13, 49–51. Reprinted in 36th Division Association, *The Fighting 36th: A Pictorial History*, Paducah, Kentucky: Turner Publishing Company, 1995. N.p.

Stubinski, Michael. "Mike in the Service." Unpublished memoir, World War II Veterans Project, Special Collections, University of Tennessee, Knoxville, MS 1881, Box 28, Folder 19 (1992): 1–13, with "Excerpts" (8 pages).

———. "I Would Have Kicked Them in the Shins." 36th Division Association, *The Fighting 36th Historical Quarterly*, vol. 13, no. 4 (Winter 1993): 36.

"36th Infantry Division Artillery, Special Operations Report, Velletri-Colli Laziale Operation, May-June 1944" (After Action Reports). Headquarters 36th Infantry Division: 1–11. 36th Infantry Division Collection, Microfilmed Records and Reports, Archives Division, Texas State Library, Austin, Texas, Reel no. 3008.

"36th Infantry Division, Capture of Velletri and the Colli Laziale, 29 May-4 June 1944," 36th Infantry Division Collection, Microfilmed Records and Reports, Archives Division, Texas State Library, Austin Texas, Reel no. 2071 (19 pages).

Wagner, Robert L. *The Texas Army: A History of the 36th Division in the Italian Campaign.* Austin, Texas: State House Press, 1972.

Walker, Fred L. *From Texas to Rome: A General's Journal.* Dallas, Texas: Taylor Publishing Company, 1969.

Interviews and Correspondence

Paolo Carotenuto
Michael Stubinski (K-141)
Jack W. Wilson (D-141)

SOURCES USED IN CHAPTER 11: THE RACE FOR ROME–CLEARING THE ALBAN HILLS

Adleman, Robert H. and (Colonel) George Walton. *Rome Fell Today.* Boston: Little Brown, 1968.

Bond, Harold L. *Return to Cassino: A Memoir of the Fight for Rome.* New York: Doubleday & Company, Inc., 1964.

Doubler, Michael D. *Closing With the Enemy: How GIs Fought the War in Europe, 1944–1945.* Lawrence, Kansas: University Press of Kansas, 1994.

Doughty, R.K. "No Roman Holiday." 36th Division Association, *The Fighting 36th Historical Quarterly*, Vol. 9, No. 3 (Fall 1989): 50–53.

Fifth Army History. Part VI, Pursuit to Arno, 5 June–15 August 1944. Prepared under the direction of Lt. Col. Chester G. Starr, Jr., by Capt. Bruce K. Meyers and staff. Milan, Italy, 1945.

Hawkins, William A. "History of Operations of Company "D," 141st Infantry, June 1944" (After Action Report): 69–70. From Narrative of Action, Regimental Headquarters Company-M Company, 141st Infantry, June 1944 (After Action Reports): 40–111. 36th Infantry Division Collection, Microfilmed Records and Reports, Archives Division, Texas State Library, Austin, Texas, Reel no. 3029.

"History of Operations, 141st Infantry Regiment, Rifle, May 1944" (After Action Reports). Headquarters 36th Infantry Division: 1–12. National Archives and Records Administration, Modern Military Records, Textual Archives Services Division, College Park, Maryland.

"History of Operations, 141st Infantry Regiment, Rifle, June 1944" (After Action Reports). Headquarters 36th Infantry Division: 1–20. National Archives and Records Administration, Modern Military Records, Textual Archives Services Division, College Park, Maryland.

Kurzman, Dan. *The Race for Rome*. Garden City, New York: Doubleday, 1975.

Laurie, Clayton D. *Rome-Arno: The U.S. Army Campaigns of World War II*. Pub. 72–20, Washington, D.C.: U.S. Army Center for Military History, 1992.

Morning Report, Company D, 141st Infantry, 27 June 1944. National Personnel Records Center (NPRC), St. Louis, Missouri.

Morris, Eric. *Circles of Hell: The War in Italy, 1943–1945*. New York: Crown Publishers, 1993.

Narrative of Action, Regimental Headquarters Company-M Company, 141st Infantry, June 1944 (After Action Reports): 40–111. 36th Infantry Division Collection, Microfilmed Records and Reports, Archives Division, Texas State Library, Austin, Texas, Reel no. 3029.

141st Infantry Regiment Association. *Five Years, Five Countries, Five Campaigns*. Clifford H. Peek, ed. Munich, Germany, 1945.

Philips, Julian. "Rome-Plus Twenty Days." 36th Division Association, *The Fighting 36th Historical Quarterly,* vol. 8, no. 2 (Summer 1988): 7–18.

———. "Rome-Plus 20 Days, Part II." 36th Division Association, *The Fighting 36th Historical Quarterly*, vol. 8, no. 4 (Winter 1988): 38–57.

Sevareid, Eric. *Not So Wild A Dream*. New York: Atheneum, 1976.

Sherman, Thomas M. *Seek, Strike, Destroy: The History of the 636th Tank Destroyer Battalion.* Marquette, Nebraska: T. Sherman, 1986.

Stern, Allen E. "A Personal View of World War II, Part 1." 36th Division Association, *The Fighting 36th Historical Quarterly*, supplement to the *T-Patcher Newsletter,* vol. 15, no. 4 (Winter 1995): 20–21.

Stubinski, Michael. "Michael Stubinski," in *The Ordinary Infantrymen: Heroes Then, Heroes Now,* Imogene Woods, et al, Chapter 11: 129–43. Springfield, Missouri: I. Woods, 2003.

———. "Mike in the Service." Unpublished memoir, World War II Veterans Project, Special Collections, University of Tennessee, Knoxville, MS 1881, Box 28, Folder 19 (1992): 1–13, with "Excerpts" (8 pages).

Taney, Warren E. "WW II Diary of an Engineer." 36th Division Association, *The Fighting 36th Historical Quarterly*, vol. 9, no. 1 (Spring 1989): 62–80.

"36th Infantry Division Artillery, Special Operations Report, Velletri-Colli Laziale Operation, May-June 1944" (After Action Reports). Headquarters 36th Infantry Division: 1–11. 36th Infantry Division Collection, Microfilmed Records and Reports, Archives Division, Texas State Library, Austin, Texas, Reel no. 3008.

Wagner, Robert L. *The Texas Army: A History of the 36th Division in the Italian Campaign*. Austin, Texas: State House Press, 1972.

Walker, Fred L. *From Texas to Rome: A General's Journal*. Dallas, Texas: Taylor Publishing Company, 1969.

Interviews and Correspondence

Michael Stubinski (K-141)

SOURCES USED IN CHAPTER 12: THE ETERNAL CITY

Adleman, Robert H. and (Colonel) George Walton. *Rome Fell Today*. Boston: Little Brown, 1968.

Bond, Harold L. *Return to Cassino: A Memoir of the Fight for Rome*. New York: Doubleday & Company, Inc., 1964.

Doubler, Michael D. *Closing With the Enemy: How GIs Fought the War in Europe, 1944–1945*. Lawrence, Kansas: University Press of Kansas, 1994.

Doughty, R.K. "No Roman Holiday." 36th Division Association, *The Fighting 36th Historical Quarterly*, Vol. 9, No. 3 (Fall 1989): 50–53.

Fifth Army History, Part VI, Pursuit to Arno, 5 June–15 August. Prepared under the direction of Lt. Col. Chester G. Starr, Jr., by Capt. Bruce K. Meyers and staff. Milan, Italy, 1945.

"History of Operations, 141st Infantry Regiment, Rifle, May 1944" (After Action Reports). Headquarters 36th Infantry Division: 1–12. National Archives and Records Administration, Modern Military Records, Textual Archives Services Division, College Park, Maryland.

"History of Operations, 141st Infantry Regiment, Rifle, June 1944" (After Action Reports). Headquarters 36th Infantry Division: 1–20. National Archives and Records Administration, Modern Military Records, Textual Archives Services Division, College Park, Maryland.

Kurzman, Dan. *The Race for Rome*. Garden City, New York: Doubleday, 1975.

Laurie, Clayton D. *Rome-Arno: The U.S. Army Campaigns of World War II*. Pub. 72–20, Washington, D.C.: U.S. Army Center for Military History, 1992.

Morris, Eric. *Circles of Hell: The War in Italy, 1943–1945*. New York: Crown Publishers, 1993.

Narrative of Action, Regimental Headquarters Company-M Company, 141st Infantry, June 1944 (After Action Reports): 40–111. 36th Infantry Division Collection, Microfilmed Records and Reports, Archives Division, Texas State Library, Austin, Texas, Reel no. 3029.

141st Infantry Regiment Association. *Five Years, Five Countries, Five Campaigns.* Clifford H. Peek, ed. Munich, Germany, 1945.

Philips, Julian. "Rome-Plus Twenty Days." 36th Division Association, *The Fighting 36th Historical Quarterly,* vol. 8, no. 2 (Summer 1988): 7–18.

———. "Rome-Plus 20 Days, Part II." 36th Division Association, *The Fighting 36th Historical Quarterly*, vol. 8, no. 4 (Winter 1988): 38–57.

Sevareid, Eric. *Not So Wild A Dream.* New York: Atheneum, 1976.

Stern, Allen E. "A Personal View of World War II, Part 1." 36th Division Association, *The Fighting 36th Historical Quarterly*, supplement to the *T-Patcher Newsletter,* vol. 15, no. 4 (Winter 1995): 20–21.

Stubinski, Michael. "Michael Stubinski," in *The Ordinary Infantrymen: Heroes Then, Heroes Now,* Imogene Woods, et al, Chapter 11: 129–43. Springfield, Missouri: I. Woods, 2003.

———. "Mike in the Service." Unpublished memoir, World War II Veterans Project, Special Collections, University of Tennessee, Knoxville, MS 1881, Box 28, Folder 19 (1992): 1–13, with "Excerpts" (8 pages).

Taney, Warren E. "WW II Diary of an Engineer." 36th Division Association, *The Fighting 36th Historical Quarterly*, vol. 9, no. 1 (Spring 1989): 62–80.

"36th Infantry Division Artillery, Special Operations Report, Velletri-Colli Laziale Operation, May-June 1944" (After Action Reports). Headquarters 36th Infantry Division: 1–11. 36th Infantry Division Collection, Microfilmed Records and Reports, Archives Division, Texas State Library, Austin, Texas, Reel no. 3008.

Wagner, Robert L. *The Texas Army: A History of the 36th Division in the Italian Campaign.* Austin, Texas: State House Press, 1972.

Walker, Fred L. *From Texas to Rome: A General's Journal.* Dallas, Texas: Taylor Publishing Company, 1969.

Interviews and Correspondence

Charles A. Golub (K-143)
Michael Stubinski (K-141)

SOURCES USED IN CHAPTER 13:
PURSUIT OF THE GERMANS NORTH OF ROME

Benton, George A. "We're On Our Way." 36th Division Association, *The Fighting 36th Historical Quarterly*, vol. 11, no. 3 (Fall 1991): 36–43.

Church, William V. (Capt.). "Operations of 1st Battalion, 141st Infantry (36th Division), in the Vicinity of Nunziatell[a], Italy, 10–11 June 1944 (Rome-Arno Campaign). Personal experiences of an 81mm Mortar Platoon Leader. (603–141 1948a)." Fort Benning, Georgia: Academic Department, The Infantry School, 1948.

Connole, Dennis J. Veterans Administration (VA) File #05-075-171.

Doughty, R.K. "No Roman Holiday." 36th Division Association, *The Fighting 36th Historical Quarterly*, vol, 9, no. 3 (Fall 1989): 50–53.

———. "Strange Interlude, a new look at our tour of duty at Anzio." 36th Division Association, *The Fighting 36th Historical Quarterly*, vol. 13, no. 1 (Spring 1988), 17.

Duffey, Paul H. "Action at Anzio." 36th Division Association, *The Fighting 36th Historical Quarterly,* vol. 13, no. 1 (Spring 1993): 4–10.

Fifth Army History, Part VI, Pursuit to Arno, 5 June–15 August. Prepared under the direction of Lt. Col. Chester G. Starr, Jr., by Capt. Bruce K. Meyers and staff. Milan, Italy, 1945.

"History of Operations, 141st Infantry Regiment, Rifle, June 1944" (After Action Reports). Headquarters 36th Infantry Division: 1–20. National Archives and Records Administration, Modern Military Records, Textual Archives Services Division, College Park, Maryland.

Miller, Frank J. "Memories of My 36th Division Days." 36th Division Association, *The Fighting 36th Historical Quarterly*, vol. 9, no. 1 (Spring 1989): 42–49.

Morning Report, Company D, 141st Infantry, 27 June 1944. National Personnel Records Center (NPRC), St. Louis, Missouri.

Morris, Eric. *Circles of Hell: The War in Italy, 1943–1945*. New York: Crown Publishers, 1993.

Narrative of Action, Regimental Headquarters Company-M Company, 141st Infantry, June 1944 (After Action Reports): 40–111. 36th Infantry Division Collection, Microfilmed Records and Reports, Archives Division, Texas State Library, Austin, Texas, Reel no. 3029.

Philips, Julian. "Rome-Plus Twenty Days." 36th Division Association, *The Fighting 36th Historical Quarterly*, vol. 8, no. 2 (Summer 1988): 7–18.

———. "Rome-Plus 20 Days, Part II." 36th Division Association, *The Fighting 36th Historical Quarterly*, vol. 13, no. 4 (Winter 1988): 38–57.

Pullen, B.G. "A Combat Engineer's Experience." 36th Division Association, *The Fighting 36th Historical Quarterly*, vol. 12, no. 2 (Spring 1992): 53–64.

Stern, Allen E. "A Personal View of World War II, Part 1." 36th Division Association, *The Fighting 36th Historical Quarterly*, supplement to the *T-Patcher Newsletter,* vol. 15, no. 4 (Winter 1995): 20–21.

Stubinski, Michael. "Michael Stubinski," in *The Ordinary Infantrymen: Heroes Then, Heroes Now,* Imogene Woods, et al, Chapter 11: 129–43. Springfield, Missouri: I. Woods, 2003.

Taney, Warren E. "WW II Diary of an Engineer." 36th Division Association, *The Fighting 36th Historical Quarterly*, vol. 9, no. 1 (Spring 1989): 62–80.

Wagner, Robert L. *The Texas Army: A History of the 36th Division in the Italian Campaign.* Austin, Texas: State House Press, 1972.

Walker, Fred L. *From Texas to Rome: A General's Journal.* Dallas, Texas: Taylor Publishing Company, 1969.

Interviews and Correspondence

George E. Bennett (I-142)
John Paul Jones (D-141)

Rosaire J. Rajotte (A-141)
David C. Rosenbluth (A-141)
Terry Rosenbluth (son of David C. Rosenbluth)
Michael Stubinski (K-141)
Jack W. Wilson (D-141)

SOURCES USED IN CHAPTER 14: THE BATTLE
OF NUNZIATELLA, JUNE 10–12, 1944

Benton, George A. "We're On Our Way." 36th Division Association, *The Fighting 36th Historical Quarterly*, vol. 11, no. 3 (Fall 1991): 36–43.

Carotenuto, Paolo. *La battaglia di Velletri, 23 maggio–2 giugno 1944*. Rome: Omnimedia S.r.l., Viale del Policlinico, 131–00161, 2004.

Church, William V. (Capt.). "Operations of 1st Battalion, 141st Infantry (36th Division), in the Vicinity of Nunziatell[a], Italy, 10–11 June 1944 (Rome-Arno Campaign). Personal experiences of an 81mm Mortar Platoon Leader. (603–141 1948a)." Fort Benning, Georgia: Academic Department, The Infantry School, 1948.

Connole, Dennis A. "A Bloody Encounter North of Rome." *World War II Magazine*, vol. 20, no. 5 (September 2005): 34–40.

Connole, Dennis J. Veterans Administration (VA) File #05-075-171.

Doughty, R.K. "No Roman Holiday." 36th Division Association, *The Fighting 36th Historical Quarterly*, vol, 9, no. 3 (Fall 1989): 50–53.

———. "Strange Interlude, a new look at our tour of duty at Anzio." 36th Division Association, *The Fighting 36th Historical Quarterly*, vol. 13, no. 1 (Spring 1988), 17.

Duffey, Paul H. "Action at Anzio." 36th Division Association, *The Fighting 36th Historical Quarterly*, Vol. 13, No. 1 (Spring 1993): 4–10.

Eastberg, Ralph J. Silver Star Citation, 11 June 1944. "Silver Star Awards, 2 Jun-19 Sept. 1944." National Archives and Records Administration (NARA), Modern Military Records, Textual Archives Services Division, College Park, Maryland. See Microfilmed Records and Reports, 36th Division, Texas State Library, Reel no. 2079. This document includes awards before 2 June 1944 (307 pages).

Fifth Army History, Part VI, Pursuit to Arno, 5 June–15 August. Prepared under the direction of Lt. Col. Chester G. Starr, Jr., by Capt. Bruce K. Meyers and staff. Milan, Italy, 1945.

Hawkins, William A. Silver Star Citation, 11 June 1944. "Silver Star Awards, 2 Jun-19 Sept. 1944." National Archives and Records Administration (NARA), Modern Military Records, Textual Archives Services Division, College Park, Maryland. See Microfilmed Records and Reports, 36th Division, Texas State Library, Reel no. 2079. This document includes awards before 2 June 1944 (307 pages).

"History of Operations, 141st Infantry Regiment, Rifle, June 1944" (After Action Reports). Headquarters 36th Infantry Division: 1–20. National Archives and Records Administration, Modern Military Records, Textual Archives Services Division, College Park, Maryland.

Light, Royal B. Silver Star Citation, 11 June 1944. "Silver Star Awards, 2 Jun-19 Sept. 1944." National Archives and Records Administration (NARA), Modern Military

Records, Textual Archives Services Division, College Park, Maryland. See Micro-
    filmed Records and Reports, 36th Division, Texas State Library, Reel no. 2079. This
    document includes awards before 2 June 1944 (307 pages).

Materra, Ralph A. Silver Star Citation, 11, June 1944. "Silver Star Awards, 2 Jun-19
    Sept. 1944." National Archives and Records Administration (NARA), Modern Mil-
    itary Records, Textual Archives Services Division, College Park, Maryland. See Mi-
    crofilmed Records and Reports, 36th Division, Texas State Library, Reel no. 2079.
    This document includes awards before 2 June 1944 (307 pages).

Miller, Frank J. "Memories of My 36th Division Days." 36th Division Association,
    The Fighting 36th Historical Quarterly, Vol. 9, No. 1 (Spring 1989): 42–49.

Morning Report, Company D, 141st Infantry, 27 June 1944. National Personnel
    Records Center (NPRC), St. Louis, Missouri.

Morris, Eric. *Circles of Hell: The War in Italy, 1943–1945*. New York: Crown Pub-
    lishers, 1993.

Narrative of Action, Regimental Headquarters Company-M Company, 141st Infantry,
    June 1944 (After Action Reports): 40–111. 36th Infantry Division Collection, Mi-
    crofilmed Records and Reports, Archives Division, Texas State Library, Austin,
    Texas, Reel no. 3029.

Philips, Julian. "Rome-Plus Twenty Days." 36th Division Association, *The Fighting
    36th Historical Quarterly,* vol. 8, no. 2 (Summer 1988): 7–18.

———. "Rome-Plus 20 Days, Part II." 36th Division Association, *The Fighting 36th
    Historical Quarterly*, vol. 13, no. 4 (Winter 1988): 38–57.

Pullen, B.G. "A Combat Engineer's Experience." 36th Division Association, *The
    Fighting 36th Historical Quarterly*, vol. 12, no. 2 (Spring 1992): 53–64.

Slavinski, Edward J. Silver Star Citation, 11 June 1944. "Silver Star Awards, 2 Jun-
    19 Sept. 1944." National Archives and Records Administration (NARA), Modern
    Military Records, Textual Archives Services Division, College Park, Maryland. See
    Microfilmed Records and Reports, 36th Division, Texas State Library, Reel no.
    2079. This document includes awards before 2 June 1944 (307 pages).

Stern, Allen E. "A Personal View of World War II, Part 1." 36th Division Association,
    The Fighting 36th Historical Quarterly, supplement to the *T-Patcher Newsletter,*
    vol. 15, no. 4 (Winter 1995): 20–21.

Taney, Warren E. "WW II Diary of an Engineer." 36th Division Association, *The
    Fighting 36th Historical Quarterly*, vol. 9, no. 1 (Spring 1989): 62–80.

Wagner, Robert L. *The Texas Army: A History of the 36th Division in the Italian Cam-
    paign*. Austin, Texas: State House Press, 1972.

Walker, Fred L. *From Texas to Rome: A General's Journal*. Dallas, Texas: Taylor Pub-
    lishing Company, 1969.

Interviews and Correspondence

George E. Bennett (I-142)
John Paul Jones (D-141)
Rosaire J. Rajotte (A-141)
David C. Rosenbluth (A-141)

Terry Rosenbluth (son of David C. Rosenbluth A-141)
Michael Stubinski (K-141)
Jack W. Wilson (D-141)

SOURCES USED IN CHAPTER 15: PREPARATION AND PLANNING FOR THE INVASION OF SOUTHERN FRANCE.

Benton, George A. "We're On Our Way." 36th Division Association, *The Fighting 36th Historical Quarterly*, vol. 11, no. 3 (Fall 1991): 36–43.

Blumenson, Martin. *Liberation*. Alexandria, Virginia: Time-Life Books, 1978.

Breuer, William B. *Operation Dragoon: The Allied Invasion of the South of France*. Novato, California: Presidio Press, 1987.

Caraccilo, Dominic J. "Dragoon Clears the Rhone Valley." *Veterans of Foreign Wars Magazine*, vol. 81, no. 11 (August 1994): 14, 16. Reprinted in 36th Division Association, *The Fighting 36th Historical Quarterly*, supplement to the *T-Patcher Newsletter*, vol. 14, no. 3 (Fall 1994): 10–11.

Clarke, Jeffrey J. *Southern France: The U.S. Campaigns of World War II*. Pub. 72–31, Washington, D.C.: U.S. Army Center of Military History, 1992.

Courington, Morris, "and Seven Buddies From the 36th Division." *Cruel Was the Way*. Park Forest, Illinois: Velletri Books, 2000.

Duffey, Paul H. "The Invasion of France's Southern Coast." 36th Division Association, *The Fighting 36th Historical Quarterly*, vol. 13, no. 1 (Spring 1993): 52–63.

Golub, Charles A. "The Band Played On." *In City Times* (Worcester, Mass.) 1 Nov. 14–Nov. 2002, 3, 5.

Hewitt, Admiral H. Kent (Retired). *"Anvil-Dragoon: Planning and Operation."* 36th Division Association, *The Fighting 36th Historical Quarterly,* Vol. 3, No. 4 (Winter 1983): 6–33. Original title: "Planning Operation Anvil-Dragoon," published July 1954, *U.S. Naval Institute Proceedings*, vol. 80, no. 7, Annapolis, Maryland: 730–45.

"History of Operations in France, 141st Infantry Regiment, Rifle, August 1944" (After Action Reports). Headquarters 36th Infantry Division: 1–28. National Archives and Records Administration, Modern Military Records, Textual Archives Services Division, College Park, Maryland.

Hyman, Pfc. John A., ed. "From the Riviera to the Rhine, A T-Patch [36th Division newspaper] Anniversary Supplement." Described as "Excerpts from a book in preparation by the Public Relations Section, with the cooperation of official sources," 1945.

Lee, Rod. *God Is Our Co-pilot: The Life and Times of Ross Rajotte–An American Patriot*. Whitinsville, Mass.: Old Colony Stationery, 2002.

Lockhart, Col. Vincent M. *T-Patch to Victory: The 36th "Texas" Division, France–Germany–Austria*. Canyon, Texas: Staked Plains Press, 1981.

Morison, Samuel Eliot. *History of the United States Naval Operations in World War II, The Invasion of France and Germany 1944–1945* (15 vols.), vol. XI. Boston: Little, Brown, 1957.

Morning Report, Company D, 141st Infantry, 13 September 1944. National Personnel Records Center (NPRC), St. Louis, Missouri.

141st Infantry Regiment Association. *Five Years, Five Countries, Five Campaigns.* Clifford H. Peek, ed. Munich, Germany, 1945.

Philips, Julian. "Anvil to Draguignan." 36th Division Association, *The Fighting 36th Historical Quarterly*, vol. 5, no. 3 (Fall 1985): 44–57.

Quinn, Francis S., Jr. "Assault in Southern France," in *Seek, Strike, Destroy: The History of the 636th Tank Destroyer Battalion* by Thomas M. Sherman. Marquette, Nebraska: T. Sherman, 1986: 103–08.

Scott, Jack L. *Combat Engineer.* Baltimore: American Literary Press, Inc., 1999.

Sherman, Thomas M. *Seek, Strike, Destroy: The History of the 636th Tank Destroyer Battalion.* Marquette, Nebraska: T. Sherman, 1986.

Sizemore, Arlis D. *Hidden Memories of World War II.* Topeka, Kansas: Learning Resources, Inc., 2002.

Stevenson, Eleanor B. and Pete Martin. *I Knew Your Soldier.* New York: Penguin Books, 1945.

Stubinski, Michael. "Michael Stubinski," in *The Ordinary Infantrymen: Heroes Then, Heroes Now,* Imogene Woods, et al, Chapter 11: 129–43. Springfield, Missouri: I. Woods, 2003.

——. "Mike in the Service." Unpublished memoir, World War II Veterans Project, Special Collections, University of Tennessee, Knoxville, MS 1881, Box 28, Folder 19 (1992): 1–13, with "Excerpts" (8 pages).

36th Division Association. *The Fighting 36th: A Pictorial History* (reprint of the 1945 edition). Paducah, Kentucky: Turner Publishing Company, 1995. N.p.

Truscott, Lt. Gen. Lucian K. *Command Missions: A Personal Story.* New York: Dutton, 1954.

"Vets pay tribute to a 'brute' of a boat" (The Associated Press). *Worcester Sunday Telegram* 7 November 1999, A2.

Interviews and Correspondence

Charles A. Golub (A-141)
Arlis D. Sizemore (D-141)
Michael Stubinski (K-141)

SOURCES USED IN CHAPTER 16:
D-DAY—AUGUST 15, 1944, FRANCE

Benton, George A. "We're On Our Way." 36th Division Association, *The Fighting 36th Historical Quarterly*, vol. 11, no. 3 (Fall 1991): 36–43.

Breuer, William B. *Operation Dragoon: The Allied Invasion of the South of France.* Novato, California: Presidio Press, 1987.

Clarke, Jeffrey J. *Southern France: The U.S. Campaigns of World War II*. Pub. 72–31, Washington, D.C.: U.S. Army Center of Military History, 1992.

"Company E's D-Day." *Stars and Stripes,* 3–4. N.d. (c. August 1944). Copy of article sent to author by William F. Hartung, Sr.

Courington, Morris, "and Seven Buddies From the 36th Division." *Cruel Was the Way*. Park Forest, Illinois: Velletri Books, 2000.

Doughty, R.K. "Zero." 36th Division Association, *The Fighting 36th Historical Quarterly*, vol. 8, no. 2 (Summer 1988): 28–35.

Duffey, Paul H. "The Invasion of France's Southern Coast." 36th Division Association, *The Fighting 36th Historical Quarterly*, vol. 13, no. 1 (Spring 1993): 52–63.

"General Orders, No. 7, Battle Honors, Presidential Citation, 1st Battalion, 141st Infantry Regiment, War Department." Washington, D.C., January 15, 1947.

Hartung, William F., Sr. "Company E's D-Day . . . : writer recalls U.S. invasion of southern France beaches in 1944." Originally published in the *Record-Courier* (Ravenna-Kent, Ohio) 22 August 1979, 5. Reprinted in the *The Fighting 36th Historical Quarterly*, vol.4, no. 4 (Winter 1984): 68–71.

———. "Reflections of World War II." 36th Division Association, *The Fighting 36th Historical Quarterly* supplement to the *T-Patcher Newsletter,* vol. 24, no. 4 (Winter 2004): 11–12.

———. "Small invasion large when you're in it, vet says." *Record-Courier* (Ravenna-Kent, Ohio) N.d., n.p. (c. August 1994). Copy of article sent to author by William F. Hartung, Sr.

Hewitt, Admiral H. Kent (Retired). *"Anvil-Dragoon: Planning and Operation."* 36th Division Association, *The Fighting 36th Historical Quarterly,* Vol. 3, No. 4 (Winter 1983): 6–33. Original title: "Planning Operation Anvil-Dragoon," published July 1954, *U.S. Naval Institute Proceedings*, vol. 80, no. 7, Annapolis, Maryland: 730–45.

Hinkle, Paul D. "Honorary Texan." 36th Division Association, *The Fighting 36th Historical Quarterly,* vol. 12, no. 1 (Spring 1992): 42–45. See also "Memories Never Forgotten." <http://www.kwanah.com/36division/ps/ps900337.htm> (2001).

———. "Morning 30 Aug. 1944." 36th Division Association Message Board, posted July 1, 2000. <http://p081.ezboard.com/36th-InfantryDivision/btexasmilitaryforces museum> (1999–2007).

"History of Operations in France, 141st Infantry Regiment, Rifle, August 1944" (After Action Reports). Headquarters 36th Infantry Division: 1–28. National Archives and Records Administration, Modern Military Records, Textual Archives Services Division, College Park, Maryland.

Hyman, Pfc. John A., ed. "From the Riviera to the Rhine, A T-Patch [36th Division newspaper] Anniversary Supplement." Described as "Excerpts from a book in preparation by the Public Relations Section, with the cooperation of official sources," 1945.

Kennett, Lee B. *G.I.: the American Soldier in World War II*. Norman, Oklahoma: University of Oklahoma Press, 1997.

Lee, Rod. *God Is Our Co-Pilot: The Life and Times of Ross Rajotte–An American Patriot*. Whitinsville, Mass.: Old Colony Stationery, 2002.

Morison, Samuel Eliot. *History of the United States Naval Operations in World War II, The Invasion of France and Germany 1944–1945* (15 vols.), vol. XI. Boston: Little, Brown, 1957.

Morning Reports, Company D, 141st Infantry, 15 August–5 September 1944. National Personnel Records Center (NPRC), St. Louis, Missouri.

141st Infantry Regiment Association. *Five Years, Five Countries, Five Campaigns.* Clifford H. Peek, ed. Munich, Germany, 1945.

Philips, Julian. "Anvil to Draguignan." 36th Division Association, *The Fighting 36th Historical Quarterly*, vol. 5, no. 3 (Fall 1985): 44–57.

Phillippi, Wendell C. *Dear Ike.* Nashville, Indiana: Two Star Press, 1988.

———. "A Day of Forgiving." 36th Division Association, *The Fighting 36th Historical Quarterly*, vol. 10, no. 1 (Spring 1990): 46–47.

Quinn, Francis S., Jr. "Assault in Southern France," in *Seek, Strike, Destroy: The History of the 636th Tank Destroyer Battalion* by Thomas M. Sherman. Marquette, Nebraska: T. Sherman, 1986: 103–08.

Raithel, Glenn. *All the Way with the 36th Infantry Texas Division in WW II.* Chicago: G. Raithel, 1991.

"Report of Operations in France, 36th Division, August 1944, Narrative" (After Action Reports). Headquarters 36th Infantry Division: 1–12. 36th Infantry Division Collection, Microfilmed Records and Reports, Archives Division, Texas State Library, Austin, Texas, Reel no. 2070.

Scott, Jack L. *Combat Engineer.* Baltimore: American Literary Press, 1999.

Sherman, Thomas M. *Seek, Strike, Destroy: The History of the 636th Tank Destroyer Battalion.* Marquette, Nebraska: T. Sherman, 1986.

Sizemore, Arlis D. *Hidden Memories of World War II.* Topeka, Kansas: Learning Resources, Inc., 2002.

Stubinski, Michael. "Michael Stubinski," in *The Ordinary Infantrymen: Heroes Then, Heroes Now,* Imogene Woods, et al, Chapter 11: 129–43. Springfield, Missouri: I. Woods, 2003.

———. "Mike in the Service." Unpublished memoir, World War II Veterans Project, Special Collections, University of Tennessee, Knoxville, MS 1881, Box 28, Folder 19 (1992): 1–13, with "Excerpts" (8 pages).

36th Division Association. *The Fighting 36th: A Pictorial History* (reprint of the 1945 edition). Paducah, Kentucky: Turner Publishing Company, 1995. N.p.

Truscott, Lt. Gen. Lucian K. *Command Missions: A Personal Story.* New York: Dutton, 1954.

Wilson, Jack W. *Living on the Edge.* 2003.

Interviews and Correspondence

William F. Hartung, Sr. (E-143)

Rex B. Hoon (F-141)

Edward Langdon (son of Ernest E. Langdon, B and D-141)

Rosaire J. Rajotte (A-141)

Arlis D. Sizemore (D-141)

Michael Stubinski (K-141)
Jack W. Wilson (D-141)

SOURCES USED IN CHAPTER 17: TRUSCOTT'S PLAN

Blumenson, Martin. *Liberation*. Alexandria, Virginia: Time-Life Books, 1978.

Breuer, William B. *Operation Dragoon: The Allied Invasion of the South of France*. Novato, California: Presidio Press, 1987.

Butler, Fredrick B. "Task Force Butler, Part 1." *Armored Cavalry Journal*, vol. 57, no. 1 (Jan.–Feb. 1948): 12–18.

———. "Task Force Butler, Part 2." *Armored Cavalry Journal*, vol. 57, no. 2 (March–April 1948), 30–38.

Caraccilo, Dominic J. "Dragoon Clears the Rhone Valley." *Veterans of Foreign Wars Magazine*, vol. 81, no. 11 (August 1994): 14, 16. Reprinted in 36th Division Association, *The Fighting 36th Historical Quarterly*, supplement to the *T-Patcher Newsletter*, vol. 14, no. 3 (Fall 1994): 10–11.

Clarke, Jeffrey J. *Southern France: The U.S. Campaigns of World War II*. Pub. 72–31, Washington, D.C.: U.S. Army Center of Military History, 1992.

Dear, I.C.B., General Editor, and M.R.D. Foot, Consultant Editor. *The Oxford Companion to World War II*. Oxford: Oxford University Press, 1995.

"History of Operations in France, 141st Infantry Regiment, Rifle, August 1944" (After Action Reports). Headquarters 36th Infantry Division: 1–28. National Archives and Records Administration, Modern Military Records, Textual Archives Services Division, College Park, Maryland.

Lockhart, Col. Vincent M. *T-Patch to Victory: The 36th "Texas" Division, France–Germany–Austria*. Canyon, Texas: Staked Plains Press, 1981.

Mitchell, Joseph B. and Sir Edward S. Creasy. *Twenty Decisive Battles of the World*. New York: Macmillan, 1964.

141st Infantry Regiment Association. *Five Years, Five Countries, Five Campaigns*. Clifford H. Peek, ed. Munich, Germany, 1945.

"Report of Operations in France, 36th Division, August 1944, Narrative" (After Action Reports). Headquarters 36th Infantry Division: 1–12. 36th Infantry Division Collection, Microfilmed Records and Reports, Archives Division, Texas State Library, Austin, Texas, Reel no. 2070.

Talley, Richard E. "Wild as a Buck." 36th Division Association, *The Fighting 36th Historical Quarterly*, vol. 7, no. 4 (Winter 1987): 40–47.

36th Division Association. *The Fighting 36th: A Pictorial History* (reprint of the 1945 edition). Paducah, Kentucky: Turner Publishing Company, 1995. N.p.

Truscott, Lt. Gen. Lucian K. *Command Missions: A Personal Story*. New York: Dutton, 1954.

Interviews and Correspondence

Michael Stubinski (K-141)

SOURCES USED IN CHAPTER 18: SETTING THE TRAP

Blumenson, Martin. *Liberation.* Alexandria, Virginia: Time-Life Books, 1978.

Breuer, William B. *Operation Dragoon: The Allied Invasion of the South of France.* Novato, California: Presidio Press, 1987.

Butler, Fredrick B. "Task Force Butler, Part 1." *Armored Cavalry Journal*, vol. 57, no. 1 (Jan.–Feb. 1948): 12–18.

———. "Task Force Butler, Part 2." *Armored Cavalry Journal*, vol. 57, no. 2 (March–April 1948): 30–38.

Caraccilo, Dominic J. "Dragoon Clears the Rhone Valley." *Veterans of Foreign Wars Magazine*, vol. 81, no. 11 (August 1994): 14, 16. Reprinted in 36th Division Association, *The Fighting 36th Historical Quarterly*, supplement to the *T-Patcher Newsletter*, vol. 14, no. 3 (Fall 1994): 10–11.

Clarke, Jeffrey J. *Southern France: The U.S. Campaigns of World War II.* Pub. 72–31, Washington, D.C.: U.S. Army Center of Military History, 1992.

Dear, I.C.B., General Editor, and M.R.D. Foot, Consultant Editor. *The Oxford Companion to World War II.* Oxford: Oxford University Press, 1995.

Doughty, R.K. "Zero." 36th Division Association, *The Fighting 36th Historical Quarterly*, vol. 8, no. 2 (Summer 1988): 28–35.

Hinkle, Paul D. "Honorary Texan." 36th Division Association, *The Fighting 36th Historical Quarterly,* vol. 12, no. 1 (Spring 1992): 42–45. See also "Memories Never Forgotten." <http://www.kwanah.com/36division/ps/ps900337.htm> (2001).

———. "Morning 30 Aug. 1944." 36th Division Association Message Board, posted July 1, 2000. <http://p081.ezboard.com/36th-InfantryDivision/btexasmilitary-forcesmuseum> (1999–2007).

"History of Operations in France, 141st Infantry Regiment, Rifle, August 1944" (After Action Reports). Headquarters 36th Infantry Division: 1–28. National Archives and Records Administration, Modern Military Records, Textual Archives Services Division, College Park, Maryland.

Hyman, Pfc. John A., ed. "From the Riviera to the Rhine, A T-Patch [36th Division newspaper] Anniversary Supplement." Described as "Excerpts from a book in preparation by the Public Relations Section, with the cooperation of official sources," 1945.

Lockhart, Col. Vincent M. *T-Patch to Victory: The 36th "Texas" Division, France–Germany–Austria.* Canyon, Texas: Staked Plains Press, 1981.

MacCombie, Herbert E. "Memoirs." Unpublished manuscript (1978), Chaplains of the 36th Division, 36th Division Association website.<http://www.kwanah.com/txmilmus/gallery/36div.htm> (2001).

141st Infantry Regiment Association. *Five Years, Five Countries, Five Campaigns.* Clifford H. Peek, ed. Munich, Germany, 1945.

Pincetl, Marcel F. ("as told to John Coyne"). "Invasion Day August 15th 1944." 36th Division Association, *The Fighting 36th Historical Quarterly*, vol. 13, no. 4 (Winter 1993): 33–34.

Raithel, Glenn. *All the Way with the 36th Infantry Texas Division in WW II.* Chicago: G. Rathiel, 1991.

"Report of Operations in France, 36th Division, August 1944, Narrative" (After Action Reports). Headquarters 36th Infantry Division: 1–12. 36th Infantry Division Collection, Microfilmed Records and Reports, Archives Division, Texas State Library, Austin, Texas, Reel no. 2070.

Stubinski, Michael. "Michael Stubinski," in *The Ordinary Infantrymen: Heroes Then, Heroes Now,* Imogene Woods, et al, Chapter 11: 129–43. Springfield, Missouri: I. Woods, 2003.

———. "Mike in the Service." Unpublished memoir, World War II Veterans Project, Special Collections, University of Tennessee, Knoxville, MS 1881, Box 28, Folder 19 (1992): 1–13, with "Excerpts" (8 pages).

———. "Montelimar." 36th Division Association, *The Fighting 36th Historical Quarterly*, supplement to the *T-Patcher Newsletter*, vol. 14, no. 2 (Summer 1994): 21.

———. "Task Force Butler–General Butler." Eight page paper. N.d. A hand written account of Stubinski's experiences with TFB.

Talley, Richard E. "Wild as a Buck." 36th Division Association, *The Fighting 36th Historical Quarterly*, vol. 7, no. 4 (Winter 1987): 40–47.

36th Division Association. *The Fighting 36th: A Pictorial History* (reprint of the 1945 edition). Paducah, Kentucky: Turner Publishing Company, 1995. N.p.

Truscott, Lt. Gen. Lucian K. *Command Missions: A Personal Story*. New York: Dutton, 1954.

Interviews and çorrespondence

Paul D. Hinkle (L-141)

Michael Stubinski (K-141)

SOURCES USED IN CHAPTER 19:
THE BATTLE OF MONTELIMAR BEGINS

Blumenson, Martin. *Liberation*. Alexandria, Virginia: Time-Life Books, 1978.

Butler, Fredrick B. "Task Force Butler, Part 1." *Armored Cavalry Journal*, vol. 57, no. 1 (Jan.–Feb. 1948): 12–18.

———. "Task Force Butler, Part 2." *Armored Cavalry Journal*, vol. 57, no. 2 (March-April 1948): 30–38.

Clarke, Jeffrey J. *Southern France: The U.S. Campaigns of World War II*. Pub. 72–31, Washington, D.C.: U.S. Army Center of Military History, 1992.

Connole, Dennis J. Veterans Administration (VA) File #05-075-171.

Hinkle, Paul D. "Honorary Texan." 36th Division Association, *The Fighting 36th Historical Quarterly,* vol. 12, no. 1 (Spring 1992): 42–45. See also "Memories Never Forgotten." <http://www.kwanah.com/36division/ps/ps900337.htm> (2001).

———. "Morning 30 Aug. 1944." 36th Division Association Message Board, posted July 1, 2000. <http://p081.ezboard.com/36th-InfantryDivision/btexasmilitaryforces museum> (1999–2007).

"History of Operations in France, 141st Infantry Regiment, Rifle, August 1944" (After Action Reports). Headquarters 36th Infantry Division: 1–28. National Archives and Records Administration, Modern Military Records, Textual Archives Services Division, College Park, Maryland.

Hyman, Pfc. John A., ed. "From the Riviera to the Rhine, A T-Patch [36th Division newspaper] Anniversary Supplement." Described as "Excerpts from a book in preparation by the Public Relations Section, with the cooperation of official sources," 1945.

Jones, Remus L. "Notes of World War II." 36th Division Association, *The Fighting 36th Historical Quarterly*, vol. 9, no. 2 (Summer 1989): 56–80.

Lockhart, Col. Vincent M. *T-Patch to Victory: The 36th "Texas" Division, France–Germany–Austria*. Canyon, Texas: Staked Plains Press, 1981.

Morning Report, Company A, 141st Infantry, 24 August 1944. National Personnel Records Center (NPRC), St. Louis, Missouri.

Morning Report, Company D, 141st Infantry, 28 August 1944. National Personnel Records Center (NPRC), St. Louis, Missouri.

141st Infantry Regiment Association. *Five Years, Five Countries, Five Campaigns*. Clifford H. Peek, ed. Munich, Germany, 1945.

Quinn, Francis S., Jr. "Assault in Southern France," in *Seek, Strike, Destroy: The History of the 636th Tank Destroyer Battalion* by Thomas M. Sherman. Marquette, Nebraska: T. Sherman, 1986: 103–08.

"Report of Operations in France, 36th Division, August 1944, Narrative" (After Action Reports). Headquarters 36th Infantry Division: 1–12. 36th Infantry Division Collection, Microfilmed Records and Reports, Archives Division, Texas State Library, Austin, Texas, Reel no. 2070.

36th Division Association. *The Fighting 36th: A Pictorial History* (reprint of the 1945 edition). Paducah, Kentucky: Turner Publishing Company, 1995. N.p.

Truscott, Lt. Gen. Lucian K. *Command Missions: A Personal Story*. New York: Dutton, 1954.

Interviews and Correspondence

John M. Hockenbury (F-142)
David C. Rosenbluth (A-141)
Terry Rosenbluth (son of David C. Rosenbluth)

SOURCES USED IN CHAPTER 20: GERMAN FORCES SUCCEED IN DRIVING UNITS OF THE 36TH DIVISION FROM THE MONTELIMAR RIDGE (AUGUST 24, 1944)

Butler, Fredrick B. "Task Force Butler, Part 1." *Armored Cavalry Journal*, vol. 57, no. 1 (Jan.–Feb. 1948): 12–18.

———. "Task Force Butler, Part 2." *Armored Cavalry Journal*, vol. 57, no. 2 (March–April 1948): 30–38.

Clarke, Jeffrey J. *Southern France: The U.S. Campaigns of World War II*. Pub. 72–31, Washington, D.C.: U.S. Army Center of Military History, 1992.

Critchfield, Col. James M. "Setting the Record Straight on the Battle of Montelimar." 36th Division Association, *The Fighting 36th Historical Quarterly*, supplement to the *T-Patcher Newsletter*, vol. 15, no. 2 (Summer 1995): 22–24.

Golwitzer, Frank A. Silver Star Citation, 24 August 1944. "Silver Star Awards, 2 Jun-19 Sept. 1944." National Archives and Records Administration (NARA), Modern Military Records, Textual Archives Services Division, College Park, Maryland. See Microfilmed Records and Reports, 36th Division, Texas State Library, Reel no. 2079. Includes awards before 2 June 1944 (307 pages).

"History of Operations in France, 141st Infantry Regiment, Rifle, August 1944" (After Action Reports). Headquarters 36th Infantry Division: 1–28. National Archives and Records Administration, Modern Military Records, Textual Archives Services Division, College Park, Maryland.

Lindsey, John H. "Lost in the Rhone Valley." 36th Division Association, The Fighting 36th Historical Quarterly, supplement to the T-Patcher Newsletter, vol. 15, no. 2 (Summer, 1995): 22–24.

Lockhart, Col. Vincent M. T-Patch to Victory: The 36th "Texas" Division, France–Germany–Austria. Canyon, Texas: Staked Plains Press, 1981.

Morning Reports, Company D, 141st Infantry, 20 August-15 September 1944. National Personnel Records Center (NPRC), St. Louis, Missouri.

"Report of Operations in France, 36th Division, August 1944, Narrative" (After Action Reports). Headquarters 36th Infantry Division: 1–12. 36th Infantry Division Collection, Microfilmed Records and Reports, Archives Division, Texas State Library, Austin, Texas, Reel no. 2070.

36th Division Association. *The Fighting 36th: A Pictorial History* (reprint of the 1945 edition). Paducah, Kentucky: Turner Publishing Company, 1995. N.p.

Truscott, Lt. Gen. Lucian K. *Command Missions: A Personal Story*. New York: Dutton, 1954.

Wilson, Jack W. *Living on the Edge*. 2003.

Interviews and Correspondence

Robert W. Brickman (D-141)
Arlis D. Sizemore (D-141)
Ernest R. Smeltzer (D-141)
Jack W. Wilson (D-141)

SOURCES USED IN CHAPTER 21: THE NIGHT OF AUGUST 24–25, 1944

Becher, John C. *The John C. Becher Playscript Collection* (1940–1953). Special Collections & Archives, George Mason University, Fairfax, Virginia. <http://www.gmu.edu/library/specialcollections/theater.htm>. See Introduction.

Connole, Dennis J. Veterans Administration (VA) File #05-075-171.

McManus, John C. *The Deadly Brotherhood: The American Combat Soldier in World War II.* Novato, California: Presidio Press, 1998.

Martin, Ralph G. *The GI War, 1941–1945.* Boston: Little, Brown, 1967.

Morning Reports, Company D, 141st Infantry, 15 August-30 August 1944. National Personnel Records Center (NPRC), St. Louis, Missouri.

"History of Operations in France, 141st Infantry Regiment, Rifle, August 1944" (After Action Reports). Headquarters 36th Infantry Division: 1–28. National Archives and Records Administration, Modern Military Records, Textual Archives Services Division, College Park, Maryland.

"Report of Operations in France, 36th Division, August 1944, Narrative" (After Action Reports). Headquarters 36th Infantry Division: 1–12. 36th Infantry Division Collection, Microfilmed Records and Reports, Archives Division, Texas State Library, Austin, Texas, Reel no. 2070.

Interviews and Correspondence

Helen G. Palumbo
Rosaire J. Rajotte (A-141)
Kathleen M. Senior

SOURCES USED IN CHAPTER 22: BUDDIES

"Artillery Fire? Phooey!" (unsigned article). *The Star Ledger* (Newark, New Jersey). N.d., n.p. (c. June–July, 1944). Article about Phillip M. DeRiggi sent to author by his niece Beth DeRiggi.

Arvizu, David. "My Most Terrible Experiences." 36th Division Association, *The Fighting 36th Historical Quarterly*, no. 10, vol. 1 (Spring 1990): 58–62.

Bartemeier, L.H., et al. "Combat Exhaustion." *Journal of Nervous and Mental Disease*, Vol. 104, 1946.

Courington, Morris, "and Seven Buddies From the 36th Division." *Cruel Was the Way*. Park Forest, Illinois: Velletri Books, 2000.

———. "To Remember or Forget." 36th Division Association, *The Fighting 36th Historical Quarterly*, supplement to the *T-Patcher Newsletter*, vol. 16, no. 3 (Fall 1996): 14–15.

Ellis, John. *The Sharp End: The Fighting Man in World War II*. New York: Scribner, 1980.

Gans, Robert J. "Best of Ink Stains." 36th Division Association, *The Fighting 36th Historical Quarterly*, supplement to the *T-Patcher Newsletter*, vol. 22, no. 4 (Winter 2002): 15.

Hartung, William F. "Memories." 36th Division Association, *The Fighting 36th Historical Quarterly*, supplement to the *T-Patcher Newsletter*, vol. 24, no. 2 (Spring 2004): 15.

Linderman, Gerald F. *The World Within War: America's Combat Experience in World War II*. New York: Free Press, 1997.

McManus, John C. *The Deadly Brotherhood: The American Combat Soldier in World War II.* Novato, California: Presidio Press, 1998.

Marshall, S.L.A. *Men Against Fire: The Problem of Battle Command in Future War.* Washington, D.C.: William Morrow & Company, 1947.

Mauldin, Bill. *Up Front.* New York: H. Holt and Company, 1945.

Palmer, Bennett J., Sr. *The Hunter and the Hunted: A Combat Soldier's Story.* Holland, New York, B. Palmer, 2002.

Stouffer, Samuel A., et al. *The American Soldier: Combat and its Aftermath, vol. 2.* Princeton, New Jersey: Princeton University Press, 1949.

Interviews and Correspondence

Greg DeRiggi (nephew of Ernest DeRiggi, D-141)
William F. Hartung, Sr. (E-143)
Sulo O. Ruuska (H-181)
Ernest R. Smeltzer (D-141)

SOURCES USED IN CHAPTER 23: CHANGES

Ellis, John. *The Sharp End: The Fighting Man in World War II.* New York: Scribner, 1980.

Estepp, James E. "Combat Soldier." 36th Division Association, *The Fighting 36th Historical Quarterly*, vol. 13, no. 2 (Summer 1993): 7–9.

Fussell, Paul. *The Boy's Crusade: The American Infantryman in Northwestern Europe, 1944–1945.* New York: Modern Library, 2003.

Kennett, Lee B. *G.I.: The American Soldier in World War II.* Norman, Oklahoma: University of Oklahoma Press, 1997.

Mauldin, Bill. *Up Front.* New York: H. Holt and Company, 1945.

Palmer, Bennett J., Sr. The *Hunter and the Hunted: A Combat Soldier's Story.* Holland, New York: B. Palmer, 2002.

SOURCES USED IN CHAPTER 24—HOME AGAIN:

Connole, Dennis J. U.S. Army "Enlisted Record and Report of Separation Honorable Discharge, 27 June 45." Form WD AGO 53–55, November 1944.

———. Veterans Administration (VA) File # 05-075-171.

"Pfc. Dennis J. Connole Returns By Plane to U.S" (unsigned article). *Evening Gazette* (Worcester, Mass.) 19 June 1945, 7.

Sandrof, Ivan. "How Veterans and Families Are Finding Life at Lincolnwood: State's Biggest Veterans' Project Houses 1200." Supplement to the *Worcester Sunday Telegram,* Fall 1947. N.p.

This Fabulous Century: 1940–1950. Alexandria, Virginia: ("by the editors of") Time-Life Books, 1969.

"Troops Begin to Return By Daily Plane Schedule" (unsigned article). *New York Times* 17 June 1945, 6.

The Twentieth Century: Postwar Prosperity and the Cold War (1946–1963), Vol. IV. Matthew T. Downey, ed. New York: Macmillan Publishing Company, 1992.

"2 City GIs in First Group Flown Home From Europe" (unsigned article). *Worcester Sunday Telegram* 17 June 1945, 5.

Interviews and Correspondence

Helen G. Palumbo

CHAPTER 25: WOUNDS OF THE MIND

American Psychiatric Association (APA). "Posttraumatic Stress Disorder." Arlington, VA: 1999.

Connole, Dennis J. Veterans Administration (VA) File #05-075-171.

Courington, Morris, "and Seven Buddies From the 36th Division." *Cruel Was the Way.* Park Forest, Illinois: Velletri Books, 2000.

———. "To Remember or Forget." *The Fighting 36th Historical Quarterly*, supplement to the *T-Patcher Newsletter*, vol. 16, no. 3 (Fall 1996): 14–15.

Decade of Triumph, the 40s. Alexandria, Virginia: ("by the editors of") Time-Life Books, 1999.

Field Manual FM 22–51, Leader's Manual for Combat Stress Control. See Chapter 6, "Post-traumatic Stress Disorder." Washington, D.C.: Headquarters, Department of the Army, December 29. 1994.

Harrison, Rex. "Flashbacks." 36th Division Association, *The Fighting 36th Historical Quarterly*, vol. 8, no. 3 (Fall 1988): 36–39.

Hinkle, Paul D. "The Reluctant Veteran." 36th Division Association Message Board, posted November 24, 2000. <http://p081.ezboard.com/36thInfantryDivision/btex-asmilitaryforcesmuseum> (1999–2007).

McManus, John C. *The Deadly Brotherhood: The American Combat Soldier in World War II.* Novato, California: Presidio Press, 1998.

Mauldin, Bill. *Up Front.* New York: H. Holt and Company, 1945.

National Institute of Mental Health (NIMH). "Facts About Post-Traumatic Stress Disorder." Pub. No. OM-99 4157. Bethesda, Maryland: Revised Sept. 1999.

———. "Reliving Trauma." Pub. No. 01–4597. Bethesda, Maryland: Oct. 2001.

———. "A Real Illness: Post-Traumatic Stress Disorder." Pub. No. 02–4675. Bethesda, Maryland: Reprint Sept. 2002.

———. "Anxiety Disorders." Departments of Health and Human Services. Pub. No. 02–3879. Bethesda, Maryland, Reprint Sept., 2002.

Onofrey, Delilah. "Ravenna WW II vet walks through time." *Record-Courier* (Ravenna-Kent, Ohio) 7 October 1991. N.p. Copy of article sent to author by William F. Hartung, Sr.

U.S. Department of Health and Human Services. "Mental Health: A Report of the Surgeon General-Executive Summary." Rockville, Maryland, 1999.

Interviews and Correspondence

Peter Androne (D-141)
Reneta Benenati (widow of Carl G., D-141)
William Claude Harrelson (D-141)
Romeo C. LeBlanc (H-181)
Charles B. Price (HQ, 3rd Bn., 142)
Arlis D. Sizemore (D-141)

Index